Predictive Intelligence Using Big Data and the Internet of Things

P.K. Gupta
Jaypee University of Information Technology, India

Tuncer Ören
University of Ottawa, Canada

Mayank Singh
University of KwaZulu-Natal, South Africa

A volume in the Advances in Computational
Intelligence and Robotics (ACIR) Book Series

Published in the United States of America by
  IGI Global
  Engineering Science Reference (an imprint of IGI Global)
  701 E. Chocolate Avenue
  Hershey PA, USA 17033
  Tel: 717-533-8845
  Fax: 717-533-8661
  E-mail: cust@igi-global.com
  Web site: http://www.igi-global.com

Library of Congress Cataloging-in-Publication Data

Names: Gupta, P. K., 1976- editor. | Oren, Tuncer I., editor. | Singh,
  Mayank, 1982- editor.
Title: Predictive intelligence using big data and the internet of things
  / P.K. Gupta, Tuncer Oren, and Mayank Singh, editors.
Description: Hershey, PA : Engineering Science Reference, an imprint of IGI
  Global, [2019] | Includes bibliographical references and index.
Identifiers: LCCN 2018003843| ISBN 9781522562108 (hardcover) | ISBN
  9781522562115 (ebook)
Subjects: LCSH: Internet of things. | Big data. | Artificial intelligence. |
  Prediction theory--Data procesing.
Classification: LCC TK5105.8857 .H36 2019 | DDC 006.3--dc23 LC record available at https://lccn.loc.gov/2018003843

This book is published in the IGI Global book series Advances in Computational Intelligence and Robotics (ACIR) (ISSN: 2327-0411; eISSN: 2327-042X)

British Cataloguing in Publication Data
A Cataloguing in Publication record for this book is available from the British Library.

For electronic access to this publication, please contact: eresources@igi-global.com.

Advances in Computational Intelligence and Robotics (ACIR) Book Series

Ivan Giannoccaro
University of Salento, Italy

ISSN:2327-0411
EISSN:2327-042X

MISSION

While intelligence is traditionally a term applied to humans and human cognition, technology has progressed in such a way to allow for the development of intelligent systems able to simulate many human traits. With this new era of simulated and artificial intelligence, much research is needed in order to continue to advance the field and also to evaluate the ethical and societal concerns of the existence of artificial life and machine learning.

The **Advances in Computational Intelligence and Robotics (ACIR) Book Series** encourages scholarly discourse on all topics pertaining to evolutionary computing, artificial life, computational intelligence, machine learning, and robotics. ACIR presents the latest research being conducted on diverse topics in intelligence technologies with the goal of advancing knowledge and applications in this rapidly evolving field.

COVERAGE

- Synthetic Emotions
- Computational Logic
- Evolutionary computing
- Brain Simulation
- Computational Intelligence
- Machine Learning
- Artificial life
- Pattern Recognition
- Heuristics
- Fuzzy systems

IGI Global is currently accepting manuscripts for publication within this series. To submit a proposal for a volume in this series, please contact our Acquisition Editors at Acquisitions@igi-global.com or visit: http://www.igi-global.com/publish/.

Titles in this Series

For a list of additional titles in this series, please visit: www.igi-global.com/book-series

701 East Chocolate Avenue, Hershey, PA 17033, USA
Tel: 717-533-8845 x100 • Fax: 717-533-8661
E-Mail: cust@igi-global.com • www.igi-global.com

Table of Contents

Detailed Table of Contents

Section 1
Predictive Intelligence and Big Data

Big-data-analyzed finding patterns derive meaning and make decisions on data to produce responses to the world with intelligence. It is an emerging area used in business intelligence (BI) for competitive advantage to analyze the structured, semi-structured, and unstructured data stored in different formats. As the big data technology continues to evolve, businesses are turning to predictive intelligence to deepen the engagement to customers with optimization in processes to reduce the operational costs. Predictive intelligence uses sets of advanced technologies that enable organizations to use data stored in real time that move from a historical and descriptive view to a forward-looking perspective of data. The comparison and other security issue of this technology is covered in this book chapter. The combination of big data technology and predictive analytics is sometimes referred to as a never-ending process and has the possibility to deliver significant competitive advantage. This chapter provides an extensive review of literature on big data technologies and its usage in the predictive intelligence.

Chapter 2

This chapter covers the essentials of big data analytics ecosystems primarily from the business and technology context. It delivers insight into key concepts and terminology that define the essence of big data and the promise it holds to deliver sophisticated business insights. The various characteristics that distinguish big data datasets are articulated. It also describes the conceptual and logical reference architecture to manage a huge volume of data generated by various data sources of an enterprise. It also covers drivers, opportunities, and benefits of big data analytics implementation applicable to the real world.

Chapter 3

Heterogeneous data types, widely distributed data sources, huge data volumes, and large-scale business-alliance partners describe typical global supply chain operational environments. Mobile and wireless technologies are putting an extra layer of data source in this technology-enriched supply chain operation. This environment also needs to provide access to data anywhere, anytime to its end-users. This new type of data set originating from the global retail supply chain is commonly known as big data because of its huge volume, resulting from the velocity with which it arrives in the global retail business environment. Such environments empower and necessitate decision makers to act or react quicker to all decision tasks. Academics and practitioners are researching and building the next generation of big-data-based application software systems. This new generation of software applications is based on complex data analysis algorithms (i.e., on data that does not adhere to standard relational data models). The traditional software testing methods are insufficient for big-data-based applications. Testing big-data-based applications is one of the biggest challenges faced by modern software design and development communities because of lack of knowledge on what to test and how much data to test. Big-data-based applications developers have been facing a daunting task in defining the best strategies for structured and unstructured data validation, setting up an optimal test environment, and working with non-relational databases testing approaches. This chapter focuses on big-data-based software testing and quality-assurance-related issues in the context of Hadoop, an open source framework. It includes discussion about several challenges with respect to massively parallel data generation from multiple sources, testing methods for validation of pre-Hadoop processing, software application quality factors, and some of the software testing mechanisms for this new breed of applications

Due to an increase in the number of digital transactions and data sources, a huge amount of unstructured data is generated by every interaction. In such a scenario, the concepts of data mining assume great significance as useful information/trends/predictions can be retrieved from this large amount of data, known as big data. Big data predictive analytics are making big inroads into the educational field because with the adoption of new technologies, new academic trends are being introduced into educational systems. This accumulation of large data of different varieties throws a new set of challenges to the learners as well as educational institutions in ensuring the quality of their education by improving strategic/operational decision-making capabilities. Therefore, the authors address this issue by proposing a support system that can guide the student to choose and to focus on the right course(s) based on their personal preferences. This chapter provides the readers with the requisite information about educational frameworks and related data mining.

Section 2
Predictive Intelligence and IoT

Chapter 5

Vijayalakshmi Kakulapati, SNIST, India
Mahender Reddy S., SNIST, India

Sensor data takes the microcontroller and sends it to doctors through the wi-fi network and provides real-time healthcare parameter monitoring. The clinician can analyze the sensor generated information. Patients provide their measures to the arrangement and identify their fitness status without human intervention. In this chapter, MapReduce algorithm is used to identify the patient health status. The controller is connected with the signal to alert the attendee about dissimilarity in sensor output data. If the situation is sever, an alert message is sent to the doctor through the IOT devices that can provide quick provisional medication to the ill person. The system improves usability of medical devices with less power consumption, simple setup, and high performance and response.

Chapter 6

Mayank Singh, University of KwaZulu-Natal, South Africa
Umang Kant, Krishna Engineering College, India
P. K. Gupta, Jaypee University of Information Technology, India
Viranjay M. Srivastava, University of KwaZulu-Natal, South Africa

Predictive computing is a relatively new area of research. Predictive computing helps people to predict the future or unknown events. It combines various statistical approaches like predictive analytics, predictive modeling, data mining, big data, and machine learning. Predictive computing uses current and historical facts to predict future events. It looks for relationships and patterns between data variables. The outcomes of data variables can be predicted if we know the values of explanatory variables. Cloud computing is another new technology that provides everything-as-a-service (XaaS) and is used widely in various businesses. All storage and computing devices use cloud platform due to its elasticity, scalability, and dynamicity. Cloud-based predictive computing is a technology that uses data available on the cloud. Presently, the data from the social sites (e.g., Facebook, Gmail, LinkedIn, election data, etc.) are stored on cloud, and the volume of this data is enormous which needs innovative predictive computing design and architecture. This chapter represents the cloud-based predictive intelligence and its security model. Architecture for predictive intelligence is proposed and compared with the existing models. An attack prediction algorithm is also proposed and compared for the accuracy in the predictive intelligence.

Chapter 7

Afreen Mohsin, UTL Technologies, India
Siva S. Yellampalli, UTL Technologies, India

This chapter aims to reduce the extent of human presence all along the cold chain by means of a powerful tool in the form of the IoT. It should also be ensured that any details regarding instances of equipment failure leading to product spoilage or an event of a successful delivery must be communicated to the manufacturer's end. It also seeks to fill gaps involving location tracking and environment control by means of a GPS module and an IoT-based sensor platform respectively used here.

Chapter 8

Jutika Borah, Gauhati University, India

Kandarpa Kumar Sarma, Gauhati University, India

Pulak Jyoti Gohain, Gauhati University, India

Of late, home surveillance systems have been enhanced considerably by resorting to increased use of automated systems. The automation aspect has reduced human intervention and made such systems reliable and efficient. With the proliferation of wireless devices, networking among the connected devices is leading to the formation of internet of things (IoT). This has made it essential that home surveillance systems be also automate using IoT. The decision support system (DSS) in such platforms necessitates that automation be extensive. It necessitates the use of learning-aided systems. This chapter reports the design of IoT-driven learning-aided system for home surveillance application.

Chapter 9

Anil Kumar Bisht, MJP Rohilkhand University, India

Ravendra Singh, MJP Rohilkhand University, India

Rakesh Bhutiani, Gurukul Kangri Vishwavidhayalaya, India

Ashutosh Bhatt, Birla Institute of Applied Sciences, India

Predicting the water quality of rivers has attracted a lot of researchers all around the globe. A precise prediction of river water quality may benefit the water management bodies. However, due to the complex relationship existing among various factors, the prediction is a challenging job. Here, the authors attempted to develop a model for forecasting or predicting the water quality of the river Ganga using application of predictive intelligence based on machine learning approach called support vector machine (SVM). The monthly data sets of five water quality parameters from 2001 to 2015 were taken from five sampling stations from Devprayag to Roorkee in the Uttarakhand state of India. The experiments are conducted in Python 2.7.13 language (Anaconda2 4.3.1) using the radial basis function (RBF) as a kernel for developing the non-linear SVM-based classifier as a model for water quality prediction. The results indicated a prediction performance of 96.66% for best parameter combination which proved the significance of predictive intelligence in water quality forecasting.

Chapter 10

Weston Mwashita, Vaal University of Technology, South Africa

Marcel Ohanga Odhiambo, Vaal University of Technology, South Africa

The snowballing of many different electronic gadgets connected to different networks and to the internet is a clear indication that the much-anticipated internet of things (IoT) is fast becoming a reality. It is generally agreed that the next generation mobile networks should offer wireless connection to anything and anyone with a proper enabling device at any time leading to the full realization of IoT. Device-to device (D2D) communication is one technology that the research community believes will aid the implementation of the next generation of mobile networks, specifically 5G. Full roll out of D2D is however being impeded by the resulting interference. This chapter looks at the state-of-the-art research works on interference management technologies proposed for device-to-device communications. A comprehensive analysis of the proposed schemes is given and open challenges and issues that need to be considered by researchers in D2D communication for it to become a key enabler for 5G technology are highlighted and recommendations provided.

Preface

Big data and the Internet of Things (IoT) are ultimately two sides of the same coin, yet extracting, analyzing, managing and transforming data into meaningful and usable forms by applying various machine learning based approaches. Accordingly, proper analytics infrastructures/platforms should be used to analyse this data. Information technology (IT) allows people to upload, retrieve, store and collect information, which ultimately forms big data. The use of big data analytics and machine learning has grown tremendously in just the past few years. With the growth of computing technology, now it has become possible to perform predictive computing using Big data and IoT. Predictive computing uses data, statistical algorithms and machine learning techniques to identify the prospects of future outcomes based on the current and historical data. Predictive intelligence is an advanced branch of data engineering which generally predicts some occurrence or probability based on data collected in real-time. The aim of predictive intelligence is to go beyond understanding what has already happened, to come up with the best analysis of what might happen in the future. It will personalize and optimize data for individuals, private organizations, and government sectors.

Predictive intelligence is relatively a new area of research and helps people to make prediction about future or unknown events. It combines various statistical approaches like predictive computing, predictive modeling, data mining, big data, Internet of Things and machine learning. It also looks for relationships and patterns between data variables. The outcomes of data variables can be predicted intelligently, if we know the values of explanatory variables.

This book highlights state-of-the-art research based on predictive intelligence using big data and the Internet of Things, along with related areas to ensure quality assurance, efficient and Internet-compatible IoT systems. Accepted chapters discuss Big Data based architectures, and techniques for predictive intelligence along with the cloud based predictive intelligence and its security model, and various other applications of IoT for predictive intelligence. This book also describes various methods, frameworks, algorithms and security concerns for predictive intelligence, Big data, and Internet of Things. It also highlights various predictive application scenarios to discuss these breakthroughs in real-world settings. Further, this book explores possible automated solutions in daily life, including structures for smart cities and automated home systems based on IoT technology, as well as health care systems that manage large amounts of data to improve clinical predictive decisions.

This book has attracted 44 chapter proposals from around the globe and all the chapter proposals along with complete chapter submissions have been strictly reviewed by least three reviewers consisting of guest editors and external reviewers, with 10 high-quality chapters accepted in the end. Below, we briefly summarize the highlights of each accepted chapter.

In Chapter 1, "Big-Data-Based Techniques for Predictive Intelligence," Singh et al. have discussed and presented the detailed technical survey related to Big data based techniques and its usage in predictive intelligence. It focuses on various hot key areas, where big data based techniques and frameworks can be applied to enhance predictive intelligence. They have also stated that the combinations of big data technology and predictive analytics sometimes referred to never ending process and have the possibility to deliver significant competitive environment for the advantage of business.

In Chapter 2, "Big-Data-Based Architectures and Techniques: Big Data Reference Architecture," G.K. Behera has presented the essentials of Big Data Analytics ecosystem primarily from the business and technology context. It delivers insight into key concepts and terminology that define the essence of Big Data and the promise it holds to deliver sophisticated business insights. The various characteristics that distinguish Big Data datasets are articulated. This chapter also describes the conceptual and logical reference architecture to manage huge volume of data generated by various data sources of an enterprise and also covers drivers, opportunities and benefits of Big Data Analytics implementation applicable to real world. He has also focused on the discussion about several challenges with respect to massively-parallel data generation from multiple sources, data characterization, software application quality factors, and some of the software testing mechanisms for this new breed of applications.

In Chapter 3, "Quality Assurance Issues for Big Data Applications in Supply Chain Management," Kamlendu Pal has emphasized on testing of Big Data-based applications and considered it as one of the biggest challenge faced by modern software design and development communities. It is because of lack of knowledge on what to test and how much data to test. Big Data-based applications developers have been facing a daunting task in defining the best strategies for structured and unstructured data validation, setting up an optimal test environment, and working with non-relational databases testing approaches. This chapter mainly focuses on Big Data-based software testing and quality assurance related issues in the context of Hadoop, an open source framework. It includes discussion about several challenges with respect to massively-parallel data generation from multiple sources, data characterization, software application quality factors, and some of the software testing mechanisms for this new breed of applications.

In Chapter 4, "Big Data Analytics: Educational Data Classification Using Hadoop-Inspired MapReduce Framework," Guleria and Sood have discussed the requisite information about educational frameworks, related data mining and learning analytics in the educational sector. In addition to discussing the role of data mining in education and predictive intelligence, they have also discussed the MapReduce framework and its applicability to provide guidance to the learners as well as the institutions with in the educational systems.

In Chapter 5, "Improved Usability of IoT Devices in Healthcare Using Big Data Analysis," Kakulapati and Reddy S have evaluated the cost optimization models for preservation in business regions, illustration terminations on their applicability in the medical division. In this chapter, for identifying the patient health status Mapreduce algorithm has been used. The controller is connected with the signal to alert the attendee about dissimilarity in sensor output data. In the severity of the situation alert message is sent to the doctor through the IOT devices which can provide quick provisional medication to the ill person. The proposed system improves usability of medical devices with less power consumption, simple setup, and high performance and time to time response.

In Chapter 6, "Cloud-Based Predictive Intelligence and Its Security Model," Singh et al. have represented the cloud based predictive intelligence and its security model. Architecture for predictive intelligence is proposed and compared with the existing models. An attack prediction algorithm is also proposed and compared for the accuracy in the predictive intelligence.

In Chapter 7, "IoT-Based Cold Chain Logistics Monitoring," Mohsin and Yellampalli have discussed an effective Cold Chain is a complete combination of three main elements which should ensure proper transport, storage and handling of the products/commodities being transported. The Cold Chain Logistics System is proposed within distribution centres generate wireless monitoring solution specifically for end to end cold chain protection. They have implemented an ARM7 based Cold Chain Logistics System using the IoT platform that monitors the temperature and humidity through the controller.

In Chapter 8, "Learning-Aided IoT Set-Up for Home Surveillance Applications," Borah et al. have discussed the design and implementation of a home surveillance system designed using legacy devices connected in line of IoT framework. Proposed surveillance system is formulated using an embedded system connected to a control unit. Most security arrangements based on vision require human intervention for decision making. Therefore, there is a necessity to urgently automate the mechanism using learning aided tools so that the system is independent of human intervention once it is deployed. The primary mechanism of which will revolve around the working of the learning aided decision support system (DSS) which continuously learns to discriminate between authorized and unauthorized entries. A series of experiments are performed to fix the configuration of the recognition block which is a multi-layer set-up.

In Chapter 9, "Application of Predictive Intelligence in Water Quality Forecasting of the River Ganga Using Support Vector Machines," Bisht and co-authors contributed to the development of various prediction models for forecasting or predicting the quality of the river Ganga in prospective of India based on collection of the previous historical times-series authentic data and then selecting the best one on the basis of their forecasting performance. In this chapter, authors have emphasized firstly on one of the modern approach of machine learning named Support Vector Machines (SVM). Secondly, the research will determine an efficient predictive model among the developed models by comparing their performances via several experiments. Finally, they have proposed an optimal model that can be used as a decision support system for proactive planning and performing actions in order to maintain the water quality of rivers.

Finally, in Chapter 10, "Interference Management Techniques for Device-to-Device Communications," Mwashita and Odhiambo have represented the state-of-the-art research works on interference management technologies proposed for Device-to-Device communications (D2D). A comprehensive analysis of the proposed schemes is given and open challenges and issues that need to be considered by researchers in D2D communication. A qualitative comparison of the latest interference mitigation schemes is also presented, and the technical challenges have been analysed. Open challenges and issues that need to be considered by researchers in D2D for it to become a key enabler for 5G technologies are highlighted and recommendations provided in this chapter.

These 10 selected chapters basically can reflect the new horizon in the field of predictive intelligence using Big Data and IoT. Finally, we would like to thank all authors for their contributions, the reviewers for reviewing these high-quality papers, Editorial Board Members of IGI Global, and Assistant Development Editor, Amanda Fanton, for their support and guidance throughout the process.

We believe that this book will be of interest to graduate students, teachers and active researchers in academia, and engineers in industry who need to understand or implement predictive intelligence using Big Data and IoT. We hope this book will provide reference to many of the techniques used in the field as well as generate new research ideas to further advance the field.

P. K. Gupta
Jaypee University of Information Technology, India

Mayank Singh
University of KwaZulu-Natal, South Africa

Tuncer Ören
University of Ottawa, Canada

Section 1
Predictive Intelligence and Big Data

Chapter 1
Big–Data–Based Techniques for Predictive Intelligence

Dharmpal Singh
JIS College of Engineering, India

Madhusmita Mishra
JIS College of Engineering, India

Sudipta Sahana
JIS College of Engineering, India

ABSTRACT

Big-data-analyzed finding patterns derive meaning and make decisions on data to produce responses to the world with intelligence. It is an emerging area used in business intelligence (BI) for competitive advantage to analyze the structured, semi-structured, and unstructured data stored in different formats. As the big data technology continues to evolve, businesses are turning to predictive intelligence to deepen the engagement to customers with optimization in processes to reduce the operational costs. Predictive intelligence uses sets of advanced technologies that enable organizations to use data stored in real time that move from a historical and descriptive view to a forward-looking perspective of data. The comparison and other security issue of this technology is covered in this book chapter. The combination of big data technology and predictive analytics is sometimes referred to as a never-ending process and has the possibility to deliver significant competitive advantage. This chapter provides an extensive review of literature on big data technologies and its usage in the predictive intelligence.

INTRODUCTION

The continuous evolvements of big data technology turn the businesses to predictive analytics to help them deepen engagement with customers, optimize processes, and reduce operational costs. The combination of real time data streams and predictive analytics sometimes referred to as processing that never stops has the potential to deliver significant competitive advantage for business. Enterprises performed the analysis to structured data like transactions and customer information stored in relational database

DOI: 10.4018/978-1-5225-6210-8.ch001

management systems (RDBMSs) and unstructured data stored in form of videos, images, audio, click streams, weblogs, text, and e-mail for long used business intelligence (BI) for competitive advantage. The massive scale and growth of data (structured and unstructured) do not cope well with the heterogeneity of big data. It may be possible the organizations have rich data, but new analytic processes and technologies are needed to unlock the potential of big data.

Analytics of big data required the stimulation of advanced computer processing power, database technology, and tools of Predictive analytics to set advanced technologies that enable organizations to use data, both stored and real-time. The predictive intelligence used the two method (Inductive and deductive) to performed the analysis's on the data and deductive methods work well with structured data whereas predictive analytics used inductive reasoning in big data to its sophisticated quantitative methods such as machine learning, neural networks, robotics, computational mathematics, and artificial intelligence to explore all the data and to discover interrelationships and patterns. Inductive methods used in algorithms to perform complex calculations to run against highly varied or large volumes of data. The predictive model used these techniques on a real-world business problem to know what algorithms and data to be use to test and create the predictive model. According to the survey of IT managers participating in Intel's 2012 on big data, the batch and real-time data processing would shift to two-thirds of the workload by 2015. Many experts use the term predictive analytics broadly to describe the future-oriented use and scenarios for big data into the future to provide insight into what will happen and includes what-if scenarios and risk assessment for forecasting, hypothesis testing, risk modeling, and propensity modeling. Bid data provide the insight to predictive intelligence for further used of its techniques like statistics, modeling and deployment to predict the what would happen based on different alternatives and scenarios, and then choosing best options, and optimizing what's ahead. It's used the stimulated of advances in computer processing power, database technology, and tools for big data. Predictive intelligence is also used in e-learning by (Linlin Zhang, & Kin Fun Li, 2018).

This chapter provides an extensive review of literature on big data, technologies of big data and how the predictive intelligence used it. It gives detail to the reader about the fundamental concepts in this emerging field of Big data.

Finally, the paper concludes with the findings of our study and has outlined future research directions in this field.

BACKGROUND

The authors (Agarwal & Dhar, 2014) opined that magnitude of data generated and shared by businesses, public administrations numerous industrial and not-to-profit sectors, and scientific research, has increased immeasurably in form of textual content (i.e. structured, semistructured as well as unstructured) and multimedia content (e.g. videos, images, audio) on a multiplicity of platforms (e.g. machine-to-machine communications, social media sites, sensors networks, cyber-physical systems, and Internet of Things [IoT]). According the report of Dobre and Xhafa (2014), every day the world produces around 2.5 quintillion bytes of data (i.e. 1 exabyte equals 1 quintillion bytes or 1 exabyte equals 1 billion igabytes), with 90% of these data generated in the world being unstructured.

Gantz and Reinsel (2012) assessed that by 2020, over 40 Zettabytes (or 40 trillion gigabytes) of data will have been generated, imitated, and consumed. With this overwhelming amount of complex and heterogeneous data pouring from any-where, any-time, and any-device, there is undeniably an era of

Big Data – a phenomenon also referred to as the Data Deluge. The potential of BD is evident as it has been included in Gartner's Top 10 Strategic Technology Trends for 2013 (Savitz, 2012a) and Top 10 Critical Tech Trends for the Next Five Years (Savitz, 2012b).

The massive amount of data needs to be analyzed in an iterative, as well as in a time sensitive manner (Jukic, Sharma, Nestorov, & Jukic, 2015). With the availability of advanced BD analysing technologies (e.g. NoSQL Databases, BigQuery, MapReduce, Hadoop, WibiData and

Skytree), insights can be better attained to enable in improving business strategies and the decision-making process in critical sectors such as healthcare, economic productivity, energy futures, and predicting natural catastrophe, to name but a few (Yi, Liu, Liu, & Jin, 2014).

(Brown, Chui, & Manyika, 2011), rich business intelligence for better informed business decisions (Chen & Zhang, 2014), and support in enhancing the visibility and flexibility of supply chain and resource allocation (Kumar, Niu, & Ré, 2013). On the other hand, the challenges are significant such as data integration complexities (Gandomi & Haider, 2015), lack of skilled personal and sufficient resources (Kim, Trimi, & Chung, 2014), data security and privacy issues (Barnaghi, Sheth, & Henson, 2013), inadequate infrastructure and insignificant data warehouse architecture (Barbierato, Gribaudo, & Iacono, 2014), and synchronising large data (Jiang, Chen, Qiao, Weng, & Li, 2015). Advocates such as Sandhu and Sood (2014) perceive that the potential value of BD cannot be unearthed by simple statistical analysis.

Predictive analytics used to find the relationships of current or stale data to discover the patterns for estimating the future considering. Predictive analytics based on statistical methods has been described by (Gandomi & Haider, 2015), Gandomi, A., and Haider, M. (2015) in many disciplines.

Big data is a combination of structured, semi-structured and unstructured real time data originating from a variety of sources. Predictive analytics provides the methodology in tapping intelligence from large data sets. Many visionary companies such as Google, Amazon, etc. have realized the potential of big data and analytics in gaining competitive advantage. These techniques provide several opportunities like discovering patterns or better optimization algorithms. Managing and analyzing big data also constitutes a few challenges- namely size, quality, reliability and completeness of data.

From the literature, it has been observed that most of authors have described merit and demerit of big data and Predictive intelligence but how to use the big data technology in predictive intelligence has not been clearly stated.

The main objective this paper is to show the clearly relation to use the Big data technology for the predictive analysis.

Introduction of Big Data

Big data is a so large or complex that traditional data processing application software is inadequate to deal with the challenges which includes capture, storage, analysis, data duration, search, sharing, transfer, visualization, querying, updating and information privacy of data set

The term "big data" simple to use for predictive analytics, user behavior analytics, or certain other advanced data analytics methods that extract value from data, and seldom to a particular size of the data set.

Scientists, business executives, practitioners of medicine, advertising and governments alike regularly meet difficulties with large data-sets in areas including Internet search, finance, urban informatics, and business informatics due to limitation of e-Science work, including meteorology, complex physics simulations, biological and environmental research.

The data can be gathered from cheap and numerous information-sensing mobile devices, aerial (remote sensing), software logs, cameras, microphones, radio-frequency identification (RFID) readers and wireless sensor networks and due to this reason, per-capita capacity to store information has roughly doubled every 40 months since the 1980s; as of 2012, every day 2.5 Exabytes (2.5×1018) of data are generated. One question for large enterprises is to determine initiatives that affect the storage of the big data.

The work of Big data required massively parallel software running on tens, hundreds or even thousands of servers to produce the desired result which is not possible by relational database management systems and desktop statistics and visualization-packages, processing system The term "big data" varies on the capabilities of the users and their tools, and expanding capabilities make big data a moving target. Most definitions of big data focus on the size of data in storage. Size matters, but there are other important attributes of big data, namely data variety and data velocity. The three Vs of big data (volume, variety, and velocity) constitute a comprehensive definition, and they bust the myth that big data is only about data volume. In addition, each of the three Vs has its own ramifications for analytics. (https://www.sas.com/content/dam/SAS/en_us/doc/research2/big-data-analytics-105425.pdf)

Problem in Big Data

The big data are used to preserve the number of relevant, disparate datasets for analysed of new patterns, trends and insights in the dataset. Government agencies, along with cyber expert are also required to understand linking and analysis for preserving privacy rights of the individual. The big data faced the following furnished problem to adhere the aforesaid right of the individual.

Meeting the Need for Speed

In today's business competitive environment, companies not only find and analyze the relevant data, but they have to also think about how quick find the value in the data. Visualization helps to organizations to the performed analysis and makes decisions much more quickly, but the challenge is going through the complete volumes of data and accessing the level of detail needed at a high speed. The one possible solution is to use cloud computing for powerful parallel processing to crunch large volumes of data extremely quickly.

Understanding the Data

It takes a lot of understanding to know the user of the data received from social media, education, organization and business organization for general sense, such as a customer using a particular set of products and understand what it is you're trying to visualize out of the data. Without some sort of context, visualization tools are likely to be of less value to the user.

Addressing Data Quality

The concept of decision-making purposes will be jeopardized to the consumer if the data is not analyzed accurate or timely. This is a challenge with any data analysis, but when considering the volumes of information involved in big data projects, it becomes even more pronounced to clean the data in proper format for further used for processing. To address the aforesaid issue, companies need to have a data governance or an information management process in place to ensure the data is clean or not. It's always best to have a proactive method to address data quality issues so problems won't arise later.

Displaying Meaningful Results

Displaying meaningful result in the form of a graph becomes difficult when dealing with extremely large amounts of information or a variety of categories of information. One way to resolve these issues to create clusters of smaller groups of data become and used "binning," for more effectively visualize of data.

Dealing With Outliers

The graphical representations of data made possible by visualization can communicate trends and outliers much faster than tables containing numbers and text. Users can easily spot issues that need attention simply by glancing at a chart of outliers which is typically represented about 1 to 5 percent of data, but when you're working with massive amounts of data, viewing 1 to 5 percent of the data is rather difficult. Thereafter, how is possible to represent those points without getting into plotting issues? . Therefore, the possible solutions is to remove the outliers from the data (and therefore from the chart) or to create a separate chart for the outliers.

Market and Business Drivers for Big Data Analytics

Big data is everywhere these days. Marketing materials are bursting with references to how products have been enhanced to handle big data. Consultants and analysts are busy writing new articles and creating elegant presentations. But the sad reality is that big data remains one of the most ill-defined terms, we've seen in many a year.

The problem is that data volume is a metric that tells us little about the data characteristics that allow us to understand its sources, its uses in business and the ways we need to handle it in practice. Even the emerging approach of talking about big data in terms of volume, velocity and variety leaves a lot to be desired in terms of clarity about what big data really are.

The concept of the Big data can be applied to every area of the life for better understanding the data value and use of the resource for futuristic performance.

Separating the Big Data Reality From Hype

The origins of big data as a concept and phrase can be traced back to the scientific community. Researchers in astronomy, physics, biology and other fields have long been at the forefront of collecting vast quantities of data from ever more sophisticated sensors. By the early 2000s, they encountered significant problems in processing and storing these volumes and coined the term *big data* probably as a synonym for big headaches. We see here the beginnings of the business driver mentioned above, as science today is founded largely on statistical analysis of collected data. What begins with pure science moves inexorably to engineering and finally emerges in business and, especially, marketing.

The second class, also machine-sourced, consists of computer event logs tracking everything from processor usage and database transactions to click streams and instant message distribution. While machine-generated, data in both of these classes are proxies for events in the real world. In business terms, those that record the results of human actions are of particular interest. For example, measurements of speed, acceleration and braking forces from an automobile can be used to make inferences about driver behavior and thus insurance risk. In classes three and four, we have social media information directly created by humans, divided into the more highly structured textual information and the less structured multimedia audio, image and video categories. Statistical analysis of such information, gives direct access to people's opinions and reactions, allowing new methods of individual marketing and direct response to emerging opportunities or problems. Much of the current hype around big data comes from the insights into customer behavior that Web giants like Google and eBay and mega-retailers such as Walmart can obtain by analyzing data in these classes especially the textual class, so far. However, in the longer term, machine-generated data, particularly from the metrics and measures class, is likely to be the biggest game-changer simply because of the number of events recorded and communicated.

Understanding the Business Drivers

By now, you've probably noticed that there are many different options that you can select for your big data analytics program. Options include vendor tool types and tool features, users' techniques and methodologies, and team or organizational structures. The list is long and complex, and it includes a few items you probably haven't considered seriously. Regardless of what project stage you're in with big data analytics, knowing the available options is foundational to making good decisions about approaches to take and software or hardware products to evaluate.

To quantify these and other issues, TDWI presented survey respondents with a long list of options for big data analytics. The list includes options that arrived fairly recently (clouds, MapReduce, complex event processing), have been around for a few years, but are just now experiencing broad adoption (data visualization, predictive analytics), or have been around for years and are firmly established (statistical analysis, hand-coded SQL). The list is a catalog of available options for big data analytics, and responses to survey questions indicated what combinations of analytic functions, platforms, and tool types users are employing today, as well as which they anticipate using in a few years. From this information, we can deduce priorities that can guide users in planning. We can also quantify trends and project future directions for advanced analytics and big data.

(<https://www.sas.com/content/dam/SAS/en_us/doc/research2/big-data-analytics-105425.pdf>)

Business driver also used the following furnished points to understand the data of business driver.

The quest for Business agility, Increased data volumes being captured and stored, increased data volumes pushed into the network, Growing variation in types of data assets for analysis, alternate and unsynchronized methods for facilitating data delivery rising demand for real-time integration of analytical results, Technology Trends Lowering Barriers to Entry,

TECHNOLOGY OF BIG DATA

In the era of Big Data where data volume and variety is too bulky, it is difficult for older generations of technology to manage this. Therefore new classes of technologies are evolving to handle this.

Selection of Big Data Technology

This new technologies arise in response to handle Big data creation and storage, retrieving and analyzing which further encounter operational vs. analytical Big Data solutions. Selection of operational vs analytical Big Data solution isn't the right way to think about the challenge. These two technologies are complementary to each other and someone may require both to develop a complete Big Data solution. Presently two Big data technologies like MongoDB and Hadoop are integrated together for solutions with an API integration.

Operational vs. Analytical

In Big data, Operational abilities comprise of capturing and storing data in real time where as analytical abilities include complex analysis of all the data. These two technologies are complementary to each other and hence deployed simultaneously.

In Big Data, Operational and analytical technologies have different necessity and in order to attend those requirements different architectures have developed. Operational systems consist of No-SQL database deals with responding to concurrent requests. Analytical Systems work on complex queries which handle almost all the data. Both system work in cycle and handle hundreds of terabytes of data across billion of records.

The comparison of the Operational Vs Analytical based different attributes has been furnished as Table 1.

MapReduce

MapReduce is a programming model for processing massive data sets with a parallel, distributed algorithm on a cluster. Therefore MapReduce is coupled with Hadoop Distributed File System (HDFS) to handle Big data.

The basic unit of information, used in MapReduce is a Key-value pair. All types of structured and unstructured data need to be translated to this basic unit, before feeding the data to MapReduce model. As the name suggests, MapReduce model consist of two separate routines, namely Map-function and Reduce-function. The computation on an input (i.e. on a set of pairs) in MapReduce model occurs in three stages: The MapReduce model is furnished in figure 1.

Table 1. Operational Vs Analytical

Attributes/Technique	Operational	Analytical
Latency	1 ms - 100 ms	1 min - 100 min
Concurrency	1000 - 100,000	1 - 10
Access Pattern	Writes and Reads	Reads
Queries	Selective	Unselective
Data Scope	Operational	Retrospective
End User	Customer	Data Scientist
Technology	NoSQL	MapReduce, MPP Database

Figure 1. MapReduce Architecture

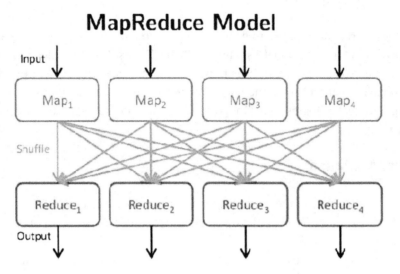

Step 1: The map stage.
Step 2: The shuffle stage.
Step 3: The reduce stage.

Semantically, the map and shuffle phases distribute the data, and the reduce phase performs the computation. In this chapter, each of these stages will be dicussed in detail.

MapReduce logic, unlike other data frameworks, is not restricted to just structure datasets. It has an extensive capability to handle unstructured data as well. Map stage is the critical step which makes this possible. Mapper brings a structure to unstructured data. For illustration, if I want to count the number of photographs on my laptop by the location (city), where the photo was taken, I need to analyze unstructured data. The mapper makes key-value pairs from this data set. In this case, key will be the location and value will be the photograph. After mapper is done with its task, we have a structure to the entire data-set.

In the map stage, the mapper takes a single key-value pair as input and produces any number of key-value pairs as output.

The shuffle stage is works automatically and implementing MapReduce routes all of the associated values with an individual key to the same reducer.

The reduce stage, takes all of the values associated with a single key k and outputs any number of key-value pairs. It takes the user designs a function as the input values associated with a single key and outputs any number of pairs.

The MapReduce paradigm used many rounds (usually called jobs) of different map and reduce functions to performed the desired output.

Hadoop

With a boost in the access of internet and the habit of the internet, the data captured by different search engine increased exponentially year on year.

The Hadop software framework has been designed to supports HDFS and MapReduce to solve the aforesaid problem.

Hadoop is an absolute eco-system of open source projects to provide us the framework to deal with big data. But it may face the following furnished challenges.

1. High processing capacity server with High capital investment
2. Enormous time taken
3. Time will be wastage if error occurred at last stage of long query.
4. Difficulty in program query building

Despite these problem, Hadop provide following furnished way to solve these issue.

1. **High Processing Capacity Server with High Capital Investment:** Hadoop works on clusters way with maximum of 4500 machines together and also keep multiple copies to ensure reliability of data.
2. **Enormous Time Taken:** Its works as paralle processing way on broken data into pieces and hence saving time.
3. **Time Will Be Wastage if Error Occurred at Last Stage of Long Query:** Hadoop takes back up data set data-sets at every level with the executes of query on duplicate datasets to avoid process loss in case of individual failure. These steps make Hadoop processing more precise and accurate.
4. **Difficulty in Program Query Building:** Hadop query is simple as coding of any language.

MEMORY DATABASE

The evolution of memory technology created an impact on storage and computer architectures with changes in software.

Figure 2. In Memory Technology Market

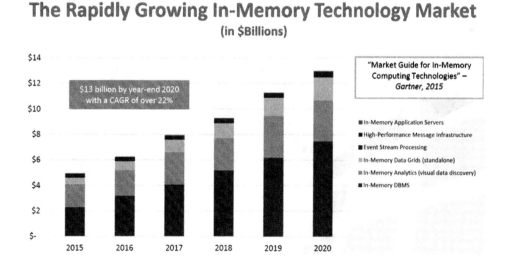

Therefore, In Memory Computing technology has been increasingly to speed up data-related operations to solve the big data mantra..

HTAP (hybrid transactional and analytical processing) have a single database backend to support both transactional and analytical workloads and many IMC solutions emphasize HTAP,build their case.

According to Abe Kleinfeld, GridGain CEO puts it, "traditionally in databases memory was a valuable resource, so you tried to use it with caution. In our case, we always go to memory first and avoid touching the disk at all cost. The algorithms we use may be the same -- it's all about cache and hits and misses after all -- but the thinking is different."

Massively Parallel Computing

An MPP database is a type of database that works in parallel for many operations to performed by many processing units at a time. It used coordinated processing of a program on different parts of the program to make it multiprocessing. Therefore, it use multiple processors, multi-core processors, and servers, and storage appliances equipped for parallel processing. Greenplum database processing of MPP has been furnished in Figure 3.

1. **Master Host:** Separate physical server with its own OS/CPU/storage/memory. Hosts master database..
2, 3, 4. **Represents the Segment Hosts:** Individual physical servers with their own OS/CPU/storage/memory..
5. **Interconnect Switch:** Segment server databases communicate through an interconnect switch

Figure 3. Greeplum Physical Architecture
Note: This configuration is only used to demonstrate the working of Greenplum database.

Data Mining Grid

In the last decade, the revolution of Internet and the boom in Web applications, momentum us towards process integration and cooperative computing with supercomputing facilities and world of Web-based tools. Therefore, for new perspectives in industrial and scientific computational processes, an emerging technology has been being proposed as the most natural way to pursue such a goal named as grid computing (GC).

Grid computing is (GC) is a model of distributed computing that uses geographical and disparate resources (a logical entity such as a distributed file or a computing cluster) that are found on the network (grid network). These resources may include processing power, storage systems, catalogs, data, network resources, sensors and other hardware such as input and output devices. In grid computing, individuals' users can access computers and data transparently without having to consider location, operating systems and other details.

It used networks of computers as a single, unified computing tool and clustering or coupling a wide variety of facilities over a wide geographical region along with supercomputers, storage systems, data sources, and special classes of devices, and using them as a single unifying resource (computational grid).

At the beginning, it was used to link supercomputing sites but now a days it used collaborative engineering, data exploration, high-throughput computing (HTC), meta application, and high-performance computing (HPC), .

Scientific computing involves the use of computers to analyse and solve scientific and engineering problems as well as construction of numerical solutions and mathematical model techniques. In practical terms, computational science is the application of computer simulations and other forms of computations to problem in various science and engineering research disciplines like the FUTA community that is an institution where research is taken to be the root to all development of the entire department.

Distributed Database (DB)

By selecting a distributed storage DB, we succeeded in constructing IT infrastructure capable of high-speed processing at a large number of manufacturing sites. In the new IT infrastructure, we achieved resource leveling of the application server and improvement of data processing time. It is expected that data file stagnation and DB registration delay can be resolved.

Distributed File System

A distributed file system is a client/server-based application where clients can access and process data stored on the server as if it were on their own computer. Whenever, a user want to accesses a file on the server, the server sends copy of the file to user, with cached on the user's computer. The concept of distributed file system has been used to organize the file and directory services of individual servers into a global directory to all the users of the global file system and organization it in hierarchical and directory-based.

As more than one client may be access the same data therefore the server must have a mechanism to organize the updates the client with recent data Distributed file systems normally used file or database replication (distributing copies of data on multiple servers) to protect against data access failures and enhance availability of data..

Examples of Distributed File systems are Sun Microsystems' Network File System (NFS), Novell NetWare, Microsoft's Distributed File System, and IBM/Transarc's DFS are some examples of distributed file systems.

PREDICTIVE INTELLIGENCE

Predictive Intelligence is the collection and interpretation of data often automatically or through refined algorithms, so as to gain a perception of future events. For example, collection of behavioral data about consumers from a variety of sources and then analyzing this data to identify characteristics patterns and then using that to deliver relevant communications and offers to consumers to influence them to engage more with a business to meet its goals.

Introduction of Predictive Intelligence

Predictive Intelligence is closely related with terms like Predictive Recommendation, Predictive Marketing and Predictive Analytics. Although there are some minor variations among the terms, but in general view they all essentially mean the same thing.

This revolutionary method in e-business majorly concentrates on developing connections between a business and its consumers. Companies now have access to more information about their consumers than ever before and data analysis can now be done using better tools that assists in understanding this data. This data is voluminous in nature, and the perceptions drawn are so exact, that companies can move beyond simply responding to consumer needs; they can actually predict them.

The maturity level of the IT organization and the leveraged tools are considered under a natural progression of reactive, proactive, and predictive technology. The position of the organization does not matter in terms of e, the end goal is the same: to efficiently administer an increasingly intricate infrastructure. To accomplish this objective, IT organizations must be able to forecast and solve problems before they affect the customer.

In broad-spectrum, there are three approaches to IT administration, which are as follows:

A *reactive* approach concentrates on an IT problem or occurrence after it has already taken place. Clearly, this approach poses the largest hazard of prolonged service disruptions, as the recognition and resolution of each occurrence is not started until an incident is reported.

A *proactive* approach engages in setting pre-determined "lines" or thresholds for key performance measurements, and endorses alert triggering each time these thresholds are crossed. For example, if a server's utilization exceeds a predefined percentage of the total capacity available, an alert is raised before service delivery is impacted.

Predictive intelligence technology gathers and collects data, then correlates and analyzes this information to help IT identify, isolate, and resolve threats to mission critical applications at the earliest possible opportunity, in advance of a service disruption.

While monitoring the performance of every infrastructure component for *abnormal* behavior is a critical part of successful management, it is equally crucial that the infrastructure be able to automatically adapt and adjust to *normal* changes as they happen.

Predictive intelligence technology, through advanced measurement and analysis functionality, actually *learns* what is normal for your organization. This is achieved by automatically establishing and adjusting to a band of normal operation for every attribute within your environment - a practice referred to as dynamic thresholding. As your infrastructure changes, the technology adapts, quickly learning, anticipating, and adjusting to how the system will behave on a Monday morning versus a Sunday evening for instance. This virtually eliminates the need to manually create and maintain constant thresholds, or manually set and maintain rules-based alarms.

Organizations are turning to predictive analytics to help them solve difficult problems and uncover new opportunities. Common uses include:

Detecting Fraud: Combining multiple analytics methods can improve pattern detection and prevent criminal behavior. As cyber security becomes a growing concern, high-performance behavioral analytics examines all actions on a network in real time to spot abnormalities that may indicate fraud, zero-day vulnerabilities and advanced persistent threats.

Predictive Intelligence and it's analytics monitors communications between persons and systems to recognize all the details that are happing inside a traffic, and successfully identifies and stops threats in internal network. Organizations have the right to monitor employees' emails, track all the online activity and observe their post on social media.

Big data analytics can help us in this era. The procedure can find anomalies in big cluster, as divergent to scrutinizing a solitary individual's measures. By reviewing huge data set, pattern of standard actions can be recognized, drawing attention to irregular activities that might call for additional analysis. This pattern and anomaly revealing makes easy to predict threats while retaining user privacy.

Specific tools are there to assist agencies predict and prevent external threats. Most organizations have arrangements to provide secure networks or observe traffic to avoid an attack. Big data algorithms and intelligent tools take this protection one more step further, letting agency gather and investigate massive amounts of data to predict threats.

The Predictive Intelligence Services allow customers to employ industry accepted encryption standard to protect Customers' data during transmissions by including 128 - bit TLS Certificates and 2048 - bit RSA public keys at a minimum.

- **Optimizing Marketing Campaigns:** Predictive analytics are used to determine customer responses or purchases, as well as promote cross-sell opportunities. Predictive models help businesses attract, retain and grow their most profitable customers.
- **Improving Operations:** Many companies use predictive models to forecast inventory and manage resources. For example, airlines use predictive analytics to set ticket prices, hotels try to predict the number of guests for any given night to maximize occupancy and increase revenue.
- **Reducing Risk:** Predictive analysis allows us to use historical data for drawing beneficial insights about the present and the future. Such detailed information helps us to handle the present situations more efficiently along with being better equipped for the future, thus reducing the risk in any situation. For example, hospitals can use this technology to assess the number of patients or critical cases at present and also in the future and utilize the available resources in an efficient manner or arrange for alternatives in case of dearth of resources thus reducing the number of casualties.

Problems in Predictive Intelligence

As is the case with every human creation limitations exist in the usability of data as well; a few among them are listed below:

- **Incompleteness of Data:** Data does not come with any guarantee for completeness. more often than not data sets are incomplete, thus reducing its usefulness.

A classic example of such a situation would be a system built to analyze the weather of a region having only past 2 or 3 years of data to refer to, this leads to the system making assumptions, and the minute there is a significant change in the weather in that region the system fails to cope.

- **Inaccuracy of Data:** Like completeness there is no guarantee about the correctness or accuracy of data as well.

For example people may get conscious while sharing personal information like their eating or drinking habits, exercise regime and so on. This may lead them to answer questions incorrectly while participating in surveys etc. Now if a system uses data from such surveys to derive results the conclusion is bound to be distorted.

- **Variation in Data Obtained from Different Sources:** Data gathered from different sources like company websites, emails, social media, online forms and surveys have different formats and also vary in quality. Such data is often incompatible and needs to undergo extensive processing before it can be used for analysis.

In order to understand the limitations of your data follow certain processes like:

- Look for boundary values and eliminate them if need be.
- Ensure that your system has access to a large database of training data.
- Be mindful of data integration when the data is derived for diverse sources.
- Select data-sets capable of representing the entire population.
- Choose appropriate attributes for your system's analysis.
- Check the data for completeness and take account of missing data, etc.

Even after taking care of all this your data may still need to undergo pre-processing before it can be used for analysis to address various issues with the original data, such as missing data values, errors / inconsistency in the data, duplicities in the data, etc.

BIG DATA TECHNOLOGY IN PREDICTIVE INTELLIGENCE

Countries across the world are viewing data as the latest resource for combative benefit. We generate an unfathomable amount of data each day from a range of different sources starting from social networking sites to monetary transactions and photographs. Such huge and complicated data collection is named Big data and is extremely challenging to manage using the traditional database management processes.

Big data has certain important characteristics like bulk, origin, speed, diversity and accuracy. The bulk or magnitude of data will affect every individual on the planet and even then we are analyzing less than 1% of the total volume of data available at present.With each passing day the speed at which data is generated and the number of origins of data is also increasing at a maddening pace. And along with the growth of data the expectations regarding the use of this data is also increasing at a steady pace. This is because Big data is a consists of both structured and unstructured and analysis of such data sets calls for new age technologies like data-mining, statistical data processing, predictive analysis, optimized methods and so on.

The traditional Business Intelligence (BI) processes fail to use Big data to it's fullest capacity and organizations often experience hardships while trying to perform advanced analysis using their current infrastructure. This is where Big Data Analytics comes into the picture. It applies new age analytic methods like Hadoop, Mapreduce, Data-mining grids etc to extensive data sets, which the traditional analytic processes fail to do. The results produced by Big Data Analytics have the potential to transfigure businesses by shaping future business decisions through increased business acumen.

The value of Big Data lies in its capability to draw results by analysis of data through pattern recognition, understanding meaning, decision making and finally presenting intelligent outputs to the world. With the evolution of Big data technology, organizations are becoming excessively dependent on Predictive Analytics for increasing involvement with consumers, process optimization and cutting down the business expenses. The Predictive Analytics and real time data union is an infinite task that has the capability to generate noteworthy combative leverage for industries.

Limitation and Future Scope

Driving the utility of big data analytics to the point where the perception gained from it can be used to make decisions calls for resources like latest technologies, operations and talent. Below listed are some of the limitations of big data analytics:

Limitation

- **Proper Infrastructure:** Big data analytics requires high-end infrastructure in order to be able to reinforce the increasing needs of big data among its users. Such infrastructure comprises of latest technologies capable of dealing with cloud computing, level based database, grid computing, distributed network etc.
- **Analytic Ability:** Big data analytics calls for engagement in the latest and most powerful analytic tools like Natural language processing (NLP), rule engines, interactive visuals etc.
- **Mobility:** Ease of access is an important aspect of any technology today, and with the increasing popularity of Big data analytics its users would look for mobile options for accessing it.
- **Data Protection:** Information security is a huge concern associated with all upcoming technologies. Big data analytics needs to comply with the security rules and regulations currently in place, however risk assessment becomes an excessively challenging task when dealing with unstructured data.

- **Skilled Personnel:** Companies often struggle with procuring talented resources who can work with Big data.

Future Scope

It has been observed that there is a huge demand for Big Data Analytics due to its awesome features which have the tremendous growth on the various domains where analytics has been utilized. The image below depicts the job opportunities on various domains of real life.

Big Data Analytics with predictive intelligence will be play a vital role in the defense, text mining, combining machine learning, security threat prediction, detection, and deterrence and prevention programs and ontology modeling to provide easy and incorporated way to deal with problems.

It is the blasting in many countries with lots of accessible chances in the market. Occupations in this field fulfill the need of company and develop there in the current circumstances of business. Understanding the business situations and able to handle them with a enormous will enhances the money related position of the companies. Thus, future of Big Data Analytics with predictive intelligence is very bright and promising in all domains of real life in many countries.

Figure 4. Big Data Analytic Survey

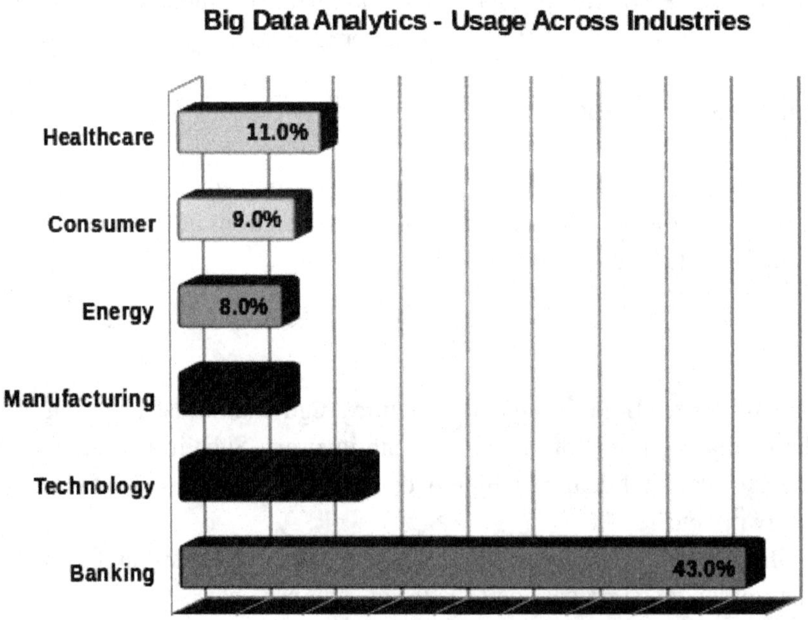

Big Data Analytics - Usage Across Industries

Source: Peer Research – Big Data Analytics Survey

CONCLUSION

Analytics does not remove the need for human insights and become the gripping need for skilled people to understand the data, think about the data from the business point of view and come up with useful insights. Therefore, it is very much necessity for the technology professionals with Analytics skill to finding a high demand and powerful tools to solve the harness of the business.. A professional with the big data Analytical with predictive intelligence can be the master the ocean of Data and become a vital asset to an organization, to boosting their business and with career advancement.

REFERENCES

Agarwal, R., & Dhar, V. (2014). Editorial – big data, data science, and analytics: The opportunity and challenge for is research. *Information Systems Research*, *25*(3), 443–448. doi:10.1287/isre.2014.0546

Barbierato, E., Gribaudo, M., & Iacono, M. (2014). Performance evaluation of No SQL big data applications using multi-formalism models. *Future Generation Computer Systems*, *37*, 345–353. doi:10.1016/j.future.2013.12.036

Barnaghi, P., Sheth, A., & Henson, C. (2013). From data to actionable knowledge: Big data challenges in the web of things. *IEEE Intelligent Systems*, *28*(6), 6–11. doi:10.1109/MIS.2013.142

Brown, B., Chui, M., & Manyika, J. (2011). Are you ready for the era of Big Data? *The McKinsey Quarterly*, *4*, 24–35.

Chen, C. L. P., & Zhang, C. Y. (2014). Data-intensive applications, challenges, techniques and technologies: A survey on big data. *Information Sciences*, *275*, 314–347. doi:10.1016/j.ins.2014.01.015

Dobre, C., & Xhafa, F. (2014). Intelligent services for big data science. *Future Generation Computer Systems*, *37*, 267–281. doi:10.1016/j.future.2013.07.014

Gandomi, A., & Haider, M. (2015). Beyond the hype: Big data concepts, methods, and analytics. *International Journal of Information Management*, *35*(2), 137–144. doi:10.1016/j.ijinfomgt.2014.10.007

Gandomi, A., & Haider, M. (2015). *Beyond the hype: Big data concepts, methods, and analytics*. Academic Press.

Gandomi, A., & Haider, M. (2015). Beyond the hype: Big data concepts, methods, and analytics. *International Journal of Information Management*, *35*(2), 137–144. doi:10.1016/j.ijinfomgt.2014.10.007

Gantz, J., & Reinsel, D. (2012). *The Digital Universe in 2020: Big data, bigger digital shadows, and biggest growth in the Far East*. IDC – EMC Corporation. Available at http://www.emc.com/collateral/analyst-reports/idc-the-digital-universe-in2020.pdf

Jiang, H., Chen, Y., Qiao, Z., Weng, T. H., & Li, K. C. (2015). Scaling up MapReduce-based big data processing on multi-GPU systems. *Cluster Computing*, *18*(1), 369–383. doi:10.100710586-014-0400-1

Jin, X., Wah, B. W., Cheng, X., & Wang, Y. (2015). Significance and challenges of big data research. *Big Data Research*, 2(2), 59–64. doi:10.1016/j.bdr.2015.01.006

Kim, G. H., Trimi, S., & Chung, J. H. (2014). Big-data applications in the government sector. *Communications of the ACM*, 57(3), 78–85. doi:10.1145/2500873

Kumar, A., Niu, F., & Ré, C. (2013). Hazy: Making it easier to build and maintain big-data analytics. *Communications of the ACM*, 56(3), 40–49. doi:10.1145/2428556.2428570

Sandhu, R., & Sood, S. K. (2014). Scheduling of big data applications on distributed cloud based on QoS parameters. *Cluster Computing*, 18, 1–12.

Savitz, E. (2012a). *Gartner: Top 10 strategic technology trends for 2013*. Available at http://www.forbes.com/sites/ericsavitz/2012/10/23/gartner-top-10-strategictechnology-rends-for-2013/

Savitz, E. (2012b). *Gartner: 10 critical tech trends for the next five years*. Available at http://www.forbes.com/sites/ericsavitz/2012/10/22/gartner-10-critical-techtrends-for-the-next-five-years

Yi, X., Liu, F., Liu, J., & Jin, H. (2014). Building a network highway for big data: Architecture and challenges. *IEEE Network*, 28(4), 5–13. doi:10.1109/MNET.2014.6863125

Chapter 2
Big-Data-Based Architectures and Techniques:
Big Data Reference Architecture

Gopala Krishna Behara
Wipro Technologies, India

ABSTRACT

This chapter covers the essentials of big data analytics ecosystems primarily from the business and technology context. It delivers insight into key concepts and terminology that define the essence of big data and the promise it holds to deliver sophisticated business insights. The various characteristics that distinguish big data datasets are articulated. It also describes the conceptual and logical reference architecture to manage a huge volume of data generated by various data sources of an enterprise. It also covers drivers, opportunities, and benefits of big data analytics implementation applicable to the real world.

INTRODUCTION

In Information Age, we are overwhelmed with data, ways to store, process, analyze, interpret, consume and act upon the data. The term Big Data is quite vague and ill defined. The word "Big" is too generic and the question is how "Big" is considered as "Big" and how "Small" is small (Smith, 2013) is relative to time, space and circumstance. The size of "Big Data" is always evolving and the meaning of Big Data Volume would lie between Terabyte (TB) and Zettabyte (ZB) range. The concept of big data is the explosion of data from the Internet, cloud, data center, mobile, Internet of things, sensors and domains that possess and process huge datasets. Cisco claimed that humans have entered the ZB era in 2015 (Cisco, 2017).

DOI: 10.4018/978-1-5225-6210-8.ch002

Based on social media statistics 2018, the face book claimed that, there are over 300 million photos uploaded to Facebook every day (Nowak & Spiller, 2017). On an average 300 hours of videos are uploaded every minute on You Tube (YouTube, 2017). Approximately, 42 billion texts are sent and 1.6 billion photos shared through Whatsapp daily (Stout, 2018). Since 2005, business investment in hardware, software, talent, and services has increased as much as 50 percent, to $4 trillion (Rijmenam, 2018).

In 2005, Roger Mougalas from O'Reilly Media coined the term Big Data for the first time. It refers to a large set of data that is almost impossible to manage and process using traditional business intelligence tools. During the same year, Yahoo created Hadoop. This was built on top of Google's MapReduce. Its goal was to index the entire World Wide Web (Rijmenam, 2018).

In 2009, the Indian government decides to take an iris scan, fingerprint and photograph of all of its 1.2 billion inhabitants. All this data is stored in the largest biometric database in the world (Chandra, 2018).

In 2010, at Technomy conference, Eric Schmidt stated, "There were 5 Exabyte's of information created by the entire world between the dawn of civilization and 2003. Now that same amount is created every two days." (Schmidt, 2010).

In 2011, McKinsey released a report on Big Data which claimed that, the next frontier for innovation, competition, and productivity, states that in 2018 the USA alone will face a shortage of 140.000 – 190.000 data scientist as well as 1.5 million data managers (Manyika, 2011).

Another detailed review was contributed by Visualizing.org (Hewlett Packard Enterprise, 2017) in Big Data. It is focused on the time line of how to implement Big Data Analytics. Its historical description is mainly determined by events related to the Big Data push by many internet and IT companies such as Google, YouTube, Yahoo, Facebook, Twitter and Apple. It emphasized the significant impact of Hadoop in the history of Big Data Analytics.

In the past few years, there has been a massive increase in Big Data startups, trying to deal with Big Data and helping organizations to understand Big Data and more and more companies are slowly adopting and moving towards Big Data.

Figure 1 shows the history of Big Data and its eco system.

Figure 1. History of Big Data

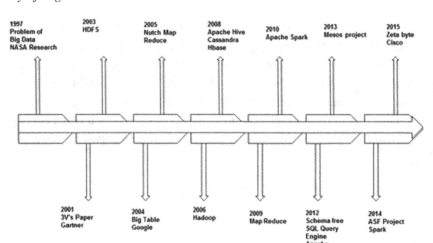

The data sources and their formats are continuous to grow in variety and complexity. Few list of sources includes the public web, social media, mobile applications, federal, state and local records and databases, commercial databases that aggregate individual data from a spectrum of commercial transactions and public records, geospatial data, surveys and traditional offline documents scanned by optical character recognition into electronic form. The advent of the more Internet enabled devices and sensors expands the capacity to collect data from physical entities, including sensors and radio-frequency identification (RFID) chips. Personal location data can come from GPS chips, cell-tower triangulation of mobile devices, mapping of wireless networks, and in-person payments (Manyika, 2011). The big challenge is, how do we consume those data sources and transform them into actionable information Big Data describes a data management strategy that integrates many new types of data and data management alongside traditional data.

There exist many sources, which predict exponential data growth toward 2020 and beyond. Human- and machine-generated data is experiencing an overall 10x faster growth rate than traditional business data, and machine data is increasing even more rapidly at 50x the growth rate.

IDC predicts that by 2020, 50% of all business analytics software will incorporate prescriptive analytics built on cognitive computing technology, and the amount of high-value data will double, making 60% of information delivered to decision makers actionable (Hewlett Packard Enterprise, 2017). 75% of Big Data is helping government departments to improve the quality of citizen's life style (Mullich, 2013; Wedutenko & Keeing, 2014).

The objective of this chapter is to describe the aspects of big data, definition, drivers, principles, scenarios, best practices and architectures.

BACKGROUND

Today, the data that we deal with is diverse. Users create content like blog posts, tweets, social network interactions, etc. To tackle the challenges of managing this data, a new breed of technologies has emerged.

Data architecture earlier designed primarily for batch processing of mostly structured data and created to address specific Business Units, Enterprise needs. It lacks in the ability to support data democratization, ad-hoc analytics, machine learning/artificial intelligence (ML/AI), complex data governance and security needs - all of which are critical to building a true data driven enterprise.

These new technologies are more complex than traditional databases. These systems can scale to vastly larger sets of data, but using these technologies effectively requires a fundamentally new set of techniques.

Enterprises that do not actively transform themselves to become data driven are left behind, their basic existence questioned. CXOs recognize the threat and the opportunity, and are eager to deploy a modern data architecture that can not only help them store a wide variety of large amounts volume of data but also provides an enterprise-wide analytic platform. This can empower every single employee in the organization to take data driven decisions in real-time, with little or no support from IT.

Big data addresses large, diverse, complex, longitudinal, and/or distributed datasets generated from instruments, sensors, Internet transactions, email, video, click streams, and/or all other digital sources available today and in the future (National Science Foundation, 2012). It describes a holistic information management strategy that includes and integrates many new types of data and data management alongside traditional data. The boundaries of what constitutes a Big Data problem are also changing due to the ever shifting and advancing landscape of software and hardware technology.

Thirty years ago, one gigabyte of data could amount to a Big Data problem and require special purpose computing resources. Now, gigabytes of data are commonplace and can be easily transmitted, processed and stored on consumer-oriented devices. Data within Big Data environments generally accumulates from enterprise applications, sensors and external sources. Enterprise applications consume this processed data directly or can fed into a data warehouse to enrich existing data there.

The results obtained through the processing of Big Data can lead to a wide range of insights and benefits, such as,

- Operational optimization
- Actionable intelligence
- Identification of new markets
- Accurate predictions
- Fault and fraud detection
- Improved decision-making

Concepts and Terminology

The following are the fundamental concepts and terms used in Big Data Architectures and Techniques.

Datasets: Collections or groups of related data. Each group or dataset member shares the same set of attributes or properties as others in the same dataset. Some examples of datasets are:

- Tweets stored in a flat file
- A collection of image files in a directory
- An extract of rows from a database table stored in a CSV formatted file
- Historical weather observations that are stored as XML files

Data Analysis: Process of analyzing data to find facts, relationships, patterns, insights and trends. The overall goal of data analysis is to support better decision making.

Big Data: A massive volume of both structured and unstructured data that is so large that it's difficult to process with traditional database and software techniques

Data Analytics: A discipline that includes the management of the complete data lifecycle, which covers collecting, cleansing, organizing, storing, analyzing and governing data. Data analytics enable data-driven decision-making with scientific backing so that the decisions based on factual data and not just on experience.

Highlighted below are the four categories of analytics,

1. **Descriptive Analytics**: It addresses to answer questions about events that have already occurred. This form of analytics contextualizes data to generate information.
2. **Diagnostic Analytics**: It aim to determine the cause of a phenomenon that occurred in the past using questions that focus on the reason behind the event. The goal is to determine the information related to the phenomenon in order to enable answering questions that seek to determine why something has occurred.

3. **Predictive Analytics**: It helps to determine the outcome of an event that might occur in the future. Enriched information with meaning to generate knowledge that conveys how that information is related. The strength and magnitude of the associations form the basis of models to generate future predictions based on past events.

4. **Prescriptive Analytics**: Built upon the results of predictive analytics by prescribing actions be taken. This type of analytics used to gain an advantage or mitigate a risk.

Types of Data: The data processed by Big Data solutions can be human-generated or machine-generated. Human-generated data is the result of human interaction with systems, such as online services and digital devices. Software programs and hardware devices in response to real-world events generate machine-generated data. The primary types of data are:

- Structured data
- Unstructured data
- Semi-structured data

Structured Data: Conforms to a data model or schema and is often stored in tabular form. Used to capture relationship between different entities. The data is often stored in a relational database. Generally, generation of structured data is by enterprise applications and information systems like ERP and CRM systems.

Unstructured Data: Data that does not conform to a data model or data schema. Unstructured data has a faster growth rate than structured data. This form of data is either textual or binary and often conveyed via files that are self-contained and non-relational. A text file may contain the contents of various tweets or blog postings. Binary files are often media files that contain image, audio or video data.

Semi Structured Data: This type of data has a defined level of structure and consistency, but is not relational in nature. Instead, semi-structured data is hierarchical or graph-based. This kind of data is commonly stored in files that contain text. XML and JSON files are common forms of semi-structured data.

Metadata: It provides information about a dataset's characteristics and structure. This type of data is mostly machine-generated data. The tracking of metadata is crucial to Big Data processing, storage and analysis because it provides information about the pedigree of the data and its provenance during processing. Examples of metadata include:

- XML tags providing the author and creation date of a document
- Attributes providing the file size and resolution of a digital photograph governments

CHARACTERISTICS OF BIG DATA

Big Data Analytics is an integrated Business Intelligence and Data Analytics, which includes conventional and Big Data. Comparing to the traditional data, big data has five major characteristics: Volume, Velocity, Variety, Veracity and Value (Normandeau, 2013; Hilbert, 2016; Hilbert, 2015).

- **Volume:** It indicates more data. The volume of data that processed by Big Data solutions is substantial and ever growing. High data volumes impose distinct data storage and processing demands, as well as additional data preparation, curation and management processes. Big Data requires processing high volumes of data, that is, data of unknown value. For example, twitter data feeds, clicks on a web page, network traffic, sensor-enabled equipment capturing data and many more. Typical data sources that are responsible for generating high data volumes are:
- Online transactions
- Scientific and research experiments
- Sensors, such as GPS sensors, RFIDs, smart meters and telematics
- Social media, such as Facebook and Twitter
- **Velocity**: In Big Data environments, data can arrive at fast speeds, and enormous datasets can accumulate within very short periods. From an enterprise's point of view, the velocity of data translates into the amount of time it takes for the data processing, once it enters the enterprise's perimeter. Coping with the fast inflow of data requires the enterprise to design highly elastic and available data processing solutions and corresponding data storage capabilities. Some Internet of Things (IoT) applications have health and safety ramifications that require real-time evaluation and action. Other internet-enabled smart products operate in real-time or near real-time. As an example, consumer e-commerce applications seek to combine mobile device location and personal preferences to make time sensitive offers.
- **Variety**: New unstructured data types. Unstructured and semi-structured data types, such as text, audio, and video require additional processing to both derive meaning and the supporting metadata. Unstructured data has many of the same requirements as structured data, such as summarization, lineage, auditability, and privacy. Further complexity arises when data from a known source changes without notice.
- **Veracity**: Quality or fidelity of data. Assessment of Data that enters Big Data environments for quality, which can lead to data processing activities to resolve invalid data and remove noise. Data with a high signal-to-noise ratio has more veracity than data with a lower ratio. Data that is acquired in a controlled manner, for example via online customer registrations, usually contains less noise than data acquired via uncontrolled sources, such as blog postings
- **Value**: There is a range of quantitative and investigative techniques to derive value from data. The cost of data storage and compute has exponentially decreased, thus providing an abundance of data from which statistical sampling and other techniques become relevant, and meaningful.

Figure 2. Big Data Characteristics

Volume	Velocity	Variety	Veracity	Volume
Data at Scale	Data in Motion	Data in Many Forms	Data Uncertainty	Data Usage
Terabytes to petabytes of data	Batch to Streaming Analysis of streaming data to enable decisions within fractions of a second	Structured, unstructured, text, multimedia	Managing the reliability and predictability of inherently imprecise data types	Managing the Cost, Storage and Time for data processing

DRIVERS OF BIG DATA

Easy and timely retrieval and analysis of related and unrelated information is crucial for enterprise to meet and improve mission requirements that vary across business units. Enterprises are collecting, procuring, storing and processing increasing quantities of data. This is occurring in an effort to find new insights that can drive more efficient and effective operations, provide management the ability to steer the business proactively and allow the C-suite to better formulate and assess their strategic initiatives. Ultimately, enterprises are looking for new ways to gain a competitive edge. Thus, the need for techniques and technologies that can extract meaningful information and insights has increased. Computational approaches, statistical techniques and data warehousing have advanced to the point where they have merged, each bringing their specific techniques and tools that allow the performance of Big Data analysis. The maturity of these fields of practice inspired and enabled much of the core functionality expected from contemporary Big Data solutions, environments and platforms.

Data continues to be generated and digitally archived at increasing rates driven by customer initiatives, sensors, customer interactions and program transactions. For example, Government organizations are beginning to deploy Big Data technologies to analyze massive data sets as well as mine data to prevent bad actors from committing acts of terror and/or to prevent waste, fraud, and abuse (Kalil, 2012; Department of Defense, 2012).

Figure 3 depicts the drivers of Big Data. Big Data drivers are explained below.

Business

Enterprises today are looking for improvement in marketing, enhance customer experience, improve operational efficiencies, identify fraud and waste, prevent compliance failures and achieve other outcomes that directly affect top- and bottom-line business performance. Big Data analytics helps in discovering new business initiatives. This is the opportunity to enable innovative new business models.

Figure 3. Drivers of Big Data and Analytics

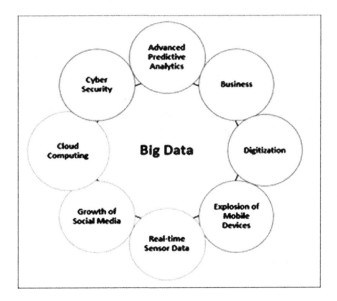

Digitization

Today for all businesses, digital mediums have replaced physical mediums as the de facto communications and delivery mechanism. The use of digital artifacts saves both time and cost as distribution is supported by the vast pre-existing infrastructure of the Internet. As consumers connect to a business through their interaction with these digital substitutes, it leads to an opportunity to collect detailed data by leveraging Big Data Analytics. Collecting detailed data can be important for businesses because mining this data allows customized marketing, automated recommendations and the development of optimized product features.

Explosion of Mobile Devices

The increased use of smart phones Users expect to be able to access their information anywhere and anytime. To the extent that visualizations, analytics, or operationalized big data/analytics are part of the mobile experience.

Real-Time Sensor Data

The coverage of Internet and Wi-Fi networks has enabled more people and their devices to be continuously active in virtual communities. Usage of Internet based connected sensors, Internet of Things and Smart Internet connected devices has resulted in massive increase in the number of available data streams demanding the need for Big Data Analytics. These data streams are public and channeled directly to corporations for analysis.

Growth of Social Media

Customers today are providing feedback on product/item to enterprise, in near real time through various channels. This leads the businesses to consider customer feedback on their service and product offerings in their strategic planning. As a result, businesses are storing increasing amounts of data on customer interactions within their customer relationship management systems (CRM) and from harvesting customer reviews, complaints and praise from social media sites. This information feeds Big Data analysis algorithms that surface the voice of the customer in an attempt to provide better levels of service, increase sales, enable targeted marketing and even create new products and services. Businesses have realized that branding activity no longer managed by internal marketing activities. In addition, enterprises and its customers are co-creating the product brands and corporate reputation. For this reason, businesses are increasingly interested in incorporating publicly available datasets from social media and other external data sources.

Cloud Computing

Cloud computing plays an essential role in data analytics. In many scenarios, it act as a data source, providing real-time streams, analytical services, and as a device transaction hub. Businesses have the opportunity to leverage highly scalable, on-demand IT resources for storage and processing capabilities provided by cloud environments in order to build-out scalable Big Data solutions that can carry out large-scale processing tasks. The ability of a cloud to dynamically scale based upon load allows for the creation of resilient analytic environments that maximize efficient utilization of ICT resources. Cloud computing can provide three essential ingredients required for a Big Data solution: external datasets, scalable processing capabilities and vast amounts of storage.

Cyber Security

Big Data security strategy should be align with the enterprise practices and policies already established, avoid duplicate implementations, and manage centrally across the environments.

Enterprise security management seeks to centralize access, authorize resources, and govern through comprehensive audit practices. Adding a diversity of Big Data technologies, data sources, and uses adds requirements to these practices.

Advanced Analytical Capability

Technological advancement in data collection, storage, analytics and visualization allows the enterprises to increase the amount of data they generate and produce actionable intelligence to support real time decision making. It helps the capability to foresee key events and take appropriate and timely actions. Better utilization of data, not merely for producing statistical reports on the past but intelligent reports that throw light on the future.

PRINCIPLES OF BIG DATA

Architecture principles provide a basis for decision making when developing Big Data solutions and design. These principles will be extended with Organization specific architecture principles and requirements (Blockow, 2018; Forrest, 2016). They form a structured set of ideas that collectively define and guide development of a solution architecture, from values through to design and implementation, harmonizing decision making across an organization.

The following are the principles to guide enterprises in their approach to big data.

- **Data is an Asset**: Data is an asset that has a specific and measurable value to the Enterprise and managed
- **Data is Shared**: Users have access to the data necessary to perform their duties; therefore, data is shared across enterprise functions and organizations
- **Data Trustee**: Each data element has a trustee accountable for data quality.
- **Common Vocabulary and Data Definitions**: Data definition is consistent throughout Enterprise, and the definitions are understandable and available to all users.
- **Data Security**: Data is protected from unauthorized use and disclosure.
- **Data Privacy**: that privacy and data protection is considered throughout the entire life cycle of a big data project. All data sharing will conform to relevant regulatory and business requirements
- **Data Integrity and the Transparency of Processes**: Each party to a big data analytics project must be aware of, and abide by their responsibilities regarding: the provision of source data and

the obligation to establish and maintain adequate controls over the use of personal or other sensitive data

- **Data Skills and Capabilities**: Skills and expertise in data analytics were shared amongst enterprises and industry, where appropriate. Resources such as data sets and the analytical models used to interrogate them, as well as the infrastructure necessary to perform these computations and shared amongst business units where appropriate and possible to do so.
- **Collaboration with Industry and Academia**: The industry, research and academic sectors have been working on big data analytics projects for some time and continue to invest heavily in the skills, technologies and techniques involved with big data analysis.

BIG DATA ARCHITECTURE FRAMEWORK

The diagram below depicts the high-level architecture framework of traditional data, structured in nature. It has two data sources that use integration (ELT/ETL/Change Data Capture) techniques to transfer data into a DBMS data warehouse or operational data store, and then offer a wide variety of analytical capabilities to reveal the data. Some of these analytic capabilities include dashboards, reporting, EPM/BI applications, summary and statistical query, semantic interpretations for textual data, and visualization tools for high-density data.

A big data architecture, designed to handle the ingestion, processing, and analysis of data that is too large or complex for traditional database systems. Conceptual Architecture of the Big Data Analytics shown in Figure below. It illustrates key components and flows and highlights the emergence of the Data repository and various forms of new and traditional data collection.

Big data solutions typically involve one or more of the following types of workload:

- Batch processing of big data sources at rest.
- Real-time processing of big data in motion.
- Interactive exploration of big data.
- Predictive analytics and machine learning.

Description of these primary components:

Figure 4. Traditional Architecture Components

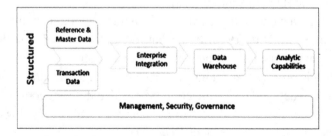

Figure 5. Conceptual Reference Architecture

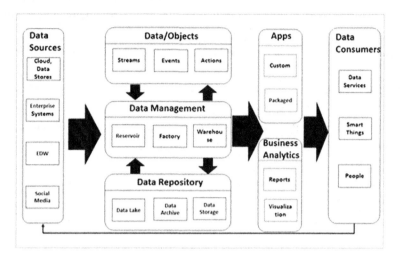

- **Stream Data:** Components that process data in-flight (streams) to identify actionable events and then determine next best action based on decision context and event profile data and persist in a durable storage system. The decision context relies on data in the data reservoir or other enterprise information stores.
- **Reservoir:** Economical, scale-out storage and parallel processing for data that does not have stringent requirements for data formalization or modelling. Typically manifested as a Hadoop cluster or staging area in a relational database.
- **Factory:** Management and orchestration of data into and between the Data Reservoir and Enterprise Information Store as well as the rapid provisioning of data.
- **Warehouse**: Large scale formalized and modelled business critical data store, typically manifested by a Data Warehouse or Data Marts.
- **Data Repository:** A set of data stores, processing engines, and analysis tools separate from the data management activities to facilitate the discovery of new knowledge. Key requirements include rapid data provisioning and sub setting, data security/governance, and rapid statistical processing for large data sets.
- **Business Analytics:** A range of end user and analytic tools for business Intelligence, faceted navigation, and data mining analytic tools including dashboards, reports, and mobile access for timely and accurate reporting.
- **Applications:** A collection of prebuilt adapters and application programming interfaces that enable all data sources and processing directly integrated into custom or packaged business applications.

BIG DATA LOGICAL ARCHITECTURE

The following diagram shows logical application architecture of Big Data Analytics System with key components and layers. A detailed description of these components and layers are provided in this section. While there exist many standard logical architectures for the Big Data Analytics (Wu, 2014;

Angelov, 2012; Chen, 2014; Ahmed & Karypis, 2012; Klein, 2017), the author tried to arrive a detailed and concise Big Data Logical Reference Architecture based on practical experience across various domains and technologies.

Below is the brief description of each of the logical application architecture layers,

Data Sources and Types

The data sources provide the insight required to solve the business problem. The data sources are structured, semi-structured, and unstructured, and it comes from many sources. Big Data Analytics solution

Figure 6. Logical Application Architecture View

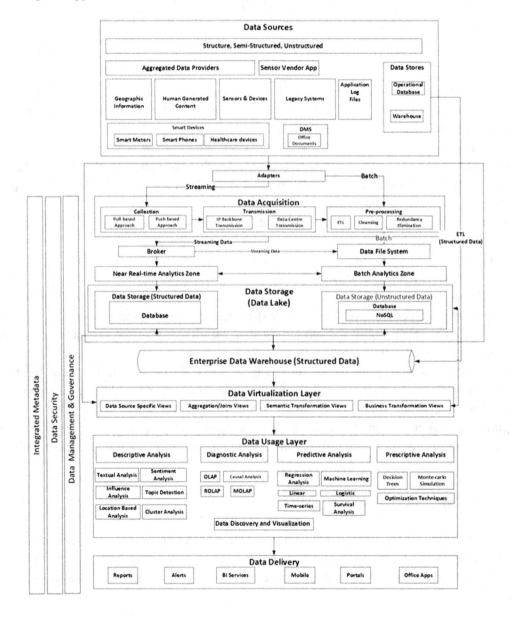

shall support processing of all types of data from a variety of sources. Given below is an indicative list of data sources, and categories. All big data solutions start with one or more data sources. Examples include,

- Application data stores, such as relational databases.
- Static files produced by applications, such as web server log files.
- Real-time data sources, such as IoT device.

Data Acquisition and Enrich

Relevant push or pull-based mechanisms are used for collecting data from various data sources. Data acquisition provide the capability to hold and transmit raw data collected from various sources to data. The acquisition layer provides the mechanism to cleanse different types of data like traditional, sensor based, log data and data from internet.

- **Streaming Data**: Streaming data comprises of unstructured data coming in from various sources. The data shall be held in a buffer area and when a set limit is reached, it shall be transmitted to Data Analytics system (Hold-Transmit). After capturing real-time messages, the solution must process them by filtering, aggregating, and otherwise preparing the data for analysis. The processed stream data is written to an output sink.
- **Batch Data**: Batch data is normally extracted from enterprise systems using ETL or ELT processes. Structured data may be loaded directly to Data Warehouse, and unstructured/semi structured data to Hadoop or equivalent(or better) unstructured data processing platform. Both ETL and ELT support complex transformations such as cleansing, reformatting, aggregating, and converting large volumes of data from many sources. Because the data sets are so large, often a big data solution must process data files using long-running batch jobs to filter, aggregate, and otherwise prepare the data for analysis.
- **Near Real-Time Data Analytics Zone**: It process incoming stream data in real time to provide quick insights into the data. This data may then be persisted on Hadoop system. Near real-time analytics shall provide capabilities like log stream analysis, sensor data analysis etc. The real-time analytics system must be able to quickly identify useful data and that is not useful. Near real-time data shall augment insights obtained from batch analysis.

Table 1. Structured and Unstructured data for Internal and External systems

Category	Internal
Structured	Departmental Database, Data Hubs, Data Warehouse, Data Marts
Semi/Unstructured	e-Mails, Documents, XML documents
Category	**External**
Structured	
Semi/Unstructured	Sensor Data, Log Stream Data, Web sites, Satellite Data, Social media, Bioinformatics, Blogs/Articles Documents, E-mails, Audio-visuals, Stream data and Web Analytics data

- **Batch Data Analytics Zone**: Batch data zone ingest large amount of data in batch mode, and also insights obtained in Real-time analytical zone.

Data Storage

Data for batch processing operations is typically stored in a distributed file store that can hold high volumes of large files in various formats. This type of data store is called Data Lake.

- **Data Lake**: A data lake is a storage repository that holds a vast amount of raw data in its native format, including structured, semi-structured, and unstructured data. The data structure and requirements are not defined until the data is needed. It stores all data while making it faster to get up and running with batch, streaming and interactive analytics. The lake can serve as a staging area for the data warehouse, the location of more carefully treated data for reporting and anlaysis in batch mode. The data lake accepts input from various sources and can preserve both the original data fidelity and the lineage of data transformations.

The features of the Data lake are:

- **Collect Everything:** A Data Lake contains all data, both raw sources over extended periods of time as well as any processed data.
- **Dive in Anywhere:** A Data Lake enables users across multiple business units to refine, explore and enrich data on their terms.
- **Flexible Access:** A Data Lake enables multiple data access patterns across a shared infrastructure: batch, interactive, online, search, in-memory and other processing engines.

Enterprise Data Warehouse

A Data warehouse stores whole of enterprise data, comprising of structured data from enterprise database and data hubs. The data warehouse supports massively Parallel processing and share-nothing architecture and provide optimal performance considering structured and unstructured data. It designed in such a way; it has no single point of failure.

Data Virtualization Layer

Data Virtualization acts as the intermediary and abstraction layer between the information consumers and all sources of data that may contribute to the interaction. It hides cryptic names of tables and columns from users and provide business friendly definitions of data that be used to create reports even by non-technical people. In addition, the data abstraction layer has the capability to access structured, unstructured, or both data in a single query. The query language is standard RDBMS, and query initiated at any level should have ability to process data from all data stores (structured and unstructured). The layer supports a strong optimizer to tune query execution, for response time as well as throughput.

Data Consumers and Delivery

It describes how enterprise users and applications consume output from Big Data Analytics system. This may be in the form of Big Data Analytics Services, alerts on emails and phones, actions, integration with office applications like word, excel etc., collaboration(discussion threads etc.), mobile and so on. The Delivery layer supports delivery through the following mechanisms:

1. **Big Data Analytics Services**: It offers ability to embed actions, alerts, and reports in other application, tool or UI. They shall have ability to refresh automatically based on predefined schedule.
2. **Alerts**: This is to notify stakeholders if a certain event has occurred. Alerts may be delivered in the form of email, reports, or messages.
3. **Actions**: Enable users take some action based on alerts or reports. For example: removing a duplicate record or fixing a corrupted data.
4. **Portal**: Portals provide mechanism to catalogue and index, classify, and search for Big Data Analytics objects such as reports or dashboards. All Big Data Analytics reports to be made available to department users on the portals, based on the roles and responsibilities.
5. **Mobile:** Reports, dashboards, and portals shall be accessible on Mobile devices too.
6. **Office Applications**: The system should integrate with Standard Office products at the minimum. The data and reports should be importable and exportable from/to Office products.

Integrated Meta Data Management

Metadata repository needs to be created for both Structured and Unstructured data. Whether it is for structured data or unstructured, metadata contain enough information to understand, track, explore, clean, and Transform data. Big Data Analytics has the capability to apply metadata on incoming data without any manual intervention.

- **Metadata for Structured Data (DWH)**: It includes Technical, Business, and Process metadata. Besides these, rules of precedence such as which source tables can update which data elements in which order of precedence must be defined and stored.
- **Metadata for Unstructured Data**: Contains rules, definitions, and datasets that help filter out valuable data from incoming data streams or batch load, and persist only such data that are useful. Metadata should enable lineage tracking of data that is loaded into Big Data Analytics system
- **Reusing Data Objects**: Standard queries, models, and metadata can be moved into one layer and virtualise it so that these objects may be reused

Data Security

Data security considerations specific to big data include:

- Increased value of the information asset as enterprises enrich their data, its aggregation and the insights derived from it.
- The increasing range of data acquisition channels and their potential vulnerability.
- The unknowability of the content of unstructured data sources upon acquisition.

- Increased distribution of physical and virtual locations of data storage.

More details about the Big Data Security is explained in the Secuirty Architecture Section of this chapter.

Data Usage Layer

Different users may want different types of outputs based on their role, responsibilities, and functions. The goal of most big data solutions is to provide insights into the data through analysis and reporting. To empower users to analyze the data, the architecture may include a data modeling layer, such as a multidimensional OLAP cube or tabular data model in Azure Analysis Services. It might also support self-service BI, using the modeling and visualization technologies in Microsoft Power BI or Microsoft Excel. Analysis and reporting can also take the form of interactive data exploration by data scientists or data analysts. Big Data Analytics shall provide the following usage capabilities:

- **Reports and Ad-hoc Queries**: Analytical reporting (based on data warehouse/Datamart). The system shall provide scripting language, ability to handle complex headers, footers, nested subtotals, and multiple report bands on a single page.
- The system shall support simple, medium, and complex queries against both structured and unstructured data.
- **Online Analytical Processing (OLAP)**: Slicing and dicing, measuring dependent variables against multiple independent variables. It enables users regroup, re-aggregate, and re-sort by dimensions.
- **Advanced Analytics**: This includes predictive, prescriptive, descriptive, causal, statistical, spatial, and mathematical analysis, using structured and unstructured data
- **Dashboards**: Displays variety of information in one page/screen. Typically they display Key Performance Indicators visually.
- **Textual Analytics**: Textual analytics refers to the process of deriving high-quality information from text in documents, emails, Government orders, web, etc. This is useful in sentiment analysis, understand hot topics of discussion in public, and maintaining government image.
- **Performance Management**: Analytical data can be used by departments to understand their performance, and reasons for current levels of performance measured in terms of KPIs.
- **Data Mining, Discovery, and Visualisation**: It is about searching for patterns and values within data streams such as sensor based data, social media, satellite images etc. Data exploration is primarily used by Data scientists or statisticians to create new Analytical models and test them so that they can be used for Analytics.

Data Management and Governance

Data Governance is a process of managing data assets of an enterprise. It includes the rules, policies, procedures, roles and responsibilities that guide overall management of an enterprise's data. It provides the guidance to ensure that data is accurate and consistent, complete, available and secure. Governance is not a onetime event - it is a continual process of maintaining, monitoring and improving the enterprise important asset.

Enterprises have the governance responsibility to align disparate data types and certify data quality. Governance provides the structure to enable:

- The decision making processes that an enterprise uses to ensure the integrity of its key data items.
- Fast and effective decision making in times of ambiguity.
- Adherence to policies, standards and alignment to overall data management approach.

Improved Governance

- Data-analysis-based insights improving quality of governance.
- Data-analysis-driven decisions leading to right planning and right targeting.
- Insights leading to effective regulation and better governance.
- Recommendations and interventions to improve performances.

Principles of Data Governance are:

- **Enterprise Asset**: Data is recognized as a key business asset and will be organized, stored, distributed and managed to allow sharing across the Enterprise.
- **Conformance**: The logical structure of data will be independent of Applications and will conform to defined Logical Data Models and common data formats.
- **Stewards and Owership**: Each data element has a corporate steward accountable for data ownership and data quality.
- **Shared**: Users have access to the data necessary to perform their duties; therefore, data is shared across Enterprise functions and Business Units.
- **Accessible**: Data is accessible for users to perform their functions from any location and by any approved mechanisms.
- **Secure**: Data is protected from unauthorized use and disclosure.
- **Timely:** The Systems, Applications and Databases will be designed to make data available anytime and anyplace.
- **Available:** All shared data will have the capability to be continuously available based on agreed business need.
- **Interoperable Information**: Data must be managed in such a way as to achieve information interoperability.
- **Common Vacabulary**: Data is defined consistently throughout the Enterprise, and the definitions are understandable and available to all users.
- **Meta Data Repository**: An integrated, centralized Metadata Repository.
- **Data Capture**: All primary data will be captured once at the point of creation and stored and managed to enable appropriate levels of sharing across the Enterprise.

BIG DATA SECURITY ARCHITECTURE

Security today involves far more than just password protection, anti-malware solutions, and network encryption. It requires a continuous application of security measures to manage and control access to valuable electronic assets of an enterprise. Big Data security approach shall ensure that the right people, internal or external, get access to the appropriate data and information at right time and place, within the right channel (National Security Agency, Central Security Services, 2011; Smith & Hallman, 2013). The security prevents and safeguards against malicious attacks and protects enterprise data assets by securing and encrypting data while it is in-motion or at-rest. It also enables organizations to separate roles and responsibilities and protect sensitive data without compromising privileged user access.

Based on the author experience in Big Data Architectures, the core components of the Big Data Security Framework are classified as:

- **Data Management**: Secure data storage and transaction logs
- **Identity and Access Management:** Role based access control for data components
- **Data Protection and Privacy:** Scalable privacy preserving data mining and analytics
- **Network Security:** Network access control allows traffic to approved levels
- **Infrastructure Security and Integrity:** Secure computations in distributed programming

Figure 7 is the logical architecture for the big data security approach:
The various data security capabilities are:

- Authentication and authorization of users, applications and databases
- Privileged user access and administration
- Data encryption and redaction, application level cryptographic protection
- Data masking and sub setting, performed in batch or real time
- Separation of roles and responsibilities, role based access control
- Transport security
- Network security, data protection in transit and network zoning and authorization components
- Database activity monitoring, alerting, blocking, auditing and compliance reporting

Figure 7. Big Data Security Architecture View

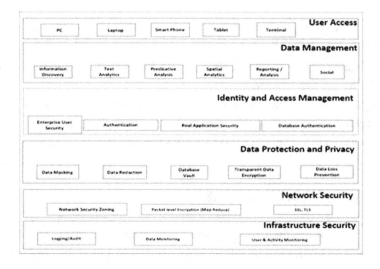

IOT ANALYTICS ARCHITECTURE

Imagine a world where billions of objects can sense, communicate and share information and are inter connected over public or private Internet Protocol (IP) networks. These interconnected objects have data regularly collected, analyzed and used to initiate action, providing a wealth of intelligence for planning, management and decision-making. This is called Internet of Things (IOT) (Morris, 2014; Wang, 2017; Greenough, 2014; Rohling, 2014).

These devices are producing Zetabytes of data every month. The transmissions typically consist of high velocity semi-structured data streams that must land in highly scalable data management systems. The following diagram depicts the IoT logical reference architecture as three tiers: 1.) Edge; 2.) Platform, and; 3.) Enterprise. These tiers process the data flows and control flows based on usage activities across the enterprise systems.

1. **Edge**: Consists of IoT devices and the IoT gateway. The architectural characteristics of this tier, including its breadth of distribution and location, depend on the specific use cases of the enterprise.

It is common for IoT devices to communicate using a relatively short range and specialized proximity network, due to power and processing limitations.

The IoT gateway contains a data store for IoT device data, one or more services to analyze data streaming from the IoT devices or from the data store, and control applications.

The IoT gateway provides endpoints for device connectivity, facilitating bidirectional communication with the enterprise systems. It also implements edge intelligence with different levels of processing capabilities.

2. **Platform**: Receives, processes and forwards control commands from the Enterprise tier to the Edge tier. The Platform tier consolidates, processes and analyses data flows from the Edge tier, and provides management functions for devices and assets. It also offers non-domain-specific services such as data operations and analytics.

Figure 8. IoT Analytics Architecture View

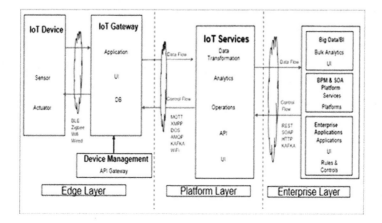

3. **Enterprise**: Receives data flows from the Edge and Platform tiers, and issues control commands to these tiers. The Enterprise tier implements enterprise domain-specific applications and decision support systems, and provides interfaces to end users, including operations.

The different networks used to connect these three tiers are:

1. The *proximity network* connects the sensors, actuators, devices, control systems and assets, collectively called edge nodes. It typically connects these edge nodes in one or more clusters to a gateway that bridges to other networks.
2. The *access network* enables data and control flows between the Edge and the Platform tiers. It may be a corporate network, or a private network overlaid over the public Internet or a 4G/5G network.
3. The *service network* enables connectivity between the services in the platform tier and the enterprise tier, and the services within each tier. It may be an overlay private network over the public Internet, or the Internet itself, allowing enterprise-grade security between end-users and various services.

Users of the IoT system include both humans and digital users. Humans typically interact with the IoT system using one or more kinds of user devices – smartphones, personal computers, tablets or specialized devices. In all cases, the IoT system provides some form of application that connects the human user with the rest of the IoT system.

In some scenarios, immediate action must be taken when data is first transmitted (as when a sensor reports a critical problem that could damage equipment or cause injury) or where it would be possible alleviate some other preventable situation (such as relieving a highway traffic jam). Event processing engines designed to take certain pre-programmed actions quickly by analyzing the data streams while data is still in motion or when data has landed in NoSQL database front-ends or Hadoop. The rules applied usually based on analysis of previous similar data streams and known outcomes.

BIG DATA ANALYSIS TECHNIQUES

Big Data analysis blends traditional statistical data analysis approaches with computational ones. In any fast moving field like Big Data, there are always opportunities for innovation. An example of this is the question of how to blend statistical and computational approaches for a given analytical problem. Statistical techniques are commonly preferred for exploratory data analysis, after which computational techniques that advantage the insight gleaned from the statistical study of a dataset can be apply (Buhler, 2016; We, 2014; Oracle Corporation, 2015; Lopes & Ribeiro, 2015; NIST, 2015; Labrinidis & Jagadish, 2012).

The shift from batch to real-time presents other challenges, as real-time techniques need to leverage computationally efficient algorithms. The following are the basic types of data analysis:

*   Quantitative analysis
*   Qualitative analysis
*   Data mining
*   Statistical analysis
*   Machine learning

- Semantic analysis
- Visual analysis
- **Quantitative Analysis**: Quantitative analysis is a data analysis technique that focuses on quantifying the patterns and correlations found in the data. Based on statistical practices, this technique involves analysing a large number of observations from a dataset. Since the sample size is large, the results can be applied in a generalized manner to the entire dataset. Quantitative analysis results are absolute in nature and used for numerical comparisons.
- **Qualitative Analysis**: Qualitative analysis is a data analysis technique that focuses on describing various data qualities using words. It involves analysing a smaller sample in greater depth compared to quantitative data analysis. Extending these results to entire dataset is not possible due to the small sample size. The analysis results state only that the figures were "not as high as," and do not provide a numerical difference.
- **Data Mining**: Data mining, also known as data discovery, is a specialized form of data analysis that targets large datasets. In relation to Big Data analysis, data mining generally refers to automated, software-based techniques that sift through massive datasets to identify patterns and trends. Specifically, it involves extracting hidden or unknown patterns in the data with the intention of identifying previously unknown patterns. Data mining forms the basis for predictive analytics and business intelligence (BI).
- **Statistical Analysis**: Statistical analysis uses statistical methods based on mathematical formulas as a means for analysing data. Statistical analysis is most often quantitative, but can also be qualitative. This type of analysis commonly used to describe datasets via summarization, such as providing the mean, median, or mode of statistics associated with the dataset. In addition, it is used to infer patterns and relationships within the dataset, such as regression and correlation.
- **Machine Learning**: Humans are good at spotting patterns and relationships within data. Unfortunately, we cannot process large amounts of data very quickly. Machines, on the other hand, are very adept at processing large amounts of data quickly, but only if they know how. If human knowledge combined with the processing speed of machines, machines will be able to process large amounts of data without requiring much human intervention. This is the basic concept of machine learning.
- **Semantic Analysis**: A fragment of text or speech data can carry different meanings in different contexts, whereas a complete sentence may retain its meaning, even if structured in different ways. In order for the machines to extract valuable information, text and speech data needs to understand by the machines in the same way as humans do. Semantic analysis represents practices for extracting meaningful information from textual and speech data.
- **Visual Analysis**: Visual analysis is a form of data analysis that involves the graphic representation of data to enable or enhance its visual perception. Based on the premise that humans can understand and draw conclusions from graphics more quickly than from text, visual analysis acts as a discovery tool in the field of Big Data. The objective is to use graphic representations to develop a deeper understanding of the data being analysed. Specifically, it helps identify and highlight hidden patterns, correlations and anomalies. Visual analysis, directly related to exploratory data analysis as it encourages the formulation of questions from different angles.

INDICATIVE BUSINESS SCENARIOS OF BIG DATA IN GOVERNMENT

The following lists summarizes representative categories where Big Data Analytics system will be used to improve Government and department processes.

Integrated Services

- Analyzing the content in electronic and social media and other sources to understand public sentiment on the programs of the Government, conducting a root-cause analysis and suggesting appropriate interventions and mid-course corrections to improve the delivery of the programs.
- Predicting a disaster and identifying the areas likely to be affected, and suggesting advance interventions required to mitigate the adverse impact on the population.
- Analyzing the Text inputs (unstructured data) in the Grievance system and the popular print media, identifying of key problem areas (Region / Type of Problem / Frequency/Severity) and suggesting suitable remedial action.
- Designing a Happiness Index, appropriate to the socio-economic profile of the Government agency, supporting the Government in conducting approriate sample surveys, Analyzing the results and making suitable recommendations for enhancement of the Index.

Service Delivery

- Analyzing the medium-term impact of development and welfare schemes, identifying the gaps and realigning the schemes for enhanced effectiveness.
- Analyzing the geographical spread of various schemes and making corrections for even distribution.
- Conduct sentiment analysis based on social media and electronic media, and provide appropriate inputs for action by the municipality.
- Qualitative and Quantitative analysis of potable drinking water supplied to the rural people in the habitations as per defined norms through implementation of various water supply schemes under different programs in the government.

Statistics

- Analyzing the patterns of public expenditure on top 10 sectors of the economy, identifying the correlations with the progress in achieving the relevant Sustainable Development Goals and suggesting the desired areas and sectors for intervention.
- Analyzing the trends of growth of GSDP, geographically and sector-wise, identifying causal factors for high and low growth rates and suggesting the right mix of interventions required to optimize the growth rate of the economy of the Government.
- Analysis of trends of cropped areas and economics of various crops area wise over the last 5 years, and the demand-supply position for different agricultural produce across the country and to arrive at the optimised crop area planning for various crops in different agro-climatic regions of the Government and giving decision support to agricultural planners.

- Analysis of soil health records of the last 5 years, along with the crops grown during the period, rainfall, irrigation, yield and other parameters, to arrive at a plan for maximising micro-nutrient corrections, through focused interventions.

Productivity Gain

- To monitor the condition of the roads and provide advance recommendations on optimal resource utilisation for producing best impact on taxpayers.
- Identify leakages of taxes and other major revenues, conduct causal analysis and provide decision support.
- Monitor the sanitary conditions, analyse w.r.t climatic and othe rconditions and predict the outbreak of communicable diseases to enable the department to take corrective action.
- Analysis of global commodity prices and provision of advisories to farmers on the export markets to be preferred for exporting grain and horticultural products.
- Integrating climatic, economic, and social data along with quality of healthcare provided, identify geographic regions that are vulnerable to Viral diseases and providing decision support to the department (realtime).
- Usage of IOT for Smart City to improve the quality of the life of the Citizen.

BIG DATA BEST PRACTICES

The following are the best practices for the Big Data Architectures:

Business

- **Align Big Data with Business Goals**: Advice business of an enterprise on how to apply big data techniques to accomplish their goals. For example, understand e-commerce behaviour, derive sentiment from social media and customer support interactions and understand statistical correlation methods and their relevance for customer, product, manufacturing, or engineering data. Even though Big Data is a newer IT frontier and there is an obvious excitement to master something new, it is important to base new investments in skills, organization, or infrastructure with a strong business-driven context to guarantee ongoing project investments and funding. Determine how Big Data support and enable enterprise business architecture and top IT priorities.
- **Consolidate Enterprise Data**: Today enterprises have an overwhelming amount of data available in the form of structured and unstructured application data (documents, files, logs, click streams, events, social media, images, videos and more). All this data is either poorly captured or not easily accessible by employees due to the siloed nature of old data architectures. Big Data Analytics helps in establishing an enterprise-wide common data platform that makes data available from a central location.
- **Align with the Cloud Operating Model**: Big Data processes and users require access to broad array of resources for both iterative experimentation and running production jobs. Data across the data realms (transactions, master data, reference, and summarized) is part of a Big Data solution.

Private and Public cloud provisioning and security strategy plays an integral role in supporting these changing requirements.

- **Manage Operations**: Operationalizing insights requires a repeatable and scalable process for developing numerous analytic models and a reliable architecture for deploying these models into production applications. Ease of operationalization is an important characteristic of a successful modern data architecture.

Technical

- **Unstructured and Structured Data**: It is certainly valuable to analyse Big Data on its own. However, by connecting and integrating low density Big Data with the structured data you are already using today, you can bring even greater business clarity. For example, there is a difference in distinguishing all sentiment from that of only your best customers. Whether you are capturing customer, product, equipment, or environmental Big Data, an appropriate goal is to add more relevant data points to your core master and analytical summaries, which can lead to better conclusions. For these reasons, many see Big Data as an integral extension of enterprise existing business intelligence and data warehousing platform and information architecture.
- **Partition Data**: Partition data files and data structures such as tables, based on temporal periods that match the processing schedule. That simplifies data ingestion and job scheduling, and makes it easier to troubleshoot failures.
- **Schema-on-Read Semantics**: Use *schema-on-read* semantics, which project a schema onto the data when the data is processing, not when the data is stored. This builds flexibility into the solution, and prevents bottlenecks during data ingestion caused by data validation and type checking.
- **Cloud**: Incorporate on premise and cloud Organizations have different criteria for determining which workloads run on premise vs cloud. The criteria could involve internal or external policies regarding location of data stored; availability of an application/system in the cloud; availability of capacity for running a specific workload, etc. It is important for a modern architecture to support a hybrid environment as it is fast becoming the new operating reality for enterprises.
- **Process Data In-Place**: Traditional BI solutions often use an extract, transform, and load (ETL) process to move data into a data warehouse. With larger volumes data, and a greater variety of formats, big data solutions generally use variations of ETL, such as transform, extract, and load (TEL). With this approach, the data processed within the distributed data store, transforming it to the required structure, before moving the transformed data into an analytical data store.
- **Orchestrate Data Ingestion**: In some cases, existing business applications may write data files for batch processing directly into data storage, where Data Lake Analytics consume it. To orchestrate the ingestion of data from on-premises or external data sources into the data lake. Use an orchestration workflow or pipeline, to achieve a predictable and centrally manageable fashion.
- **Automate Processes:** At a time when data volume, variety and number of sources are ever-increasing, automation plays a key role in keeping the data driven culture alive. Data pipeline automation, automation of data cataloging (using ML/AI) and such, help in near real-time availability of consumable data.

Governance

- **Support from Management**: Get C-suite support Building a data driven enterprise needs deep collaboration between various functions across the organization. Many challenges pertaining to people, policies, data ownership and sharing will arise. For the initiative to succeed, a top-down mandate with a clear mission and approval framework to resolve logjams is required.
- **Culture Cultivation**: Develop a data driven culture Building a data driven enterprise is more about people and culture than technology. To ensure employees replace their gut-based decision making with a more thoughtful, data driven approach, it is important to sensitize employees to the need for, and advantages of, being data driven. Orientation and training sessions on how to use data and analytics as part of their daily operations will play a key role in the successful implementation and adoption of a modern data architecture.
- **Data Governance**: Data is a shared asset for any enterprise. Data governance assumes an important role and needs a well thought out enterprise wide strategy coupled with strong execution. It needs a framework that transcends enterprise silos to establish how data assets managed, accessed by employees. Data quality, lineage, security, discovery, self-serve access, compliance, legal hold and information lifecycle management need to be given due importance as part of the data governance strategy. To achieve a comprehensive governance strategy, put together a strategy team representing the legal and compliance departments, IT operations, line of business stakeholders, and application/ information owners. Further, enterprises need to implement a comprehensive communication program to sensitize employees about the need for the governance policy and their adherence to it.
- **Data Community**: Build a data community Data democratization needs trusted guardians who can help data consumers use the right data in its relevant form. Building a data community comprising IT managers, data engineers, data scientists and functional experts is crucial for enabling a trusted data environment for business users. This community is responsible for the availability of centralized data dictionaries, MDM, data enrichment, data preparation, pre-prepared data models, business formulae, algorithms and such to the business users. This greatly helps business users to quickly extract insights without having to worry about the data quality or the trustworthiness of the data available.
- **Skills and Governance**: Organizations implementing Big Data solutions and strategies should assess skills requirement early and often and should proactively identify any potential skills gaps. Skills gaps can be addressed by training / cross-training existing resources, hiring new resources, or leveraging consulting firms.
- **No Big Bang**: Do not try to do everything at once. Deploying a modern data architecture is a big initiative and is heavily influenced by technology, policies and people. Though it is important to approach this in a holistic manner, it is not necessary to do it all at once. Enterprises can realize benefits by implementing modern data architecture even for a single function and use the lessons learned for the next phase.

FUTURE RESEARCH DIRECTIONS

Big data analytics is gaining so much attention these days and there were number of research problems that need to be addressed going forward. Few research directions for the future are highlighted below.

Many different models like fuzzy sets, rough sets, soft sets, neural networks, their generalizations and hybrid models are used in analyzing the data. The challenges in analyzing the data may affect performance, efficiency and scalability of the data intensive computing systems. Fast processing while achieving high performance and high throughput, and storing it efficiently for future use is another issue. Expressing data access requirements of applications and designing programming language abstractions to exploit parallelism are an immediate need.

- **Data Life Cycle of Big Data Analytics:** Most of the customer requirements today demanding real-time performance of the big data analytics. This leads for the definition of data life cycle, the value it can provide and the computing process to make the analytics process real time. This increases the value of the analysis (Boyd & Crawford, 2012). A proper data filtering techniques need to be developed to ensure correctness of the data (Nielsen & Chuang, 2000) in Big Data Analysis. The availability of data that is complete and reliable is a big challenge. In most of the cases, data is very limited and do not show clear distribution, resulting to misleading conclusions. A method to overcome these problems needs proper attention and sometimes handling of unbalanced data sets leads to biased conclusion.
- **Storage and Retrieval Data:** Multidimensional data should be integrated with analytics over big data. With the explosion of smart phones, the Images, Audios and Videos are being generated at an unremarkable pace. However, storage, retrieval and processing of these unstructured data require immense research in each dimension.
- **Big Data Computations:** Apart from current big data paradigms like Map-Reduce, other paradigms such as YarcData (Big Data Graph Analytics) and High-Performance Computing cluster (HPCC explores Hadoop alternatives), are being explored.
- **Algorithms for Real Time Processing:** The pace at which data is being generated and the expectations from these algorithms may not be met, if the desired time delay is not met.
- **Smart Storage Devices:** The demand for storing digital information is increasing continuously. Purchasing and using available storage devices cannot meet this demand. Research towards developing efficient storage device that can replace the need for HDFS systems that is fault tolerant can improve the data processing activity and replace the need for software management layer.
- **Quantum Computing for Big Data Analytics:** A quantum computer has memory that is exponentially larger than its physical size and can manipulate an exponential set of inputs simultaneously (Hashem, 2015). Quantum computing provides a way to merge the quantum mechanics to process the information. In traditional computer, information is presented by long strings of bits which encode either a zero or a one. On the other hand a quantum computer uses quantum bits or qubits. The difference between qubit and bit is that, a qubit is a quantum system that encodes the zero and the one into two distinguishable quantum states. Therefore, it can be capitalized on the phenomena of superposition and entanglement. It is because qubits behave quantumly. For example, 100 qubits in quantum systems require 2100 complex values to be stored in a classic computer system. It means that many big data problems can be solved much faster by larger scale

quantum computers compared with classical computers. Hence it is a challenge for this generation to built a quantum computer and facilitate quantum computing to solve big data problems.

- **Cloud Computing for Big Data Analytics:** Big data application using cloud computing should support data analytic and development. The cloud environment should provide tools that allow data scientists and business analysts to interactively and collaboratively explore knowledge acquisition data for further processing and extracting results. This can help to solve large applications that may arise in various domains (Chen, 2012). In addition, cloud computing should also enable scaling of tools from virtual technologies into new technologies like spark, R, and other types of big data processing techniques. The major issues are privacy concerns relating to the hosting of data on public servers, and the storage of data from human studies. All these issues will take big data and cloud computing to a high level of development.

- **IoT for Big Data Analytics:** An IoT device generates continuous streams of data and the researchers can develop tools to extract meaningful information from these data using machine learning techniques. Understanding these streams of data generated from IoT devices and analyzing them to get meaningful information is a challenging issue and it leads to big data analytics. Machine learning algorithms and computational intelligence techniques is the only solution to handle big data from IoT prospective. Key technologies that are associated with IoT are also discussed in many research papers.

- **Machine Learning for Big Data Analytics:** Research in the area of machine learning for big data has focused on data processing, algorithm implementation, and optimization. Many of the machine learning tools for big data are started recently needs drastic change to adopt it. Author, argue that while each of the tools has their advantages and limitations, more efficient tools can be developed for dealing with problems inherent to big data. These efficient tools to be developed must have provision to handle noisy and imbalance data, uncertainty and inconsistency, and missing values.

CONCLUSION

Modern businesses are evolving and are constantly demanding more from their Information Management systems. No longer satisfied with standardized reporting by a limited set of users, modern businesses manage by fact, demanding faster and more pervasive access to information on which to base critical business decisions. This change to the volume, velocity and reach of the information is in turn forcing changes to the solution architecture and technology that underpins the solutions.

Big Data employs the tenet of "bringing the analytical capabilities to the data" versus the traditional processes of "bringing the data to the analytical capabilities through staging, extracting, transforming and loading," thus eliminating the high cost of moving data.

In Big Data world, data storage platforms are not restricted to a predefined rigid data model and data systems are capable of handling all kinds of structured and unstructured data. Big data offers capabilities such as deploying data storage/processing from new sources such as external social media data, market data, communications, interaction with customers via digital channels, etc. with unconstrained scalability and flexibility to adapt to constantly changing data landscape.

The following are the Outcome and recommendations on the usage of Big Data Analytics:

- To provide insights into how current business scenario's are performing, and Why(Descriptive and Causal Analyses).
- Design of Better Projects by being more customer centric and effective.
- To determine likely future scenarios and recommend best courses of action (Predictive and Prescriptive Analyses).
- To gauge sentiments of customers, and understand their perceptions of and attitudes towards enterprise products, policies.
- To provide a system of dashboards that enable administrators monitor and implement enterprise programs effectively.
- To improve collaboration among various stakeholders.
- To provide a tool for research in Data Sciences and statistical analysis.
- Enhanced customer Satisfaction through participation in decision-making.
- Formulation of the Right Policies that factor the needs of the people.
- Enhanced transparency of public institutions through feedback & social audit.
- Increased Trust between enterprise & customer allows the free flow of the information.
- Real-time fraud monitoring can be done by integrating large amounts of diverse, structured and unstructured high-velocity data.
- Real-time location information to provide more accurate traffic and drive-time information by analyzing the commute patterns, drive times to and from work.

Big Data also opens up a range of new design and implementation patterns that can make Information Management solutions less brittle, speed development reduce costs and generally improve business delivery. When designed appropriately, they can combine these benefits without giving up the things the business has come to expect and value such as good governance, data quality and robustness.

Finally, Big Data Analytics is not about adopting a technology solution. It is about leveraging tools that enable enterprise to operate more effectively through making informed decisions and where needed, in real time.

ACKNOWLEDGMENT

The author would like to thank Hari Kishan Burle, Raju Alluri of Architecture Group of Wipro Technologies for giving us the required time and support in many ways in bringing this chapter as part of Global Enterprise Architecture Practice efforts. This research received no specific grant from any funding agency in the public, commercial, or not-for-profit sectors.

REFERENCES

Ahmed, R., & Karypis, G. (2012). Algorithms for Mining the Evolution of Conserved Relational States in Dynamic Networks. *Knowledge and Information Systems, 33*(3), 603–630. doi:10.100710115-012-0537-2

Angelov, S., Grefen, P., & Greefhorst, D. (2012). A framework for analysis and design of software reference architectures. *Journal of Information and Software Technology, 54*(4), 417–431. doi:10.1016/j.infsof.2011.11.009

Blockow, D. (2018). *Big Data Architecture Principles*. Data to Decision CRC. Retrieved from https://www.d2dcrc.com.au/blog/big-data-architecture-principles/

Boyd & Crawford. (2012). *Six Provocations for Big Data. Proceeding of A Decade in Internet Time: Symposium on the Dynamics of the Internet and Society*. Retrieved from: https://papers.ssrn.com/sol3/papers.cfm?abstract_id=1926431

Buhler, P. (2016). *Big Data Fundamentals: Concepts, Drivers & Techniques*. Prentice Hall.

Chandra, S. (2018). *India's Biometric Identity Program Is Rooting Out Corruption*. Retrieved from: https://slate.com/technology/2018/08/aadhaar-indias-biometric-identity-program-is-working-but-privacy-concerns-remain.html

Chen, M., Mao, S., & Liu, Y. (2014). Big data: A survey. *Mobile Networks and Applications, 19*(2), 171–209. doi:10.100711036-013-0489-0

Chen, X. (2012). Article. *Research on Key Technology and Applications for Internet of Things, 33*, 561–566.

Cisco. (2017). *The Zettabyte Era: Trends and Analysis*. Retrieved from: http://www.cisco.com/c/en/us/solutions/collateral/service-provider/visual-networking-index-vni/VNI_Hyperconnectivity_WP.html

Department of Defence. (2012). *Big Data Across the Federal Government*. Executive Office of the President. Retrieved from: https://www.hsdl.org/?view&did=742609

Enterprise, H. P. (2017). *The Exponential Growth of Data*. Retrieved from: https://insidebigdata.com/2017/02/16/the-exponential-growth-of-data/

Forrest, C. (2016). 5 architectural principles for building big data systems on AWS. *TechRepublic*. Retrieved from: https://www.techrepublic.com/article/5-architectural-principles-for-building-big-data-systems-on-aws/

Greenough, J. (2014). *The 'Internet of Things' Will Be The World's Most Massive Device Market And Save Companies Billions Of Dollars. BI Intelligence reports*. Retrieved form: https://www.businessinsider.in/The-Internet-of-Things-Will-Be-The-Worlds-Most-Massive-Device-Market-And-Save-Companies-Billions-Of-Dollars/articleshow/44766662.cms

Hashem, I., Yaqoob, I., Anuar, N. B., Mokhtar, S., Gani, A., & Ullah Khan, S. (2015). The rise of "big data" on cloud computing: Review and open research issues. *Information Systems, 47*, 98–115. doi:10.1016/j.is.2014.07.006

Hilbert, M. (2015). What is Big Data. *YouTube*. Retrieved from: https://www.youtube.com/watch?v=XRVIh1h47sA

Hilbert, M. (2016). Big Data for Development: A Review of Promises and Challenges. *Development Policy Review, 34*(1), 135–174. doi:10.1111/dpr.12142

Kalil, T. (2012). *Big Data is a Big Deal*. The White House. Retrieved from: https://obamawhitehouse.archives.gov/blog/2012/03/29/big-data-big-deal

Klein, J. (2017). *Reference Architectures for Big Data Systems*. Carnegie Mellon University Software Engineering Institute. Retrieved from: https://insights.sei.cmu.edu/sei_blog/2017/05/reference-architectures-for-big-data-systems.html

Labrinidis, A., & Jagadish, H. V. (2012). Challenges and opportunities with big data. *Proceeding of VLDB Endowment, 5*(12), 2032–2033.

Lopes & Ribeiro. (2015). GPUMLib: An Efficient Open-source GPU Machine Learning Library. *Machine Learning for Adaptive Many-Core Machines - A Practical Approach, 7*, 15–36.

Manyika. (2011). *Big data: The next frontier for innovation, competition, and productivity*. McKinsey Global Institute. Retrieved from: http://www.mckinsey.com/insights/business_technology/big_data_the_next_frontier_for_innovation

Morris, H. (2014). *A Software Platform for Operational Technology Innovation*. International Data Corporation. Retrieved from: https://www.predix.com/sites/default/files/IDC_OT_Final_whitepaper_249120.pdf

Mullich, J. (2013). *Closing the Big Data Gap in Public Sector*. SAP, Bloomberg Inc.

National Science Foundation. (2012). *Core Techniques and Technologies for Advancing Big Data Science & Engineering (BIGDATA)* (Publication Number: 12-499). Retrieved from: http://www.nsf.gov/pubs/2012/nsf12499/nsf12499.pdf

National Security Agency, Central Security Services. (2011). *Groundbreaking Ceremony Held for $1.2 Billion Utah Data Center*. NSA Press. Retrieved from: https://www.nsa.gov/news-features/press-room/press-releases/2011/utah-groundbreaking-ceremony.shtml

Nielsen & Chuang. (2000). Quantum Computation and Quantum Information. Cambridge University Press.

NIST. (2015). *NIST Big Data Interoperability Framework: Use Cases and General Requirements*. NIST Big Data Public Working Group (Publication number 1500-3). Retrieved from: https://bigdatawg.nist.gov/_uploadfiles/NIST.SP.1500-3.pdf

Normandeau. (2013). *Beyond Volume, Variety and Velocity is the Issue of Big Data Veracity*. Big Data Innovation Summit. Retrieved from: https://insidebigdata.com/2013/09/12/beyond-volume-variety-velocity-issue-big-data-veracity/

Nowak & Spiller. (2017). *Two Billion People Coming Together on Facebook*. Facebook News.

Oracle Corporation. (2015). *An Enterprise Architect's Guide to Big Data*. Oracle Corporation. Retrieved from: https://www.oracle.com/technetwork/topics/entarch/articles/oea-big-data-guide-1522052.pdf

Rijmenam, M. (2018). *A Short History Of Big Data*. Retrieved from: https://datafloq.com/read/big-data-history/239

Rohling, G. (2014). *Facts and Forecasts: Billions of Things, Trillions of Dollars*. Siemens - Internet of Things: Facts and Forecasts. Retrieved from: https://www.siemens.com/innovation/en/home/pictures-of-the-future/digitalization-and-software/internet-of-things-facts-and-forecasts.html

Schmidt, E. (2010). *Techonomy*. Retrieved from: https://www.youtube.com/watch?utm_source=datafloq&utm_medium=ref&utm_campaign=datafloq&v=UAcCIsrAq70

Smith, T. P. (2013). *How big is big and how small is small, the size of everything and why*. Oxford University Press.

Smith & Hallman. (2013). NSA Spying Controversy Highlights Embrace Of Big Data. *The Huffington Post*. Retrieved from: https://www.huffingtonpost.in/entry/nsa-big-data_n_3423482

Stout. (2018). *Social Media Statistics 2018: What You Need to Know*. Retrieved from: https://dustn.tv/social-media-statistics/

Wang, J. (2017). Big Data Driven Smart Transportation: the Underlying Story of IoT Transformed Mobility. *The WIOMAX SmartIoT Blog*. Retrieved from: http://www.wiomax.com/big-data-driven-smart-transportation-the-underlying-big-story-of-smart-iot-transformed-mobility/

We, H. (2014). *SAP and Hortonworks Reference Architecture*. SAP AG.

Wedutenko & Keeing. (2014). *Big data and the public sector: strategy and guidance*. Clayton Utz Insights.

Wu, X. (2014). Data Mining with Big Data. *IEEE Transactions on Knowledge and Data Engineering*, *26*(1), 97–107. doi:10.1109/TKDE.2013.109

YouTube. (2017). *YouTube by the Numbers*. Retrieved from: https://www.youtube.com/yt/about/press/

KEY TERMS AND DEFINITIONS

Cloud Computing: Cloud computing is an ICT sourcing and delivery model for enabling convenient, on-demand network access to a shared pool of configurable computing resources (e.g., networks, servers, storage, applications, and services) that can be rapidly provisioned and released with minimal management effort or service provider interaction.

Data Exhaust: Data exhaust (or digital exhaust) refers to the by-products of human usage of the internet, including structured and unstructured data, especially in relation to past interactions.

ETL: Extract, transform, load.

OLAP: Online analytical processing.

OLTP: Online transaction processing.

Open Data: Data which meets the following criteria: accessible (ideally via the internet) at no more than the cost of reproduction, without limitations based on user identity or intent. In a digital, machine readable format for interoperation with other data; and free of restriction on use or redistribution in its licensing conditions.

Structured Data: The term-structured data refers to data that is identifiable and organized in a structured way. The most common form of structured data is a database where specific information is stored based on a methodology of columns and rows. Structured data is machine readable and efficiently organized for human readers.

Unstructured Data: The term unstructured data refers to any data, that has little identifiable structure. Images, videos, email, documents, and text fall into the category of unstructured data.

Chapter 3
Quality Assurance Issues for Big Data Applications in Supply Chain Management

Kamalendu Pal
City, University of London, UK

ABSTRACT

Heterogeneous data types, widely distributed data sources, huge data volumes, and large-scale business-alliance partners describe typical global supply chain operational environments. Mobile and wireless technologies are putting an extra layer of data source in this technology-enriched supply chain operation. This environment also needs to provide access to data anywhere, anytime to its end-users. This new type of data set originating from the global retail supply chain is commonly known as big data because of its huge volume, resulting from the velocity with which it arrives in the global retail business environment. Such environments empower and necessitate decision makers to act or react quicker to all decision tasks. Academics and practitioners are researching and building the next generation of big-data-based application software systems. This new generation of software applications is based on complex data analysis algorithms (i.e., on data that does not adhere to standard relational data models). The traditional software testing methods are insufficient for big-data-based applications. Testing big-data-based applications is one of the biggest challenges faced by modern software design and development communities because of lack of knowledge on what to test and how much data to test. Big-data-based applications developers have been facing a daunting task in defining the best strategies for structured and unstructured data validation, setting up an optimal test environment, and working with non-relational databases testing approaches. This chapter focuses on big-data-based software testing and quality-assurance-related issues in the context of Hadoop, an open source framework. It includes discussion about several challenges with respect to massively parallel data generation from multiple sources, testing methods for validation of pre-Hadoop processing, software application quality factors, and some of the software testing mechanisms for this new breed of applications

DOI: 10.4018/978-1-5225-6210-8.ch003

INTRODUCTION

All business today understands the value and importance of building an effective supply chain, as part of organizational growth and profitability (Pal, 2017). A supply chain is a network of suppliers, factories, warehouses, distribution centers and retailers, through which raw materials are procured, transformed into intermediate and finished products, and finally delivered the finished products to customers. In this way, a supply chain consists of all the activities associated with the flow and transformation of raw materials stage, through to the end-customers; and as well as the associated information flows. Supply Chain Management (SCM) is a set of synchronized decision and activities, utilized to effectively integrate all relevant business processes to deliver the right products, to the right locations, and at the right time, to optimize system wide costs while satisfying customer service level. Information and Communication Technology (ICT) applications have ushered enormous opportunities to retail supply chain management; and helping it to grow at faster pace. Figure 1 shows a simple diagrammatic representation of a retail supply chain, which highlights some of the main internal business activities.

In addition, retail businesses are evolving into new forms based on knowledge and networks in response to a globalized environment characterized by indistinct organizational boundaries and fast-paced change. These enterprises have understood the importance of enforcing performance tracking of the goals defined by their corporate strategy through metrics-based management (Kaplan & Norton, 1993). The strategic fit requires that a retailer's supply chain achieve the balance between responsiveness and efficiency that best support the business's competitive strategy. A supply chain's performance in terms of responsiveness and efficiency is best on interaction between the following logistical cross-functional drivers of business: demand forecasting, warehousing, scheduling, delivery, inventory planning, and distribution. The performance drivers and some of the related issues are highlighted in Figure 1. Demand forecasting helps more accurate estimation of demand by accessing data of sales, market trends, competitor analysis, and relevant local and global economic factors. Warehousing deals with real-time Big Data-based analysis within the Enterprise Resource Planning (ERP) system and identifying inventory levels, delivery miss-matches, and incoming deliveries. Scheduling plays an important role in SCM. It could help directly increasing visibility of inventory levels, demand, and manufacturing capacity; hence more accurate and distributed scheduling is necessary for global SCM.

Increased internationalization of retail business is changing the operational practices of global retail supply chains, and many retailers have adopted new models, either by outsourcing or by establishing business-alliances in other countries. Globalization has also led to changes in operational practices, where products are manufactured in one part of the world and sold in another. The retail supply chain has become more global in its geographical scope; the international market is getting more competitive and customer demand oriented. Customers are looking for more variety as well as better quality products and services.

Increased customer demand, fierce competitive market conditions, structural complexity of global operations, corporate aspiration of customer satisfying products and services, advances in technological innovation, ICT, have added extra challenges in designing and managing retail supply chains. Over the years, the concepts and practices of SCM have undergone many changes that have been reflected in its '*constantly evolving*' nature. From its initial cost efficiency focus to modern responsive and agile nature, SCM has witnessed a transformational change at the operational frontier. To survive under unpredictable business environment, it has become imperative to function with information driven strategies wherein collaborative business practice among supply chain partners is one of the crucial success factors.

Figure 1. A simple diagrammatic representation of retail supply chain

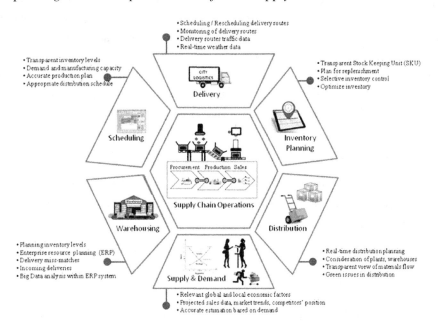

In this way, sharing of business operational information enhances customer services and financial performances by offering correct and relevant real-time information. It also improves supply chain's operational visibility to its collaborative business partners. This also arranges and checks key performance indicators to focus variances and sloppiness and tackles the *bullwhip effect* which is basically happened due to the *mismatch* of demand information while moving from downstream to upstream. However, timely and efficiently an enterprise can formulate an appropriate forward-looking strategy has become a crucial factor in the context of modern SCM. Probing the rich oracles of *Business Intelligence* (BI) and *Business Analytics* (BA) application software, retail enterprises can take the advantages of Big Data-driven insight to work with optimal-lead time and enhance prediction of future to cope-up with uncertainties.

With the rapid evolution and adoption of ICT by the retail industries, deluge of data is being produced all pervasively from each business activity along retail supply chain. This creates a huge chance for retail enterprises to properly use such vast amount of data for making judicious business decisions. As the retail enterprises are changing towards a new kind of ICT laid digital infrastructure, where every object linked with a supply chain is now acting like as a continuous producer of data in structured and unstructured form. This is ushering a new era of digitized supply chain, which can act as an intelligent ICT based decentralized real-time data production system. In this system, the real and virtual worlds are connected through a cyber-physical connectivity wherein the products and machineries independently exchange and respond to information for managing end-to-end processes. It offers a technological platform to agglutinate production technologies and smart process to establish a smart factory. It is providing organizations an unprecedented opportunity to leverage informed supply chain strategy for leveraging competitive advantage. Managing such mega volume of data, commonly referred to as Big Data, is a challenging task. Understanding and tracking of data generation and then processing of data for deriving useful information to operate a smart supply chain stands as the key to success. Analytics thus play a vital role in formulating smart strategies for enhancing the performance of a retail supply chain.

Retail supply chain managers are increasingly seeking to *'win with data'*. They are reliant upon data to gain visibility into expenditure, looking for trends in corporate operational cost and related performance, and support process control, inventory monitoring, production optimization, and process improvement efforts. In fact, many retail businesses are awash in data, with many seeking to capture data analysis as a means for gaining a competitive advantage (Davenport, 2006). In this way, appropriate data capture, data cleaning, and different data analysis techniques are each thought to be part of an emerging competitive area that will transform the way in which retail supply chains are designed and managed. In addition, due to the huge volume of generated data, the fast velocity of arriving data, and the large variety of heterogeneous data, the Big Data-based applications bring new challenges. It is a hard job to test the correctness of a Big Data-based software system due to its enormous size and timeliness. This is an important concern for Big Data-based software system practitioners who are motivated to come up with innovative ways of thinking about how data is produced, organized, and analyzed. Thus, Big Data-based systems quality assurance plays a crucial role.

BIG DATA AND THEIR IMPACT ON SUPPLY CHAIN MANAGEMENT

Big Data is one of the most *'hyped'* terms in the business information systems world now-a-days; however, there is no consensus as to how to define it. The term is often referred to data, which goes beyond the processing capacity of the standard relational database management systems. Moreover, to the aspect that sheer size of Big Data (e.g. an enormous number of transactions, real-time data streams from sensors, mobile devices) is a key factor. This type of data is typically generated by controlled interactions between enterprise and its customers and other internal / external stakeholders through a defined set of enterprise applications and interfaces. The structure of this data is decided in design time and generally relational in nature. For example, data generated by ecommerce, Enterprise Resource Planning (ERP), Customer Relationship Management (CRM), Human Resource Management (HRM), and Accounting Information Systems (AIS) including general ledger are all part of transactional data. In addition, retail business observational data are also part of this deluge of raw information source. This type of data is typically generated by automated machines / sensors as ancillary to the main application data while business processes get executed. The structure of this data through typically decided in design time; but they are non-relational in nature. The examples include data arising from blogs, sensors that monitor specific events, customer call logs in call centers, and so on. There are also issues around how to identify dedicated techniques to analyses this huge volume of data to unlock business critical information from it. Doing so would lead subsequently to important knowledge used to manage the retail supply chain.

This also forms the basis for the most used definition of Big Data, the five V's: Volume, Velocity, Variety, Veracity, Values; and some of the data sources are shown in Figure 2.

- **Volume:** The volume refers to huge amount of information involved. The huge volume of data can be advantageous for the predictive data analytics purpose. In other words, this massive volume of data may enhance the data analysis models by having more business situations available for forecasts and increase the number of factors to be considered in the models making them more realistic. On the other hand, the volume bears potential challenges for data processing infrastructures to deal with enormous amounts of data, when considering its second V-feature – velocity.

- **Velocity:** The velocity, with which data flows into the retail supply chain environment, or the expected response time to the data, is the second V-feature of Big Data. In genuine business environment, Big Data may arrive in high speed in real-time or near real-time. If data arrives too quickly the information processing infrastructures may not be able to respond timely to it, or even fail to store these data. Such adverse cases may result to data inconsistencies hazards. However, real-time or nearly real-time information makes it possible for a retail business to be much more *agile* than its competitors.
- **Variety:** Data comes from different data sources. In other words, this characteristic refers that data comes in many formats, not falling into the rigid relational structures of SQL (Standard Query Language) databases without loss of information. Some of data stream may be saved as blobs inside traditional data base. The data processing infrastructures for Big Data are referred as NoSQL (i.e. not only SQL). Examples of diverse sources and types of data are typical business documents, transactional records and unstructured data in form of images, videos, HTML web pages, text, email messages, streams from environmental monitoring sensors, GPS (Global Positioning, System) data, click stream from web queries, social media updates, and so on) data, click stream from web queries, social media updates, and so on. Social interaction data is typically gathered from voluntary participation of the stakeholders of a retail business through a defined process or casual interactions. The structure of this data is typically open / free following and not decided in design time of the enterprise processes or applications. This includes feedback from customers, information gathered from social media like Twitter, Google Plus, LinkedIn, Facebook and so on.
- **Veracity:** This feature defines in relation to two aspects: *data consistency* and *data trustworthiness* in a business environment. Consistency refers to data set must be statistically reliable; and data trustworthiness relates to number of factors (e.g. data origin, data collection and processing

Figure 2. The typical types of Big Data application systems

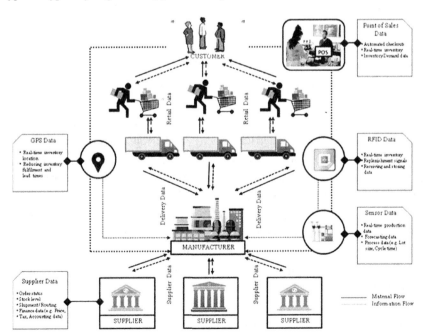

methods, facilities within Big Data-based information systems infrastructure). The data must be in a secure environment during the whole of their lifecycle from collection from trusted sources to processing on trusted software systems infrastructure.

- **Value:** The fourth V-feature for Big Data is value. The Big Data Value dimension denotes the potential value of Big Data which first requires processing, to make it useful for retail business decision making purposes. The Value feature bears special importance for retail supply chain design and management point of view.

Big Data is changing the way resources are used within retail business environment. The managerial challenges are immensely acknowledged within academics and practitioners; it is also highlighted that senior decision makers must embrace evidence-based decision-making (McAfee & Brynjolfsson, 2012). Detail analysis and interpretation from Big Data can help those in global retail business to make judicious decisions. In addition, it can help deepening customer engagement, optimize retail operational costs, able to provide business operational risks related warnings, managing resource management appropriately and capitalizing on new source of revenue. This extra demand on Big Data-based software applications for clear insights needs an innovative approach. An approach to find out meaningful value from Big Data-based software processing power as well as abilities to analyses the data (analytics) as well as appropriate skills.

In this way, data manipulation mechanisms transform data into information. Knowledge workers equipped with analytical tool identify pattern in the information and create rules and models, to be used to develop global retail business strategies. Retail enterprises gain wisdom by reviewing the impact of their strategies. Value resides in Big Data, and the insights derived from the data can be leveraged for improved operational competitive advantage. Researchers and practitioners (Davenport & Harris, 2007; Gorman, 2012) define analytics by three categories:

1. **Descriptive Analytics:** These types of analytics prepare and analyses historical data; and identify patterns from samples for reporting trends.
2. **Predictive Analytics:** These types of analytics predict future probabilities and trends; and find relationships in data that may not be clear with descriptive analysis.
3. **Prescriptive Analytics:** These types of analytics evaluate and use innovative ways to operate; consider business operational objectives; and try to mitigate all business constraints.

In addition, International Business Machines (IBM) Corporation provides the definition of Social Media Analytics and Entity Analytics (Dietrich, Plachy, & Norton, 2014). Social media analytics try to analysis data based on pattern embedded in it; and they use data classification and clustering mechanisms. The main characteristic of social media analytic is that data do not originate from within an enterprise; and which are simply considered as transactional data (e.g. data from social media). Entity Analytics focus on sorting and grouping data belonging to the same entity together. Modern computing power permits the analysis of data in a much more quickly, and detailed fashion than ever before.

In a broad range of functional areas within retail supply chain, data is being collected at unprecedented scale. Decisions that previously were based on guesswork, or on painstakingly constructed models of reality, can now be made based on the data itself. Such Big Data analysis now drives nearly every aspect of global retail business. The promise of Big Data-driven decision-making is now being recognized broadly, and there is growing enthusiasm for the research challenges within academics and practitioners. While the potential advantages of Big Data are real and significant, and some initial successes have already been achieved, there remain many technical challenges that must be addressed to fully realize this potential.

RESEARCH IN BIG DATA-BASED SUPPLY CHAIN APPLICATIONS

In recent years Big Data and Business Analytics have attracted burgeoning interest among researchers due their potential in business community (Waller & Fawcett, 2013). Particularly, a research conducted by IBM Institute for Business Value in collaboration with MIT Sloan Review revealed the importance of Big Data to business managers. The subject has been embraced in special journals including Harvard Business Review articles (McAfee & Brynjolfsson, 2012; Davenport & Patio, 2012; Barton & Court 2012); and some articles in MIT Sloan Management Review (Wixom & Ross, 2017). However, despite increasing contributions, Big Data-based software applications in supply chain management (SCM) are still in their infancy.

J R Stock (Stock, 2013) discusses Big Data driven supply chain management related issues in one of his recent publications; and he also proposes that Big Data-based analytics for SCM will allow decision makers to make faster decisions. In an industry survey conducted by Mitsubishi Heavy Industries and consulting company Deloitte (Deloitte & MHI, 2014); supply chain executives were questioned about innovations that drive supply chains. The main objective was to get the views of business executives on emerging technology trends that could dramatically impact supply chains of the future. The survey also identified areas for analytic-based SCM. The Council for Supply Chain Management Consultants published a report on Big Data in SCM, based on interviews with supply chain managers. One of the objectives of this research was to find out best practices in using Big Data for better SCM performance. Many commercial Big Data applications related to SCM are attracted the attention of academics and practitioners (Watson, Lewis, Cacioppo, & Jayaraman, 2013; Davenport, 2006; Davenport & Harris, 2007; McAfee & Brinjals, 2012; Deloitte & MHI, 2016). For example, a few researches work in corporate marketing management are showing tremendous opportunity in Big Data-based business analytics. The number of publications on supply chain network design using Big Data-based business analytics is also growing ceaselessly (Baseness, 2014; Dietrich, Plachy, & Norton, 2014; Swathi, 2012; Siegel, 2013; Watson, Lewis, Cacioppo, & Jayaraman, 2013).

It is evident from research literature review that the critically important organizational functions of SCM will evolve and adapt to Big Data analytics. An industry report (Deloitte & MHI, 2016) expressed a view about the potential of supply chains to deliver massive economic and environmental rewards for society. However, to fulfill this potential, the report suggests technological innovation will need to play a crucial role. Big Data analytics can provide step-change improvements in supply chain visibility, cost savings, and customer service. The key is to not only generate insightful data analysis, but to share it between business partners along retail supply chain so that they can act on it.

To solve a problem, Big Data-based application used intelligent reasoning in automated software environment that helps users apply analytical and scientific methods to business decision making. The software applications that focus on the retail supply chain domain are referred to as retail decision support systems, providing Big Data-based tools to support a user for global supply chain related reasoning process to come up with a solution to a problem. This type of reasoning can be considered an intellectual process by which retail managers use diverse types of artificial intelligence-based inference mechanisms (e.g. rule-based reasoning, case-based reasoning, model-based reasoning, and neutral network-based reasoning) to solve day-to-day operational problems.

Each of these approaches focuses on enriching some aspects of the traditional retail intelligent decision support systems. In addition, these automated software systems regularly make use of models that are expected to be reasonably accurate reflections of real-world work practices. In the term, *reasonably accurate*, one discovers the need of evaluation. The way these models are obtained and deployed across decision-making entities (i.e. *human* and *machine*) can introduce inconsistencies, incompleteness, redundancies, as well as problems in coordination. Consequently, there is a clear need for the evaluation of Big Data-based systems that are intended for serious business use.

Moreover, considering both the proliferation of Big Data-based analytics use for global retail business management and the fact that the data upon which these software applications (i.e. analytics) functions rely are often error-prone; there is an important need to assess the *data quality* as it pertains to the field of global retail management. As such, poor data quality can have a direct impact on retail supply chain operational decisions; and this will promote several tangible and intangible losses for global business. Retail operational managers are seeing the problems and impacts attributed to poor *data quality* growing in importance.

Many of the issues in Big Data-based retail supply chain related applications may not be new, but there is an evolving positive view of business analytics that is resulting in significant business transformations. The use of the term business analytics is now becoming standard to communicate the full life cycle of enhanced data-driven business decision making. Big data is the key ingredient in the estimation of many analytical models and the well-known garbage in, garbage out principle continues to apply. In Big Data era, the requirement that data must be accurate remains a critical issue. Data quality assurance is playing key role in different problem domains of supply chain management (e.g. sales forecasting, risk management, raw material procurement system).

BIG DATA-BASED SOFTWARE APPLICATIONS TESTING APPROACH

Testing Big Data-based applications is one of the crucial challenges faced by software development community. This is due to lack of knowledge on what to test; how to test; and how much data to test. In addition, Big Data-based application developers have been facing daunting challenges in creating the best strategies for structured and unstructured data validation; formulating an appropriate software test framework, working with broader use of existing data, integration of new sources of data, and making sure to maintain the standard of in-house quality assurance practices. These challenges are causing in inferior quality of data in production and delayed implementation and increase in total product cost. Robust Big Data-based applications testing strategy need to be defined for validating structured and unstructured data. Additionally, early identification of defects in Big Data-based software helps to minimize the overall deployment cost and time to market.

Big Data-based technologies are mainly classified into three distinct types: *file system*, *computing frameworks*, and *tools for analytics*. File system is responsible for the organization, storage, naming, sharing, and protecting files. Big Data-based application frameworks are often categorized into two: *open-source frameworks*, and *commercial frameworks*. Well known open source *frameworks* are - Apache Hadoop (Hadoop, 2017), Spark (Spark, 2017), Storm (Storm, 2017), and S4 (S4, 2017). Google offers Big Query (BigQuery, 2017) to operate on Google Big Table, Amazon support Big Data through Hadoop cluster, and NoSQL support of columnar database using Amazon DynamoDB are the few examples of commercial frameworks. The brief descriptions of the several Big Data tools can be found in academic literatures (Kune, Konugurthi, Agarwal, Chillarige, & Buyya, 2016). Technical details of these technologies are beyond the scope of this chapter.

Different software testing mechanisms (e.g. functional, non-functional) are used along with test data and test environment management to make sure that the data from different sources (e.g. retail business in-house data, data from outside sources) is processed error free and is of good quality to perform analysis. Functional testing mechanisms, like validation of map reduce process, structured and unstructured data validation, data storage validation are essential to make sure that the data is correct, in consistent format, and is of quality assured. Except functional validations other non-functional testing (e.g. *failover* testing, system *performance* testing, *service level agreement* testing) are also play crucial role in Big Data-based applications development.

To discuss different Big Data-based application testing mechanism, this chapter uses an open source software framework (i.e. Hadoop) for explanation purpose. Hadoop uses its own distributed file system, HDFS (Hadoop Distributed File System), which extends the native file system of the host operating system (e.g. UNIX, Linux, Windows). Hadoop is not actually a single product but is instead a growing collection of components and related projects. Figure 3 shows a typical Big Data architecture diagram and highlights the areas where testing should be focused. A brief description of the relevant technical terms in this architecture is explained in Table 1.

Big Data implementation deals with written complex Pig, Hive programs and running these jobs using Hadoop map educe framework on huge volumes of data across different nodes. Hadoop is a framework that allows for the distribution processing of large data sets across clusters of computers. Hadoop uses Map/Reduce, where the application is divided into many small fragments of work, each of which may be executed or re-executed on any node in the cluster. Hadoop utilizes its own distributed file system, HDFS, which makes data available to multiple computing nodes.

Figure 3. A typical Big Data architecture highlighting the areas of testing

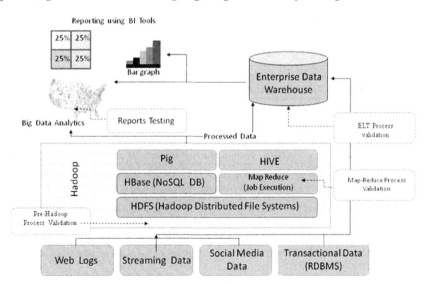

A step-by-step process need to follow in testing Big Data systems, using Hadoop ecosystem. First step loading source data into HDFS involves in extracting the data from different source systems and loading into HDFS. Data is extracted using crawl jobs web data, tools like sqoop for transactional data and then loaded in HDFS by splitting into multiple files. Once this step is completed second step perform map reduce operations involves in processing the input files and applying map and reduce operations to get a desired output. Last setup extracts the output results from HDFS involves in extracting the data output generated out of second step and loading into downstream systems which can be enterprise data warehouse for generating analytical reports or any of the transactional systems for further processing.

Big Data-Based Software Applications Testing

Poor implementation of Big Data-based software applications can lead to poor quality, and delays in testing. Performing functional testing can identify data quality issues that originate in errors with coding or distributed node configuration; effective test data and test environment management ensures that data from a variety of sources is of enough quality for accurate analysis and can be processed without error.

Apart from functional testing, non-functional testing (e.g. performance testing, failover testing) plays a key role in ensuring the scalability of the process. Functional testing is performed to identify functional coding issues and requirements issues, while non-functional testing identifies performance bottlenecks and validates the non-functional requirements. The size of Big Data applications often makes it difficult or too costly to replicate the entire system in a test environment; a smaller environment must be created

Table 1. Technical description in Hadoop framework

Technical Term	Brief Description
Web Logs	Log files from a web server and based on the values contained in the "Log files", derives indicators about when, how, and by whom a web server is visited.
Streaming Data	Streaming data is data that is generated continuously by thousands of data sources, which typically send in the data records simultaneously, and in small size (order of kilobytes). Streaming data includes a wide variety of data such as log files generated by customers using their mobile device or web-based applications, and so on.
Social Data	Social data is information that social media users publicly share, which includes metadata such as the user's location, language spoken, biographical data and / or shared links. Social data is valuable to marketers looking for customer insights that may increase sales of a particular retail product.
Transactional Data	Transactional data are information directly derived as a result of transactions. Unlike other sorts of data, transactional data contains a time dimension which means that there is timeliness to it and over time.
HDFS	Hadoop uses its own distributed file system, HDFS (Hadoop Distributed File System), which extends the native file system of the host operating system (e.g. UNIX, Linux, Windows).
HBase	Apache HBase is an open source; non-relational database modeled after Google's Bigtable and is written in Java. It runs on top of HDFS. It provides a fault-tolerant way of storing enormous quantities of *sparse data*.
PIG	Apache Pig provides an alternative language to SQL (Structured Query Language), called Pig Latin, for querying data stored in HDFS. Pig does not require the data to be structured as relational database tables.
HIVE	Hive is a software tool that structures data in Hadoop into the form of relational-like tables and allows queries using a subset of SQL.
EDW	Enterprise Data Warehouse (EDW) is a database that stores all information associated with a business. EDW contains data related to areas that the business wants to analyze for business intelligence (BI) operation.

instead, but this introduces the risk that applications that run well in the smaller test environment behave differently in production.

Therefore, it is necessary that the system engineers are careful when building the test environment, as many of these concerns can be mitigated by carefully designing the system architecture. A proper systems architecture can help eliminate performance issues (such as an imbalance in input splits or redundant shuffle and sort), but, of course, this approach alone doesn't guarantee a system that performs well.

The numerical stability of algorithms also becomes an issue when dealing with statistical or machine learning algorithms. Applications that run well with one dataset may abort unexpectedly or produce poor results when presented with a similar but poorly conditioned set of inputs. Verification of numerical stability is particularly important for customer-facing systems.

Two key areas of the testing problem are: (1) establishing efficient test datasets and; (2) availability of Hadoop-centric testing tools (e.g. PigUnit, Junit for Pig).

Testing should include all four phases shown in Figure 4. Data quality issues can manifest themselves at any of these stages.

Testing Methods for Validation of Pre-Hadoop Processing

Big Data systems typically process a mix of both structured data (e.g. POS transactions, call detail records, general ledger transactions, and call center transactions). Unstructured data (such as user comments, insurance claims descriptions and web logs) and semi-structured social media data (from sites like Twitter, Facebook, LinkedIn and Pinterest). Often the data is extracted from its source location and saved in its raw or a processed form in Hadoop or another Big Data database management system. Data is typically extracted from a variety of source systems and in varying file formats (e.g. relational tables, fixed size records, flat CSV files with delimiters, XML files, JSON and text files).

The most important activity during data loading is to compare data to ensure extraction has happened correctly and to confirm that the data loaded into the HDFS (Hadoop Distributed File System) is a complete, accurate copy.

Typical Tests Include

1. **Data Type Validation:** Data type validation is customarily carried out on one or more simple data fields. The simplest kind of data type validation verifies that individual characters provided through user input are consistent with the expected characters of one or more known primitive data types as defined in a programming language or data storage and retrieval mechanism.
2. **Range and Constraint Validation:** Simple range and constraint validation may examine user input for consistency with a minimum/maximum range, or consistency with a test for evaluating a sequence of characters, such as one or more tests against regular expressions.

Figure 4. Testing phases

3. **Code and Cross-Reference Validation:** Code and cross-reference validation includes tests for data type validation, combined with one or more operations to verify that the user-supplied data is consistent with one or more external rules, requirements or validity constraints relevant to an organization, context or set of underlying assumptions. These additional validity constraints may involve cross-referencing supplied data with a known look-up table or directory information service.

4. **Structured Validation:** Structured validation allows for the combination of any number of various basic data type validation steps, along with more complex processing. Such complex processing may include the testing of conditional constraints for an entire complex data object or set of process operations with a system.

Testing Methods for Hadoop MapReduce Processes

Hadoop MapReduce: Hadoop MapReduce, as shown in Figure 5, is a software framework for easily written applications that process vast amounts of data (multi-terabyte datasets) in-parallel on large cluster (thousands of nodes) of commodity hardware in a reliable fault-tolerant manner.

A MapReduce job usually splits the input dataset into independent chunks that are processed by the map tasks in a completely parallel manner. The framework sorts the outputs of the maps, which are then input to the reduce tasks. Typically, both the input and the output of the job are stored in a file system. The framework takes care of scheduling tasks and monitoring them and re-executed the failed tasks.

ETL Process: ETL is a variation of the Extract, Transform, Load (ETL), a data integration process in which transformation takes place on an intermediate server before it is loaded into the target. This capability is most useful for processing the large data set required for BI and BA.

Testing Methods for Data Extract and EDW Loading

The major part of the data warehouse system is data extraction, transformation and loading (ETL). The goal is to extract the data, often from a variety of different systems, and transform it so that it is uniform in terms of format and content, and, finally, to load the data into a warehouse where it can serve as the basis for business intelligence needs.

Figure 5. Hadoop MapReduce software framework

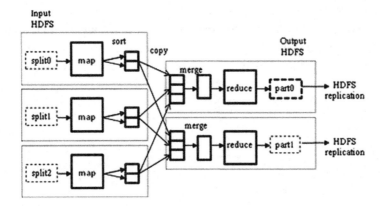

The integrity of the data must be maintained at every step. It must be stored clearly and concisely without loss and should be accessible to all authorized professionals. So, for the data warehouses to deliver value, they require carful ETL testing to ensure that processes work as required.

The different methods for ETL testing depend on the challenges faced in performing this testing. The following are some of the main challenges to overcome.

- **No User Interface**: In data warehouse testing, no user interface is present by only data and its relations are there. To test this type of data, the ability to look at data, validate data processing rules, and analyze final data output are required. Consequently, knowledge of database query languages like SQL is essential for testers to do this accurately, where traditional manual testing skills are not enough.
- **Huge Volume of Data**: Millions of transactions can be happening every day. It is a challenge to verify the extraction, transformation and loading of that data in the real-time environment as the code is updated.
- **Variety of Sources**: Typically, a wide variety of systems feed daily transactional data to a data warehouse. Some of the data may even come from systems used in cloud computing or hosted by a third party. Similarly, the format and content of the data will vary. It is often a huge challenge to merge the data while making sure that everything gets processed consistently and in relation to each other.
- **Bad or Missing Data**: The information collected from the various source systems may not be complete, may have many special cases requiring exception processing, or may be of poor quality generally.
- **Non-Static Rules**: The source systems will likely change over time because of release upgrades with attendant changes in data content and structure. There should be ways to cope with these changes without having to change the design of the data warehouse.

Testing Methods for Reports

Big Data analytics solutions are built to report and analyze data from data warehouses. They can vary in size and complexity depending on the needs of the business, underlying data stores, number of reports and number of users. The key focus is on validating layout format as per the design mock-up, style sheets, prompts and filter attributes and metrics on the report. Verification of drilling, sorting and export functions of the reports in Web environment is also done. Data generated on the reports should be corrected as per business logic. The test team needs to target the lowest granularity that is present in the data warehouse, understanding each report and the linkages of every field displayed in the report with the schema. Tracing its origin back to the source system is a big challenge and a time-consuming process.

SCOPE AND PROCESS OF BIG DATA APPLICATION QUALITY ASSURANCE

Big Data-based software Quality Assurance (QA) has its roots in assuring the quality of manufactured physical product. In manufacturing product QA is performed by inspecting the product and evaluating its quality near its completion or at various stages of production process. However, software is not as tangible as manufactured engineering products which are much more physical items by nature. But a software product is *'invisible in nature'* and it is characterized by its functionalities. This invisible nature of software product creates extra problems of assessing its quality. In this way, engineering manufactured products are visible, whereas software engineering products are invisible. Majority of the defects in an industrial engineering product can be detected during the manufacturing and fabrication processes. However, defects in software products are invisible that makes its incorrectness identification much harder and as a result software quality assurance is very complex. Moreover, there are additional problems with assessing software quality; and this is attributed to its recent trend of software product design and development. For example, now-a-days software products are often developed by global teams of professional spanning multiple countries, multiple development platforms, and multiple layers of interfaces between software components.

Different academics and practitioners have different views on the source of the software quality attributes. Juran and his fellow practitioners (Juran & Gryna, 1970) define software quality as 'fitness for use' and 'customer impression' and later 'freedom of deficiencies'. A second view is that of Crosby (Crosby, 1979) who defines quality as both the 'conformance to requirements' and 'non-conformance implies defects. A third view is that of Roger Pressman (Pressman, 2000) who states that there are three requirements for software quality, namely 'specific functional requirements', 'adhering to quality standards in the contract' and lastly 'good software engineering practices.

These views on software quality has suggested to approaches of measuring the quality of Big Data-based software applications. The entire process of Big Data-based software development is guided by software engineering techniques and the assessment of the quality of the software is carried out during the quality assurance process. In software engineering, different techniques are used to design and develop software applications based on business requirements. At the same time, software quality assurance (SQA) mechanisms manage quality of software during the software development process. SQA defines and measures the inputs and outputs of the development processes and qualifies the quality of the software in terms of defects. To assess the software quality, it is advantageous to identify what aspect of software need to measure.

Factors that Impact Software Application Quality

McCall (McCall, 1977) has identified three different categories of factors that software quality can come under. The factors are spread over the lifespan of the application and not only its original development. The first set of factors is associated with the original operation of the software product by a user. The second set of factors is directed towards the revision of the product from an existing product to new or enhanced product and how the quality of the original design and code allows for this revision. The last set of factors is concerned with the transaction of the product to another target environment, such as a new database or operating system. The factors are outlined in the Table 2.

In this chapter, software quality assurance (SQA) is considered as a process for the measurement of deliverables and activities during each stage of Big Data-Based software application development lifecycle. The objective of SQA is to quantify the quality of the products and the activities giving rise to them and to guide a quality improvement effort. For discussion, this chapter considers that Big Data-based software applications assurance activities take place at each development stage of the application development lifecycle. The stages are categorized into areas for requirements capture, system design, coding and testing, and finally release.

Table 2. McCalls Quality factors for new software development

Quality Factors for New Software Development s for		
Product Operational	**Product Revision**	**Product Transaction**
Correctness Reliability Efficiency Integrity Usability	Maintainability Flexibility Testability	Portability Reusability Interoperability

In general, Big Data-based application quality assurance refers to the study and application of various assurance process, methods, standards, criteria, and systems to ensure the quality of Big Data system in terms of a set of quality parameters. Figure 6 shows a sample scope of validation for quality assurance of Big Data-based supply chain management applications.

Conventional system quality parameters such as performance, robustness, security, etc., can be applicable to Big Data systems. These are listed below:

- **System Reliability:** Software systems reliability means the ability of an application (e.g. product or service) to perform as expected over time; and this is usually measured in terms of the probability of it performing as expected over time.
- **System Data Security:** Software systems data security could be used to evaluate the security of Big Data applications indifferent perspectives. Using this criterion, data security could be evaluated in various aspects at various levels of software system application user hierarchy.
- **System Consistency:** The absence of difference, when comparing two or more test case outputs in software testing environment.

Figure 6. The scope of validation for Big Data application system quality

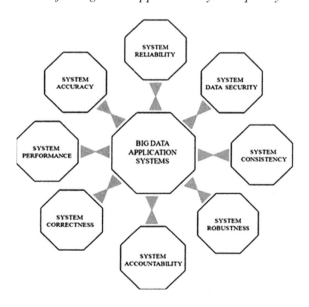

Figure 7. A quality test process for Big Data-based application systems

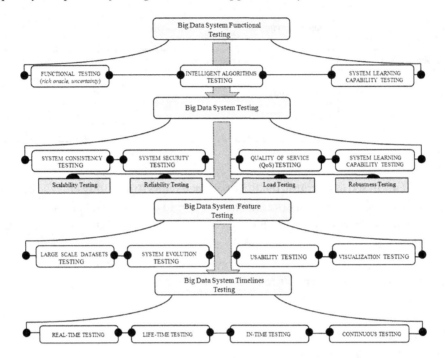

- **System Robustness:** System robustness complements correctness. Correctness addresses the behavior of a system in case covered by its specification; robustness characterized what happens outside of the specification. In this way, robustness is the ability of software systems to react appropriately to abnormal conditions.
- **System Accountability:** System accountability quality factor can be divided up into three processes. First, one must identify relevant parties, for what they are accountable, and to whom they are accountable. Second, if a condition verifies for which a party was previously identified as accountable, a forum of some kind convenes to gather the necessary information and passes a judgement as to the accountability of the said party. Third, one must assign positive or negative sanctions to the responsible party.
- **System Correctness:** System correctness is the very essential quality criteria for Big Data analytic applications. It is the quality criteria of software applications to perform their specific tasks, as specified by their specification. If a Big Data-based analytic application does not do what it is meant to do, everything else (e.g. nice graphical user interface, appropriate algorithm to data processing) about it matters little.
- **System Performance:** This quality criterion indicates the performance of the system, such as availability, response time, throughput, scalability, and so on.
- **System Accuracy:** System accuracy criterion indicates the results of Big Data-based software systems as anticipated.

The promise of Big Data-driven decision making is now being recognized broadly, and there is a growing enthusiasm for business analytics quality assurance related testing methods. Heterogeneity, scale, timeliness, and privacy problems with supply chain Big Data impede process at all phases of the pipeline that can create value from this huge data set. The problems start right away during operational data acquisition, data cleaning, and selecting the right data for decision-making software applications. One of the main problems about what data to keep and what data to discard, and how to store that make data to be reliable for the indented applications. Much supply chain operational data today is not natively structured format; for example tweets and blogs are weakly structured pieces of text, while images and video are structured format for storage and display. Therefore, getting the appropriate data set is a challenging task.

Nevertheless, this chapter will highlight a simplistic view of Big Data-based software testing that consists of systems functional testing aspects (e.g. rich oracle, uncertainty), intelligent algorithms testing (e.g. scalability, reliability, load, robustness), and system learning capability testing. A brief over view of Big Data-based software testing is shown in Figure 7.

There are two typical Big Data applications: (a) recommendation systems, and; (b) prediction systems. Figure 8 summarizes the typical quality factors for prediction and recommendation systems in a fishbone diagram, and a brief description of those factors are presented in the next section.

Quality Factors for Prediction Systems

- **System Correctness:** System Correctness is a quality factor used to evaluate the correctness of the Big Data applications. Unlike the conventional system, Big Data applications are hard to validate for correctness. For instance, prediction-related software is mainly developed to make predictions about real world activities. Hence, it is difficult to determine the correct output for those types of software. Correctness is related to the prediction pattern or model. For instance, some models are more likely used to predict point of inflexion values while some other models do well in predicting continuity. Thus, to verify the correctness of the system effectively, engineers need to evaluate the capability of prediction in the specified conditions and environments.

- **System Accuracy:** System Accuracy is used to evaluate if the system yields true (no systematic errors), and consistent (no random errors) results. Some Big Data applications are developed to find previous unknown answers; thereby only approximate solutions might be available. This can be called uncontrollable prediction. Some prediction is used to prevent something happening in the future, and the prediction result will affect actions or behaviours. In turn, those actions can promote the prediction result.

- **System Stability:** System Stability reflects the stability of the system prediction while the environment or data changes. For example, the prediction capability of a system is stable with minor changes when statistical data are acquired from different timeframes.

- **System Consistency:** System Consistency is a quality indicator useful to evaluate the consistency of the targeted system in different perspectives. Due to the inherent uncertainties in system models, some applications do not produce a single correct output for a given set on inputs. This leads to hardly determining the expected behaviours of the software. In such situations, domain-specific experts could provide opinions to support system consistency.

- **Duration:** Duration indicates the expected prediction period. It can measure how up-to-date the data is, and whether it is correct despite the possibility of modifications or changes that impact time and date values. For instance, commonly-used prediction duration in enterprise management can be divided into short term, middle term, and long term.

Figure 8. Big Data Application System Quality Factors

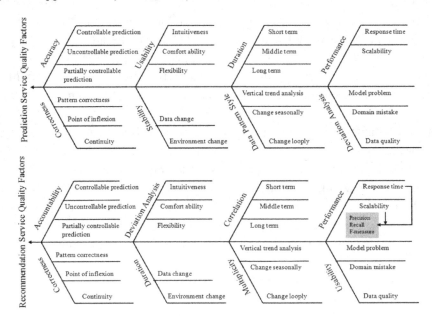

- **Deviation Analysis:** Deviation Analysis is used to analyze the prediction deviation within an accepted range or confidence interval.
- **System Usability:** System usability is a parameter that indicates how well the Big Data application service can be used. This can be very subjective due to different developers and users having diverse user experiences. The typical usability factors include intuitiveness, comfortability, and flexibility.

This aspect concerns understandability – the users' effort for recognizing the logical concept and its applicability; learnability – the users' effort for learning its application; operability – the users' effort for operation and operation control.

- **System Performance:** System Performance is a distinct quality factor for Big Data application service. It is useful to evaluate how well Big Data is structured, designed, collected, generated, stored, and managed to support large-scale prediction services.

QUALITY FACTORS FOR RECOMMENDATIONS

- **Correctness:** This quality factor reflects if the recommended service or commodity meets the demands of customers. Correctness could be subjective between different persons. Thus, how to measure correctness is still a challenge for quality assurance engineers.
- **Correlation:** This quality factor evaluates the degree of correlation of the recommended service. This involves various recommendation strategies, such as user content-based, behavior-based, and collaboration filtered-based.

- **Multiplicity:** This quality factor refers to the measurements for repeatability of recommended service. For instance, a poor-quality system probably recommends too many repeated or similar commodities to users.
- **Category Coverage:** This indicator is useful to evaluate the coverage rate for diverse categories. This factor measures the completeness of recommendation within a selected domain.
- **Accountability:** This quality parameter is very important and mandatory for both Big Data service applications and users. This could be measured in a quantitative way, such as user rating similarity, domain trust value, domain related degree, and social intimacy degree.
- **Duration:** This factor indicates the expected recommendation period. For instance, commonly-used recommendation duration in enterprise management can be divided into short term, middle term, and long term.
- **Deviation Analysis:** This factor is used to analyze the recommendation deviation within an accepted range or confidence interval.
- **System Usability:** This parameter indicates how well the Big Data application service can be used. This can be very subjective due to different developers and users having diverse user experiences.
- **System Performance:** This is a distinct quality factor for Big Data application service, and it is useful to evaluate how well Big Data is structured, designed, collected, generated, stored, and managed to support large-scale recommendation services.

In addition to the typical applications discussed above, there are more Big Data related applications such as machine learning system, ranking system, and search systems.

SYSTEM VALIDATION METHODS FOR BIG DATA-BASED APPLICATIONS

Software testing process attempt to verify and validate the capability of a software system to meet its required attributes and functionality. This aims at evaluating an attribute or capability of a software system and determining that it meets its required results. Although crucial to software quality and widely deployed by programmers and testers, Big Data-based application systems validation remains an art, due to limited understanding of the principles of software. The difficulties in software testing and validation stems from the complexity of software. The purpose of validation can be quality assurance, verification and reliability estimation.

This section presents the existing software testing methods which have been used to validate several types of Big Data-based applications including intelligent systems, data mining systems, and learning-based systems.

Program-Based Software Testing

Program-based software testing methods have been used in many Big Data-based applications. In this software testing mechanism systematically searches for errors in MapReduce applications and generates corresponding test cases.

Classification-Based Testing

A classification-based testing method to software systems testing usually involves two distinct steps: (a) training a classifier to distinguish failure from successful cases on a select subset of results, and then; (b) applying the trained classifier to identify failures in the main set of results. A resembling reference model is usually used to train a classifier. More specifically, there are techniques for applying pattern classifications to alleviate the test oracle problems.

Oracle Problem in Software Testing

Testing involves examining the behavior of a system to discover potential faults. Given an input for a system, the challenge of distinguishing the corresponding desired, correct behavior from potentially incorrect behavior is called the "test oracle problem". Test oracle automation is important to remove a current bottleneck that inhibits greater overall test automation. Without test oracle automation, the human should determine whether observed behavior is correct.

Machine Learning-Based Software Testing

Software testing is an investigation process which attempts to validate and verify the alignment of a software system's attributes and functionality with its intended goals. Due to this fact, automated testing approaches are desired to reduce the time and cost. Besides, automation can significantly enhance the testing process performance. Several machine learning techniques been used for automated software testing purpose. Particularly, Artificial Neural Networks (ANN), Decision Tree-based algorithms have been used for predicting potential bugs in Big Data-based applications.

Crowd-Sourced Software Testing

Software engineering no longer takes place in small, isolated groups of developers, but increasingly takes place in organizations and communities which involves delegating a variety of tasks to an unknown workforce – the crowd. There is an increasing trend towards globalization with a focus on collaborative methods and infrastructure. Driven by Web 2.0 technologies, organizations can tap into a workforce consisting of anyone with an Internet connection. Customers, or *requesters*, can advertise chunks of work, or tasks, on a crowdsourcing platform, where suppliers (i.e., individual workers) select those task that match their interests and abilities. Several potential benefits have been linked to the use of crowdsourcing in general, and these would also be applicable in the context of software development specifically: *cost reduction, faster time-to-market, higher quality through broad participation*, and usher *open innovation*. It is a cost-effective method to validate a machine-learning based application systems, such as human face recognition system. Currently, crowd-sourced testing has been used in mobile app testing and mobile Teas (Testing as a Service). One good example is test (http://www.utest.com/company).

Crowdsourcing has gained much attention in practice over the last years. Many Big Data-based applications have drawn on this concept for performing different tasks and value creation activities. Nevertheless, despite its popularity, there is still comparatively little well-founded knowledge on crowdsourcing, particularly about crowdsourcing intermediaries.

Model-Based Software Testing

There is an abundance of testing style in the disciple of software engineering. Over the last few decades, many of these have come to be used and adopted by the industry as solutions to address the increasing demand for assuring software quality. Due to popularization of object-oriented design and development of software, models are used for software implementation. There has been a growth in black box testing techniques that are collectively dubbed *model-based testing* (MBT). Model-based testing has recently gained attention with the popularization of models (e.g. UML-based models) in software design and development. Model-based testing or MBT is a general term that signifies an approach that bases common testing tasks such as test case generation and test result evaluation on a model of the application under test.

FUTURE RESEARCH DIRECTIONS

Opportunities are always followed by challenges. On the one hand, Big Data-based supply chain software applications bring many attractive opportunities; and on the other hand, Big Data-based supply chain management applications software are facing a lot of challenges. These challenges can be broadly categorized as Big Data-based software architectural aspects, system hardware performance enhancement related issues, and parallel software testing capabilities. Particularly, Big Data-based supply chain applications testing is the most expensive and critical phase of software development life cycle.

As part of the general Big Data quality assurance research initiative, the current research will continue the concurrency and parallelism issues of Big Data generation and uses in global supply chain business analytics. Therefore, in dealing with this huge amount of data and executing it on multiple nodes of processing is a highly challenging risk of having bad data and even data quality related issues may exist at every stage of design and development. Some of the future research agendas are: (1) increasing need for integration of large volume of data available from multiple sources (e.g. text, video, audio); and this integration forces global supply chain operational provision to have constantly clean and reliable data sets; (2) instant data collection and live deployment are very crucial issues in order to get appropriate business intelligences for a retail business, which can be overcome only by testing the business intelligence software applications before live deployment, and finally; (3) real-time scalability related issues of large amounts of data generated by devices equipped with sensing components along global supply chain. In addition, there are emerging needs for research problems and directions on this subject in terms of quality control models, automated validation methods, approaches, and service platforms as well as TasS (Testing-as-a-service) and test automation techniques.

CONCLUSION

With the advent of big data management technologies and analytics in supply chain management, academics and practitioners are paying much more attention to build high-quality software services for business applications. However, there are increasing quality problems resulting in erroneous data costs in global supply chain industries. Data has always been an integral part of business. Technology transformation has further reinforced this importance. The entrance of social media, mobility, and the Internet of Things (IoT) has not only blurred the lines between online and offline business, but also resulted in the availability of a huge amount of unstructured data related to consumer behavior and interests. With big insights, Big Data could indeed mean big business for supply chain management. However, industry analysts are echoing growing concerns on data quality. Quality Assurance (QA) can offer a solution to the data quality challenge, and a robust and effective QA strategy can deliver big returns from Big Data.

The design and development of Big Data-based software applications have been proven useful in a diverse area of application for solving problem in global supply chain industry – e.g., raw material procurement planning, marketing strategy formulation, and logistics planning. This chapter provides an introductory discussion on Big Data-based business intelligence software systems and their quality assurance related issues; it includes a brief discussion on the appropriate software testing mechanisms for the new breeds of Big Data-based applications.

While Big Data provides solutions to complex business problems like analyzing large volume of data to derive precise answers, analyzing data in motion it processes bigger challenges in testing these scenarios. The data is highly volatile and often unstructured as it is generated from myriad of sources – such as weblogs, radio frequency identification (RFID) devices, sensors embedded in different business applications (e.g. in artifact manufacturing machines, global positioning systems, transportation networks). The quality data plays an important role in all supply chain management applications. The quality of data is recognized as a relevant performance issue in operating processes, business decision-making activities, and business-partners cooperation requirements.

Several initiatives have been lunched in the public and private sectors, with data quality having a leading role. At the same time, information systems have been migrating from a hierarchical / monolithic structure to a networked-based structure. Here the set of potential data sources that organizations can use has dramatically increased in size and scope. The issue of data quality has become more complex and controversial because of this evolution. In network information systems, processes are involved in complex information exchanges and often operate on a priori – input obtained from external sources. Consequently, the overall quality of the data that flows across information systems can rapidly degrade over time if the quality of both processes and information inputs is not controlled. On the other hand, networked information systems offer new opportunities for data quality management, including the availability of a broader range of data sources and the ability to select and compare data from diverse sources. The aim is to detect and correct errors, and thus, improve the overall quality assurance of data, and the business applications based on this data.

Moreover, Big Data is changing definitions and benchmarks for breakthrough technologies. The need to stream and collect real time data from varied data sources and in different formats results in an exponential increase in volume. Further, there is also the need to continuously 'listen' to the stream and sift out irrelevant data. There is no point in responding to a customer tweet after a week, or having dirty, noisy data affecting business decisions.

REFERENCES

S4. (2017). Retrieved from http://incubator.apache.org/s4

Arnold, S. E. (1992). Information manufacturing: The road to database quality. *Database*, *15*(5), 32–39.

Baesens, A. (2014). *Analytics in a big data world: The essential guide to data science and its applications*. Hoboken, NJ: John Wiley & Sons.

Ballou, D. P., & Pazer, H. L. (1985). Modeling data and process quality in multi-input, multi-output information systems. *Management Science*, *31*(2), 150–162. doi:10.1287/mnsc.31.2.150

Ballou, D. P., Wang, R., & Pacer, H. (1998). Modeling information manufacturing systems to determine information product quality. *Management Science*, *44*(4), 462–484. doi:10.1287/mnsc.44.4.462

Battani, C., Cappelli, C., Francians, C., & Maurino, A. (2009). Methodologies for data quality assessment and improvement. *Association for Computing Machinery Computing Surveys*, *41*(3), 1–52.

Blake, R., & Mangiameli, P. (2011). The effects and interactions of data quality and problem complexity on classification. *Association for Computing Machinery Journal of Data and Information Quality*, *2*(2), 1–28. doi:10.1145/1891879.1891881

Cooke, J. A. (2013). Three trends to watch in 2013, Perspective. *Supply Chain Quarterly*, *1*, 11.

Crosby, P. (1995). *Philip Crosby's Reflections on Quality*. McGraw-Hill.

Davenport, T. H., Barth, P., & Bean, R. (2012, Fall). How Big Data is different. *MIT Sloan Management Review*, 22–24.

Davenport, T. H., & Harris, J. G. (2007). *Competing on analytics – the new science of wining*. Boston: Harvard Business School Publishing Corporation.

Davenport, T. H., Harris, J. G., & Morison, R. (2010). *Analytics at work – smart decisions, better results*. Boston: Harvard Business Press.

Davenport, T. H., & Prusiks, L. (2000). *Working knowledge: how organizations manage what they know*. Boston: Harvard Business Press.

Deloitte & MHI. (2014). *The 2014 MHI Annual Industry Report – Innovation the driven supply chain*. Charlotte, NC: MHI.

Deloitte & MHI. (2016). *The 2016 MHI Annual Industry Report – Accelerating change: How innovation is driving digital, always-on Supply Chains*. MHI.

Deming, W. E. (2000). *The New Economics for Industry, Government, Education* (2nd ed.). MIT Press.

Dietrich, B., Plachy, E. C., & Norton, M. F. (2014). *Analytics across the enterprise: How IBM realize business value from big data and analytics*. Boston: IBM Press Books.

Emery, J. C. (1969). *Organizational planning and control systems: Theory and management*. New York: Macmillan.

Hadoop. (2017). Retrieved from http://hadoop.apache.org

Haug, A., & Arlbjorn, J. S. (2011). Barriers to master data quality. *Journal of Enterprise Information Management*, *24*(3), 288–303. doi:10.1108/17410391111122862

Haugh, A., Arlbjorn, J. S., & Pedersen, A. (2009). A classification model of ERP system data quality. *Industrial Management & Data Systems*, *109*(8), 1053–1068. doi:10.1108/02635570910991292

HBR. (2012, October). Getting Control of Big Data. *Harvard Business Review*.

Huh, Y. U., Keller, F. R., Redman, T. C., & Watkins, A. R. (1990). Data quality. *Information and Software Technology, 32*(8), 559–565. doi:10.1016/0950-5849(90)90146-I

Imminent, A., Pacemen, P., & Alaska, E. (2015). Evaluating the quality of social media data in big data architecture. *IEEE Access: Practical Innovations, Open Solutions, 3*, 2028–2043. doi:10.1109/ACCESS.2015.2490723

Jones-Farmer, L. A., Ezell, J. D., & Hazen, B. T. (2013). Applying control chart methods to enhance data quality. *Technometrics*.

Jurak, J. M., & Godfrey, A. B. (1999). *Juran's Quality Handbook* (5th ed.). McGraw-Hill.

Kahan, B. K., Strong, D. M., & Wang, R. Y. (2002). Information quality benchmarks: Product and service performance. *Communications of the ACM, 45*(4), 184–192. doi:10.1145/505248.506007

Kaplan, R. S., & Norton, D. P. (1993, September). Putting the Balanced Scorecard to Work. *Harvard Business Review*, 4–17.

Kune, R., Konugurthi, P. K., Agarwal, A., Chillarige, R. R., & Buyya, R. (2016). The anatomy of big data computing. *Software, Practice & Experience, 46*(1), 79–105. doi:10.1002pe.2374

Lee, Y. W., Pipino, L., Strong, D. M., & Wang, R. Y. (2004). Process-embedded data integrity. *Journal of Database Management, 15*(1), 87–103. doi:10.4018/jdm.2004010104

Lee, Y. W., Strong, D. M., Kahn, B. K., & Wang, R. Y. (2002). AIMQ: A methodology for information quality assessment. *Information & Management, 40*(2), 133–146. doi:10.1016/S0378-7206(02)00043-5

March, S. T., & Hevner, A. R. (2007). Integrated decision support systems: A data warehousing perspective. *Decision Support Systems, 43*(3), 1031–1043. doi:10.1016/j.dss.2005.05.029

McAfee, A., & Brynjolfsson, E. (2012). Big data: The management revolution. *Harvard Business Review, 90*(10), 61–68. PMID:23074865

Murphy, C., Kaiser, G., Hu, L., & Wu, L. (2008). Properties of machine learning applications for use in metamorphic testing. *Proceeding of the 20th Internal Conference on Software Engineering and Knowledge Engineering (SEKE)*, 867-872.

Pal, K. (2017). A Semantic Web Service Architecture for Supply Chain Management. *Procedia Computer Science, 109C*, 999–1004. doi:10.1016/j.procs.2017.05.442

Parssian, A. (2006). Managerial decision support with knowledge of accuracy and completeness of the relational aggregate functions. *Decision Support Systems, 42*(3), 1494–1502. doi:10.1016/j.dss.2005.12.005

Pipino, L. L., Lee, Y. W., & Wang, R. Y. (2002). Data quality assessment. *Communications of the ACM, 45*(4), 211–218. doi:10.1145/505248.506010

Redman, T. C. (1996). *Data Quality for the Information Age*. Norwood, MA: Artech House Publishers.

Ronen, B., & Spiegler, I. (1991). Information as inventory: A new conceptual view. *Information & Management, 21*(4), 239–247. doi:10.1016/0378-7206(91)90069-E

Sathi, A. (2012). Big data analytics: Disruptive technologies for changing the game. MC Press Online, LLC.

Scannapieco, M., & Catarci, T. (2002). Data quality under a computer science perspective, *Archivi and Computer*, 21-15.

Siegel, E. (2013). *Predictive analytics: The power to predict who will click, buy, lie or die*. Hoboken, NJ: John Wiley & Sons Inc.

Smith, W. B. (1993). Total Customer Satisfaction as a Business Strategy. *Quality and Reliability Engineering International, 9*(1), 49–53. doi:10.1002/qre.4680090109

Spark. (2017). Retrieved from https://spark.incubator.apache.org

Stock, J. R. (2013). Supply chain management: A look back, a look ahead. *Supply Chain Quarterly, 2*, 22–26.

Storm. (2017). Retrieved from https://storm.incubator.apache.org

Svilvar, M., Charkraborty, A. & Kanioura, A. (2013). Big data analytics in marketing. OR/MS Today, October 22-25.

Wand, Y., & Wang, R. Y. (1996). Anchoring data quality dimensions in ontological foundations. *Communications of the ACM, 39*(11), 86–95. doi:10.1145/240455.240479

Wang, R. Y. (1998). A product perspective on total data quality management. *Communications of the Association for Computer Machinery, 41*(2), 58–65. doi:10.1145/269012.269022

Wang, R. Y., & Kon, H. B. (1993). Towards total data quality management (TDQM). In R. Y. Wanf (Ed.), *Information technology in action: Trends and perspectives*. Englewood Cliffs, NJ: Prentice-Hall.

Wang, R. Y., Storey, V. C., & Firth, C. P. (1995). A framework for analysis of data quality research. *IEEE Transactions on Knowledge and Data Engineering, 7*(4), 623–640. doi:10.1109/69.404034

Wang, R. Y., & Strong, D. M. (1996). Beyond Accuracy: What data quality means to data consumers. *Journal of Management Information Systems, 12*(4), 5–33. doi:10.1080/07421222.1996.11518099

Watson, M., Lewis, S., Cacioppo, P., & Jayaraman, J. (2013). *Supply chain network design – applying optimization and analytics to the global supply chain*. FT Press.

Watts, S., Shankaranarayanan, G., & Even, A. (2009). Data quality assessment in context: A cognitive perspective. *Decision Support Systems, 48*(1), 202–211. doi:10.1016/j.dss.2009.07.012

Williamson, O. (1996). *The Mechanisms of Governance*. New York: Oxford University Press.

Wixom, B. H., & Ross, J. W. (2017). How to Monetize Your Data, MIT Sloan Management Review. *Spring Issue, 58*(3), 10–13.

Zeithaml, V. A., Berry, L. L., & Parasuraman, A. (1990). *Delivering quality service: Balancing customer perceptions and expectations*. New York: Free Press.

KEY TERMS AND DEFINITIONS

Big Data Analytics: Analytics is the discovery, interpretation, and visualization of meaningful patterns in big data. To do this, analytics use data classification and clustering mechanisms.

Decision-Making Systems: A decision support system (DSS) is a computer-based information system that supports business or organizational decision-making activities, typically resulting in ranking, sorting, or choosing from among alternatives. DSSs serve the management, operations, and planning levels of an organization (usually mid and higher management) and help people make decisions about problems that may be rapidly changing and not easily specified in advance (i.e., unstructured and semi-structured decision problems). Decision support systems can be either fully computerized, human-powered or a combination of both.

Radio Frequency Identification (RFID): This is a wireless technology used to identify tagged objects in certain vicinities. Generally, it has got three main components: a tag, a reader, and a back-end. The tag uses the open air to transmit data via radio frequency (RF) signal. It is also weak in computational capability. RFID automates information collection regarding an individual object's location and actions.

Supply Chain Management: A supply chain consists of a network of key business processes and facilities, involving end users and suppliers that provide products, services and information. In this chain management, improving the efficiency of the overall chain is an influential factor; and it needs at least four important strategic issues to be considered: supply chain network design, capacity planning, risk assessment and management, and performances monitoring and measurement. Moreover, the details break down of these issues need to consider in the level of individual business processes and sub-processes; and the combined performance of this chain. The coordination of these huge business processes and their performance are of immense importance.

Chapter 4
Big Data Analytics:
Educational Data Classification Using Hadoop-Inspired MapReduce Framework

Pratiyush Guleria
Himachal Pradesh University, India

Manu Sood
Himachal Pradesh University, India

ABSTRACT

Due to an increase in the number of digital transactions and data sources, a huge amount of unstructured data is generated by every interaction. In such a scenario, the concepts of data mining assume great significance as useful information/trends/predictions can be retrieved from this large amount of data, known as big data. Big data predictive analytics are making big inroads into the educational field because with the adoption of new technologies, new academic trends are being introduced into educational systems. This accumulation of large data of different varieties throws a new set of challenges to the learners as well as educational institutions in ensuring the quality of their education by improving strategic/operational decision-making capabilities. Therefore, the authors address this issue by proposing a support system that can guide the student to choose and to focus on the right course(s) based on their personal preferences. This chapter provides the readers with the requisite information about educational frameworks and related data mining.

INTRODUCTION

Educational data mining is one of the most promising areas for getting new insight into the trends and predictions in our educational systems supporting continuous integration of newer technologies and corresponding transformations. The inclusion of various modes of e-learning and other online educational resources into the teacher-taught paradigm, in the formal as well as informal education sectors, results into a collection of huge volumes of data. For this structured, semi-structured or unstructured data to make reasonable sense to the stakeholders of the systems, the emerging trends of data mining need to be explored for processing this data available on distributed systems with parallel computations.

DOI: 10.4018/978-1-5225-6210-8.ch004

With the adoption of these new mining techniques, educational sector is the beneficiary because of faster decision-making with a support from analyses of data fetched from students. The data from students and other stakeholders may include: a) preferences for the courses, course outcomes, trainings especially vocational trainings, industry, industry oriented courses as optional subjects, job profiles, etc.; b) choices of the appropriate existing subjects; c) available options at the national and international levels, and; d) in-house training needs for the employees and management and so on.

Big data is the emerging field that uses data mining and provides answers to resolve the problems arising due to accumulation of large amount of data obtained from academia. In big data, mining techniques process the data in the form of small chunks and distribute it on multiple machines for processing and finally aggregate it to present the results. Big data perform these operations with the help of its programming paradigm i.e. Hadoop. It is a framework for distributed processing of datasets so large and/or complex where traditional data processing applications are incompetent to deal with them. Big data is the term for collection of datasets which are large, complex and becomes difficult to process using on-hand database management tools. Big data includes gathering of data for storage and analysis purpose which gain control over operations like searching, sharing, visualization of data, query processing, updation and maintain privacy of information. In Big data, there is extremely large dataset that is analyzed computationally to reveal patterns, trends and associations. It deals with unstructured data which may include Microsoft Office files, PDF, Text etc whereas structured data may be the relational data. Hadoop is one technique of big data and answer to problems related to handling of unstructured and massive data.

In Educational sector, data mining is the area for getting new insight into educational system where with increase in technologies as well with transformation of class room teaching to online learning and other educational resources, it results into collection of huge volume of data which may be structured, semi-structured or completely unstructured. With data-processing and decision driven technologies like "Big Data", educational sector will be the beneficiary as decision-making will be faster with analyses of data fetched from students in terms of their feedback for the courses, syllabi curriculum in preference for industry oriented courses as optional subjects, in-house trainings for the staff members etc.

Educational System Design

With the rapid development of technologies (Begona Gros, 2016), flexible and efficient learning methods for learners are being developed. The students usually acquire basic knowledge and core skills in the classroom. Learning goals and processes always are the same for each student in traditional classroom. But students (Tomlinson & McTighe, 2006) with different backgrounds have different needs. The interactions in the classrooms should therefore, be differentiable and responsive enough to accommodate the variations according to the learners readiness levels, interests and learning profiles (Tomlinson & Kalbfleisch, 1998). In a traditional classroom, the teacher is the main source of information and students are required to stay in the same place and participate simultaneously in the same set of activities, whereas in a situation of ubiquitous learning, activities can be conducted in a different space and time for each student. In addition, integrated teaching aids are also available to them all the time and are accessible from any device (Begona Gros, 2016). The paradigm shift in educational system from traditional classroom teaching to smart learning environment is shown in Figure 1(a) and 1(b).

Figure 1. (a), (b) Educational system design

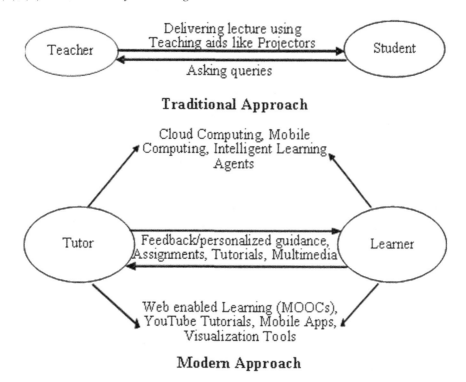

Traditional Approach

Modern Approach

Smart Learning Environments

Smart learning is a learning system that provides advising learners to learn in the real world. In smart learning environment, the use of intelligent technologies such as cloud computing, learning analytics or big data focuses on how learning data can be captured, analysed and directed towards improved learning, teaching and supporting the development of personalised and adaptive learning (Mayer, Schonberger, & Cukier, 2013; Picciano, 2012).

Research Framework of Smart Education

(Zhu & He, 2012) stated that "the essence of smart education" is to create intelligent environments by using smart technologies, so that smart pedagogies can be facilitated as to provide personalized learning services and empower learners. Authors (Zhu, Yu, & Riezebos, 2016) have proposed research framework of smart education shown in Figure 2. The framework describes 3 essential elements in smart education: (a) Smart environments; (b) Smart pedagogy, and; (c) Smart learner.

The smart pedagogies consists of: (a) Mass-based generation learning; (b) Individual based personalized learning; (c) Group-based collaborative learning, and; (d) Class-based differentiated instruction. Authors (Zhu, Yu, & Riezebos, 2016) have proposed 4-tier architecture of smart pedagogies in Figure 3.

Author Gwo-Jen Hwang (2014) has proposed another smart learning environment framework which is illustrated in Figure 4.

Figure 2. Research framework of smart education (Zhu,Yu, & Riezebos, 2016)

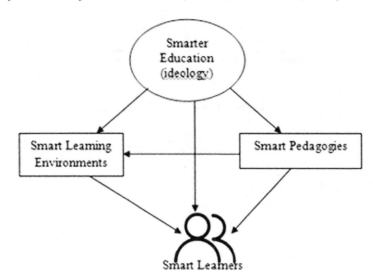

Figure 3. 4-tier architecture of smart pedagogies (Zhu,Yu, & Riezebos, 2016)

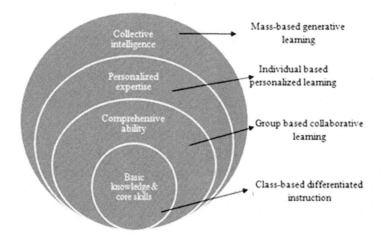

Policies and Practices in Education

Quality teaching (Henard & Roseveare, 2012) is the use of pedagogical techniques to produce learning outcomes for students. It involves dimensions like: (a) effective design of curriculum; (b) course content; (c) variety of learning contexts i.e. project-based learning, collaborative learning, experimentation; (d) feedback; (e) effective assessment of learning outcomes; (f) student support services; (g) student query response systems; (h) intelligent tutoring system; (i) integration of degree/diploma programmes with employment/placements, and; (j) adoption of skill oriented courses.

According to Sahlberg (2007), Finland nation education policies are intended to raise student achievements built upon ideas of: (a) sustainable leadership that place strong emphasis on teaching and learning; (b) intelligent accountability; (c) encouraging schools to craft optimal learning environments, and; (d) implement educational content that best helps their students reach the general goals of schooling.

Figure 4. Smart learning framework (Gwo-Jen Hwang, 2014)

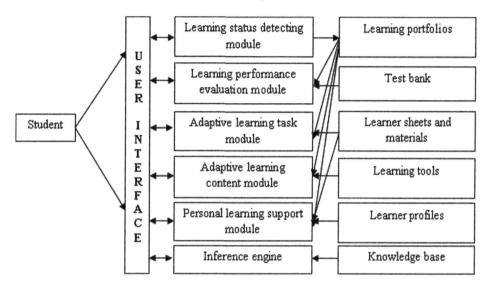

A study conducted by Slater et al. (2009) that finds a relationship between observable teacher characteristics and student performance. The authors investigate whether observable characteristics of teachers correlate with measures of teacher effectiveness.

The National Council of Teachers of Mathematics in the US describes teachers' knowledge of their students as being the ability to influence their performance (NCTM 2000). In a South African context, Fleisch (2004) discussed the relationship between higher levels of teacher resources and student performance.

The relationship between teacher characteristics (both qualification and demographic characteristics) and student performance is important for education policy. It is the responsibility of policymakers to employ best suited and most able teachers to enhance student performance (Armstrong, 2015).

Pointers for Policies and Practices

- Alignment of teaching and learning process as well as student assessment to the teaching and learning framework.
- Students' viewpoint to be included in the development of educational framework.
- Engagement of academia, researchers, technocrats, policymakers to share their ideas for best practices in quality teaching.
- Conduct of workshops, seminars, conferences and symposiums for students to give them exposure and become part of learning process.
- Provide support for faculty involved in fostering quality education.
- Research inspired teaching to be promoted.
- Development of support system using new tools of ICT and e-learning.
- Inclusion of smart learning environment framework for imparting quality education.
- Recognition and reward for innovative and effective teaching.
- Awards for teaching excellence and students with good academic record.

- Need to develop pedagogical competencies with the objective of improving quality education.
- Techniques for gathering and using students' feedback to courses and curricula.
- Funding and financial support for carrying out research.
- Use of multimedia techniques and access of library, updated books, journals, research papers, electronic, digital documents to students.

ROLE OF DATA MINING IN EDUCATION

Educational data mining (Bakhshinategh, Zaiane, Elatia, & Ipperciel, 2018) is the field using data mining techniques in educational environments. Data Mining is playing an important role in educational systems where education is primary factor for society. Educational data mining is receiving great attention due to some reasons like: (a) to increase the quality of education; (b) to find solution to problems arising from complex educational dataset; (c) competitive environment among the academic institutions. The main challenge of institutions is to deeply analyze their performance in terms of student performance, teaching skills and academic activities. There are some important factors related to students like performance in sessional marks, attendance, lab work etc for analyzing and predicting student class result. Some of the widely used data mining techniques i.e. decision trees, neural networks, nearest neighbour, naive bayes etc are being used in educational data mining. Using these techniques, many kinds of knowledge can be discovered such as classification, clustering and association rules which becomes helpful in increasing quality of education.

Data mining techniques applied on educational data is significant to educational organizations as well as for students for effective decision support system. It enhances our understanding of learning by finding educational trends which includes improving student performance, course selection, in-house trainings and faculty development. There are some factors correlated to students' academic performance obtained using linear regression analysis (Bhardwaj & Pal, 2011). According to author (Liebowitz, 2017), adaptive/ personalized learning, educational data mining, data visualization, visual analytics, knowledge management and blended/e-learning play growing roles to better inform higher education officials and teachers.

Educational data mining helps in facilitating utilization of resources related to student performance, predicting placement results and finding new educational trends. There are tools like WEKA, Rapid-Miner, SPSS, Matlab, Orange, KEEL, Python etc for performing data mining in the area of education. Authors (Slater, Joksimovic, Kovanovic, Baker, & Gasevic, 2017) have reviewed the tools frequently used for data mining/analytics in the area of education. The field seeks to develop and improve methods for exploring the educational data in order to discover new insights related to students learning activities in educational system and helps in improving students' retention rate, increase educational improvement ratio and enhance students' learning outcome.

Data Mining comprises of machine learning, statistical and visualization techniques to find and extract knowledge. In order to collect data, questionnaires and feedback forms are filled up from students which include certain parameters to know student's approach towards educational patterns or trends, interest towards technologies, teaching methodologies to be adopted. The data collected is to be analyzed using techniques like decision tree, neural networks, naive bayes, support vector machines, k-means etc which helps in predicting results like students' behavior patterns, interest in course, predict student retention, predict course suitability, and personalized intervention strategy (Zhang, Oussena, Clark, & Kim, 2010).

Necessity of Educational Data Mining

With competitive environment prevailing among the educational institutions, the main objective of higher education institutes is to disseminate quality education to its students and to improve the quality of managerial decisions. Quality of education can be improved by gaining knowledge from educational data which facilitate academic planners in higher education institutes to enhance their decision-making process, to improve students' academic performance, better understand students' behavior, to assist instructors, to improve teaching and many other benefits and for achieving this, data mining plays an important role. Data mining is necessary in organizations to enhance competitive advantage and decision making. Through data mining, we can share, develop and apply this knowledge for organizational growth. With the usage of data mining, educational data can be analyzed and it helps in developing model for improving institutional effectiveness. Educational data mining is key area in mining student's performance and helpful in predicting educational institutions performance taking into consideration parameters like:

- Teaching skills
- Soft skills
- Course content,
- Infrastructure requirement
- Faculty development programmes
- Students preference for industrial trainings
- Academic trends
- Social and emotional learning

GENESIS OF THE PROBLEM

Educational data mining is an upcoming field related to several well-established areas of research including e-learning, web mining, text mining etc. Data mining techniques are used to analyze educational data and extract useful information from large amount of data.

The KDD (Knowledge Discovery in Databases) field is related to development of methods and techniques which make the data relevant. Data mining is required in many fields to extract the useful information from the large amount of data. In educational sector, softwares and visualization techniques can be developed using data mining techniques which not only predict student's performance in examinations as well as helps us to cluster those students who need special attention in their studies. Knowledge discovery in databases results in better decision-making related to latest technologies useful in classroom teaching as well as faculty enhancement programs and in-house trainings etc. Using data mining techniques we can achieve refined data from distributed databases.

Data Mining is an efficient tool for improving institutional effectiveness and student learning. Knowledge acquired by educational data mining not only help teachers to manage their classes, improves their teaching skills, students learning processes but also provide feedback to institutions to improve their infrastructures and quality. For making this approach successful and to increase its scope, more data can be collected from educational institutions and queries can be performed on it.

IDENTIFICATION OF GAP

One of the biggest challenges our educational system is facing is related to quality and skill driven education, better placements of students, lacking in adopting new educational patterns as per market requirement. Decision-Making Process becomes more complex with the increase in educational entities. An educational institute seeks more efficient approaches to manage and support decision-making procedures. There are data mining techniques to extract meaningful knowledge from large datasets but their applications in the area of education sector have largely remained unexplored till now. These unexplored areas are:

- To improve the quality education and;
- To gather useful information about requirements in current educational system, improvement in students learning styles;
- There is need to provide new knowledge related to the educational trends and that knowledge can be extracted from historical and operational educational datasets using data mining techniques so that these trends can be further used to fill up the existing gaps in:
- Students learning style and instructor teaching style
- Assessment of students
- Evaluation of tutor's teaching
- predicting student behavior
- Predicting student placements based on certain parameters like attendance in class, GPA, technical skills, aptitude, communication skills, lab assignments etc.
- Learning abilities, knowledge and interests
- Introduction of skill driven courses into syllabi
- Adoption of learning analytics
- Adoption of those patterns into syllabi which becomes helpful to crack the competitive exams

Challenges Exist in the Educational Data Classification

In educational sector, there is enormous growth in Big data and the data of educational field is different from other fields in following terms: (a) there are increasing learning resources; (b) dataset vary in formal/non-formal sector; (c) updation in the curricula; (d) students behavioral attributes; (e) criteria for assessing students vary from institution to institution; (f) demographic factors; (g) data fetched from web enabled sources like MOOCs,Moodle,e-learning are different from formal education sector; (h) dataset varies in regular and distance learning modes; (i) academic and non-academic skills of students, and; (j) data varies in multiple streams of engineering like computers, IT, Electronics & communication, electrical, mechanical, textile, civil etc. The major challenges exist in the educational data classification are:

- Non-availability of relevant datasets
- No set of agreed common attributes in datasets
- Plausibility of attribute values
- Checking data completeness
- Data redundancy
- Collection of new datasets, preprocessing, cleaning and mining

- Inability to measure the quality of insights
- Regular updates in the educational frameworks
- Educational patterns vary from schools to university
- Measurement of the quality of output obtained from algorithms
- Timespan, priavcy and security issues
- Outlier detection
- Input data formats vary in algorithmic tools i.e. data may be accepted in numeric or may be in string format

UNDERSTANDING BIG DATA ANALYTICS

An analysis is a process to get the solution to a problem from the raw data with determined objective. The whole process of analysis works in a phased manner with problem understanding followed with data collection, preparation, data designing using a data modelling technique, analyzing the relationship, data evaluation and deployment.

In Big Data Analytics, analysis consists of decision-oriented and action oriented analytics. In decision-oriented approach, results obtained from unstructured data strengthen the decision making and in action oriented approach, an action is implemented based on the specific trend obtained or predicted.

Usage of Data Science in Education

Data science is the study of the generalizable extraction of knowledge from data (Dhar, 2013). According to (Provost & Fawcett, 2013), data science is a set of fundamental principles that support and guide the principled extraction of information and knowledge from data.

Data science plays important role in future education by promoting academic as well non-academic skills in students. The academic skills involve students: (a) language; (b) learning; (c) self-management/organization; (d) literacy; (e) integrity; (f) time management; (g) motivation etc whereas the non-academic skills involves: (1) Non-cognitive skills; (2) Soft skills, and; (3) Social and emotional learning. These skills (Liu & Huang, 2017) play an important role in shaping student achievements, workplace readiness and adult well-being.

Predictive Analytics

Predictive Analytics uses the historical data, combined the data with insights obtained from various sources in the form of feedback forms, survey reports, questionnaires to predict future events. The predictive analytics enables the institutions to use this data to move from a historical view to a future looking perspectives of the people. The Big data is analyzed to make future predictions based on present behavior or trends. Big data analytics helps improvement in the: (a) technological research; (b) in defence sector; (c) medical sciences, and; (d) helps improvement in customer relationship management and educational sector by enabling better monitoring.

Learning Analytics

Learning Analytics is the process of using data to improve learning and teaching using analytic tools (Tanya Elias, 2011). The patterns are discovered within the data. These patterns are then used to better predict future events and make informed decisions aimed at improving outcomes (Educause,2010). Learning Analytics emphasizes measurement and data collection as activities that institutions need to undertake and understand, focuses on the analysis and reporting of the data (U.S.Department of Education Report, 2012). It does not generally address the development of new computational methods for data analysis but instead addresses the application of known methods and models to answer important questions that affect student learning and organizational learning systems.

Learning Analytics in educational environment enables: (a) human tailoring of responses, such as discussion with at-risk students, feedback; (b) analyze students' performance in real time, and; (c) modifies teaching methods based on the data discovered. Learning analytics process aimed at the continual improvement of learning and teaching is illustrated in Figure 5.

Author has (Scheffel, Drachsler, Stoyanov, & Specht, 2014) mentioned quality indicators for learning analytics. These indicators are:

- Teacher-student awareness with learning material processes and progress.
- **Learning-Support:** An early detection of students of risk and ability to explain what could help them to improve further.
- **Learning Measures and Output:** It involves learning outcome where results are measured with traditional measure, learning performance.
- Data aspects which involves open access, privacy issues of data.
- Organizational aspects.

Figure 5. Learning analytics process

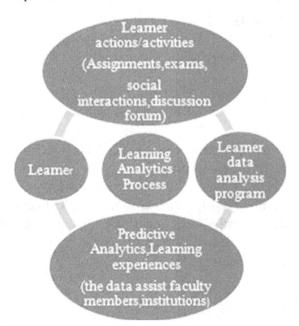

Intelligent Tutoring and Adaptive Learning

An intelligent tutoring system or an adaptive learning system is developed for supporting students to probe and acquire knowledge based on their learning status and personal factors such as: (a) learning progress; (b) knowledge level; (c) learning styles, and; (d) cognitive styles and preferences (Mampadi, Chen, Ghinea, & Chen, 2011; Papanikolaou, Grigoriadou, Magoulas, & Kornilakis, 2002; Yang, Liu, & Fu, 2010).

Adaptive learning doesn't take into account the real-world context. It adapts learning content for individual learner and provides personalized feedback or guidance. Adaptive learning also considers the online learning status of learners whereas ubiquitous learning situates learners into real-world scenarios, facilitates both formal and informal learning. Ubiquitious learning facilitates interaction with users via multiple channels like in smart learning environment. E.g smartphones whereas in adaptive learning environment, online learning systems use data to change in response to student performance.

Big Data Analytics as an Opportunity For:

- Cost effective storage system for huge datasets.
- Provide ways to analyze information quickly and make decisions.
- Next generation opportunities.
- Improved services or products.
- Evaluation of customer needs and satisfaction.

Big data analytics has played important roles in business analytics, social networking, online shopping trends etc but with growth in educational sector there is increase in data along with computing power and due to the absence of knowledge discovery process approach on educational dataset it becomes complex for analyzing and consolidating the data, therefore there is need of analyzing, evaluating huge unstructured data using educational data mining techniques for effective decision making and predicting academic trends.

Role of Big Data Analytics in Education

Big data incorporates educational data mining as one of the research areas in higher education (Daniel, 2017). Big data plays an important role in educational sector and is fruitful in e-learning as learning material is analyzed based on the usefulness and acceptability to make it readily available for all at the same time. Another benefit is that it gives teachers access to information that can help them to improve as per the instructions based on students learning habits. There are two areas that are specific to the use of big data in education are: (1) Educational data mining, and; (2) Learning analytics. Educational data mining discovers new patterns in data and develops new algorithms/models while learning analytics applies known predictive models in instructional systems (Prakash, Hanumanthappa, & Kavitha, 2014).

From the student's viewpoint, big data and predictive analytics can assist the candidate to shortlist colleges that best fit their profile. It also guides the applicants to choose the best match to their profile. With big data, students have more options than ever before. For student enrolments, big data and predictive analytics have the ability to prepare databases for analytical purpose which helps academia with fast, actionable, decisive information. This information helps them to take smart enrollment decisions and allocate both staff time and financial resources to raise enrolment from current markets.

Big Data Challenges

- Data generation at rapid pace and need response in real time.
- Unstructured data generated from multiple sources and has multiple forms with challenge of storage and processing.
- Prediction of meaningful information and trends is challenge for organisations.
- Analyzing of large growing data and decision-making of handling the data.
- The reliability and organizing data is another challenge.
- The analysis of big data in a understandable form for making decisions from visualisations.
- Hiring of personnel's for data management of structured, unstructured data and making insights from it.
- Effective utilization of structured and unstructured data for decision making.
- Sharing of data is the biggest challenge to data privacy.

Future Scope of Big Data Analytics

The Big data involves different phases for handling the data which involves data collection, storage, data organization, data analysis, visualization, and action or result utilization. Big data job opportunities include specialized programmers, statistical analysts, business analysts, advanced mathematics etc.

The Big data future scope involves a career prospect in: (a) marketing and analysis; (b) statistics; (c) applied mathematics; (d) data visualization and movement; (e) cloud computing; (f) relational databases, and; (g) product placement and management etc.

Further, the scope of Big Data scientists is in various fields like:

- Public sector undertakings
- Academics
- Big data organizations
- Commercial organizations
- Corporate information technology companies
- Marketing departments and business
- Risk management organizations

There are many application areas of big data where there are future research scopes which can benefit a lot to society. The Natural Language Processing helps in obtaining the meaningful information from unstructured data such as text messages, voice calls, emails etc so that predictive models for analyzing human behaviors can be programmed and for that Hadoop framework can help in solving the problem using Apache SPARK, which is built on top of Hadoop.

Another research area involves: (a) GIS (Geographic Information systems) for better decisions about the location and maps; (b) weather forecasting; (c) response systems for disaster management.

There is massive scope of big data analytics in bio-informatics, medical sciences for diagnostic systems for patient treatments, understanding of genomic information and analyzing it using bio-informatics.

In other fields where big data is showing its presence is: (a) traffic data monitoring and analysis; (b) multimedia analysis; (c) social networking; (d) body sensor networks for sensing, communication, and; (e) energy gathering techniques and processing of various physiological parameters.

BIG DATA AND CLOUD COMPUTING

Big data is a field which requires involvement of various technologies and equipment for handling of huge amount of unstructured data and deliver hassle free services to customers. The challenges faced by big data is related to infrastructures cost, software delivery and platform services. To overcome these problems, big data needs to utilize the services of cloud computing technology. Cloud computing is the latest computing paradigm that delivers hardware and software resources as virtualized services in which users are free from the burden of worrying about the low-level system administration details. Cloud computing is internet-based computing, where all IT-resources like software, data and other devices are provided on-demand. Cloud computing is a new way of delivering computing resources. Computing services ranging from data storage and processing to software, such as email handling, are now available instantly, commitment-free and on-demand. Cloud computing can help companies accomplish more by eliminating the physical bonds between an IT infrastructure and its users. Users can purchase services from a cloud environment that could allow them to save money and focus on their core business.

The main aim of the cloud computing technology is to move any application stored on a computer to a remote location, eliminating all the standard components, including operating system and hard drives, which are necessary in today's computers and make them accessible on line for users through a standard browser. It is an emerging computing paradigm in which applications, data and IT resources are provided as a service to users over the Internet.

Deployment Models of Cloud

The four deployment models are as follows:

1. **Public Cloud:** In simple terms, public cloud services are characterized as being available to clients from a third party service provider via the Internet. The term "public" does not always mean free, even though it can be free or fairly inexpensive to use. A public cloud does not mean that a user's data is publically visible. The public cloud vendors typically provide an access control mechanism for their users.
2. **Private Cloud:** A private cloud offers many of the benefits of a public cloud computing environment, such as being elastic and service based. The difference between a private cloud and a public cloud is that in a private cloud-based service, data and processes are managed within the organization without the restrictions of network bandwidth, security exposures and legal requirements that using public cloud services might entail.
3. **Community Cloud:** A community cloud is controlled and used by a group of organizations that have shared interests, such as specific security requirements or a common mission. The members of the community share access to the data and applications in the cloud.

4. **Hybrid Cloud:** A hybrid cloud is a combination of a public and private cloud that interoperates. In this model users typically outsource non-business critical information and processing to the public cloud, while keeping business critical services and data in their control.

Cloud Services

There are three types of services offered by cloud computing. These are SaaS (Software as a Service), PaaS (Platform as a Service), IaaS (Infrastructure as a Service).The term services in cloud computing is the concept of being able to use components across a network, provided by web service providers. This is widely known as "as a service."

Software as a Service (SaaS)

Companies host applications in the cloud that many users access through internet connections. In Software as a service, customer needs not to purchase the Software or install it. The required software applications are accessible from wherever they want. The example of Software as a Service is Gmail, face book etc.

Platform as a Service (PaaS)

Developers can design, build and test applications that run on the cloud provider's infrastructure and then deliver those applications to end users from the provider's servers. Here, user applications are provided a platform for writing code and executing it through the PaaS Cloud. These services are used by the developers of the web applications. The example of Platform as a service is google app engine.

Infrastructure as a Service (IaaS)

The IT companies obtain general processing, storage, database management and applications through the network and pay only for gets used. These services are used by the IT companies so as to reduce the infrastructure cost for their companies.

The infrastructure as a Service provides customers related to storing of data in the form of photos, videos, music files etc or it can be backup of daily reports taken by the clients. The virtual machines, load balancing and network attached storage are some examples of IaaS.

LITERATURE REVIEW

Knowledge Discovery in Databases

According to Romero and Ventura (2007), data mining and knowledge discovery in databases are related to each other and to other related fields such as machine learning, statistics, and databases. Data mining is one of the steps in the overall process of KDD that consists of collection and pre-processing of data, data mining, interpretation, evaluation of discovered knowledge and finally post processing.

Fayyad et al.(1996) have discussed the KDD field's basic objective to make data meaningful by developing methods and techniques of mining but major problem faced by the KDD process is to map huge and heterogeneous data into understandable, more abstract and useful form.

Data Mining and Techniques

Data Mining introduced in the year 1990's and it is the combination of many disciplines like database management systems (DBMS), Statistics, Artificial Intelligence (AI), and Machine Learning (ML) (Shapiro & Gregory, 2000). Data Mining produce useful patterns by applying algorithmic methods on observational data.

There are different data mining techniques which are used to extract information from a data set and transform it into an understandable format for further use. Table 1 shows different data mining techniques and their roles.

Statistics

Statistics is a vital component in data selection, sampling, data mining, and knowledge evaluation. In data cleaning process, statistics offer the techniques to detect outliers to simplify data when necessary, and to estimate noise, it deals with missing data using estimation techniques (Bala & Ojha, 2012).

Classification and Prediction

One of the most useful data mining techniques for e-learning is classification. Weiss and Kulikowski (1991) proposed that classification is learning a function that maps (classifies) a data item into one of several predefined classes. Apte and Hong (1995) suggested that classification methods of data mining are used as part of knowledge discovery applications which includes classifying trends in financial markets, education and identifying objects of interest from large dataset of images. Classification methods consist of techniques for prediction. Examples includes feed forward neural networks, adaptive spline methods, projection pursuit regression that maps data item to a prediction variable, multi-layer perceptrons, generalized linear models (Elder & Filzmoser, 2008), bayesian networks, decision trees, and support vector machines.

Classification maps data into predefined group of classes. It is supervised learning approach because the classes are determined before examining the data. The example of classification in education sector is the: (a) prediction of student's performance with high accuracy, and; (b) for identifying low academic performance of the students at the beginning.

Classification (Sarma & Rahul Roy, 2010) is the processing of finding a set of models which describe and distinguish data classes or concepts. The derived results may be represented in various forms, such as classification (IF-THEN) rules, decision trees, or neural networks. Models then can be used for predicting the class label of data objects. In many applications, there is need to predict some missing data values rather than class labels. E.g. case when the predicted values are numerical data, and is often specifically referred to as prediction.

Table 1. Data mining techniques and their roles

Techniques	Roles
Classification	Pre-Defined Examples
Clustering	Identification of similar classes of objects.
Prediction	Regression Technique.
Association Rules	Find frequent item set findings among large data sets.
Neural Networks	Derive meaning from complex or imprecise data and can be used to extract patterns and detect trends that are complex.
Decision Trees	Represent set of decisions using CART (Classification and Regression Trees) and CHAID (Chi Square Automatic Interaction and Detection), C4.5, ID3.
Nearest Neighbor method	Classify each record in a dataset Based on a combination of the classes of the K-records which are most similar in historical dataset.

Clustering

Clustering groups the data, which is not predefined and it can identify dense and sparse regions in object space. It is a descriptive task where we identify a finite set of categories or clusters to describe the data.E.g identifying those students who are short of attendance and shown poor performance in sessionals Unlike classification and prediction, which analyze class labelled data objects, clustering analyses data objects without consulting a known class label. The class labels are not present in the training data and clustering can be used to generate such labels.

Clusters of objects are formed so that objects within a cluster have high similarity in comparison to one another, but are very dissimilar to objects in other clusters. Each cluster formed can be viewed as a class of objects, from which rules can be, derived (Shapiro & Gregory, 2000).

Application of clustering in education can help in finding academic trends, student's performance analysis in class. Authors (Cheeseman & Stutz, 1996) suggested examples of clustering applications in a knowledge discovery context which include discovering similar groups.

Association Rule Mining

According to author Hu (2010), association rule learning is a method for discovering interesting relations between variables in large databases.ARM task (Liu & Wong, 2000) is to discover the hidden association relationship between the different item sets in transaction database.

Association rule mining is to find set of binary variables that occurs in the transaction database repeatedly. Apriori measures are the association rule mining algorithm. Association analysis is the discovery of association rules showing attribute-value conditions that occur frequently together in a given set of data. The association rule A=>B shows those database tuples that satisfy the conditions in A as well as in B.

Garcia et al. (2011) has described a collaborative educational data mining tool based on association rule mining. This tool helps in improvement of e-learning courses and allows teachers to analyze and discover hidden information based on interaction between the students and the e-learning courses.

Goh and Ang (2007) have applied ARM approach in social-science related fields such as education and councelling. A case study is conducted by authors (Danubianu, Pentiuc, & Tobolcea, 2011) on mining association rules inside a relational database. Kumar and Chadha (2012) have analysed students' assessment data using association rule mining. Author (Oladipupo and Oyelade) presents data mining in education environment that identifies student's failure patterns using ARM technique.

Learning Content Management Systems

Data mining and text mining technologies are used in Web-based educational systems for shared learning. Text mining is used for discussion board for expanded correspondence analysis. Learners select the relevant category which represents his/her comment and the system provides evaluations for learner's comments between peers.

Dringus and Ellis (2005), Abdous et al., (2012) proposed text mining approach as a strategy for determining conversations among irregular discussion forums. Text mining techniques also helps in evaluating the progress of a thread or user group discussions. Authors Ha et al. (2000), Romero et al. (2005) have proposed the concept of Web mining in distance education. Using web mining, data can be retrieved from pdf interactive multimedia productions for helping the evaluation of multimedia presentations for statistics purpose and for extracting relevant data.

Web-based educational systems help in collection of large amount of student data from web log history which can be further analyzed for deriving meaningful patterns.

Robust and Intelligent Web-Based Educational Systems

A prototype is proposed to formulate a personalized web based application by which mining can be done on both framework and structure of the courseware. Keyword-driven text mining algorithms are used to select articles for distance learning students (Tang, Tiffany, & Gordon, 2002).

Big Data and Hadoop

Author Tole (2013) has stressed upon the infrastructures high cost for processing of big data. Manjulatha et al. (2016) have discussed the tools of data mining like MangoDB, an open-source database and Apache Hadoop. Data Mining Techniques using these tools help students in choosing their course curriculum. Bhosale et al. (2014) have presented review paper on Big Data and Hadoop. The paper has focused on technical challenges and highlighted Map Reduce techniques proposed by different authors. Dean and Ghemawat (2010) discussed that MapReduce scales to large array of machines comprising of thousands of machines which solves large computational problems. Apriori algorithm is implemented (Woo, 2012) and high performance is achieved using Map Reduce Technique of Hadoop framework to collect item sets frequently occurred in dataset.

According to Author (Sin & Muthu, 2015), big data techniques are the necessity in learning environments. In present scenario, accumulation of large amount of unstructured data and introduction of Massive open online courses in education has stressed upon the need for data mining in education. (Nasser and Tariq) has discussed the challenges encountered during the processing of big data. The big data challenge characteristics like volume, volatility, velocity, variety and quality are discussed by author. Tajunisha and Anjali (2015) have used Map Reduce programming paradigm for predicting student's performance.

Patil and Kumar (2017) have performed classification of data using Map Reduce and proposed data mining model for effective data analysis of higher education students. Yang et al. (2010) have mainly addressed the challenges of using Map Reduce model for computing parallel application of Apriori.

PREDICTIVE ANALYTICS USING HADOOP

Big data using Hadoop helps in data processing of data which can be structured, unstructured or semi-structured on single node clusters or multimode clusters using the MapReduce which is a programming framework and runs on hadoop layer to facilitate the parallel processing of distributed data and faster processing of data. In Hadoop, with faster processing, it also helps in load balancing with the scaling of data and provides data reliability.

Hadoop is an open-source programming paradigm which performs parallel processing of applications on clusters. The characteristics of Hadoop are shown in Figure 6. The Big data problem solution using Hadoop approach can help colleges, institutions, universities to get a comprehensive aspect about the students. It helps in answering questions related to the learning behaviors, better understanding and curriculum trends, and future course selection for students which helps to create captivating learning experiences for students. The problem of enormously large size of dataset can be solved using Map Reduce Techniques. Map Reduce jobs run over Hadoop clusters by splitting the big data into small chunks and process the data by running it parallel on distributed clusters.

The prerequisite for the predictive models is data, as predictive models learn from the past experiences which can be called as the training data. The predictive models help us in: (a) classification; (b) clustering; (c) statistical analysis, and; (d) correlation and regression.

Building Blocks of Hadoop Platform

The key building blocks of Hadoop ecosystem which includes support for Hadoop HDFS, Hadoop MapReduce, Hive, HBase, Pig, Sqoop and Zookeeper are shown in Table 2.

Working Principle of Hadoop Cluster

Hadoop is a schema that allows to store and process large datasets in parallel and distributed pattern. In Hadoop, HDFS is for storage which means Hadoop distributed file system and MapReduce for processing. HDFS is the storage unit of Hadoop and it divides input files into smaller chunks and stores it across the cluster. Hadoop distributed file system stores metadata which may be structured, semi-structured or unstructured. Hadoop cluster consists of two core components i.e. Name node and Data node.

Figure 6. Characteristics of Hadoop

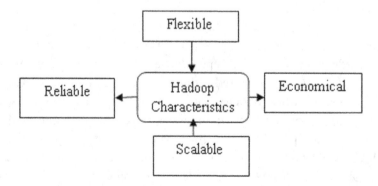

Table 2. Building blocks of hadoop ecosystem

SrNo	Name of the Building Block	Description
1.	MapReduce	It works on the Hadoop layer that simplifies the creation of processes for analyzing huge amount of unstructured and structured data. MapReduce consists of combination of Map and Reduce features. Using Map function, problem is distributed across the large number of systems and reduces function shows the aggregated results.
2.	Hive	In Hive, large volume of data is aggregated using database queries. It built on top of Apache hadoop for providing data summarization, query and analysis.
3.	Pig	It is a scripting language used for batch processing of huge amount of data. Pig programming language creates programs that run on Apache Hadoop. Pig latin can execute its Hadoop jobs in MapReduce.
4.	HBase	It is a column oriented database that provides fast access for handling the data. HBase is a Hadoop database, a distributed and scalable for real-time read/write access to Big data.
5.	Sqoop	It refers to a command line tool that can import tables, columns or entire database files into the distributed file system on data warehouse. Using Sqoop command line interface, data transferring is done between relational databases and Hadoop.
6.	Zookeeper	It coordinates multiple Hadoop instances and nodes in distributed synchronization. It provides protection to every node from failure because of overloading of data.
7.	Mahout	It is a scalable maching learning and data mining library for classification, clustering of data. It also performs association rule mining for frequent item sets.

- The Name node is the main node that contains summarization about the data stored. The Name node is the main feature of Hadoop distributed file system. The name node stores all the metadata for the file system using yarn command i.e. Yet another Resource Negotiator (YARN), which is the core Hadoop service having two major services, one is resource Manager and other is application master. The progress and schedule of the jobs running in cluster can be viewed through resource manager. The resource manager determines all the available cluster resources and help in managing the distributed applications. It works with node manager and application master. The name node uses RAM space.
- Data node is the storage of data that is the asset hardware in the distributed environment. Data node stores the actual data in HDFS.Here, data node is known as Slave and Name node is known as Master. There is master-slave communication between Name node and Data node. When data node starts, it communicates to the namenode along with blocks list managed by it. The datanode uses hard disk space.

In Figure 7 dataset in the form of input files is being processed across multiple nodes and each node is offering local computation and storage as per requirement. Here, each process is handling the tasks independently and parallely. The Figure 7 also depicts that job tracker residing on the name node is the main node for complete execution of the tasks submitted. The job tracker resides on name node when only one task to be accomplished and for multiple tasks, job tracker resides on Data node. Job tracker plays an important role for complete execution of the tasks submitted. The overall progress of each job

Figure 7. Working principle of Hadoop cluster

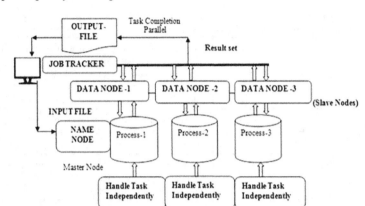

is tracked through Job tracker whereas Task tracker is a node in the cluster that accepts tasks related to MapReduce which involves operations like Map, Reduce and Shuffle.

The Task tracker is composed with set of slots which indicate the number of tasks it can accept. The Task tracker also ensures and monitors the endurance to process failure. The task tracker regularly communicates as acknowledgement to the Job tracker as assurance of its working and about the updation. The results sets obtained finally combined together into the output file in name node and the task is done.

Six Major Services Which Are Required To Successfully Run Hadoop Cluster

1. **Datanode:** Datanode is the data storage in the Hadoop Distributed File System. On adding more data, nodes data replicates across them. The Figure.8 displays the data node information using Hadoop on Ubuntu Machine.
2. **Nodemanager:** The Nodemanager is answerable for launching and administering containers on a node which are responsible for executing tasks. Nodemanager keeps updated with the Resource Manager and track node health.

Figure 8. Web interface displaying datanode information

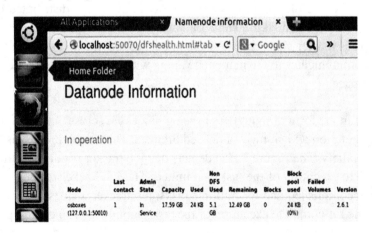

Figure 9. Web interface of Hadoop cluster displaying cluster metrics information

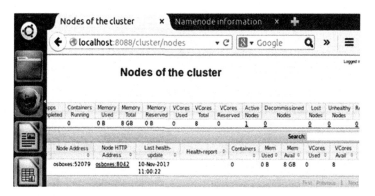

Each slave node in Yet another Resource Negotiator (YARN) has a node manager, which regularly reports to the Resource Manager about the data processing resources on its node. The Nodemanager with cluster information and cluster metrics is shown in Figure 9.

3. **JPS:** JPS command keep check on all the Hadoop daemons which are running on the machine.
4. **Namenode:** Namenode is the core of the HDFS and it keeps the hierarchical tree of all the files in the file system. It stores the data dictionary of HDFS.
5. **Secondary Namenode:** It is a dedicated node in HDFS cluster whose function is to make checkpoints and make copy of the file system, log files and metadata present on Namenode.
6. **Resource Manager:** The Resource Manager is responsible for tracking the resources in a cluster and scheduling applications. It is the master service that arbitrates all the available cluster resources and helps in managing the distributed application running on the YARN System. The resource manager works together with the per node Nodemanager which tracks the resource utilization of CPU, disk, network, memory by the application and reports it to the resource manager. For each running application, there exists an application master which notifies the NodeManager.The application masters are responsible for resource negotiation with the resource manager and works with the nodemanager to start the containers.

MAP REDUCE FRAMEWORK

Hadoop divides the task into map and reduce tasks. The components of hadoop distributed file system are discussed below. The MapReduce program transforms lists of input data elements into list of output data elements and it will be done using twice by Map and Reduce.

The organization structure of MapReduce framework is shown in Figure.10 which represents that input data in the form of input data file first splits and then mapped followed with shuffling. The unstructured data after shuffling filtered to obtain output which is also called "Reduce Phase".

Features of MapReduce

MapReduce has the following unique features:

Figure 10. Organization structure of MapReduce framework

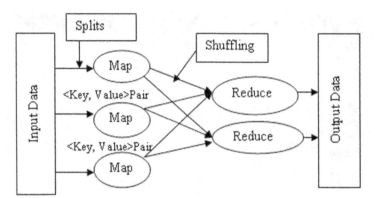

- It can manage the issues related to parsing text, troubleshooting through web logs and reading from huge raw databases effectively and efficiently.
- MapReduce uses extract, load and transform tool for reading data from input sources, map the data in the form of key, value pair and finally summarizes the data in a meaningful manner for analytical purpose.

Phases of Map Reduce Framework

- **Mapper**

In Map function, individual jobs transform records into intermediate records. There is multiplicity in the input pair which map to zero or one to many output pairs. Map task process each input splits and performs the local sorting and aggregation of the results obtained in the form of key, value pair. The further aggregation is done using combiner. A combiner consolidates the data so as to reduce the amount of data that must be transferred to reduce tasks.

- **Reducer**

In Reducer function, the set of intermediate value share key of smaller set of values which reduces the overhead of the system. In reducer, output is obtained after merging. The reduce phase aggregates the results from the map phase into final results. The final results are smaller than the input set as reduction is carried out by parallel reducing tasks. The reduce function performs in phases like sorting, merging the copied results into a single sorted set of (key, value) pair. The final results obtained are stored in HDFS.

Data Processing Using MapReduce Framework

MapReduce refers to a software framework that enables distributed processing of huge amounts of data on different clusters of computers.

The main task of MapReduce is to solve the large computational problems using the principle of divide and conquer. A large input dataset is split into independent chunks which are later processed together by machines that perform the map function. The results obtained from the mappers are then provided to the reducers as input.

Data Description

Table 3 shows the dataset of courses preferred by students of Computer Science or Information Technology of engineering and technology fields. Here, each tuple is considered as event occurrence and each tuple comprises of a combination of attributes.

The objective here is to predict the interest of a student in training course(s) from various available combinations for training from the dataset. This dataset has been synthesized for the purpose of experimental exploration in the area of Computer Science Engineering and Information Technology fields only. In real life, the proposed system shall include all the areas of study at secondary and tertiary levels of education in formal as well as informal education sector. The output obtained using the proposed methodology can be tested on such practical applications which may run into Tera Bytes of data in size.

Life Cycle of MapReduce Framework

The MapReduce life cycle performs Mapper and Reducer functions with the help of Job tracker and TaskTracker. In Figure 11 it shows that the input dataset in Table 3 is submitted as MapReduce job to Hadoop, then the local job client prepares the job for submission and it is handed to the Job tracker which runs as a single master node on Hadoop cluster configuration.

The job tracker performs job scheduling and distributes the mapping work among the Task Trackers for parallel processing. In turn, each TaskTraker running on the nodes spawns a Map Task and on regular interval of time intimates job tracker about the progress information of nodes. After mapping, when results in the form of key, value pair becomes available, the Job Tracker distributes the reduce work among task trackers for faster parallel processing. Here, again TaskTraker spawns a Reduce Task to perform the work. The Reduce tasks can start processing as soon as the map task begins completing.

Table 3. Dataset for course selection

Course Curriculum	Preferable Course
Java,J2EE	Android
HTML,Javascript	PHP
C,C++	Asp.Net
J2EE,Java	Android
C,C++	Java
C,C++,Dot Net	Java
Matlab	Hadoop
HTML,Web Designing	PHP
SQL, MySQL	MangoDB
Machine Learning	Python
---------	------------
n technologies	n courses

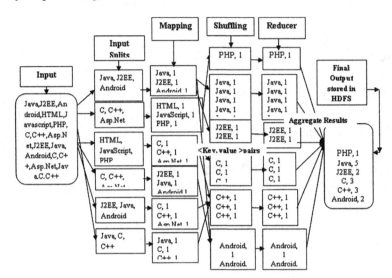

Figure 11. Stages of MapReduce framework

The following are the broad level steps to process the application on Hadoop for parallel processing:

1. **Defining the Objective:** The input dataset shown in Table 3 consists of course curriculum and the preferable choice of students for industrial training programmes. The said dataset may be structured, semi-structured or unstructured and from that data it becomes complex for students to select right course curriculum for trainings and strengthen their decision-making. The objective is to summarize the data in the form of maximum frequency of preferable course chosen by the students so that faculty members guide the students to undergo the industrial trainings in technology which has more demand as per industry norms.

2. **Deciding the Action:** Hadoop MapReduce programs are implemented for performing text mining and processing of input dataset shown in Table 3.

3. **Breaking the Program Modules:** The program is break into Map and Reduce functions for summarization of results.

4. **Results and Discussions:** The results obtained using Hadoop MapReduce program using linux Ubuntu machine are shown in Figure 12.

The Table 4 shows the summarized output obtained from MapReduce framework. The result also shows that the maximum students have shown their interest in technologies like Android, Hadoop, Java courses among all the technologies in the input dataset.

These results: (a) helps management as well faculty members to know about the interest of students to incorporate these courses into their course curriculum; (b) helpful for industries to get the skilled candidates in the latest technologies, and; (c) imparting skill oriented training to students.

From the Figure 12, it also determines that after mapping, shuffling task condense the relevant records obtained from Mapping Phase in the form of key value pair. The output in the form of {key, value} pair obtained from the MapReduce task is shown in Table 5.

Figure 12. Output obtained from MapReduce framework

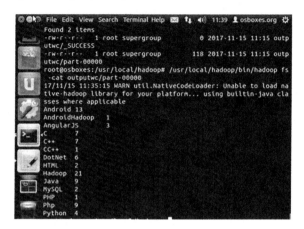

Guidelines While Implementing MapReduce Applications

There should be right number of maps and reducers for the benefit of applications. There should be balanced use of maps and reducers for processing applications because:

- Use of excessive mappers results into scheduler and infrastructure overhead as excessive use of mappers can terminate a jobtracker. However, excessive mappers improve resource utilization and execution time.
- The use of fewer mappers can lead to underutilization of some parts of the storage and results in overburden on other parts of the storage.
- Another important factor is the proper utilization of reducers for the application, as it is an important function for the application. The use of more reducers generates a corresponding no. of output documents which has negative impact on the Namenode whereas having few reducers results into underutilization of resources.

Benefits of Proposed Approach and its Suitability for Educational System

A microscopic examination of the experimental results show that the rules mined out of the datasets can guide students in right selection of course(s) as per their preferences and strengthen their decision making capabilities with a certain degree of confidence. The faculty members also get the feedback to incorporate in-demand course specializations into their syllabi, conduct in-house workshops/trainings and suggest students to choose the right course specializations for industrial trainings. Pursuing the right course(s) is going to help the students in bridge the skill gaps, however small or large it may be, and also in enhancing their employability prospects after completion of course(s).

The experiment results in the easier on-the-fly scaling of data processing over multiple computing nodes. These results if consumed rightly by right people at right place and at a right time can also facilitate right decision-making by teachers, mentors and/or management in reference to the education being imparted to the students. As a future scope, this experimentation is also intended to promote targeted

Table 4. MapReduce framework summarized output information

Map input records	Map Output Records	Map output bytes	Input split bytes	Combine input records	Combine output records	Reduce input groups	Reduce shuffle bytes	Reduce Input records	Reduce output records	Spilled Records	Shuffled Maps	Merged Map outputs	CPU time spent(ms)	Physical memory(bytes) snapshot	Virtual memory(bytes) snapshot	Total committed heap usage(bytes)
3	183	4272	303	0	0	37	4657	183	37	366	3	3	3400	436776960	1269108736	379858944

Table 5. <Key, Value> pair of output

Courses<Key, Value>Pair	Count
<Android,13>	13
<Android Hadoop,1>	1
<AngularJS,3>	3
<C,7>	7
<C++,7>	7
<CC++,1>	1
<DotNet,6>	6
<HTML,2>	2
<Hadoop,21>	21
<Java,9>	9
<MySQL,2>	2
<PHP,10>	10
<Python,4>	4
---	---
<n,n courses>	<n count>

skill/ capacity oriented intelligent and crisp approach among the parents/ guardians/ teachers/ mentors and their children/ wards/ students so that the future career paths of the students can be planned well in advance at any age.

CONCLUSION AND FUTURE WORK

In this chapter, the authors have discussed the role of educational data mining and learning analytics in educational sector. Apart from it, the authors have synthesized an experimental dataset that consists of courses related to the field of ICT and their attributes. The dataset is processed through proposed methodology of MapReduce algorithm which runs the task in parallel on a single node cluster using Hadoop distributed file system. The file system converts the data into individual tuples in the form of key/value pair. The output obtained from reducer function of MapReduce classifies the data and display the courses preferred more in number by students. The results and their analysis show that MapReduce can be used to provide the students with appropriate academic guidance support so as to strengthen their decision-making in opting for appropriate course(s) for training activities as per industry requirements. Here, the experimentation has been limited only to the internship/training requirements of Computer Science Engineering and Information Technology fields.

In future, the authors intend to involve all the branches of Engineering and Technology in the first phase, other professional courses in the second phase and lastly, authors intend to go for a generic career counselling system with necessary appropriate enhancements. The results so obtained are surely going to help educational institutions in formal as well as informal sectors to find answers to some of the yet unanswered questions related to academic guidance. All these propositions have the potential to improve the quality of education, and the employment prospects of the students at the centre of focus. The proposed methodology is going to be the pivotal point in designing and implementing such support system that will facilitate intelligent decision-making by parents, teachers and mentors related to the careers of their children/ wards/ students and strengthening of in-house training programmes.

REFERENCES

Abdous, M., He, W., & Yen, C. J. (2012). Using Data Mining for Predicting Relationships between Online Question Theme and Final Grade. *Journal of Educational Technology & Society*, *15*(3), 77–88. Available Online at www.sciencedirect.com

Apte, C., & Hong, S. J. (1995). *Predicting Equity Returns from Securities Data with Minimal Rule Generation. In Advances in Knowledge Discovery and Data Mining*. AAAI Press.

Armstrong, P. (2015). Teacher characteristics and student performance: An analysis using hierarchical linear modelling. *South African Journal of Childhood Education*, *5*(2).

Bakhshinategh, B., Zaiane, O. R., Elatia, S., & Ipperciel, D. (2018). Educational data mining applications and tasks: A survey of the last 10 years. *Education and Information Technologies*, *23*(1), 537–553. doi:10.100710639-017-9616-z

Bala, M., & Ojha, D. B. (2012). Study of applications of Data Mining Techniques in Education. *International Journal of Research in Science and Technology, 1*(4).

Bhardwaj, B. K., & Pal, S. (2011). Mining Educational Data to Analyze Students Performance. *International Journal of Advanced Computer Science and Applications, 2*(6), 2011.

Bhosale, H. S., & Gadekar, D. P. (2014). A Review Paper on Big Data and Hadoop. *IJSRP, 4*(10).

Cheeseman, P., & Stutz, J. (1996). Bayesian Classification (AUTOCLASS): Theory and Results. In *Advances in Knowledge Discovery and Data Mining*. AAAI Press.

Daniel, B. K. (2017). Thoughts on Recent Trends and Future Research Perspectives in Big Data and Analytics in Higher Education. In *Big Data and Learning Analytics in Higher Education* (pp. 7–17). Cham: Springer. doi:10.1007/978-3-319-06520-5_1

Danubianu, M., Pentiuc, S. G., & Tobolcea, I. (2011). *Mining Association Rules Inside a Relational Database – A Case Study, ICCGI 2011. Sixth International Multi-Conference on Computing in the Global Information Technology.*

Dean, J., & Ghemawat, S. (2010). *MapReduce: Simplified Data Processing on Large Clusters.* Google, Inc.

Dhar, V. (2013). Data Science and Prediction. *Communication of the ACM, 56*(12), 64-73. doi:10.1145/2500499

Dringus, L. P., & Ellis, T. (2005). Using data mining as a strategy for assessing asynchronous discussion forums. *Computers & Education, 45*(1), 141–160. doi:10.1016/j.compedu.2004.05.003

Educause. (2010). *7 Things you should know about analytics*. Retrieved October 1, 2010 from https://www.educause.edu/ir/library/pdf/ELI7059.pdf

Elder, J. (n.d.). Non Linear Classification and Regression. In *Introduction to Machine Learning and Pattern Recognition*. CSE 4404/5327.

Elias, T. (2011). Learning Analytics: Definintions, Processes and Potential. *Learning,* 1-22.

Fayyad, U., Shapiro, G. P., & Smyth, P. (1996). From Data Mining to Knowledge Discovery in Databases. *American Association for Artificial Intelligence, 17*(3), 1996.

Filzmoser, P. (2008). Linear and Nonlinear Methods for Regression and Classification and applications in R. *Forschungsbericht CS-2008-3.*

Fleisch, B. (2004). Does higher education expenditure generate higher learner achievement?A study of historically disadvantaged schools in Gauteng. *South African Journal of Education, 24*(4), 264–269.

García, E., Romero, C., Ventura, S., & Castro, C. D. (2011). A collaborative educational association rule mining tool. *Internet and Higher Education, 14*(2), 77–88. doi:10.1016/j.iheduc.2010.07.006

Goh, D. H., & Ang, R. P. (2007). An introduction to association rule mining: An application in counseling and help-seeking behavior of adolescents. *Behavior Research Methods, 39*(2), 259–266. doi:10.3758/BF03193156 PMID:17695353

Gros, B. (2016). The design of smart educational environments. *Smart Learning Environments, 3*(1), 15. doi:10.118640561-016-0039-x

Ha, S. H., Bae, S. M., & Park, S. C. (2000). Web mining for distance education. In IEEE international conference on management of innovation and technology (pp. 715–719). IEEE.

Henard, F., & Roseveare, D. (2012). *Fostering Quality Teaching in Higher Education:Policies and Practices.* OECD,.

Hu, R. (2010). Medical Data Mining Based on Association Rules. *Computer and Information Science, 3*(4).

Hwang, G.-J. (2014). Definition, framework and research issues of smart learning environments-a context-aware ubiquitous learning perspective. *Smart Learning Environments, 1*(1), 4. doi:10.118640561-014-0004-5

Jain, A. K., Murty, M. N., & Flynn, P. J. (1999). Data clustering: A review. *ACM Computing Surveys, 31*(3), 264–323. doi:10.1145/331499.331504

Kouskoumvekaki, I. (2011). *Non-linear Classification and Regression Methods.* Academic Press.

Kumar, V., & Chadha, A. (2012). Mining Association Rules in Student's Assessment Data. *International Journal of Computer Science Issues, 9*(5).

Liebowitz, J. (2017). Thoughts on Recent Trends and Future Research Perspectives in Big Data and Analytics in Higher Education. In *Big Data and Learning Analytics in Higher Education* (pp. 7–17). Cham: Springer. doi:10.1007/978-3-319-06520-5_2

Liu, B., & Wong, C. K. (2000). *Improving an association rule based classifier.* Journal In Principles of Data Mining and Knowledge Discovery.

Liu, M. C., & Huang, Y. M. (2017). *The use of data science for education:The case of social-emotional learning. Smart Learning Environments, 4(1).* doi:10.118640561-016-0040-4

Mampadi, F., Chen, S. Y. H., Ghinea, G., & Chen, M. P. (2011). Design of adaptive hypermedia learning systems:a cognitive style approach. *Computers & Education, 56*(4), 1003–1011. doi:10.1016/j.compedu.2010.11.018

Manjulatha, B., Venna, A., & Soumya, K. (2016). Implementation of Hadoop Operations for Big Data Processing in Educational Institutions. *International Journal of Innovative Research in Computer and Communication Engineering, 4*(4).

Mayer, V., Schonberger, K., & Cukier, K. (2013). *Big data: A revolution that will transform how we live,work,and think.* Boston: Houghton Mifflin Harcourt.

Nasser, T., & Tariq, R. S. (2015). Big data challenges. *Journal of Computer Engineering & Information Technology.* doi:10.4172/2324-9307.1000135

NCTM (National Council of Teachers of Mathematics). (2000). *Principles and standards for school mathematics.* Reston, VA: NCTM.

Oladipupo, O.O., & Oyelade, O.J. (n.d.). Knowledge Discovery from Students' Result Repository: Association Rule Mining Approach. *International Journal of Computer Science & Security, 4*(2).

Papanikolaou, K. A., Grigoriadou, M., Magoulas, G. D., & Kornilakis, H. (2002). Towards new forms of knowledge communication:the adaptive dimension of a web-based learning environment. *Computers & Education, 39*(4), 333–360. doi:10.1016/S0360-1315(02)00067-2

Patil, S. M., & Kumar, P. (2017). Data Mining Model for Effective Data Analysis of Higher Education Students Using MapReduce. *IJERMT, 6*(4).

Picciano, A. G. (2012). The evolution of big data and learning analytics in American Higher Education. *Journal of Asynchronous Learning Networks, 16*(3), 9–20.

Prakash, B.R., Hanumanthappa, M., & Kavitha, V. (2014). Big data in Educational Data Mining and Learning Analytics. *International Journal of Innovative Research in Computer and Communication Engineering, 2*(12).

Provost, F., & Fawcett, T. (2013). Data science and its relationship to big data and data-driven decision making. *Big Data, 1*(1), 51–59. doi:10.1089/big.2013.1508 PMID:27447038

Romero, C., & Ventura, S. (2007). Educational data mining: A survey from 1995 to 2005. *Expert Systems with Applications, 33*(1), 135–146. doi:10.1016/j.eswa.2006.04.005

Romero, C., Ventura, S., & Bra, P. D. (2004). Knowledge Discovery with Genetic Programming for Providing Feedback to Courseware Authors. *User Modeling and User-Adapted Interaction, 14*(5), 425–464. doi:10.100711257-004-7961-2

Sahlberg, P. (2007). Education policies for raising student learning: The Finnish approach. *Journal of Education Policy, 22*(2), 147–171. doi:10.1080/02680930601158919

Sarma, P. K. D., & Roy, R. (2010). A Data Warehouse for Mining Usage Pattern in Library Transaction Data. *Assam University Journal of Science &Technology: Physical Sciences and Technology, 6*(2), 125–129.

Scheffel, M., Drachsler, H., Stoyanov, S., & Specht, M. (2014). Quality indicators for learning analytics. *Journal of Educational Technology & Society, 17*(4), 117–132.

Shapiro, P. (1999). The Data-Mining Industry Coming of Age. *IEEE Intelligent Systems, 14*(6), 32–34. doi:10.1109/5254.809566

Sin, K., & Muthu, L. (2015). Application of Big Data in Education Data Mining and Learning Analytics – A Literature Review. *ICTACT Journal on Soft Computing, 5*(4).

Slater, H., Davies, N., & Burgess, S. (2009). *Do teachers matter? Measuring the variation in teacher effectiveness in England.* Centre for Market and Public organisation (CMPO), Working paper series no. 09/212.

Slater, S., Joksimovic, S., Kovanovic, V., Baker, R. S., & Gasevic, D. (2017). Tools for Educational Data Mining: A Review. *Journal of Educational and Behavioral Statistics*, *42*(1), 85–106. doi:10.3102/1076998616666808

Tajunisha, N., & Anjali, M. (2015). Predicting Student Performance Using MapReduce. *IJECS*, *4*(1), 9971–9976.

Tang, T. Y., & Gordon, M. (2002). Student modeling for a web-based learning environment: a data mining approach. *AAAI*, 967-968.

Tole, A. A. (2013). Big Data Challenges. Database Systems Journal, 4(3).

Tomlinson, C. A., & Kalbfleisch, M. L. (1998). Teach Me, Teach my Brain: A call for differential classrooms. *Educational Leadership*, *56*(3), 52–55.

Tomlinson, C. A., & McTighe, J. (2006). *Integrating differentiated instruction & understanding by design: Connecting content and kids.* Alexandria, VA: ASCD.

U.S. Department of Education. (2012). *Enhancing Teaching and Learning Through Educational Data Mining and Learning Analytics*: *An Issue Brief.* Available online: https://tech.ed.gov/wp-content/uploads/2014/03/edm-la-brief.pdf

Weiss, S. M., & Kulikowski, C. A. (1991). *Computer systems that learn: classification and prediction methods from statistics, neural nets, machine learning, and expert systems.* Morgan Kaufman Publishers.

Williamson, B. (2017). *Big data in education: The digital future of learning, policy and practice.* Sage.

Woo, J. (2012). Apriori-Map/Reduce Algorithm. *Proceedings of the International Conference on Parallel and Distributed Processing Techniques and Applications (PDPTA).*

Yang, X. Y., Liu, Z., & Fu, Y. (2010). MapReduce as a Programming Model for Association Rules Algorithm on Hadoop. In *Information Sciences and Interaction Sciences (ICIS) 2010: Proceedings of 3rd International Conference.* IEEE.

Zhang, Y., Oussena, S., Clark, T., & Kim, H. (2010). Use Data Mining to improve student retention in higher education – A Case Study. *Proceedings of the 12th International Conference on Enterprise Information Systems, 1*,.

Zhu, Z.-T., Yu, M.-H., & Riezebos, P. (2016). A research framework of smart education. *Smart Learning Environments, 3*(4). doi:10.118640561-016-0026-2

Zhu, Z. T., & He, B. (2012). Smart Education: New frontier of educational informatization. *E-education Research, 12*, 1–13.

KEY TERMS AND DEFINITIONS

Analytics: Analytics is the process of statistics in which the data revelation, perception, and communication of meaningful patterns in data is obtained.

Classification: A classification is allocation, categorization, and analysis of data according to its similarities.

Clustering: Clustering is the task of grouping a set of objects in such a way that similarity of objects in the same group are compared to another group and discover that object in which group are more similar to each other than to those in other groups.

Correlation: Correlation is the statistical analysis technique, which is used to compute the organization between two continuous variables which can be between an independent and a dependent variable or between two independent variables.

HDFS: HDFS means Hadoop distributed file system, which provides the extensible, fault-tolerant, and cost-efficient storage for metadata.

KEEL: KEEL is a data mining and learning analytics tools. KEEL means knowledge extraction based on evolutionary learning.

MOOCs: Massive open online courses are free online courses available for anyone to enroll.

Regression: Regression is the statistical analysis technique used to examine the relationship between one dependent and one independent variable. The regression performs the prediction of the dependent variable when the independent variable is known.

SPSS: SPSS means statistical package for the social sciences used for statistical analysis acquired by IBM in 2009.

WEKA: WEKA means Waikato environment for knowledge analysis. It is a machine learning software written in Java, developed at the University of Waikato, New Zealand.

YARN: Apache Hadoop YARN is known as Yet another resource negotiator, which is a cluster management technology. YARN acts as a resource manager that coordinates the resources for the applications using the Hadoop resources and monitors the operations on cluster nodes using TaskTraker and regularly communicates to Job Tracker which is the Master Node.

Section 2
Predictive Intelligence and IoT

Chapter 5
Improved Usability of IOT Devices in Healthcare Using Big Data Analysis

Vijayalakshmi Kakulapati
SNIST, India

Mahender Reddy S.
SNIST, India

ABSTRACT

Sensor data takes the microcontroller and sends it to doctors through the wi-fi network and provides real-time healthcare parameter monitoring. The clinician can analyze the sensor generated information. Patients provide their measures to the arrangement and identify their fitness status without human intervention. In this chapter, MapReduce algorithm is used to identify the patient health status. The controller is connected with the signal to alert the attendee about dissimilarity in sensor output data. If the situation is sever, an alert message is sent to the doctor through the IOT devices that can provide quick provisional medication to the ill person. The system improves usability of medical devices with less power consumption, simple setup, and high performance and response.

INTRODUCTION

There are numerous research studies are done to assessment the new trends in efficiency in healthcare providers. The effectiveness (Wang, Fedele, & Pridgen, 1999) of the hospital accomplish by analyzing data which showed high inadequacy into a number of clinics acknowledged. The major inadequacy of clinics exists in the accessibility of clinical facilities, the quantity of operating devices and clinical staff. Hospital inefficiency estimating method (Rosko, & Chilingerian, 1999) by identification of the communicated case mix indicator condensed inefficiency by 50%. As a result, the optimization of diagnostic practice is improving the efficiency of healthcare services.

DOI: 10.4018/978-1-5225-6210-8.ch005

Using of independent systems allow the observation and tracking of physiological factors at some time and everywhere is called as biofeedback which falls under the new patterns of clinical services and might be achieved by therapeutic sensors (Sawyer, Aziz, Backinger, Beers, Lowery, & Sykes, 1996) placed on the body of long suffering. All these can be accomplished by correlating message panels by means of sensors empowering Wi-Fi.

Patients utilized by carrying body sensor are able to collect diverse anatomical or genetic factors consistently, as involved in various pathologies and healing rule. The extensively utilized body sensors are: monitoring the temperature of the body, monitoring heartbeat, beat oximeter, oxygen saturation (SPo2), blood pressure monitoring, the electrocardiogram (ECG), with accelerometers (movement), and electroencephalogram (EEG).

There is a growing approval of the connections among the design of therapeutic devices, reduced usability, individual inaccuracy and long-suffering protection. To scale back the possibility of inaccuracy, therapeutic device devise must take the description of requires of all users, in addition to the assortment of environments wherein the devices may be utilized. Categorizing the connection among design, individual fault and patient protection, the narrow necessities for therapeutic devices are insertion a growing stress on usability and different user-associated issues.

The Internet of Things is predicted to facilitate a diversity of healthcare providers in which each examines provide a set of medical resolutions. In the medical environment, there is no typical explanation of the Internet of Thing examinations. Though, here may be few cases where a service cannot be independently illustrious from a scrupulous explanation or appliance. Now, recommends that an examination is via some indicates common in life and have the impending to be a structure chunk for a position of resolutions or appliances. Additionally, it should be note-down those common services and procedures needed for the Internet of things structures may need insignificant alterations for their fitting utility in medical situations. These contain warning checks, resource distribution checks, online checks, annoyed-connectivity procedures for diverse medical devices, and connection procedures for the most important connectedness.

The uncomplicated, rapid, protected, and low-power detection of apparatus and examinations can be supplementary to this catalog. Conversely, a conversation on analogous simplified checks of IoT is further than the extent of this research. The fascinated persons who read is referred to the writing for an additional complete perceptive of this issue.

The objective of this chapter is to control the conventional heuristic investigation method of evaluating software service with the intention that it will be useful to therapeutic apparatus and utilized to calculate the patient protection affecting to individual devices through recognition and evaluation of service issues. The other objective is to reduce patient uneasiness, to reduce patient delaying the diagnosis to be accomplished with enhancement of medical equipment consumption. The major goal is optimization of medical diagnosis with the intention of achieve it in improving investigative processes, to decrease the number and diagnosis cost for each patient, to reduce point from the beginning of the diagnostic procedure to till ending of the diagnosis and to personalize the process for every patient.

In this chapter, we tend to amend a usability production method known as heuristic assessment with the estimation of usage issues in therapeutic devices. During the recognition of usage problems, ultimately recognize therapeutic devices' impending difficulty marks that are probable to origin medicinal faults. Describing the usage heuristics customized for the assessment of medicinal devices, the proportions of the severity evaluation of usage issues, and also the process of moving away a heuristic assessment.

RELATED WORK

Several investigation results, therapeutic fault descriptions, and different records demonstrate a clear association among usability concerns and client fault (Obradovich & Woods, 1996; Lin, Isla, Doniz, Harkness, Vicente, & Doyle, 1998). According to the FDA's report, Do it By Design (Sawyer, Aziz, Backinger, Beers, Lowery, & Sykes, 1996), and illustrates a variety of fault consequences from the therapeutic device interface be determined. Assessment of Heuristic methods, when adapted for medicinal apparatus, is a helpful, productive and minimal effort technique for assessing persistent security highlights of restorative devices through the recognition of usage issues and their severities (Jiajie Zhang & Caldeira, 2003).

In 2020, through IOT more than 25 billion devices will be connected according to Gartner prediction. With these connected devices, how many will be medical and/or monitoring devices. Now- a-days in health informatics numerous wearable devices, measuring heart rates, weight, ECG, daily steps, and intensity level of workouts; patients may aware of these facts and maintain the health by utilizing wearable devices (kellton-tech-blog).

Patients are able to recognize the usage of sophisticated monitoring devices such as blood report levels, hydration, lung capacity, diabetic levels, BMI (Body Mass Index), mood swings and blood flow.

Doctors are utilizing smart phones to convey health related issues and even fix appointment and summaries which are available in the form of text. EHR (electronic health records) are stored in the patient's medical history.

IOT devices reduce the gap between patient and doctor. Physicians will track from the sensor data to monitor the patient's health issues from remote. Patient can register for a remote health checkup through live streaming offered by online health monitoring systems. As a result, physicians utilize data to diminish severe health conditions. Medical devices connected through IOT will help physicians to diagnosis abnormalities. For example, if a patient fell due to high blood pressure at remote place, an alert will be sent to the physician and immediately team will be sent by health care provider to the site for assistance.

In the year 2017 wearable devices are suffering with the problem of fitness (iot-trends-2018) by receiving features. The majority of the devices were incapable of deliver precise extents and utilizing functions of fitness. Medical device services such as diabetic tests, electrocardiogram, CT scan, x-ray or even a simple medical treatment will be a part of an electronic record. Health care providers and clinics will be adopted with advanced sensors able to transfer live data using IoT and automatic medical processes.

The majority of patient acquaintance mechanism oscillations, which are characterized by segments of under scaled and deliberate faction, and spilling over unstructured movement (João Massano & Bhatia, 2012). Researchers have proposed automating the evaluation with wearable sensors (Bjoern, Eskofier, Lee, Daneault, Golabchi, Ferreira-Carvalho... Bonato, 2016; Patel, Lorincz, Hughes, Huggins, Growdon, Standaert... Bonato, 2009). However, most approaches to date have been narrow to regulated mechanism assignments in medical settings (Ossig Antonini, Buhmann, Classen, Csoti, Falkenburger, Schwarz... Storch, 2016). To enable automated evaluation of motor states which covers an extensive assortment of indications transversely enduring, a huge amount of medical wearable sensor data in every day existing situations is required (Silvia Del Din, Godfrey, Mazza, Lord, & Rochester, 2016). Deep learning (DL) approaches (LeCun, Benigo, & Hinton, 2015) provide a promising methodology to the arrangement with the huge inconsistency of data (Bjoern, Eskofier, Lee, Daneault, Golabchi, Ferreira-Carvalho... Bonato, 2016; Plotz, 2015; Ken, Kubota, Chen, & Little, 2016).

Big data processing is widely using mapreduce the framework in terms of handling large data which consist of Text mining (Jia, Tian, Shenc, & Tran, 2016), extraordinary learning (Xin, Wang, Qu, Yu, & Kang, 2016), disseminated learning (Zhan, Chen, Chen, & Tek, 2016), categorization (Bechini, Marcelloni, & Segatori, 2016), image segmentation (Saeed Shahrivari, & Jalili, 2016), clustering (Li, Song, Zhang, Ouyang, & Khan, 2016) etc. The major problem of optimization in terms of disseminated work is profound require of communication. In each and every step of optimization algorithm require to swap data with the intention of investigate optima.

Body sensor data fault identification of imagine physiological factors have associations among them. Such as, heart beat is determined because the quantity of periods in an electrocardiogram indication. The rate of breath is relative to the heart beat, however fluctuates for dissimilar persons. Furthermore, body temperature of one degree centigrade appends approximately 10–15 beats for every moment to the heart beat (Rotariu & Manta, 2012). Moreover, incidents of hypoglycemia (low glucose) can activate an arrhythmia, which regularly carries on like a flying heart (Nguyen, Su, & Nguyen, 2013). Taking everything into account, breath rate and body temperature are for the most part emphatically corresponded with the heart beat.

In Genetic algorithm, the fitness of devices is based on the prospect of reproduction. Though, assigning fitness values to devices based on a fitness function by using fittest. The optimal solution of the device is outlined or the utmost generations achieved (Reeves, 2003; Math Works).

For a range of device issues and optimization, genetic algorithm is often utilized. The list of medical equipment is optimized by the Genetic algorithm to make best use of the number of clinical devices taking into the usability

The general purpose optimization algorithm, GA depends on the local searches that impersonate the principles instigated to assess fitting solutions to device related issues (Khurana, Rathi, & Akshatha, 2011). Generally, genetic algorithm initiates with an observations of accidentally generated amplifications (Aickelin & Dowsland, 2004). Generating novel observations are the rule of continued existence of the fittest by concerning operators.

Several researchers study about evaluation and improve device consistency in their intension or built-up considerations with no considering assessments and protection approaches of these devices operating maintain. In (Wang, Ozcan, Wan, & Harrison, 2010) explained about breakdown codes to calculate continuation usefulness for several types of clinical devices.

HEALTH-IOT ECOSYSTEM

The present therapeutic designs are usually proprietary, not interoperable, and rely upon experts to give inputs and review yields; components of such apparatus have a tendency to be stove-piped and not interoperable among the remaining components of devices. Patient is fixing to numerous apparatus at a time so that physicians should examine all apparatus in parallel amalgamate data, and take action on their perceptions, which can be influencing by pressure, fatigue, or factors.

The architecture of therapeutic device architecture is consisting of wired and wireless interfaces to assisting for communication of enduring data. Devices intend to control individually with informal attempts to combined data transversely can prompt to unintended or fortuitous results. Developing of such potentials as personal medical services, telemedicine, and investigation of the online clinical lab emphasizes the focal part of cutting edge organizing and disseminated correspondence of health care in the health systems.

Present medical devices, enhance techniques are sufficient for the high- certainty devise and complex in manufacture, interoperable therapeutic apparatus software and structures which probably incorporate nano/bio apparatus, bionics, or programmable natural systems. The devices are inspecting and testing approaches depends on system-life-cycle development activities, which are inadequate in the assortment variety and unpredictability of segments and associations in developing medicinal devices and structures.

Observation techniques of imperative tasks and enhancing measurements are doing by combining sensors, wireless communication, 3G, RFID and Bluetooth. There are numerous applications are existing in medical fields associated with the IoTs. The transformation of IoT is reshaping the cutting edge medicinal services with promising financial and social prospects. The vast amount of users develop conventional portable network service has remarkably accelerated the improvement of the IoT based personalize medical services, which is called Health-IoT.

An innovative network-determined devise approach (Pang, Tian, & Chen, 2014) and the execution of it was concluded in intend of an open-source resolution. In this ecosystem, numerous roles in diverse the public provinces are associated. Numerous collaborators in the network for instance, medical providers, medical economical resources, content providers, telegram engineer, etc., are not on target. In order to get used to the application of mobile healthcare diagnosis, in this chapter explains about healthcare application domain. Application broker describes the patient's experience and service quality, which is a joint name of application designer, platform provider and the application store. Distribution of application for health care is most important.

Modern investigation on basic medical observation by employing the Internet of Things can be divided into two types. The first type is based on variety bases on production procedure and genuine calculation (Kim, Pakzad, Culler, & Demmel, 2007; Li, Shi, & Wang, 2012). The second type executes on the origin of hypothetical algorithms which practice data and indications that have been accumulating by sensors. Recurrence reaction has frequently been utilizing for examination in these schemes adjacent to medical observing by utilizing the pulsation-based factors has been given careful considerations. The main goal of this method is detecting damages from the alteration of pulsation assessments accumulated from accelerometers connected to the apparatus. There are numerous inquires about utilizing the other damage-perceptive aspect to watch basic wellbeing.

Using IoT in Healthcare Benefits

- **Treatment Cost Reducing:** This type of healthcare make available 24/7 and monitoring patient health issues by real time. This provides to minimize avoidable clinic appointments and also reduce transportation cost too. Through online video streaming healthcare providers patient can have the physician recommendation at patient home and only when the patient fell in the critical situation may arrive at hospitals. This type of health care monitoring can decrease premiums of insurance and also patient operational leave for the medical checkup.
- **Reducing Human Error:** This type of healthcare observations, body sensors send information such as patient physical medical information like blood pressure, level of sugar in blood, etc., is accumulating move away precisely by sensors and analogous decisions taking by the big data analytics method which helps in diminishing individual errors.

- **Eliminating Barriers of Geographical:** patients can get healthcare suggestions from remote areas throughout the world wide due to physicians and patients are connected through the internet of things.
- **Reducing Formalities and Documentation:** In this IoT healthcare applications, healthcare observations maintain green technology and reducing the formalities and documentation.
- **Premature Recognition of Chronic Disorders:** Patient physical health information is by utilizing different techniques like big data analytics and data mining which is generating by medicinal sensor, to predict persistent disorders in their early stage of disease and healing can be preparing before it turns into not curable
- **Improved Medicine Supervision:** One of the immense challenges to construct and supervise medicines for medical manufacturing. For better medicine management for producers utilizing Radio-frequency Identification technology in the medicine, supply chain, supplier and consumers also? Which reduces loss as of the thief, vanish and ignore the supervision of medicines.
- **Instant Healthcare Attention:** Medical devices in the Internet of things can alarm the healthcare supplier or patient family members in case of emergency such as high blood pressure or collapse of a senior family member.
- **Enhanced Results of Treatment:** By providing *24*/7 healthcare observation and indication based healing decisions will help to heal diseases on time, which enhance the treatment results.

USABILITY EVALUATION BASICS

According to the FDA, 2018 report healthcare defines as:

- "An instrument, apparatus, implement, machine, contrivance, implant, in vitro, reagent, or other similar or related article, including a component part, or accessory, which is:
- Recognized in the official Formulary, or the United States Pharmacopoeia, or any supplement to them,
- Intended for use in the diagnosis of disease or other conditions, or the cure, mitigation, treatment, or prevention of disease, in man, or other animals, or
- Intended to affect the structure or any function of the body of man or other animals, and which does not achieve any of its primary intended purposes through chemical action within or on the body of man or other animals, and which is not dependent upon being metabolized for the achievement of any of its primary intended purposes."

Usability Stands For...

It refers to the aspect of a patient's knowledge while communicating by means of things or systems, along with online communications, applications, or devices. This will provide overall satisfaction, effectiveness and efficiency of the patient. Usability is not considered as a single or one dimensional property of artifact, arrangement or network, which is a combination of parameter. Those are:

1. Perceptive devise.
2. simplicity of learning

3. Effectiveness of usage
4. Memorization
5. Severity of Error frequency
6. Personal satisfaction

Classification of Therapeutic Devices

Long-sufferings do not require being anxious about their actions' boundaries since the structure is able to maintain portability as executes observeing constantly. Body sensors conceding by enduring are utilizing to collect diverse anatomical or natural factors uninterruptedly, as need by numerous pathologies and healing control. This sensor network provides mobility support to a reliable solution to be connected in clinics, healthcare providers; other allied health care systems and old age or incapacitated user's homes (Alemdar & Ersoy, 2010).

Medical sensors are using as wearable devices by data analysis methods is providing to monitor health condition remotely due to enhanced wireless communication. This apparatus contains \components such as the item of clothing, wrist belts, eyeglasses, socks, hats, shoes, and other devices like smart phones, headphones and wristwatches.

Generally these medical sensors can be classified into two types: body contact sensors and Peripheral Non-contact sensors.

The first category can be further classified into two types:

1. Physiological actions monitoring sensors, the compound and visual (Oximetry, tissue properties),
2. Medicine deliverance scrapes (Prescription based healing sensor), chronic pain relief (stimulus) and defibrillator (urgent situation).

The second category can be further classified into two types:

1. Evaluating action of robustness monitoring, position(GPS, inside localization)
2. Patient behavioral monitoring, patient feelings, diet and language development and technology for blinds (Hiremath, Yang, & Mankodiya, 2014).

The healthcare applications (Jeong Gil Ko, Lu, & Srivastavea, 2010) utilized therapeutic sensors and wearable devices are:

1. Essential symptoms monitoring
2. Using smart phones at home
3. Support with cruise and sensory refuse
4. Behavioral learning

The few examples of wearable medical devices with sensors are:

1. ECG monitoring is also known as Electrocardiography is the procedure of tracing the dynamic movement of the heart some undefined time frame by wires placed on the body.

2.   Blood Glucose Monitoring: It consists of a glucose sensor, a transmitter, and a little exterior monitor to analysis patient glucose levels.
3.   Calculating Body Temperature: This is one of the four major imperative symptoms that must be checked to make certain secure and efficient care
4.   Blood pressure monitoring
5.   Oxygen saturation monitoring

Evaluation Methods

User-cantered devise employing by the developing usable online content is extremely useful. For instance, "test early and often", is mainly applicable as it moves towards usability analysis. The process and the kind of testing in the user centred device, enable users to assistance contained by the improvement of content, data devise, optical approach, communication approach are developed for the user satisfaction.

The testing of the user centered device includes:

- Control usage observing on an accessible site
- Target categories, conduct reviews to develop user objectives
- Observation sorting to help with IA expansion
- Routing calculation done by wireframe observation

Medical device parameters are:

- **Performance:** The system executes an achievement appropriate to capitulate of some function. The accomplishment is a bodily action, e.g., the movement of the gantry.
- **Information:** Significance to the information, generally fraud or failure of contribution Information.
- **Exhibit:** The visual demonstration on a screen –numbers, content, or figures in diverse designs.
- **Function:** Generally a particular computation or action; a software function in individual module.
- **General:** Inadequate data to allocate to a type.
- **Contribution:** The preliminary input (typed, modeled, examine off the apparatus, the database, file or tape, etc., on a number of function is executed.
- **Production:** The output of some function; usually a result to be utilized by the subsequently function.
- **Superiority:** Patient surveillances stated that "superiority constraint was not met".
- **Reaction:** Somewhat has occurred that should not, e.g., energy released above the allocated quantity; evident in a small number of hardware utility.
- **Examine:** An individual system examination concerning several roles for example, pushing, circulate air, providing medication; usually absorbs in excess of one factor (the module, subsystem).
- **Structure:** The entire system.
- **LifeTime:** The lifetime of the device or a service of the instrument.
- **Instructions for User:** Physical or further explanations for the user.

The Internet of Things in Healthcare Systems

Data is collected from fixed medium sensor movements with wearable devices. This data collects by wearable device activity data from 3D movements and physiological data.

For example, devices are monitoring biovotion (http://www.biovotion.com), Health patch, dynamometer, apple watch, etc. The data containing variable are:

1.   Comparable to incidence/ nonexistence in a precise room (PIR motion).
2.   Increase of the rate of the precise wrist (Actimetry).
3.   Condition of the room (Temperature).
4.   No optical data (Light intensity).
5.   Interior location (only close to/distant inference potential).
6.   Exterior location (GPS location).
7.   Digital dynamometer (Physiological measures supported on wrist-wear visual and wearable patch sensors).
8.   Wrist-Wear (Skin-conductivity).

Health and Fitness Monitoring by Using the Internet of Things

Wearable IoT medical devices (JMLP Caldeira, 2012) allocate to constant observing factors of physiological for example, patient blood pressure, patient heart beat, patient body temperature, etc., assist in uninterrupted physical condition and robustness observing. These can also evaluate the accumulated medical data to establish any physical conditions or abnormalities.

*   The various form of wearable devices may be:
*   Belts
*   Wrist-bands

The Practical Usage of Wearable Medical Sensor for Specific Requirements As

*   Diverse gums to establish the grip with no skin exasperation if the device is closely connect to the body surface.
*   These devices are painless to wear and to alter.
*   These devices are having fine battery ability to avoid recurrent battery change.
*   Signal to the noise ratio.
*   Consistent data.
*   The acceptable platform for data assortment.

Structural Health Monitoring (Zhang, 2013)

*   It utilizes an association of sensors to observe the pulse levels in the systems.
*   Sensors information is accumulated and analyzed to measure the physical condition of the systems.
*   With this data used to identify faults and automatic splits, trace the breaks to a system and also predict the durability of the system.

- By utilizing systems with faults provide progress caution in the impending breakdown of the system.

Predictions

- Internet of Things based predictions of real-time fitness administration systems can calculate execution of devices by learning the scope of variation of a system from its usual working condition.
- Actual data is collected utilizing particular electrical sensors called PMU (Phasor Measurement Units).
- Investigate the huge amount of information gathered from medical device sensors which can provide forecasts for imminent faults.

Usability Evaluation focuses on how in good health users can learn and utilize an item to accomplish their objectives and also provides user satisfaction with that method. To build up this information, proficient utilize a collection of methods that collect input from users about existing methods.

EXPERIMENT ANALYSIS

IoT is an emerging technology where all (living and non living) objects is connected through the internet for data sharing and controlling remotely. Heterogeneous technologies are combined together to enable IoT applications. IoT in healthcare uses the combination of RFID technology, Sensors, Networks, wireless Communication Technology and Embedded System Technology (link lab). Physical health information gathered by the sensor is transmitted to middleware the gateway. Gateway can handle multiple technologies and multiple sensors together. This analysis and aggregate this health data and send it the internet where connected healthcare service provider and stockholders use this information and take actions accordingly.

For acquisition of adjoin-optimal problem solution is done by applying Genetic Algorithms (GAs) with reasonable execution time and limited resources. To facilitate reproduction an innovative optimisation difficulty into an inherited one, some principle elements of GAs should be characterized appropriately. The objective function of the innovative problem should correspond to the fitness function. Genetic algorithm is implemented on single machines as successive programs. Though the fundamental rule behind these algorithms isn't generally successive, as it is conceivable to choose in excess of two devices for propagation, utilize in excess of one device, and execute administrators in parallel. This algorithm can be implemented in the equivalent without altering their major rule. In progression one existing disseminated the environment is the Hadoop map reduces and its simple establishment and practicality are two key angles that added to its awesome prevalence. Each cycle of calculation creates another signal and comprises of the accompanying steps.

- **Selection:** Every condition is calculating by the fitness function. Every assessment impacts the irregular decision among the successors for the following stage. When picked the k successors are gathered into couples

- **Crossover:** The crossover point is derived by the algorithm prefers for every device separation point. At this point, the signal reproduction in which two components are made start: the principal takes the initial segment of the primary device and the second of the second device; the alternate takes the second piece of the main device and the initial segment of the second device
- **Mutation:** When the issues are created, every quality is subjected to an arbitrary change with a little autonomous probability. Based on the code utilized to represent the possible solutions of a given issue, the illustration of the genetic signs can condition the *crossover* and *mutation* steps.
- **Fitness:** For every subset of qualities, the training dataset is separated to regard the characteristics of the subset.
- **Elitism:** Optionally empowered, this progression permits to pick the best entities among the ones in the new issues and in the previous generation, so as to ensure the development of precision focus after each creation.

The dataset utilized in this chapter for the implementation purpose taking from Katarina Karagiannaki, Athanasia Panousopoulou, Panagiotis Tsakalides, (UbiComp), ACM, 2016.

The dataset contains fields are: DeviceID, accelerometer, accelerometer, accelerometerz, gyroscopex, Gyroscopey, gyroscopez, magnetometerx, magnetometery, magnetometerz, Timestamp, ActivityLabel

The dataset is collected from 15 participants wearing 5 Shimmer sensor nodes on the locations listed in the Table 1. The participants performed a series of 16 activities (7 basic and 9 postural transitions), listed in the Table 2.

ActivityLabel
Minimum: 1.000
1st Quarter: 4.000
Median: 6.000
Mean: 7.051
3rd Quarter: 11.000
Maximum: 14.000

In previous experiments, due to big larger problem size, the serial initialization population will take more time for processing. Amdahl law theory the speed-up factor is totally depends on serial components. Experimental results are showing that in MapReduce platform gives similar results to ordinary algorithm which proves for the optimization problem that needs a lot of calculation, it is possible to use MapReduce platform to divide work load and find solutions in a distributed environment.

Table 1. Locations

S.No.	Position of the Wearable Device
1.	Left Wrist
2.	Right Wrist
3.	Torso
4.	Right Thigh
5.	Left Ankle

Table 2. Activity labels

S.No.	Activity
1.	stand
2.	sit
3.	sit and talk
4.	walk
5.	walk and talk
6.	climb stairs (up/down)
7.	climb stairs (up/down) and talk)
8.	stand -> sit
9.	sit -> stand
10.	stand -> sit and talk
11.	sit and talk -> stand
12.	stand -> walk
13.	walk -> stand
14.	stand -> climb stairs (up/down), stand -> climb stairs (up/down) and talk
15.	climb stairs (up/down) -> walk
16	climb stairs (up/down) and talk -> walk and talk

Algorithm 1. Genetic algorithm of Map part, each iteration

```
1.  Map ( input assessment):
2.  entit<- ENTITYILLUSTRATION(input)
3.  Fitness <- Evaluatefitness(entity)
4.  EMIT(entity, fitness)
5.  (maintain path of the present preeminent)
6.  If fitness > maximum then
7.     Max <-fitness
8.     maxEnt<-Entity
9.  End if
10. If all entities have been processed then
11. Write best entity to global file in DFS
12. End if.
```

There were 42 warnings:
Genetic algorithm Mean = -0.4488744 | Best = -0.2424006

```
Genetic algorithm situations:
Category                = genuine-valued
Size of Population    =   50
Amount of productions =   100
```

Algorithm 2. Genetic algorithm for reducing part of each iteration

```
1.   Initialize processed ← 0, tournArray [2 −tSize], crossArray[cSize]
2.   REDUCE(input, assessment):
3.   While assessments.hasNext() do
4.   entity←ENTITYILLUSTRATION(input)
5.   Fitness← assessment.getassessment()
6.   If processed < tSize then
7.   tournArray [tSize + processed%Size]   entity
8.   else
9.   SELECTIONANDCROSSOVER()
10.  End if
11.  processed← processed +1
12.  If all entities have been processed then
13.  for k← 1 to tSize do
14.  SELECTIONANDCROSSOVER()
15.  processed ← processed +1
16.  end for
17.  end if
18.  end while
19.  SELECTIONANDCROSSOVER:
20.  crossArray[processed%Size]←TOURN(tournArray)
21.  if (processed-tSize) % cSize = cSize -1 then
22.  newEntities← CROSSOVER(crossArray)
23.  For entity in newEntities do
24.  EMIT( entity, dummyFitness)
25.  End for
26.  End if
```

```
Elitism                 =  2
Probability of Crossover =  0.8
Probability of Mutation  =  0.1
Investigate field =       x1
Minimum   10                 Maximum 150
Genetic algorithm outcomes:
Iterations               = 100
Value of Fitness function = 149.5562 .
```

Assessment reproductions elapsed comparative average

1	GA1	10	27.13	1.000	2.713
2	GA2	10	57.10	2.105	5.710

CONCLUSION

The implementation results exhibit that the underlying usability communicated intend deficiencies evident themselves like enhance devices containing ease of use related faults can be recognized during the investigation of clinical apparatus protection data. Hadoop is the preeminent option to throw genetic

Figure 1. Device fitness values by using genetic algorithm

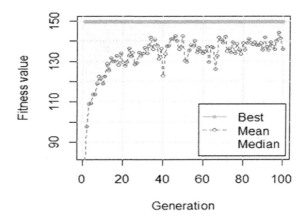

Figure 2. Residuals versus fitted values

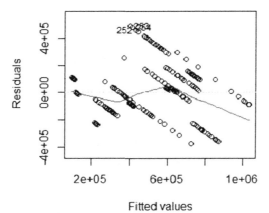

Figure 3. Normal standardized residuals and theoretical quantiles

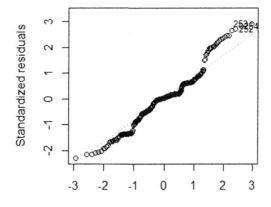

Figure 4. Fitted values scaled location

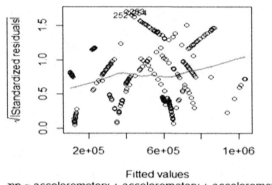

Figure 5. Residuals versus leverage values

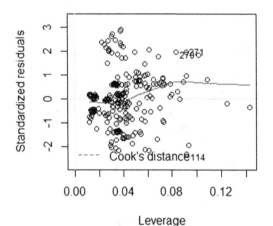

algorithm on the huge volume of data issue and demonstrated how will enhance utilizing parallel registering. MapReduce is intended for the expansive volume of the data set.

- The analytic diagnostic process has been optimising by dropping the amount of requiring examinations accomplishing enhance accuracy, Affectability and specificity additionally by presenting the dynamic analytic representation individualizing enduring.
- Minimising the analytic procedure term and holding up times between examinations keeping the dynamic circumstances of the apparatus.
- Augmenting the device reliability and availability by best possible planning of preventive protection.

FUTURE WORK

However benchmark functions which we used are not costly functions in terms of process power, for this reason experiment with more costly functions must be made for future work. Using MapReduce as distributed optimization may provide fast and easy to implement the solution for costly. The assessment of this methodology was achieving and validating by reproduction to enhance this technique and assess it in genuine situations. Also offer important insights for further medicinal services utilizing remote sensors and other networked devices.

REFERENCES

Aickelin, U., & Dowsland, K. A. (2004). An indirect genetic algorithm for a nurse scheduling problem. *Computers & Operations Research, 31*(5), 761–778. doi:10.1016/S0305-0548(03)00034-0

Alemdar & Ersoy. (2010). Wireless Sensor Networks for Healthcare: A Survey. *Computer Networks, 54*(15), 2688–710.

Bechini, Marcelloni, & Segatori. (2016). A MapReduce solution for associative classification of big data. *Information Sciences, 332*(1), 33–55.

Caldeira, J. M. L. P. (2012). Toward ubiquitous mobility solutions for body sensor network health care. *IEEE Communications Magazine, 50*(5), 108 – 115. Doi:10.1109/MCOM.2012.6194390

Del Din, S., Godfrey, A., Mazzà, C., Lord, S., & Rochester, L. (2016). Free-living monitoring of Parkinson's disease: Lessons from the field. *Movement Disorders, 31*(9), 1293–1313. doi:10.1002/mds.26718 PMID:27452964

Eskofier, Lee, Daneault, Golabchi, Ferreira-Carvalho, Vergara-Diaz, ... Bonato. (2016). Recent machine learning advancements in sensor-based mobility analysis: Deep learning for Parkinson's disease assessment. *2016 38th Annual International Conference of the IEEE Engineering in Medicine and Biology Society (EMBC)*, 655–658.

Jia, Tian, Shenc, & Tran. (2016). Leveraging MapReduce to efficiently extract associations between biomedical concepts from large text data. *Microprocessors and Microsystems*.

Khurana, N., Rathi, A., & Akshatha, P. S. (2011). Genetic algorithm: A search of complex spaces, international. *Jisuanji Yingyong, 25*, 13–17.

Ko. (2010). *Wireless Sensor Networks for Healthcare*. IEEE.

Kubota, K. J., Chen, J. A., & Little, M. A. (2016). Machine learning for large-scale wearable sensor data in Parkinson's disease: Concepts, promises, pitfalls, and futures. *Movement Disorders, 31*(9), 1314–1326. doi:10.1002/mds.26693 PMID:27501026

LeCun, Y., Bengio, Y., & Hinton, G. (2015, May 28). Deep learning. *Nature, 521*(7553), 436–444. doi:10.1038/nature14539 PMID:26017442

Li, Shi, & Wang. (2012). Automatic ARIMA Time Series Modeling for Data Aggregation in Wireless Sensor Networks. *International Journal of Digital Content Technology and its Applications, 6*(23), 438-447.

Li, Song, Zhang, Ouyang, & Khan. (2016). MapReduce-based fast fuzzy c-means algorithm for large-scale underwater image segmentation. *Future Generation Computer Systems*.

Lin, I., & Doniz, H. Vicente, & Doyle. (n.d.). *Applying human factors to the Linklabs IoT In Health Care: What You Should Know*. Retrieved from https://www.link-labs.com/blog/IoT-in-healthcare

Massano & Bhatia. (2012). Clinical Approach to Parkinson's Disease: Features, Diagnosis, and Principles of Management. *Cold Spring Harb Perspect Med, 2*(6).

Monitoring Motor Fluctuations in Patients With Parkinson's Disease Using Wearable Sensors. (2009). *IEEE Transactions on Information Technology in Biomedicine, 13*(6), 864–873. doi:10.1109/TITB.2009.2033471 PMID:19846382

Ossig, C., Antonini, A., Buhmann, C., Classen, J., Csoti, I., Falkenburger, B., ... Storch, A. (2016). Wearable sensor-based objective assessment of motor symptoms in Parkinson's disease. *Journal of Neural Transmission (Vienna, Austria), 123*(1), 57–64. doi:10.100700702-015-1439-8 PMID:26253901

Pang, Z., Tian, J., & Chen, Q. (2014). Intelligent packaging and intelligent medicine box for medication management towards the Internet-of-Things. *Proc. 16th International Conference in Advance Communication Technology (ICACT)*. 10.1109/ICACT.2014.6779193

Plotz. (2015). PD Disease State Assessment in Naturalistic Environments Using Deep Learning. In *Proceedings of the Twenty-Ninth AAAI Conference on Artificial Intelligence (AAAI'15)*. AAAI Press.

Reeves, C. (2003). *Genetic algorithms. Handbook of metaheuristics*. Springer. doi:10.1007/0-306-48056-5_3

Rotariu, C., & Manta, V. (2012). Wireless system for remote monitoring of oxygen saturation and heart rate. *Proceedings of the Federated Conference on Computer Science and Information Systems (FedCSIS)*, 193–196.

Shahrivari, S., & Jalili, S. (2016). Single-pass and linear-time k-means clustering based on MapReduce. *Information Systems, 60*, 1–12. doi:10.1016/j.is.2016.02.007

Wang, Ozcan, Wan, & Harrison. (n.d.). *Trends in Hospital Efficiency among Introduction to Human Factors in Medical Devices*. US Department of Health and Human.

Wang, B., Fedele, J., Pridgen, B., Williams, A., Rui, T., Barnett, L., ... Poplin, B. (2010). Evidence-based maintenance: part I: measuring maintenance effectiveness with failure codes. *Journal of Clinical Engineering, 35*(3), 132–144. doi:10.1097/JCE.0b013e3181e6231e

Xin, Wang, Qu, Yu, & Kang. (2016). A-ELM: Adaptive Distributed Extreme Learning Machine with MapReduce. *Neurocomputing, 174*(A), 368–374.

Zhan, C.-Y., Philip Chen, C. L., Chen, D., & Kin Tek, N. G. (1996). MapReduce based distributed learning algorithm for Restricted Boltzmann Machine" Neurocomputing Available online 17 March 2016 In Press, Corrected Proof — Note to users computer-based medical devices. *Human Factors*, *38*(4), 574–592. PMID:8976622

Zhang, H. (2013). Environmental Effect Removal Based Structural Health Monitoring in the Internet of Things. *Innovative Mobile and Internet Services in Ubiquitous Computing (IMIS), 2013 Seventh International Conference on.* DOI: 10.1109/IMIS.2013.91

Zhang, J., Johnson, T. R., Patel, V. L., Paige, D. L., & Kubose, T. (2003). Using usability heuristics to evaluate patient safety of medical devices. *Journal of Biomedical Informatics*, *36*(1-2), 23–30. doi:10.1016/S1532-0464(03)00060-1 PMID:14552844

Chapter 6

Cloud–Based Predictive Intelligence and Its Security Model

Mayank Singh
University of KwaZulu-Natal, South Africa

Umang Kant
Krishna Engineering College, India

P. K. Gupta
Jaypee University of Information Technology, India

Viranjay M. Srivastava
University of KwaZulu-Natal, South Africa

ABSTRACT

Predictive computing is a relatively new area of research. Predictive computing helps people to predict the future or unknown events. It combines various statistical approaches like predictive analytics, predictive modeling, data mining, big data, and machine learning. Predictive computing uses current and historical facts to predict future events. It looks for relationships and patterns between data variables. The outcomes of data variables can be predicted if we know the values of explanatory variables. Cloud computing is another new technology that provides everything-as-a-service (XaaS) and is used widely in various businesses. All storage and computing devices use cloud platform due to its elasticity, scalability, and dynamicity. Cloud-based predictive computing is a technology that uses data available on the cloud. Presently, the data from the social sites (e.g., Facebook, Gmail, LinkedIn, election data, etc.) are stored on cloud, and the volume of this data is enormous which needs innovative predictive computing design and architecture. This chapter represents the cloud-based predictive intelligence and its security model. Architecture for predictive intelligence is proposed and compared with the existing models. An attack prediction algorithm is also proposed and compared for the accuracy in the predictive intelligence.

DOI: 10.4018/978-1-5225-6210-8.ch006

INTRODUCTION

Cloud Computing

The concept of cloud computing came into the picture since 1960 by work of researcher John McCarthy. McCarthy's work was dedicated to making cloud computing a public utility which would benefit the society in whole. This idea of McCarthy's idea was further carried ahead by Doughlas Parkhill. Doughlas Parkhill explored the characteristics of cloud computing in his book "The Challenge of Computer Utility" in 1966 (Kaufman, 2009). The term 'cloud' roots back in the telecommunication world, where the telecommunication companies started offering reasonable quality VPN services at lower cost. Before VPN, the telecommunication service providers provided dedicated point-to-point data circuits. These dedicated point-to-point data circuits resulted in the wastage of network bandwidth. Using VPN services enables the switching of traffic to balance the utilization of the overall network. Cloud computing extends this concept to servers and network infrastructure (Jadeja & Modi, 2012). Big players in this industry have already dived and had successfully implemented cloud computing, be it Amazon, IBM, Google or other smaller companies, all are shifting their computation base to the cloud.

Internet has changed computing in a radical way from its initial days to the present day. Cloud computing has emerged in leaps and bounds since the dawn of internet in the past decade. A large number of facilities of prevalent computing are now provided over the internet. These facilities have led to the shifting and evolution of the concept of parallel computing, to grid computing, to distributed computing, and currently to cloud computing. The notion of cloud computing has been around for quite some time, but it is still an emerging field of computer science. It has spread to wide range of facilities provided over internet. Technically, cloud computing may be defined as computing environment where the computing needs of one party can be outsourced to another party via internet (NIST, 2018). There are many advantages of cloud computing, the most important is that an end user need not to invest in any infrastructure and hence not for installation. Since there is no such infrastructure or installation, no manpower is required to handle or maintain the infrastructure, which leads to a tremendous reduction in cost. Other advantages include: easy management, uninterrupted service, disaster management, green computing to name a few.

The National Institute of Standards and Technology (NIST) provides the definition of cloud computing, which says that:

Cloud computing is a model for enabling convenient, on-demand network access to a shared pool of configurable computing resources (e.g., networks, servers, storage applications, and services) that can be rapidly provisioned and released with minimal management effort or service provider interaction. (NIST, 2018)

In cloud computing, service is requested from the cloud, and the end user is not required to know the configuration and the physical location of the system which is delivering the services requested. It deals with computation resources, software, Platform and data storage services (Satish, Manjunath, & Hegadi, 2017). Cloud computing moves the data and related computing away from the personal computers to large data processing centers. Cloud computing combines all distributed resources and makes optimal use of resources to be able to solve significant computation problems and aims for higher throughput. Cloud computing deals with virtualization, scalability, interoperability, quality of service and the delivery models of the cloud, namely private, public and hybrid (Yaseen, Swathi, & Kumar, 2017). Due to many advantages of cloud computing, almost all the applications are using the cloud for computation, and one of them is Predictive Computing.

History of Predictive Computing

Predictive computing ages back to 1940s. However, the credit of the rise of predictive computing goes to the technological advances over the past 50 years. Predictive computing originated when the government started using the initial computation models. Predictive computing has become mainstream and is explored in almost all the organizations these days.

Predictive Computing

We have now entered an era of predictive computing with the rise of big data technologies. Predictive computing uses data, statistical algorithms and machine learning techniques to identify the prospects of future outcomes based on the current and historical data (Angeloy, Grefen, & Greefhorst, 2012). Work on historical information is done with the help data analytics. Predictive analysis is an advanced branch of data engineering which generally predicts some occurrence or probability based on data (Gao, Xia, & Ma, 2017). The aim of predictive computing is to go beyond understanding what has already happened, to come up with the best analysis of what might happen in the future. It will personalize and optimize data for individuals, private organizations, and government sectors. Predictive computing has revolutionized research and development within the industries. It has enabled businesses to make better and smarter decisions for the successful future of the business. It has enabled governments to reinvent the ways to run a society. Predictive computing includes a wide range of methods from modelling, statistics, data mining, machine learning, and recommender systems that analyse the historical and existing data to make predictions about future events. Record keeping standards, relational databases, new technologies such as Hadoop and MapReduce have made predictive computing an accessible tool for decision making. Predictive computing is a technology whose time has come and is here to stay. More and more organizations are opting for predictive computing to improve their work base and face the existing fierce competition and the reasons being growing volumes and varieties of data, faster cheaper computers, user-friendly software, hard-hitting economic conditions, and to survive the competition. With user friendly and interactive becoming more prevalent, predictive computing is no longer a domain of statisticians and mathematicians. Business Experts, business analysts, recommender system analysts are also using these technologies (Chen & Jinchuan, 2013).

Predictive computing can be viewed as a set of business intelligence technologies that reveal relationships and patterns within large volumes of data that can be used to predict future behavior and events. The concept of predictive computing can be easily understood by Figure 1. Unlike other business intelligence technologies, predictive analytics use the past and present events to anticipate the future. The term predictive computing can be interchanged with the term predictive analysis or predictive analytics.

Predictive analytics has been in the picture for a long time but has been more commonly identified by other terms. For many years, most people in business and commercial industry used the word "data mining" to describe the techniques and processes involved in creating predictive tools and models. In data mining, the tools allow the users to "mine" pieces or chunks of information (data) within the dimensions of respective databases. On the other hand, academicians and researchers have used the term

Figure 1. Business Predictive Analytics (Yaseen, Swathi, & Kumar, 2017)

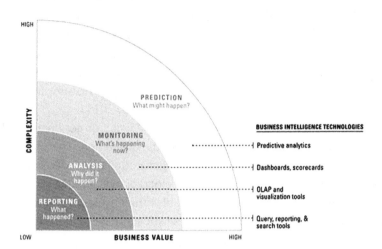

"knowledge discovery" or "knowledge discovery in databases (KDD)." KDD is a widely used and most common data mining technique. KDD is the process of discovering useful knowledge (information) from the collection of data (database). Hence the terms predictive analytics, data mining, knowledge discovery are interchangeable in different scenarios (Pearce, 2013).

Traditionally, data mining was performed manually. With the passage of time, the amount of data grew exponentially large and could no longer be maintained manually. For the successful existence of any business, discovering underlying patterns in data and predicting the future is essential. Since the process cannot be performed manually with a huge amount of data; as a result, several software tools were developed to discover data patterns and make assumptions. Today, the term data mining has been diluted so much that industrialists, business experts, and consultants now embrace the term "predictive analytics" or "advanced analytics" or just "analytics" to describe the nature of the tools or services they offer. But even here the terminologies can get fuzzy as not all analytics are predictive (Zhang, 2011).

Predictive computing is essential and essential these days from many perspectives. The most common are detecting frauds, optimizing marketing campaigns, improving the operation, and reducing risks. Banking and financial services, retail, oil, gas, utilities, governments and public sectors, insurance sector, manufacturing, health sector and many more industries are using predictive computing widely.

Cloud-Based Predictive Computing

As evident, there have been significant advances in various technologies in IT Industries. This advancement in technologies has led to the continued reduction in data storage. This continuous growth in data volume has led to data explosion and in turn has led to high data processing costs. The data has increased exponentially in the past few years, which includes human data on the social media in the form of photos, messages, blogs, tweets, digital data generated by sensors such as GPS, the business data, the classified data to name a few. It makes difficult to store, query, analyze and share the data as the available data are enormous in volume and highly complicated due to the number of data sources and their interrelationships (Chung, 2013).

Data analysis is of utmost importance in knowledge discovery and decision support in various data and application domains. Big data computing poses a severe challenge regarding the necessary hardware and software resources required for decision making. Hence we look upon to cloud technology as it offers a promising solution to these challenges by enabling ubiquitous and scalable provisioning of the computing resources (Low, 2012). Data analytics is a combination of methods, technology, data, and people. Data is collected, parsed and analyzed for relationships, and features are selected and mapped to estimate the response of a system under exploration (Shmueli, 2011).

Every business is now a data business, whether aware of the fact or not but the industry is shifted to the cloud when the data becomes large as data makes all the difference. The volume of enterprise data increases exponentially every year, which makes the organizations incredulous as the data cannot be processed as fast as the data is growing. This is when a cloud comes into the picture, and a relationship builds between the cloud and analytics. The cloud enables the business analytics to scale out the data easily and quickly, which in turn allows them to analyze silos of data to identify the developing trends. It leads to better customer satisfaction and profitability.

Predictive computing can be made more scalable, pervasive and more accessible to deploy using cloud technologies. Using cloud for predictive computing makes the computing resources delivered as a service and will provide multi-tenancy and shared resources. Various areas of opportunities can be achieved by using the cloud for predictive computing. Some of which are: pre-packed cloud-based solutions, predictive modeling with the data in the cloud, and flexible compute power among many more. The advantages are scalability, pervasiveness, deployment agility, moving analytics to data, whereas the cons are: complexity, privacy and security, regulatory issues, and transferring data to the cloud (Shmueli, 2010).

CLOUD-BASED DESIGN ARCHITECTURE

Referenced architecture would be useful in the following ways: It should facilitate the creation of concrete architectures (Tan, 2012) and increase understanding as an overall picture by containing common functionality and data flows in a cloud-based predictive computing system. Classification of technologies and products/services should facilitate decision making regarding the realization of system functionalities. Also, it would be essential to understanding architecture and performance characteristics of related technologies.

The first research question: *What steps are required for the reference architecture for predictive computing systems?*

The second research question: *How to classify technologies and products/services of predictive computing?*

A framework for design and analysis of cloud-based predictive computing reference architectures has been presented. This architecture design based on reference architecture which leads to success in cloud-based predictive computing. This is a stepwise process, which consists of multiple steps to perform predictive computing of any given problem or future prediction of any product /services.

In the present technology, predictive computing is used in various domains for technology enhancement and business future scope. Predictive computing is used for predictive analysis purpose fundamentally predictive analysis is a synonym of predictive computing.

Predictive analysis is used widely in Text Classification, Recommender Systems, Decision Support, Machine Learning, Security Management, Big Data Deployment and Strengthen Audience Engagement. Another application of predictive analytics is Aviation. There is an interest in large-scale data analytics in the aviation domain for analysis and prediction (Umadeyi & Chaturvedi, 2017).

Steps Involved in Cloud-Based Predictive Computing Architecture

The levels of a generic architecture for predictive computing are:

1. Identify data sources
2. Data Extraction from different sources
3. Data Storage and perform pre-processing
4. Data Conversion (from unstructured, semi-structured and structured data into the desired format as per application need)
5. Data Processing (generate multiple forms of data like a table, Gantt chart, graphs, etc. as per application need)
6. Data Analysis
7. Data Transformation (analysis forward to decision-making team)
8. Interfacing and Virtualization (changes will reflect customer or user application, dashboard application or virtualization application)

Figure 2. Generic Architecture of Predictive Computing

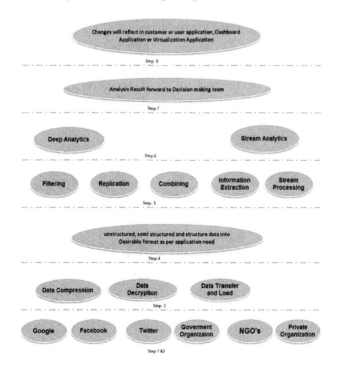

1. Identify Data Sources

In predictive architecture, we need to decide the data sources from where we will collect data for predictive computing or predictive analysis. For example, if we want to collect data for a movie review, we may collect data from website bookmyshow, big cinemas, PVR cinemas, and movie social page to predict the movie rating and future scope.

Similarly, if we want to collect data about any product, then we may receive data from Google, Facebook page, twitter page, and different individuals to analyze the current and future scope of the particular product.

Data sources are defined in two dimensions, *mobility,* and *structure* of data.

First, *in situ* refers to data, which does not move. An example of *in situ* data is a Hadoop file to be processed with MapReduce. *Streaming* data relates to a data flow to be treated in real time, e.g., a Twitter stream.

Second, the structure of the data source is defined. *Structured* data has a strict data model. An example is contents of a relational database, which is structured based on a database schema.

2. Data Extraction from Different Sources

After identifying data sources, we need to collect data from various sources. If the data is available in public domain or open access website, then we can collect easily form those sources. Otherwise, first, we need to get permission from corresponding authority and then we can access or receive data from these sources. If data is under some authority who may not grant permission to access data directly e. g. Data from hospitals or some confidential data of government agencies then we may request them and collect some sample data.

3. Data Storage and Performed Pre-Processing

After collection of data, we need to store that data securely. If the information is encrypted, then we need to decrypt data before storing in the database. Data should be stored in compressed form so that it will use storage space efficiently. Cloud data storage can be used for data storage that can expand as per our need and process efficiently.

4. Data Conversion

After storage of data, we need to convert all data as per our requirements, or we can say that we need to convert data from unstructured, semi-structured and structured data into the desired format as per application requirement.

Unstructured data is raw and flexible and is not associated with any particular data model. *Semistructured* information is not raw data or strictly typed. Other aspects of semi-structured data include irregularity, implicitness, and partiality of structure, and an evolving and flexible schema/data model. Examples of semi-structured data include XML and JSON documents. *Structured* data has a firm data model, which is not flexible. A case can be the contents of a relational database, which is structured as per a database schema (Kapasa, 2016).

5. Data Processing

In this step, we perform different processing on the data as per our requirements, like, filtering, replication, combining, information extraction and stream processing.

We Compress extracted data before operations: *transfer* and *load*. The *Raw data store* is used to hold unprocessed data. Data from the *raw data store* may be *cleaned* or *combined*, and saved into a new *Preparation data store*, which temporarily carries processed data. *Cleaning* and *combining* refer to quality improvement of the raw, unprocessed data. Raw and prepared data may be *replicated* between data stores. Also, new *information* may be *extracted* from the *Raw data store* for *Deep analytics. Information extraction* refers to storing of raw data in a structured format. The *Enterprise data store* is used for holding of cleaned and processed data. The *Sandbox store* is used for containing data for experimental purposes of data analysis.

After doing all these processing, we can generate data in multiple forms like a table, Gant chart, graphs, etc. as per application need.

6. Data Analysis

In data analysis phase, we analyze data based on past and present patterns and the basis of past result and scope we will predict future scope and opportunities for our object.

In-depth analytics refers to the execution of batch-processing jobs for *in situ* data. Results of the analysis may be stored back into the original data stores, into a separate *Analysis results store* or a *Publish and subscribe* store. *Publish and subscribe* store enables storage and retrieval of analysis results indirectly between subscribers and publishers in the system. Stream processing refers to the processing of extracted streaming data, which may be saved temporarily before analysis. *Stream analysis* relates to the analysis of *streaming* data (to be collected into *Stream analysis results*). Results of the data analysis may also be *transformed* into a *Serving data store*, which serves *interfacing and visualization applications*. A typical use for *transformation* and *Serving data store* is servicing of Online Analytical Processing (OLAP) queries (Sarkin & Maistry, 2016).

For example, if you analyze any product future scope then based on customer feedback, selling, purchasing, production, etc.. and their graphical representation with the similarity of past successful product graphical representation, you will easily be able to predict product future scope and opportunities.

7. Data Transformation

We will perform all analysis and appropriate correction and strategy changes. We will forward all analyzed data to decision-making team. With the help of above data, we can improve our business or able to predict the future scope of our product /services.

8. Interfacing and Virtualization

After final decision of audit team or decision-making team, changes will be reflected on the customer side or the user application, be it dashboard application or virtualization application.

Analysed data may be envisioned in several ways. *The dashboarding application* refers to a simple user interface, where typically crucial information (e.g., Key Performance Index (KPI)) is visualized without user control. *Visualization application* provides detailed visualization and control functions and is comprehended with a Business Intelligence tool in the enterprise domain. *The end-user application* has a limited set of control functions and could be realized as a mobile application for end users.

With the help of above architecture and step 1: Identify Data Sources, in which we analyse the problem and identify the appropriate data sources where we will get correct and useful data. In step 2: Data Extraction from different Sources, in which we will extract data from, identifies data sources. In step 3: Data Storage and performed Pre-processing, in which we will store data in a stable storage medium for next step processing. In step 4: Data Conversion, in which we will convert our stored data into a proper format which we will use for our predictive analysis. In step 5: Data Processing, in which we will process our data and generate some useful results and graphical representation by which we able to predict the future scope of product/services or future of our business. In step 6: Data Analysis, in which we will analyze our generated graphs and data. In step 7: Data Transformation, in which we will forward our data and result to senior or decision-making team to approve following changes or prediction to next authority. In step 8: Interfacing and Virtualization, in which we will reflect our changes in applications in virtualized or cloud environment.

CLOUD-BASED PREDICTIVE COMPUTING DESIGN

Cloud-based predictive computing is widely used in current era because data that need to be analyzed is big data, so it is not cost effective if the physical setup is made for this analysis purpose, so most companies are analyzed their data on cloud-based architecture like Facebook, Google, Twitter, etc.

Firstly we will make a comparison between predictive and non-predictive analysis in information security scenario:

Predictive Analytics in Information Security/Cybersecurity

Predictive analysis is widely used in information security/cybersecurity areas because an attack increases day by day very fast. So hypothesis or traditional tools are not sufficient for our data protection on the physical system or online system.

Table 1. Comparison of predictive and non-predictive analysis

Parameter	Non-Predictive Analysis	Predictive Analysis
Goals	We will make only casual hypothesis.	We will predict future basis of some predicted values
Security settings	Used only underlying concept, the relationship between values	Basis on observation and related calculated values
Prevention measures	Not able to apply correct preventions	Able to apply correct preventions.
Attack analysis	Start after an attack occurs	Saved data before the attack for the purpose of analysis
Security	Improve overall security after the attack.	Improve overall security before the attack.
Information loss	High	Very Low
Zero-day attack	Not able to detect	Able to detect

Cybersecurity is an ever-changing aspect of IT industry. Cybersecurity experts are continually working to keep up to date with the security aspects of this volatile industry. Many of the security breaches go undetected despite having sophisticated tools for dealing with them. Machine learning has somewhat provided some powered tools decreasing the time to detects these security attacks. But still some breaches go unnoticed for a long time, and by the time they have been identified, harm has already taken place. The need of today is to stay ahead of the threats and the people responsible for them and predict their next attack before destruction takes place. And cloud-based predictive computing is a solution to this need of the industry. With the help of cloud-based predictive computing, this thought can become a reality as it has a pivotal role to play. As cloud-based predictive computing is finding its way into almost every business, it's also making it importance felt in the domain of cybersecurity area. Cloud-based predictive computing is helping in determining the possibilities of cyber-attacks against organizations and setting up respective defenses before the attacks reach them. Already, many cyber security vendors are accepting this technology as the base of their security services. Shortly, no security provider will function without incorporating cloud-based predictive computing as the threats have become far too sophisticated and ever-evolving to be caught using the primitive methods.

Cloud computing is completely based on virtualization technology, and complete architecture which is used for predictive analytics is virtual that is called cloud-based predictive computing (Lu, 2015). Previously multiple solutions have been proposed for security issues that are a unique design for virtual environment and implemented by many security researchers (Ayhan, 2013). Mostly papers use data mining for security issues of virtualization and handling risk in information security.

Existing Model for Information Security

In previously existing method (Mishra & Silakari, 2012), in which data will collect from the virtual environment at regular intervals to analyze the effectiveness of our security controls. In this, they propose a step by step process for the security of the virtual environment.

Framework Comparison

In the architecture (Kapasa, 2016) shown in Figure 3, using machine learning approach in which first we train the system with the help of generated samples, but in our architecture, we use all previously exiting attack signature and traffic pattern by which our model starts working from the first installation.

In this architecture, the researcher does not have any prevention measures to prevent our system from predicted attack, but in our architecture, we do it for our system.

In this architecture, researchers do not improve security to prevent from predicted attack, but in our architecture, we suggest admin enhance the security of our virtual environments.

Design New Architecture for Above Problem

We analyse previous discussed architecture and design new architecture according to our proposed framework.

Figure 3. Proposed Framework process (Kapasa, 2016)

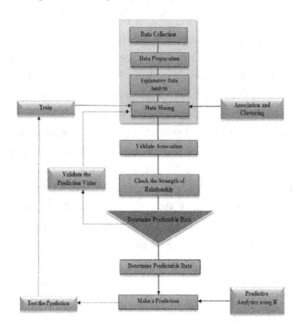

Figure 4. Working Architecture for the Previous Problem as per our proposed Framework

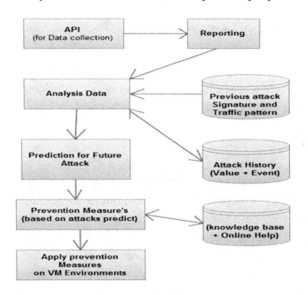

For this architecture implementation, we design an Application Programming Interface (API), which use to collect data from different sources and generate a structured report for our analysis. In the phase of review, we use existing data from various sources about all previously current attack signature and traffic pattern (in graphs form with different protocols packet patterns) for prediction of possible future attack on our virtual environment. This prediction is stored in a separate database for use in future projections. We are also taking help from the knowledge base and online databases and forwarded to higher level authority. Higher authority will analyze and implement suggested security prevention measures.

Figure 5. Previous architecture (Pearce, 2013) Vs. new Architecture

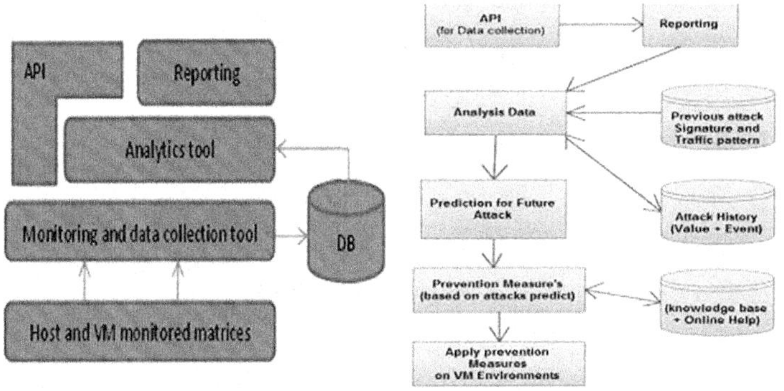

Comparison With Previous Architecture

At an earlier architecture, researchers proposed a monitoring and data collection architecture but we introduced a complete architecture after analyze entire problem discussed in research. This proposed architecture is improved and more effective as compared with previous.

In our architecture we more scope including previous architecture features, to monitor and collect data from the user system, servers, hypervisors, CPU, and Memory uses of virtual systems as well as all servers assigned to our client.

Formal Modelling

In our architecture Data analysis is a significant part which predicts a future event based on current data and previous system state that already stored in attack history.

Any vulnerability exploitation or attack is possible only when access rights are available to the attacker. We define the exploitability score e (v) as the measure of complexity in exploiting the vulnerability v.

The CVSS standard provides a framework for computing these scores using the access vector (AV), access complexity (AC), authentication (Au) and error rate **a** as follows

$$e\ (v) = a \times AC \times AV \times Au$$

In our architecture, we will use *State Transition Diagram Method* for future attack prediction. In this initial state of the system is represented by q_0 and basis on event performed by intruder we will move to next state. From the present state, we will predict future and their possibility of occurrence.

In the Figure 6, we will predict future attack prediction.

How to Calculate Attack Possibility Percentage

From state q_0, attack A is 4 passes away so at state q_0 is initial state and treated as an ideal state, so attack possibility is 0. But when the system state is a move to state q_1, one pass has been covered, so the possibility of attack A is:

Figure 6. State transition method for attack prediction

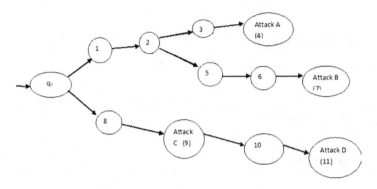

Table 2.

State	Attack	No. of Pass From Present State	Attack Probability (%)	Severity of Attack	State	Attack	No. of Pass From Present State	Attack Probability (%)	Severity of Attack
q_0	A	4	0	VL	q_1	A	3	25	L
q_0	B	5	0	VL	q_1	B	4	20	L
q_0	C	2	0	VL	q_1	C	NR	0	VL
q_0	D	4	0	VL	q_1	D	NR	0	VL
.	.	.	.	.	.	.	.	.	.
.	.	.	.	.	.	.	.	.	.
.	.	.	.	.	.	.	.	.	.
.	.	.	.	.	.	.	.	.	.

*NR= No route

Table 3. Severity level matrix

Attack Possibility (%)	Level
0-10	Very Low
10-25	Low
25-60	Medium
60-100	High

Single-pass possibility = 100/ total no of passes from q_0 = **100/4= 25**

So after one pass covered at state q_1 = 25

After one pass covered at state q_2 = 50

After one pass covered at state q_3 = 75

After one pass covered at state q_4 = 100 (attack performed)

Algorithm 1. Attack Prediction Algorithm

```
Input:      current system state
Output:  Possibility of attacks
foreach attack a1 in A do
    foreach states in s do
        p= Cal_possibility (state, no of passes from initial state D);
        Store p in P_A.
End
                Add Max (P_A) in P.
  End
Cal_possibility (state, no of passes from initial state)
Input: current state no, no of passes from initial D)
Output: p (Attack possibility in %)
        N= Calculated passes from current state to attack state a.
        Single pass possibility = 100/ D
        Attack possibility p = 100- N*(100/D)
```

Proposed Algorithm for Attack Prediction

For attack prediction algorithm following terms defined as:

A= set of all possible attacks, A= {a1, a2, a2 ...}.
P= set of possibility of attacks P= {p1, p2, p3...}
S= set of system states S= {q_0, 1, 2, 3...}.
s= subset of system states
P_A = All route possibility of attack A.
Note: Current system state is defined in term of s.

Algorithm 1 will give attack prediction is more than 90% accurate, because all previously known attack states are identified and stored beforehand in data analytics system. As much as accurate, you will recognize the states of a new attack, accuracy will maintain as much.

Figure 7. Accuracy comparison

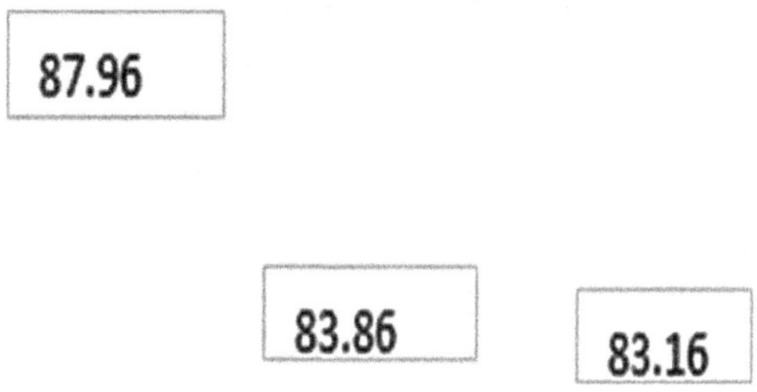

87.96

83.86   83.16

Some of previously algorithms which determine the dependency of one attribute over the other qualities. These did also use to predict the future event, but their accuracy is not up to such level.

The proposed method has been simulated on Ubuntu 14.4, with the help of traffic sniffer tool Wireshark. With the help of traffic pattern and decrypted traffic contents, find out the next possible states of our system and predict future attack possibility.

We perform the simulation for some basic attack like port scanning, ARP poisoning, DNS poisoning, Denial of service attack, etc.

REFERENCES

Angelov, G., Grefen, P., & Greefhorst, D. (2012). A framework for analysis and design of software reference architectures. *Information and Software Technology, 54*(4), 417–431. doi:10.1016/j.infsof.2011.11.009

Ayhan, S. (2013). Predictive analytics with aviation big data. *2013 Integrated Communications, Navigation and Surveillance Conference (ICNS)*, 1-13.

Chen, J., Chen, Y., Du, X., Li, C., Lu, J., Zhao, S., & Zhou, X. (2013). Big data challenge: A data management perspective. *Frontiers of Computer Science, 7*(2), 157–164. doi:10.100711704-013-3903-7

Chung, C., Khatkar, P., Xing, T., Lee, J., & Huang, D. (2013). NICE: Network Intrusion Detection and Countermeasure Selection in Virtual Network Systems. *IEEE Transactions on Dependable and Secure Computing, 10*(4), 198–211. doi:10.1109/TDSC.2013.8

Gao, X. & Ma. (2017). A new approach of cloud control systems: CCSs based on data-driven predictive control. *2017 Chinese Automation Congress (CAC)*, 3419-3422.

Jadeja & Modi. (2012). Cloud computing - concepts, architecture and challenges. *2012 International Conference on Computing, Electronics and Electrical Technologies (ICCEET)*, 877-880.

Kapasa, R. (2016). Predictive Analytics as a Security Management Tool in Virtualised Environment. *International Conference on Developments of E-Systems Engineering (DeSE)*, 102-106.

Kaufman, L. (2009). Data security in the world of cloud computing. *IEEE Security and Privacy, 7*(4), 61–64. doi:10.1109/MSP.2009.87

Low, Y., Bickson, D., Gonzalez, J., Guestrin, C., Kyrola, A., & Hellerstein, J. M. (2012). Distributed GraphLab: A framework for machine learning and data mining in the cloud. *Proceedings of the VLDB Endowment International Conference on Very Large Data Bases, 5*(8), 716–727. doi:10.14778/2212351.2212354

Lu, Y. (2015). Integrating predictive analytics and social media. *IEEE Conference on Visual Analytics Science and Technology (VAST)*, 193-202.

Mishra & Silakari. (2012). Predictive analytics: A survey, trends, applications, opportunities & challenges. *International Journal of Computer Science and Information Technologies, 3*(3), 4434–4438.

NIST. (2018). *National Institute of Standards and Technology - Computer Security Resource Center*. Retrieved form: www.csrc.nist.gov

Pearce, M., Zeadally, S., & Hunt, R. (2013). Virtualization: Issues, security threats, and solutions. *ACM Computing Surveys*, *45*(2), 1–39. doi:10.1145/2431211.2431216

Sarkin & Maistry. (2016). A Pragmatic Overview of Predictive Analytics Applications. *20th Asian Actuarial Conference*.

Satish, M., & Hegadi. (2017). E-Solution for Next Line of Business and Education Using Cloud Computing. *2017 World Congress on Computing and Communication Technologies (WCCCT)*, 105-110. 10.1109/WCCCT.2016.33

Shmueli, G. (2010). To explain or to predict? *Statistical Science*, *25*(3), 289–310. doi:10.1214/10-STS330

Shmueli, K., & Koppius. (2011). Predictive analytics in information systems research. *Management Information Systems Quarterly*, *35*(3), 553–572. doi:10.2307/23042796

Tan, Y. (2012). PREPARE: Predictive Performance Anomaly Prevention for Virtualized Cloud Systems. *2012 IEEE 32nd International Conference on Distributed Computing Systems*, 285-294.

Umadevi & Chaturvedi. (2017). Predictive load balancing algorithm for cloud computing. *2017 International conference on Microelectronic Devices, Circuits and Systems (ICMDCS)*, 1-5.

Yaseen, Swathi, & Kumar. (2017). IoT based condition monitoring of generators and predictive maintenance. *2017 2nd International Conference on Communication and Electronics Systems (ICCES)*, 725-729.

Zhang, Y. (2011). HomeAlone: Co-residency Detection in the Cloud via Side-Channel Analysis. *2011 IEEE Symposium on Security and Privacy*, 313-328. 10.1109/SP.2011.31

Chapter 7
IoT–Based Cold Chain Logistics Monitoring

Afreen Mohsin
UTL Technologies, India

Siva S. Yellampalli
UTL Technologies, India

ABSTRACT

This chapter aims to reduce the extent of human presence all along the cold chain by means of a powerful tool in the form of the IoT. It should also be ensured that any details regarding instances of equipment failure leading to product spoilage or an event of a successful delivery must be communicated to the manufacturer's end. It also seeks to fill gaps involving location tracking and environment control by means of a GPS module and an IoT-based sensor platform respectively used here.

INTRODUCTION

A new evolution in technological advancement is happening in the world these days. This increasing evolution permits the world of physical objects close in our surroundings to be connected to the internet. The design of the sensing body within the environment collects the information. Information then collected by sensing body connects itself to the cloud sensing element through a local area network. Later the network hosts information from its surroundings. This whole employment is the ideology behind giving life to IoT.

A cold chain is a temperature-controlled supply chain. It is unbroken and an uninterrupted series of refrigerated production, storage and distribution activities consisting of equipment and logistics, which maintain a desired temperature range. Cold chain logistics needs controlled surrounding environment for sensitive products. These products are suitable to use under the controlled environment. The sole assurance that tells if a certain method has been disbursed with success is the monitoring method. The use of IoT here is to observe cold chain supply leading to higher products handling and management. This book chapter describes a system which consists of a wireless microcontroller-based sensor network and a server which proves to be a perfect system to observe the temperature and humidity of cold chain logistics.

DOI: 10.4018/978-1-5225-6210-8.ch007

The meeting point between the real and the virtual world through some technologies is referred as "Internet of Things" (IoT). These technologies can be the sensor technology or mobile communication. With the ambition of giving all-pervading computing to automate the tasks or processes and to build a smart world this sort of computing system started a long time ago. The IoT is a trend with powerful technology in shaping the development of the information and communication technology (ICT). Today, the IoT consists of wide variety of items used in our daily lives, including radio frequency identification (RFID) tags, sensors, actuators, and even smart devices like mobile phones. A unique addressing scheme enables these objects to communicate and interact with other items to achieve the respective goals.

The development area like the wireless sensor networks aims at collecting contextual data. Here enhancement is being made in service-oriented architecture (SOA) which is a software approach to expanding web-based services using the capabilities of IoT (Web of Things, WoT) (Shih & Wang, 2016). Further the introduction of sensor technologies can be made doable conjointly together with technologies like artificial intelligence, nanotechnology etc. The sensor technologies create the IoT services as a knowledge domain field. Here most of the human senses are reproduced and replaced within the virtual world.

An electronic identification is given to these objects joining an IoT service. The sensors, for example, are the object/things which are the new electronic devices interacting with the real-world. A lot of chance is given to applications to contribute in building the IoT by combining sensors and mobile communications which seem to be very promising. From privacy, security, scalability and performance points of view these technologies can be improved, though they are already used (Islam, Mukhopadhyay, & Suryadevara, 2017).

The Internet within the IoT may additionally have completely different interpretations on the other hand. The present internet adapted to these new object's connectivity desires is the apparent interpretation which is more direct. With the IP addressing and routing capabilities the current internet is that of connected nodes employing a TCP/IP (internet protocol suite) protocol stack. The likelihood of planning corresponding gateways to specific nodes or networks is designed here in the internet model which runs a TCP/IP stack within the connected device (Islam, Mukhopadhyay, & Suryadevara, 2017). Adapting the TCP/IP stack to the resources of the objects involves the present internet connecting it. Within the long-standing time, the IoT seems among the leading methods to present this goal. IoT challenges the current internet model with new needs of connectivity of objects: like identifying, naming and addressing, measurability, non-uniformity, resource limitation, etc. (TCP Usage Guidance in the Internet of Things, 2018).

Regarding information visibility, IoT is currently running without any concern of autonomous decision-making. To avoid delays between data availability and choices and to alleviate from everyday decision tasks, new technologies and methods have to be compelled so it can be integrated. Autonomous cooperating logistical processes are being researched in logistics. Decentralized and hierarchal designing and management methods are used in the main set up of this idea. The combination of IoT and autonomous control (Autonomous system Internet) is an assortment of IP networks and routers below the control of one entity and additionally the IoT would provide a better level of strength in infrastructure, quantifiability and agility. To achieve subsequent level of user acceptance among the overall public they need to be easy to use and easy to assemble.

With the increasing range of deliveries either smaller or larger is been influenced by e-business in the present economy. IoT can bridge the gap between information technology and objects by the advancement of material handling and monitoring within the past years. Automated monitoring and improved data handling capabilities of the things enable the individual product identification of the product. This makes the monitoring efficient and better, because it was antecedently restricted solely to the kinds of product or a particular identification of batch of products. Massive products recall, which have led to severe monetary and company name mislaying, should be replaced by individual selective product recalls. This improves direct business-to-consumer communication. The IoT persuades to be the lacking connection between logistics and data monitoring. For connecting the things, sensors, actuators, and alternative smart technologies could be foundation for IoT. Hence this enables communication between person-to-object and object-to-object. The current changes in info technology, logistics and electronic (e-)business is aligned with the event of IoT. The IoT in logistics ideas and technologies have been applied to previous issues within the field of logistics. In transport logistics, the autonomous transport of supply objects/things from the sender to the receiver address is considered (Akulwar, 2016).

The IoT goes on the far side communication. The individual object is equipped with intelligence. On the system itself the intelligence can be placed. The product/object is permanently or temporarily linked to the IoT. The proposed system can be used for the transport of fresh fruits like for instance bananas. Traditional Storage of bananas is at 13 degrees Celsius. In Chill mode its 2 degrees Celsius. Whereas at Frozen mode -18 degrees and in deep frozen it's about -29 degrees Celsius. Condition monitoring of this kind are done by the intelligent systems as proposed in the project using ADC values. The small sensors analyze the temperature and humidity data and gather the collected information regarding the fresh products. The monitoring officer will keep a real-time track on the conditions and auto action is taken consequently. Currently, the previously proposed GPS (global positioning systems) consume high energy, they are big and expensive as well does not have the desired accuracy to be maintained (How the Internet of Things Impacts the Logistics Business, 2018).

The location tracker utilized in the proposed system overcomes these difficulties. The modern logistics is growing rapidly with the employment of IoT as the developers are working 24*7 to deal with elementary challenges. The cloud computing on the other hand can access the information using the internet instead of a computer's physical disc drive. Cloud computing and IoT technologies advancement have given vast openings within the logistics industry.

In logistics, the IoT application has for the most part currently taken root. The ability to figure out in times of volatile monetary markets and disruption of supply networks offers supply chain trading a combative advantage over opponents. The data flows in real-time inside the vicinity which is permitted by the cloud. This therefore enhances the economical communication with totally different base stations or trucks having the installed systems. All the operators will exchange data quick, streamlining operations and reducing congestion. The operators may be like fleet managers, drivers, and freight carriers.

Cloud computing can even facilitate with human error recovery. In logistics, cloud computing can even facilitate with disaster recovery as well provides a secure and solid platform to display and store the real-time information. The cloud computing can keep it safe from human error or disasters. The various actions needed to keep up with the optimum monitoring conditions are taken care of. Moreover, technologies having cloud computing even have the capability to reinforce loading and container discharge. The IoT in logistics market worldwide (Ganguli, 2016) throughout the period between 2016-2022 is anticipated to grow at a CAGR of 35.5% to touch an aggregate of $1,050.95 billion by 2022 as shown in Figure 1.

The information exchange with each other over the internet in IoT is a broad framework of interconnected devices. To come up with a lot of revenue and to open huge opportunities, IoT conjointly helps to scale back prices and employed in places like truck or in tracking the shipment. It is also employed in monitoring parameters in warehouse storage. The sensors are utilized here to monitor and keep track

Figure 1. Worldwide IoT in logistics market revenue

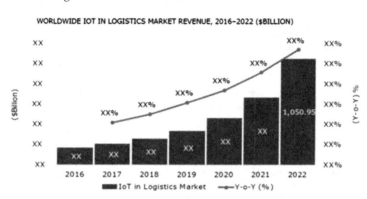

parameters like humidity and temperature. This helps the monitoring officer/driver to provide storage conditions suitable for various containers.

IoT applications usage, like WLAN in several base stations or within the truck ensures transparency in logistics. A safe transit of products from source to their destination is provided by this technology. Using GPS, the monitoring officer are in a position to check the precise location of the container products in the port or throughout transport. The movement of the trucks carrying products inside and outside the vicinity use this IoT based technology to confirm their safe destination. Containers, trucks and ships situated in varied ports with different locations are efficiently handled. Here the IoT interconnects the components situated in different areas. The IoT permits the system to gather and process information for decision-making and performance improvement at a later stage (Verma & Srivastava, 2017).

The thought process of whether the proposed system is an IoT or an WSN can be observed further. Firstly, in IoT routing isn't enforced. The sensors send their information on to the internet. Whereas, WSNs (Wireless sensor networks) nodes route traffic to reach sink node. This sink node is close to the nodes and is often accessed to read the gathered information. In IoT, things are anything ranging from sensors, humans, cameras, PCs and phones. These devices transfer their information to the internet that permits them to use in their applications. Secondly, WSN is an example of ad hoc networks and has its features. However, IoT information is send to the internet in exactly one hop. One hop transmission is against the definition of ad hoc. Thirdly, the sink node in WSN could also be connected to the internet to form IoT. In other words, all of the WSNs is one node in IoT. Hence, WSNs are simply a set of IoT. WSNs solely address the utilization of sensors specifically wirelessly-connected sensors. Major variations between WSN and IoT are shown in the Table 1. Conclusion can be made that the proposed system comes under IoT (Blaisdell, 2018).

The Internet is being exploited to control the virtual world. In IoT, there are direct implications on the physical part of the world. In reference, to being free from public attention, it's necessary for the company's professional/personal information to be treated intrinsically. New legislation is being planned to manage the misuse of personal data by employers. IoT allows additional surveillance potentialities regarding employees and consumers. Laws and regulations are improved and facilitated. However, control mechanisms which are self-regulating are additionally necessary. Power is the foremost vital limitation of the devices connected to the things. Each action taken within which the device used is power driven by batteries like using the wireless trans-receiver for sensing or for running of action devices for the proposed system. All these consume part of the energy. These devices are required to operate for days

Table 1. Major differences between WSN and IoT

Sr.No.	WSN	IoT
1	The foundation of IoT applications are the Wireless Sensor Networks.	The network of physical objects controlled and monitored over internet is IoT.
2	The network of Motes which are formed to observe, study or to monitor the physical parameters in the application desired is WSN.	In IoT application the physical parameters monitoring is done. The desired outcomes are not same but are little different. IoT is a Machine to Machine communication, smartness is brought into daily objects here.
3	For example - In Monitoring Temp-Humidity parameters or checking Soil moisture, motes are deployed in agricultural land. The gathering of data with perfect data analysis produce results about crop yields. This result may be of quality or quantity.	For example - When the device is hooked to the Thermostat, it monitors the surrounding temperature and adjusts it to the most preferred setting for user. It also learns about your habits, and help you build healthy one. All done using data analysis and some quality algorithms.

or months and even years together with an equivalent charge depending upon the battery. The protocols managing the node communication and networking for this reason should be rigorously thought-about. For future work in IoT, clustering would be accustomed to managing the power needed for the devices which represent the objects (Akkerman & Grunow, 2010).

The IoT advantages include new and advanced business opportunities with effectiveness and improved efficiency. In IoT open governance remains a major issue but there are certain levels and problems regarding security, privacy and governance that need to be considered.

Motivation

Getting the proper goods at the correct time and right place at a reduced cost is presently very important within the world market. Visibility is particularly vital in supply chain management of temperature and humidity for transportation and storage. It is of top priority to keep the standard and number of goods in the availability chain at specified levels. In case of transportation of food and medicines, the degrading quality of biodegradable foods and restricted lifespan of medicines contribute considerably to their management complexness. Properly controlled environments are required for biodegradable foods or medicines throughout the production, storage, transportation and sales processes to make sure proper food quality maintenance and cut back on major food losses. This is often referred as "Cold Chain Logistics".

The challenge of keeping perishable foods and pharmaceutical products that have diverse temperature and humidity requirements for storage and distribution environments is being addressed here. A controlled supply chain here senses the humidity and temperature parameter which refers to cold chain. The observation and management are important to maintain an unbroken and sustainable cold chain. To regulate and enhance the standard and safety potency within the cold chain logistics process the issue is taken up by the govt and enterprises and have called it a high priority discussion and crucial topic for analysis. Pharmaceutical merchandise has rigorous temperature and humidity necessities throughout the supply processes whereas in the Food business, the controlled environment varies among variety of food items. Even short amount of exposure like a couple of hours of extreme hot or cold temperatures and high or low humidity will cause a marked decrease in shelf life and loss of harvest. The supply chain is hence very crucial if quality of the merchandise is to be assured. Whereas for the medicine storage, a small variation within the humidity rate within the surroundings might produce bacteria and fungus formation. Real time data need to be communicated between the suppliers and customers to achieve controllability and visibility of each link in a cold chain. Here comes the image of WSNs which is the key element to confirm each and every product throughout its lifecycle visibility. Advanced modeling and analytics identification are the intelligent cold chains. The driver at the wheel and the monitoring staff will be assisted based on necessary safety guidelines. With the advanced choices in the action taken during imbalance of the environmental conditions, the decisions are taken in a sensible and economical way. Therefore, the need to control and monitor the environmental conditions is very crucial. IoT based Cold Chain Monitoring System, seeks to fill gaps involving location tracking and environment control by means of a GPS module and an IOT based sensor platform respectively (Mehta, Sahni, & Khanna, 2018). The sensor data is sent via Wi-Fi transmitter with receiving end involving the driver and the monitoring officer who will receive regular updates on the controlled environment parameters and the location of the transporting vehicle in real-time. The driver and the monitoring officer will have regular updates about the parameters. Automatic swift actions in cases of emergency scenarios are taken. The whole process is explained throughout the course of the book chapter.

Objective of the Product

The goal of this project is to reduce the extent of human presence all along the cold chain by means of a powerful tool in the form of IoT. The proposed idea seeks to fill gaps involving location tracking and environment control by means of a GPS module and an IOT based sensor platform respectively. Swift actions are also taken as per the requirements needed to maintain the exact environmental parameters so that the product/goods are not spoiled under uncontrolled environment conditions. Instead of using an alarm/buzzer to notify the concerned person, taking the precise action upon the condition is proven to be more effective.

Problem Statement

Technology invasion has remained crucial in the modern-day scenario of Logistics due to ever growing global presence and rising capital investments. The modern-day cold logistics companies cannot afford to slack in this ever so competitive market and so ensuring a well-managed and monitored supply chain is crucial throughout. With a rise in the number of immunizations drives and creation of new vaccines, the importance of the logistics behind their transportation cannot be stressed enough. The primary challenges faced are:

1. Increased product sensitivity, quality standards and the volume of goods involved.
2. Ever growing regulations.
3. Infrastructure gaps like location tracking issues and controlled environment monitoring all along the cold chain.

Chapter Outline

This book chapter is structured into 2 sections.

Section 1 discusses the design specifications for the system.
Section 2 discusses the IoT Development using Thinkspeak.

SECTION 1

Literature Survey

Over the last few years several techniques and ideas have been implemented for monitoring of cold chain logistics. This chapter provides content and information of previous research papers, which lays the foundation and basis for further work.

IOT is a network framework consisting of various connected real-world objects, which depend on sensors, communication, networking, and information processing technologies. The technology for IOT is RFID. It works by allowing microchips to transfer identifying data to the reader via wireless medium. Using RFID, any person can analyze, trace, and monitor the objects connected with RFID tags. The basic fundamental technology being WSNs, mainly works on intelligent sensors for sensing and monitoring. RFID finds its application in transportation of goods to consumers, production of pharmaceutical goods, retail and applies to traffic, healthcare and industrial monitoring. The advancement in both the technologies accelerate the growth of IoT (Mehta, Sahni, & Khanna, 2018). Cold Chain is the logistics system that provides to the perishable goods from the point of source to the point of consumption through thermal and refrigerated packaging methods and logistical planning to protect the quality and increase the shelf life of these shipments. A Cold Chain is a temperature-controlled supply chain, which involves temperature, and moisture controlled transportation and storage of refrigerated and frozen goods (Chen, Wang, & Jan, 2014).

Temperature is the most often measured parameters because of its critical impact on the quality of food, drugs, volatile chemicals goods transportation and logistics operations. The conventional temperature data loggers are often expensive and have very bulky form. The biggest problem is with their excessive thickness, because in packaging everything thicker than 5 mm is exposed to hazardous situations involving tearing down. High interest has been therefore raised in cost effective, thin and lightweight temperature monitoring smart tags (Pereira, 2018).

Public health care in developing countries are facing poor access to pharmaceutical care and this specific group of population are suffering from "Pharmacy tourism". ePharmacyNet was designed and implemented to meet the challenges caused by the "Pharmacy Tourism". Pharmacies at care units and pharmacies from private health sector are selected to be part of a multidisciplinary remote care system use ePharmacyNet to provide medicine and other pharmaceutical products to remote patients. The question arising here is how to deliver cost effective, secure and safe pharmaceutical products in countries where road-rail networks are in a poor state (Edoh, 2017).

The rise of the IoT paradigm is bringing with it new challenges concerning security and trust. The challenges discussed here are inherent in trust that overcomes for IoT scenarios and have introduced a framework to be used by developers to include trust concerns in IoT systems. The framework proposed here aims to assist developers when adding trust or reputation in IoT systems. Instead of having to implement each trust model from scratch, the framework facilitates the work of the developers by providing them with techniques and guidance for re-using common features of other trust models and following certain steps to carry out the implementation. In developing a framework where different trust management systems for the IoT are present, different aspects of identity management need to be considered. It is particularly crucial to properly define the identity of the 'things'. Their identity could be determined by their context (the set of things that are connected with the user for a specific purpose at a given moment in time) (Fernandez-Gago, Movano, & Lopez, 2017).

The FDA (Food and Drug Administration) and Agriculture Department within the early Nineteen Nineties had started to convey the HACCP rules (Hazard Analysis Critical Control Point) as a scientific stepping stone to safety of food. The pharmaceutical and the food trade industry have adopted identical principle. Both are presently dealing and managing with products which are sensitive to temperature. This system addresses the numerous product safety circumstances coming across. The distribution and handling of the finished product is the foremost necessary concern between them. HACCP has now become an accepted standard and universally recognized for the safety of products. The WHO standards program has adopted HACCP management system. Precautions ought to be taken at each purpose within the cold chain to make sure that the stability of the products are not affected by the any external conditions. A proof of compliance with suggested storage conditions as records of essential temperature and humidity parameters is produced. According to Salin and Nayga (Tennermann, 2012) there are several transnational eating house corporations like Burger King, McDonalds and KFC etc. The technical challenges faced in tight target markets with strict specs and exclusive offer chains are managed in these corporations, whereas the smaller corporations use ample networks to provide foreign frozen potatoes. The added worth within the supply chain and the present net value of the activities will have to be discomposed with the changes in time, temperature and distance within the chain. A thorough investigation performed the perturbation analyses. A steadiness in cold chains is necessary to assure a proper cold chain management. The time delays such as lead times and a few alternative delays will change the behavior of the supply chain.

Cold chain is a process of maintaining medication such as insulin and vaccines with-in counseled temperatures principally between 2°C to 8°C throughout the provision chain. In the pharmaceutical sector, the cold chain is concerned with the transportation, storage, and handling of pharmaceutical merchandise in very safe surrounding environment from the manufacturer end to the user end. Temperatures outside counseled temperature ranges might cut-back efficiency resulting in reduced immunity. Control of storage and transportation temperature is essential in maintaining. At the global perspective, procurement is defined as the procurance of goods, acquisition of services or works from an outdoor external source at the most effective potential price to satisfy the needs of the buyer in terms of the standard of medicines and in serving to shield the patients from sub-standard or ineffective medicines that will result from inadequate management. Lack of awareness by distributors within the management of storage and transportation temperatures will have a serious impact on quality of the goods. A survey by Agyekum (2012), conducted in Ghana, Kenya and Uganda indicates that an average of sixteen percent of the sampled facilities were not compliant to the guidelines laid out by regulatory authorities and fifty percent of these facilities had temperatures 4°c or more outside the recommended temperatures. For example, only four per cent of facilities stored vaccines in cold boxes, while the remainder used refrigerators and storage outside the recommended range. Though significant variation was observed between the countries; twenty six percent, sixteen percent, and eight percent for Ghana, Kenya, and Uganda, respectively there remains significant room to improve cold chain supply in these countries among others in Africa. In a comparison of African countries based on their cold supply chains, it was found that Ghana had developed its supply systems. It is now capable to maintain cold chain for items which are sensitive to temperature than Kenya and Uganda in spite of facing similar challenges (World Health Organization, 2010). The Ghana's regulative authorities were ready to develop validation strategies and guidelines. The aim of providing temperature assurance throughout the produce storage with transportation and delivery of cold chain items within the cold chain is the described cold chain delivery system in Ghana. There are concerned activities that provide cold chain management for foodstuff which source to food security, contract farming, and management of danger, resource and development, on-the-spot trials, coaching and education and project management (Stilmant, 2013). The various management resources were mentioned here which are utmost important while maintaining a good logistics system.

The cold chain management suggests that the combined management of food safety and transportation (Cold chain management). The individuals first judge the full cold chain then organize its transportation. The sourcing ought to be checked to confirm the food security so to contract the farming to debate the detail of contract (Food and Drug Administration, 2018). The danger involved in management is a concern just like the safety and quality of food and whether the source could also be contamination and correctly packed and handled.

Technology invasion has remained crucial in the modern-day scenario of Logistics due to ever growing global presence and rising capital investments. The modern-day cold logistics companies cannot afford to slack in this ever so competitive market and so ensuring a well-managed and monitored supply chain is crucial throughout. With a rise in the number of immunizations drives and creation of new vaccines, the importance of the logistics behind their transportation cannot be stressed enough (Domingo, 2012). The materialistic world objects are bonded with IoT with the help of internet which offers the pliability to simply manage and monitor the them. The cultural, business, social, environmental, etc. along with the environment on multiple levels have been approached with a new perception which brings about this body. The WSNs brings into picture the sensing element which is rising in IoT (Atzori, 2005).

The technological advancement of IoT has led to the rise in the quantity of physical objects being linked to the internet. The two primary entities that allow this technology to flourish are the Sensing entity that senses or collects data and the Cloud Service that plays itself as the host to the data collected (Khemapech, 2005). This meant that there was a rise in combination of wireless sensors and cloud computing strategies. IOT Analytics has emerged as a lifeline to the cold chain logistics industry due to the fact that companies have to rely on third parties (third party logistics) to self-report on performance (Hart & Martinez, 2006). Deployment of a wide array of sensors in storage locations, shipping containers and trucks is crucial in order to monitor the temperature and humidity parameters in Real Time and thereby also ensure that quick and efficient action can be taken in cases of emergencies. Thus, the IOT has offered scope to not just monitor the crucial parameters real time but also aid in preventative and remedial actions if needed through quick intimation (Peng, 2009).

A peak into AVR controller implementation, a system is developed to monitor and humidity of cold chain logistic consisting of Arduino WSN system with Xively sensor cloud service provider (Avitesh, 2017) is discussed briefly. Arduino libraries and hardware designs for connecting to the internet were integrated here. The sensor cloud service provider used here is a paid service provider whose services can be easily availed on yearly payment basis. Email service alert is also mentioned. But this system does not deal with the saving of power and faster processing issues coming across while monitoring.

Testing wireless sensing element motes primarily based within the ZigBee protocol throughout a real cargo is mentioned (Luis & Ruiz-Garcia, 2010). Information regarding water loss and condensation on the merchandise throughout shipments is concisely tested here. These motes offer data regarding temperature and humidity in a very closed container. The motes utilize the RF power isn't robust which is enough to travel along the pallets owing to the content having large amount of water of the merchandise transported. There is higher energy consumption by the readying of higher range of motes that use RF power. As well there is no mention of testing in deep trouble long run conditions.

A monitoring system using a with ZigBee WSN and GPS positioning, according to the characteristics of cold chain logistics is discussed (Mei & Wu, 2015). ZigBee has a disadvantage over WiFi. ZigBee is not secure based system. It is prone to attack from unauthorized people. Replacement cost will be high when any problem occurs in ZigBee compliant appliances and the coverage is limited. The disadvantage of this system is it requires very long battery life. An unsecure network is also a drawback.

The importance of temperature monitoring in perishable articles has been discussed (Aung & Chang, 2014). A sample dataset is included of products that have different temperatures ranging from 0 degree Celsius to 21 degrees Celsius. Methods to improve temperature control are presented and investigated to manage the cold storage of multi-temperature commodities. The author here has given light upon the Multi-commodity cold stores and mentioned the rapid growth of food delivery multi-temperature trailers, particularly for freelance grocery stores and fast food. Three methods were proposed which are used as a tool for decision making associated with cold chain logistics of perishable foods. The storage and transport facilities for a temperature-controlled supply chain require transporting a product which is temperature-sensitive from the producer to the end user. However, this provides chain management was found to be quite advanced, coping with food merchandise having completely different temperatures.

A proposed model to make a system, using IoT, which senses the room temperature and sends this data to an online cloud (Thinkspeak) for further analysis in a graphical form using API keys is presented (Mali, & Akshay, 2016). Here only the temperature is measured and tested in a room. This application can be used either for home automation, lab monitoring, etc. Humidity is not monitored and there is no mention of remedies to be taken when there is an uncontrolled environment condition in the room.

Proposed System Level Description

The System Block Diagram of IoT based Cold Chain Logistics Monitoring is as shown in Figure 2.

Figure 2 consists of components such as Humidity sensor (HSM-20G), Temperature sensor (LM35) and GPS (QUESTAR TTL) given at the input side of the microcontroller whereas 16*2 LCD and ESP8266

Figure 2. System Block Diagram

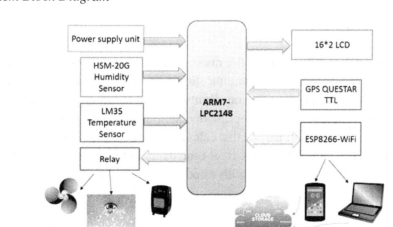

Wi-Fi module is given at the output side. The microcontroller used here is ARM7/TDMI (LPC2148). Relay circuit is connected to the devices depending upon requirement such as fan, sprinkler and heater. A Smartphone/Laptop (with TCP/IP client app) is used for real-time data acquisition.

1. Workflow of the Monitoring System

Every package should have distinctive tag name or number to spot the goods being transported which may be registered with the monitoring staff. Within the truck, the designed system consists of Temperature and Humidity Sensors installed at multiple places. Each system installed is termed as a node. Multiple nodes within the truck yield an additional sturdy observation because it can cater for various Temperature and Humidity points within the section. The monitoring officer at the specified monitoring centres or the driver at the wheel can read the information which can either be a laptop, computer, smartphone or a tablet. The block diagram can be explained in this manner by considering Figure 2, initially sensors in the nodes are going to sense the surrounding temperature and humidity. These sensors then feed the analog value to the ADC which is present in LPC2148 microcontroller. The ADC is approximation type ADC which converts analog value to digital values. The ADC values are set to specific limit depending on the environmental conditions, either displaying High/Low/Normal Temperature and High/Low/Normal Humidity Concentration. The respective action is taken on the sensed values by switching ON the fan for High Temperature or by simply switching ON the sprinkler for Low Humidity by the command given by the microcontroller.

2. IoT Implementation

The nodes embrace a WiFi Module that permits to constantly send Temperature and Humidity values to the monitoring centres or driver at the wheel can read the information which can either be a laptop, computer, smartphone or a tablet in real-time. The information gathered from the nodes at the centre or in the hand-held device(s) is transferred to the sensor cloud alongside with the location obtained from the GPS. The inventory information that is ready are sent to the respective personnel with the assistance of the TCP/IP client app within the Smartphone and using the ESP-link firmware in Laptop. The data input values from the sensor nodes given to the controller is stored as a CSV format in the server. Concurrently, the data is sent from server to client side on thingspeak.com portal using HTTP protocol.

3. Proposed System Safety

ESP-link firmware is employed that connects the micro-controller to the net using an ESP8266 WiFi module. The ESP-link's role is to facilitate communication over wireless local area network. It's doable to visualize the respective real-time data on-line. Humidity and Temperature position of the motion truck is unbroken in track to keep up with the optimum conditions needed. The location information is employed to find and trace the transport facility that calculates the coordinates by GPS. This ensures the protection of the commodities within the truck. Real-time data plotted in the graph can be observed to keep in track of the temperature and humidity with respect to the date and time of the truck.

Figure 3. Architectural Block Diagram

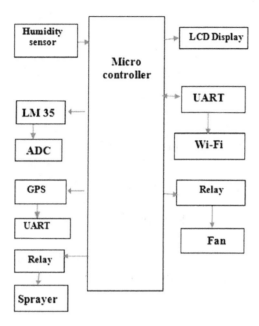

System Requirements

The aim of this project is to implement an ARM7 based Cold Chain Logistics System using the IoT platform. The system is used to monitor the temperature and humidity through the controller. The GPS location with Real-time data readings is captured in a smartphone/laptop with the help of the WiFi module. The complete overview of our architecture is defined in the diagram shown in Figure 3. In the proposed system 32-bit microcontroller (LPC2148 from NXP) is used.

Both the hardware and software specification requirements are very necessary before any development of a system. The following specifications will be explained. Based on this, the respective requirements are needed to design the system.

Table 2. Hardware specification table

Hardware	Specification
ARM7	60 MHz, v=3.3v, max 100mA capacity
RS232 USB to UART	Data rate=115.2 kbps
LM35	-55 to 150 Celsius, 60uA
HSM-20G	20-95% RH, max 2mA
LCD	16 char x 2 lines, max 3mA
GPS QUESTER TTL	3.3v, max 60-40mA
ESP8266-12E	3.6v, 2.4-2.5GHz Frequency Range, 3 power modes
RELAY FOR CONNECTED DEVICES	12v to 240v devices
ADAPTER FOR POWER SUPPLY	12v

1. Hardware Requirements

The availability of the specific part numbers in hardware and Keil IDE µvision4.0 are the ideal requirements needed for the project. Flash Magic tool in software and USB to Serial Converter for dumping the code in microcontroller is a part of hardware is used.

2. Software Requirements

The project is designed with the software module using Embedded C language and unit integration testing done with independent modules. All the initialization and operation of ADC, UART, LCD, WiFi are done by using Embedded C. IDE tool used for this software design is Keil IDE µvision4.0.

3. Specification Matching With the Proposed System

As observed the use of specified requirements mentioned in Table 2 must be matched with the proposed system. The following components are described briefly depending upon their application in the system.

a. Power Supply

The provision of electrical power is through power supply. It is a device that gives electrical energy to output load(s). This is termed as power supply unit or PSU. A 230V, 50Hz Single phase AC power supply is given to a transformer to urge 12V supply. By employing a Bridge Rectifier this voltage is regenerated to DC voltage. The capacitor filters the DC voltage and gives to LM7805 voltage regulator. This gives the constant 5V supply which further provides it to all parts within the circuit which require maximum 5V to power up the device. To make sure the power is in ON state an LED is provided for indication purpose.

b. LPC 2148

In the proposed system ARM7 TDMI-S CPU based LPC2148 microcontroller board is used. Flash memory ranges from 32 kB to 512 kB (Datasheet of ARM 7[LPC2148]. The crystal oscillator frequency is 12MHz and has 32-bit code execution. It is a "Low Power Low-Cost microcontroller".

LPC2148 is a 32-bit microcontroller manufactured by Philips semiconductors (NXP). It is very small in size as compared to other ARM controllers. Its power utilization is the lowest among other controllers. Miniaturization is a key requirement nowadays. In this case, LPC2148 based ARM7 Controller is the

Table 3. Software requirements table

Software	Requirements
IDE	Keil µvision v4
Flash Magic tool for programming	LPC2000 Flash Magic
TCP/IP client App	From Sollae systems v1.1 for Android
ESP-link firmware	Jeelabs v2.2.3

Figure 4. Power supply unit

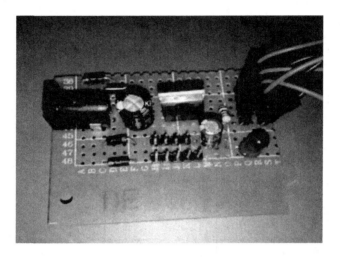

Figure 5. LPC 2148 Board

best fit. By disabling the peripheral functions and by peripheral clock scaling, it is possible to handle power optimization feature in this controller.

All industry level applications use ARM controllers. From the above comparison table, it can be observed that, power consumption is very low in ARM as compared to other controllers. Each pin in LPC2148 consumes only 3.3v and has maximum capacity of 100mA. This is best suitable industrial controller; the required remedial active devices or additional sensors can be used without worrying about huge power consumption as compared to other controllers.

c. ADC Conversion in LPC2148

For the microcontroller to process the signal/voltage and make it human readable, ADC is required which converts the analog signal into its counterpart digital number. The resolution indicates the number of digital values in ADC. A 10-bit ADC is present in LPC2148. The maximum value will be 2 raised to 10 which is equal to 1024. The digital numbers lie between 0-1024. The ADC in this controller is a 10-bit successive approximation ADC. There are two ADCs in LPC2148, namely ADC0 and ADC1 having 6-channels between AD0.1 to AD0.6 and 8-channels between AD1.0 to AD1.7 respectively. The 4.5

Table 4. Differences between different microcontrollers

Features	8051	PIC	AVR	ARM
Bus Width	8-bit	8/16/32-bit	8/32-bit	32/64-bit
Communication Protocols	UART, USART, SPI, I2C	PIC, UART, UASART, LIN, CAN, Ethernet, SPI, I2C	UART, USART, SPI, I2C,	UART, USART, LIN, I2C, SPI, CAN, USB, Ethernet, I2C, DSP, SAI (serial audio interface) IrDA
Speed	12 Clock/Instruction cycle	4 Clock/Instruction cycle	1 Clock/Instruction cycle	1 Clock/Instruction cycle
Memory	ROM, SRAM, FLASH	SRAM, FLASH	Flash, SRAM, EEPROM	Flash, SDRAM, EEPROM
ISA (Instruction Set Architecture)	CLSC	Some feature of RISC	RISC	RISC
Memory Architecture	Von Neumann architecture	Harvard Architecture	Modified	Modified Harvard architecture
Power consumption	Average	Low	Low	Low
Cost (as compared to features provide)	Very Low	Average	Average	Low
Other features	Known for its standard	Cheap	Cheap, effective	High speed operation Vast

MHz is the max operating freq. which divides the conversion time. The ADC related channel pins used in the proposed system is AD0.1 which is the pin P0.28 for LM35 and AD0.2 which is pin P0.29 for HSM-20G; both present in the 6-channel ADC port 0.

d. LCD Module (16*2 Character)

An LCD is an electronic display module. LCDs are better than 7-segment displays which consume huge power. They are economical and easily programmable. Command and Data are the registers present in LCD. There are three control signals namely, register select, read/write, enable and eight address/data pins, command register is an9instruction given to the LCD. A pre-defined task is done by the LCD by the command instruction. Data is stored by the data register which is to be displayed on the LCD. The pins P0.15 to P0.21 from LPC2148 are connected to the pins of LCD module. Figure 6 is the LCD module used in the project.

e. LM35: Temperature Sensor

The LM35 is calibrated in Kelvin. This is considered one of the most advantageous over other temperature sensors. There is no requirement of subtraction of a large constant voltage to obtain centigrade scaling. The LM35 provides typical accuracies of one-fourth degree Celsius at room temperature and about three-fourth degree Celsius. The temperature ranges between −55°C to 150°C (National Semiconductor, 2000).

LM35 temperature sensor is used in the proposed system as seen in Figure 8. It has precise inherent calibration, low output impedance and a linear. Readout is very easy in LM35. The device is used with

Figure 6. LCD Module

Figure 7. LM35

single power supply between 2.7v and 5.5v. Only 60 μA from the supply is drawn because of its self-heating capacity is low in still air.

In LM35, the output voltage is 10mV per degree centigrade. LM35 is precise and work under many environmental conditions. This proves it to be consistent between sensors and readings. They are also very inexpensive and quite easy to use. Supply voltage of 3.3v is given from the controller to the sensor and grounded accordingly. The Vout (output pin) of LM35 is connected to ADC pin AD0.1.

Figure 8. Temperature sensor

- **LM358 – Low Power Dual Amplifier:** It is a low power OPAMP IC which can amplify low level signals to readable high levels. It works on 5V supply and can give a maximum. saturated output of ~4V. It has a very low supply current drain of approximately 500 μA. It is fundamentally independent of supply voltage. Connect Pin8 to 5 V rail and Pin4 to ground rail. Connect 10kOhms variable POT pin to pin 1 and any fixed pin to pin 2 of LM358 op-amp. By setting the position of the variable by turning the pot, the temperature in the truck/room can be sensed accordingly.

f. HSM-20G: Humidity Sensor

HSM-20G is a humidity sensor which can sense, measure and report the moisture and air temperature jointly. Relative humidity (RH) is the proportion of moisture content in the air to the amount of moisture which is higher in content at a distinct temperature of air. The HSM-20G used in the proposed model is an analog humidity as well as senses temperature which gives voltage which is analog with output with respect to relative humidity and temperature (Department of Atmospheric Sciences, 2010). The Storage range is from -20°C to 70°C and the Operating range is from 0°C to 50°C. As compared to other humidity sensors, HSM-20G is one of the most used operating sensors. This sensor is used for weather forecasting. The Storage RH Range is about 0-99% RH and the Operating RH range is between 20-95% and only about 2mA of operating current, which is the required specification met for the system. The 3 basic kinds of humidity sensors are Resistive, Thermal and Capacitive sensors. A Capacitive humidity sensor is used here. A thin strip of metal oxide (whose electrical capacity changes with atmosphere's RH) is placed to measure the RH between the two electrodes. The H-out of the Humidity sensor is connected to ADC pin AD0.2. Max operating current is 2mA, hence this module consumes less current.

- **LMV324 – Single, Dual, Quad Low-Voltage, Rail-to-Rail Operational Amplifiers:** This is a cost−effective solution for the developed system application. This amplifier uses lower power consumption and saves the package space. This amplifier covers covering different voltage ranges. It includes many combinations of power consumption and gain bandwidth. Industrial temperature Range is from −40°C to +85°C. Operates from 2.7 V to 5.0 V as a Single−Sided Power Supply. Maximum input current is 10mA. Best performance for appropriate accuracy is gained from this amplifier. It requires very low supply voltage range (Texas Instruments, 2014).

Figure 9. LM358 with schematics

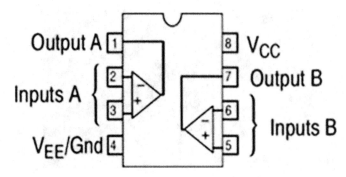

Figure 10. Humidity Sensor (Front view)

Figure 11. Humidity Sensor (Back view)

g. GPS QUESTAR TTL

The GPS QUESTAR TTL is a compact all-in-one GPS module solution used to locate the exact location of the object using the help of satellite it uses the 3D parameter i.e. the longitude, latitude, and attitude of the object and hence gives the position of the object. In areas having limited sky this GPS offers good navigation. Maximum. supply of 3.3v to 5.0v is supported which is perfect power saving module for the system. Operating temperature is from -30 °C to 80 °C. Supports lower power consumption of about 55mA at acquisition and 40mA while tracking which makes it an ideal power saving device. It has a built in RTC and EEPROM for accurate timings and storage (Datasheet of GPS QUESTAR TTL]. The UART1 pin RX1 of LPC2148 is connected to UART pin TX pin of the GPS module. Here only transmitting the coordinate values to the controller be read in the LCD. The 5V supply and ground from controller is given to GPS pins respectively.

Figure 12. GPS Module

h. USB-UART

USB-UART is a hardware device used for asynchronous serial communication. Serial data is sent from transmitter to receiver. 115200bits per second (bps) is the maximum speed of UART, here in the system baud rate of 9600 bps is used. The signal is transmitted in the form of data packets or chunks and are called as transmission characters. Each data packet consists of start bit, parity, and stop bit. Data packet is transmitted to the output serially bit by bit from Transmit (TX) and Receive (Rx) pin. MAX232 transceiver IC is present on a board where the RS232 serial port is connected to TTL converter module which is a board. Serial communication between both the ports becomes easier by allowing the required electrical signal conversion. Here is used 4 header pins with jumper cables at one end and DB9 connector is soldered at the opposite end. The microcontroller is connected to converter module through jumper cables. The DB9 connects directly to a COM port of the PC. Used to dump the code to the controller from PC/Laptop. Figure 13 shows the usage of USB-UART device in displaying name on 16*2 LCD.

i. WiFi Module - ESP8266

It is a low-cost Wi-Fi chip with a microcontroller unit and an enabled TCP/IP stack. Its range is upto 2.4 GHz. ESP series modules use lower power. It has 11 GPIO pins and a single ADC converter (ADC) present is with a 10-bit resolution. The WiFi Module used in the system for easy access of real time data is shown in Figure 14.

Figure 13. USB-UART module

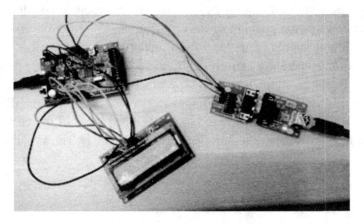

Figure 14. ESP8266 – AI THINKER

- **Why ESP8266?** The following points specifies the reasons:
  - It has good storage capabilities and processing in the board itself.
  - Permits to be integrated with application specific devices and sensors.
  - The GPIOs present have minimal loading during runtime, development is up-front.
  - Have minimal external circuitry which is designed to occupy minimal PCB area.
  - A larger server, which responded to multiple requests.
  - It offers low-level control and a very large programming memory space.
  - It executes faster and uses less resources.
  - The board is given 5v and the terminals of power connector is given to the regulator to have 3.3v resulting in minimal power requirement.
  - As per the survey and usage, a 2.4 GHz is considered better choice over 5 GHz depending upon its wireless range. 5 GHz range has limited support by devices and is of higher cost.
- What are the issues faced with ESP8266?
  - Challenges faced:
    - Endless reset on power-up
    - Power drain issues
  - Preventive measures taken:
    - Sufficient current was given. The current requirements for other components were also considered aside from the 300mA peak current needs of ESP8266. Normally, a regulated 3.3V source of at least 500ma is essential.
    - Connections were rechecked.
    - Clearing the memory. The code gets stuck somewhere in the loop and hence never returns resulting in a watchdog timer reset. Memory can be cleared by flashing the blank. bin file which comes with the nodemcu flash programmer.
    - The module needs to flash AT command set. It should respond to the "AT" command with "OK". This is the hello world for the device.
    - It can easily configure deep-sleep mode which lets the module run for 3 years on two AA batteries to rectify the power issues. The antenna is a track on the PCB which delivers good results for Wi-Fi sensitivity.

Table 5. Power consumption modes of ESP8266

Parameters	Power Consumption
Modem Sleep	15 mA
Light Sleep	0.9 mA
Deep Sleep	10 mA

ESP8266 draws almost 1 Amp of power which is very huge, but the transmission capability is from 500 meters to about few miles which is very large horsepower for such low-cost device which is in hundreds. As shown in the table above, a solution for power saving can still be rectified to an extent by using the power modes available in the module. The Wi-Fi Modem circuit shuts down to save power but requires the CPU to work in the Modem-sleep mode power mode. This is implemented with no data transmission with secure Wi-Fi connection. To maintain a 300ms of sleep time, about 15mA is the current rating. For example, in a Wi-Fi switch, the Light-sleep power mode is suspended. Without the data transmission, Wi-Fi modem circuit can be turned off and CPU is suspended to save power. To maintain a sleep of 300ms the current is 0.9mA. For Wi-Fi connection in Deep-Sleep mode is not required to be sustained. As in system developed, the temperature and humidity sensor sense the temperature and humidity at every 100s, then sleep for 300s and wakes up to connect to the Access Portal which takes about 0.3 to 1second. The total average current will come down to less than 1mA. Deep sleep is for long time between data transmission. As for the mobility of operation, with the help of a LiPo connector it can be battery operated from any PC also very useful for IoT devices which can be further enhanced in the system.

- **TCP/IP Client App for Smartphone/Tablet:** The main protocols of the IP (Internet Protocol) suite is the TCP (Transmission Control Protocol. TCP complements the IP. Hence, the TCP/IP refers to the entire suite (Fairhurst, 2003). World Wide Web, remote administration, email, and file transfer depend on TCP which are the major internet applications. By using TCP/IP communication, transmitting and receiving data after accessing specific server is allowed. The App shown in Figure 15 is used in the application.
- **What Is ESP-Link?** It is a WiFi Serial Bridge which is transparent. This is useful for inputting or debugging into a microcontroller. Communication over WiFi is done by ESP-link. The ESP-link connects TCP/UDP sockets through to the attached microcontroller. It applies most of the higher-level functionality to offload the attached microcontroller because the latter has much less flash and memory than ESP-link.
- **Role of ESP-Link in Proposed System:** The ESP-link is a platform for independent applications and supports the connected temperature and humidity sensors directly to it. The WiFi is configured for the ESP-link for the network needed. After attaching the microcontroller to ESP8266 module via a serial port the program can be uploaded. All the controller details are fed into as shown in the Figure 16. The microcontroller can use REST and MQTT which are the forthcoming functionalities requests to services. One of the online free service namely, thingspeak.com which is a sensor cloud uses the sensor values. These values get stored, then the data obtained is plotted in a graph. This can be part of the future work when the functionalities are available in the firmware. RX of ESP8266 is connected to TX of the controller and visa-versa for unit testing.

Figure 15. TCP/IP Client App

Figure 16. Configuring for ESP-link

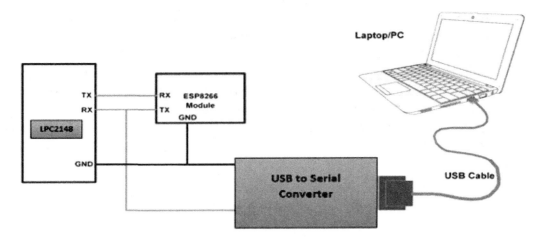

j. Other Requirements to Be Considered

- **System Maintenance and Placement During Transportation:** The proposed active system is used in a dedicated portable container of the vehicle. The nodes with the designed system in the containers are powered by on-board batteries such as the LiPo batteries which can be used to an extend of 10-12 hours per day. An external electrical power source from the vehicle can also be used to run the fans and sprinklers or if required, heaters. The microcontroller controls the activation of the cooling or heating (if required) mechanism and circulating fans and sprinklers at distributed places which help to monitor and conserve the temperature and humidity levels within specified limits around the enclosed environment.

To support the operation of those specialized vehicles, it is essential for the proper infrastructure. To have a compatible electrical connection to power the system specifically at all regular drop-off points is needed, if not using any battery supply. Particularly when the smaller vehicles are used where the system designed unit is power-driven off the vehicle engine generator. In case of battery operated connections, the batteries must be replaced after every 10-12 hours depending upon requirement. During overnight stops, these settings are critically important. In instances wherever the system is power-driven exclusively by the vehicle's engine, the engine should stay running in the slightest degree at times to avoid interruptions in maintaining correct temperature and humidity. Hence, the vehicles are equipped with an integrated continuous temperature and humidity monitoring with real-time data monitoring system. In addition, data is retrievable by logging into any PC/Laptop/Tablet/Smartphone used by the monitoring staff. The proposed system should preferably be packed to the shipped products individually to keep track of the monitoring parameters as well as the GPS location of the product or can be placed inside the truck containing all the similar products.

Flowchart of the Proposed System

Once the specification requirements are met, the system needs to be designed as proposed. The flowchart of the proposed model is as shown in Figures 17-20.

The commodity/products need to be transported are placed in the truck and the system/nodes are physically fixed at areas where the parameters can be recorded whereas the devices such as Fan and Sprinkler are also placed appropriately at necessary places. The system or node when powered by the power supply unit first displays the respective tag name or number provided to it by the manufacturer. Initialization settings are done. Temperature and Humidity sensor begin their operation by converting the ADC values obtained to respective degrees Celsius and relative humidity in percentage by using required calculations. Parallelly, the GPS module and ESP8266 sets up their platform and starts initialization. The threshold ADC values for the sensors are set accordingly beforehand depending upon the type of logistic products being transported. Here a predefined set of values have been taken for demonstration as shown in Table 6.

Figure 17. Flowchart of the real-time display part

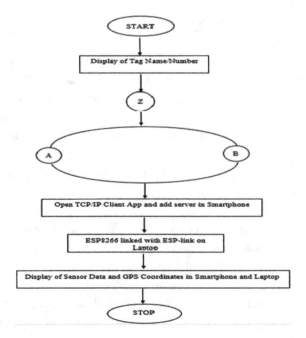

Figure 18. Flowchart of the data storage part

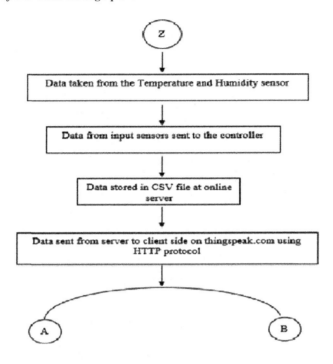

Figure 19. Flowchart of Humidity Sensor

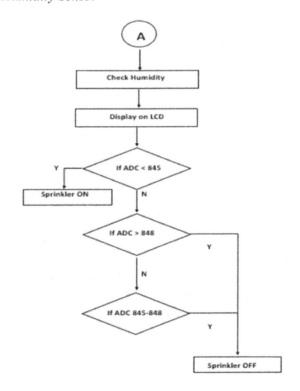

Figure 20. Flowchart of Temperature Sensor

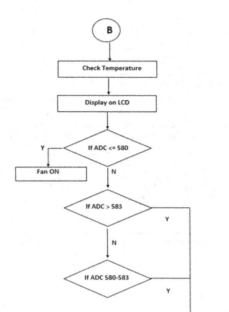

Table 6. Parameter values set for LM35 and HSM-20G

Parameter	Range	Value	Action Taken
Temperature	High Low Normal	ADC<=580 ADC>583 ADC 580-583	Turn ON Fan Turn OFF Fan Turn OFF Fan
Humidity	High Low Normal	ADC>848 ADC<845 ADC 845-848	Turn OFF Sprinkler Turn ON Sprinkler Turn OFF Sprinkler

According to Table 6, as per the set ADC values when the Temperature sensor (LM35) reads ADC value less than or equal to 580 the fan turns ON to set the environment to required temperature. When the temperature read is either less than 583 or between 580 and 583 the fan turns OFF by the command given by the controller. Simultaneously, when the ADC value read from the Humidity sensor (HSM-20G) is less than 845, this turns ON the Sprinkler which brings the humidity under control. When the relative humidity is either greater than or in between 845 to 848, the Sprinkler turns OFF. The ADC values of both are displayed in the 16x2 LCD. The system is designed to display the ADC values. These values can be adjusted as per the specific requirement. The ADC to degree Celsius values for temperature are done internally in the Embedded C program. Calculation of Relative Humidity (RH) formula is shown in equation (1) as shown,

Humidity (in %) = (ADC value * 100) / 1023 (1)

For example, an ADC value less than 522 (RH 51%) in a humid summer season results in significant reductions in allergen and mite levels for specific medications.

While the sensor operation is going on, the ESP8266 connection is set and GPS coordinates are calculated. The driver in the front wheel can keep track of the monitoring taking place with the help of the LCD display. With the help of the pre-installed app and preferred WiFi ESP_F086C selected in the smartphone/tablet a real-time data of the temperature and humidity values is monitored along with the action taken. The GPS coordinates is calculated, and the position is displayed on the app. Along with this facility the same can be seen on a PC by the monitoring officer, an online firmware called ESP-link which is a stand-alone application that support the connected sensors and GPS, displays the values on its console. By entering the IP address on the http bar of internet explorer/google chrome; by connecting to the ESP_F086C on a new page, the real-time data can be observed easily in the range of within few miles.

Results and Discussion

Results

Stepwise results obtained from the designed project is as follows:

Step 1: Turn on the Cold Chain Logistics System. The tag name is displayed.
Step 2: Temperature (LM35) and Humidity sensor(HSM-20G) will activate and sense the environmental conditions inside the truck respectively and the data is displayed on LCD.

The Figures 22 and 23 show the three ranges namely Normal, High and Low Temperatures and Low, High and Normal Humidity content for the Temperature and Humidity sensors respectively which are set according to decided ADC values. As per the products/commodities placed in the cold chain truck the values can be set.

Step 3: According to the Table 6, the test values set for High Temperature is when ADC is less than or equal to 580 and for Low Humidity is when ADC is less than 845. As per the proposed system, when temperature is high, fan turns on to reduce the heat developed in the atmosphere. When there is low humidity, sprinkler (denoted by a 10mm LED) turns on to bring the condition back to normal

Figure 21. Tag name(Title name) displayed on 16x2 LCD

Figure 22. Temperature range displayed on 16x2 LCD

Figure 23. Humidity range displayed on 16x2 LCD

humidity. This happens inside the container of the truck either on the move or stationary. In either condition, the changes can occur mostly due to the outside temperature and humidity imbalance. The following figures (Figure 24 and 25) shows the developed set-up.

Step 4: The set-up is done, readings are displayed on LCD and respective actions are taken accordingly. While displaying on LCD, real-time data readings are obtained on the smartphone/tablet by setting up the platform as follows. TCP/IP client is downloaded free from playstore for any android smartphone.

Step 5: In the PC/Laptop add and connect to ESP_F086BC connection available in the network and internet settings. For real-time data readings the IP address on PC/Laptop, the IP address of the Wireless LAN adapter Wi-Fi needs to be entered on the http bar. This will direct to the ESP-link Homepage. Click on the microcontroller console to check the real-time readings obtained. The IP address used in the proposed system is 198.168.4.2.

Figure 28 and 29 shows the home and microcontroller page console respectively in the ESP-link firmware displaying real-time values with GPS location, Sensor data and the respective action taken. This data can be obtained at the base station by the monitoring officer or can be monitored by the truck driver at the wheel.

Figure 24. System set-up with LM35 and HSM-20G

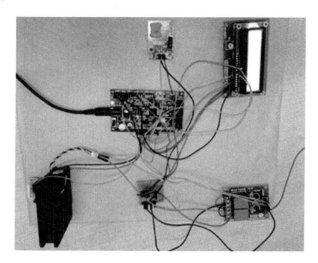

Figure 25. Complete set of proposed system model

The cold chain market in India is expected to reach INR 624 billion by the end of 2017 (Penumarthi, 2017). Cold Storage in the Indian Cold Chain Industries are the major revenue contributors. Our country's Cold Chain market is estimated to grow rapidly in the following years to come. For the cold chain infrastructure in the country to grow, private investments and favorable initiatives should be undertaken by the government on the account of rising food transportation demand.

1. **Challenges Faced:** If the solution proposed are not applied effectively this would lead to the reduction in the produce life which may affect the product nutrients to be affected.
    a. Cost involved in maintenance and monitoring. Inadequate knowledge and training of the staff in handling temperature and humidity sensitive products with the system installed is also a concerning factor.

Figure 26. TCP/IP Client App adding server and setting connection

Figure 27. Real-time readings on Smartphone

Figure 28. Home page on ESP-link

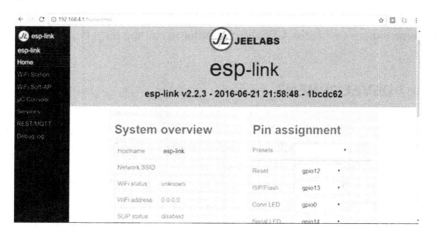

Figure 29. Microcontroller Console page on ESP-link

    b.   Issues with power back-ups and steady power supply is a longstanding problem pushes the capital investment requirement. Power issues with ESP8266 may come up during operation. Heating problem may also be faced.

    c.   The devices used here like the fan and sprinklers; continuous running or simultaneous ON/ OFF will put a huge load on the system control.

2.   Advantages of proposed system:

    a.   Wireless operated via WIFI and be installed or made detachable system as required and light weight. Battery powered lasting up to 10-12hrs per day depending on conditions. Can be re-used as necessary.

    b.   Temperature accuracy of about one-fourth degree Celsius at room temperature and three-fourth degree Celsius over the temperature ranges between −55°C to 150°C. The temperature accuracy is from positive to negative values of degree Celsius. Humidity operating RH range is between20-95%.

c.   Real time reports of location, temperature and humidity with respective action taken notification on display.

d.   Maximum capacity of 100mA by the controller to run the proposed system.

SECTION 2: IoT DEVELOPMENT

This IoT based temperature and humidity monitoring system is developed using powerful development platform ARM 7 board. This board is helpful to minimize the system hardware. This system uses Temperature (LM-35) and Humidity Sensor (HNM-20G). All these sensors are interfaced with GPIO header of ARM7 board. To get real time monitoring of data from sensors ESP8266 WiFi Module is used.

In literature, there are showcased communication using either ZigBee WSN or and BLE module where both lack security and have less frequency range compared to WiFi. The microcontroller uses the REST and MQTT functionality request for services. REST (Representational State Transfer protocol) is a scalable architecture that allows things to communicate over Hyper Text Transfer Protocol and is easily adaptable for IoT applications to provide a communication from things to a central web server. Here client is a web browser and application running on the computer or system is a server. HTTP (Hyper Text Transfer Protocol) is an application protocol used for data communication for the World Wide Web. It is the protocol which is used to exchange or transfer hypertext. HTTP functions as request-response protocol in the client-server computing model. In this system LPC2148 interfaced with the ESP8266 itself act as a server. HTTP request is sent by the client to the server. Then response message is sent by the server to the client. In the response completion status of request and requested content is sent. In that web technology such as HTTP was originally designed for human to machine communication and now utilized for machine to machine communication.

It is useful to use REST calls to update or retrieve data from a ThingSpeak channel and MQTT to update data to a ThingSpeak channel. TCP/IP client app downloaded from playstore keeps real-time values of sensors posted every 100ms.

REST (Representational State Transfer protocol) is a scalable architecture that allows things to communicate over Hyper Text Transfer Protocol and is easily adaptable for IoT applications to provide a communication from things to a central web server. Interoperability between computer systems on the internet is provided by the web services like REST or RESTful. Web service is a service offered via World Wide Web by an electronic device to another electronic device, communicating with each other.

On the system developed the WiFi module operates as a data acquisition mode and as a web server mode. It collects data from Temperature and Humidity sensor. This data is then sent to the client side using HTTP protocol. On client-side real-time data can be seen from anywhere in the world on thingspeak.com. Internet connection to the board is given by using LAN through ESP8266 module. Results on thingspeak.com are shown in graphical format. On this website one channel is created and all six fields are placed in this channel. Field 1 shows temperature, Field 2 shows humidity, Realtime data of the two fields are shown in the Figures 30 and 31.

Figure 30. Real-time Temperature monitoring in graph

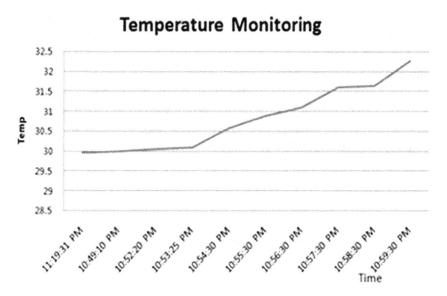

Figure 31. Real-time Humidity monitoring in graph

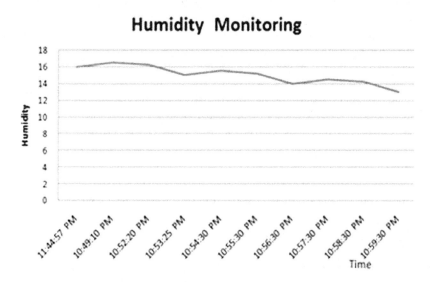

FUTURE RESEARCH DIRECTIONS

The system proposed here is Real-Time data communication received on Smartphone and PC. Data is displayed only when the device is running and not when it is switched off. By registering for a paid gateway service, data can be accessed whenever required by the monitoring officer at any part of the world. There are two on-board relays, one for Fan when encountered with high temperatures and other for Sprinklers when there is a condition of low humidity in the container. Similarly, few other sensors and devices can be added which can maintain the optimum conditions required for the commodities/

products. LEDs for indication purposes can be added such as Red LED for power on, Blue LED for breach in temperature (Fan turns on), Yellow LED for breach in humidity (Sprinkler turns on), Yellow LED for communications (On-going real-time data transfer). It can be wall mountable or placed as a tag on the commodity box in the truck.

Along with the existing features, vehicle speed/drive/idle time, fuel level efficiency and engine diagnostics can also be introduced for more precise monitoring. Alarms/buzzers can also be added for alerting the driver/officer in charge in-case of breakdown of the devices such as fan and sprinklers to receive faster and efficient service. Storage of the data can be done by external storage devices such as SD cards or EEPROMs to retrieve data log of months or years.

CONCLUSION

An Effective Cold Chain is a complete combination of three main elements which should ensure proper transport, storage and handling of the products/commodities being transported. They are namely, Trained Personal, Transport with Storage Equipment and Efficient management procedures are important to maintain cold chain logistics. The Cold Chain Logistics System within distribution centres generate wireless monitoring solution specifically for end to end cold chain protection. It is a complete cold chain standalone system whose data is monitored at distribution centres and by the driver at the wheel. It is automated temperature and humidity data collection which can run up to 10-12 hrs on battery which are replaceable. This system maintains product quality and company reputation. It reduces wastage. A greater involvement of railways and airports can also strengthen the cold chain infrastructure. There is a large scope of public partnerships in this sector. Some of the industries which use cold chain facilities are Fruits and vegetables, Floriculture, Meat and Fish products, Pharmaceutical products, Diary products, Ice cream sector and confectionaries.

REFERENCES

Akkerman, F., Farahani, P., & Grunow, M. (2010). Quality, safety and sustainability in food distribution: A review of quantitative operations management approaches and challenges. *OR-Spektrum, 32*(4), 863–904. doi:10.100700291-010-0223-2

Akulwar, K. (2016). *5 ways Internet of Things is helping logistics industry around the globe*. DreamOrbit. Retrieved from: http://dreamorbit.com/5-ways-internet-of-things-is-helping-logistics-industry-around-the-globe/

Atzori, L., Iera, A., & Morabito, G. (2005). The Internet of Things: A survey. *Journal of Computer Networks, 54*(15), 2787–2805. doi:10.1016/j.comnet.2010.05.010

Aung, M. M., & Chang, Y. S. (2014). Temperature Management for The Quality Assurance of a Perishable Food Supply Chain. *Journal of Food Control, 40*, 198–207. doi:10.1016/j.foodcont.2013.11.016

Avitesh, A. (2017). A Method of WSN and Sensor Cloud System to Monitor Cold Chain Logistics as Part of The IoT Technology. *International Journal of Multimedia and Ubiquitous Engineering, 9*(10), 145–152.

Blaisdell, R. (2018). *The risks of IoT. Rick's Cloud*. Retrieved from: https://rickscloud.com/the-risks-of-iot/

Chen, W., Wang, Y.-J., & Jan, J.-K. (2014). A novel deployment of smart cold chain system using 2G-RFID-Sys. *Journal of Food Engineering, 141*, 113–121. doi:10.1016/j.jfoodeng.2014.05.014

Department of Atmospheric Sciences. (2010). *Relative Humidity*. University of Illinois at Urbana-Champaign. Retrieved from: http://ww2010.atmos.uiuc.edu/%28Gh%29/guides/mtr/cld/dvlp/rh.rxml

Domingo, M. C. (2012). An overview of the Internet of Things for people with disabilities. *Journal of Network and Computer Applications, 35*(2), 584–596. doi:10.1016/j.jnca.2011.10.015

Edoh, T. (2017). Smart Medicine Transportation and Medication Monitoring System in EPharmacyNet. *2017 International Rural and Elderly Health Informatics Conference (IREHI)*, 1-9.

Fairhurst, G. (2003). *Transmission Control Protocol (TCP)*. Retrieved from: https://erg.abdn.ac.uk/users/gorry/course/inet-pages/tcp.html

Fernandez-Gago, M., Moyano, F., & Lopez, J. (2017). Modelling trust dynamics in the Internet of Things. *Information Sciences, 396*, 72–82. doi:10.1016/j.ins.2017.02.039

Food and Drug Administration. (2018). *Hazard Analysis Critical Control Point System (HACCP)*. Food and Drug Administration. Retrieved from http://www.who.int/foodsafety/fs_management/haccp/en/

Ganguli, S. (2016). *Worldwide IoT in Logistics Market: Drivers, Opportunities, Trends, and Forecasts*. Infoholic Research LLP. Retrieved from https://www.infoholicresearch.com/worldwide-iot-in-logistics-market-to-grow-at-a-cagr-of-35-5-over-the-period-2016-2022-to-aggregate-1050-95-billion-by-2022/

Hart & Martinez. (2006). Environmental Sensor Networks: A revolution in the earth system science. *Journal of Earth-Science Reviews, 78*(3), 177–191.

How the Internet of Things impacts the logistics business. (2018). Softweb Solutions. Retrieved from: https://www.softwebiot.com/iot-use-cases/how-iot-impacts-transportation-and-logistics-industry/

Instruments, T. (2014). *Single, Dual, and Quad General Purpose, Low-Voltage, Rail-to-Rail Output Operational Amplifiers. Datasheet of LMV321/358/324*. Texas Instruments.

Islam, M., Mukhopadhyay, S. C., & Suryadevara, N. K. (2017). Smart Sensors and Internet of Things: A Postgraduate Paper. *IEEE Sensors Journal, 17*(3), 577–584. doi:10.1109/JSEN.2016.2630124

Khemapech, I. (2005). *A Survey of Wireless Sensor Networks Technology. 6th Annual Postgraduate Symposium on the Convergence of Telecommunications, Networking and Broadcasting*, Liverpool, UK.

Mali, A. R. (2016). A novel approach for temperature sensing and monitoring through wireless sensor using IoT. *Journal of Engineering and Computer Science, 5*(12), 19657–19659.

Mehta, S., Sahni, J., & Khanna, K. (2018). Internet of Things: Vision, Applications and Challenges. *Procedia Computer Science, 132*, 1263–1269. doi:10.1016/j.procs.2018.05.042

National Semiconductor. (2000). *Precision Centigrade Temperature Sensors*. National Semiconductor.

Peng, J. (2009). Comparison of several cloud computing platforms. *Information Science and Engineering (ISISE), 2009 Second International Symposium on*, 23-27. 10.1109/ISISE.2009.94

Penumarthi, H. (2017). *Indian Cold Chain Industry – Challenges and Opportunities*. Food Marketing & Technology. Retrieved from http://fmtmagazine.in/indian-cold-chain-industry-challenges-opportunities/

Pereira, A., Bergeret, E., Benzaim, O., Routin, J., Haon, O., Tournon, L., ... Depres, G. (2018). Near-field communication tag development on a paper substrate—application to cold chain monitoring. *Flexible and Printed Electronics*, *3*(1), 014003. doi:10.1088/2058-8585/aaaeca

Ruiz-Garcia, L., Barreiro, P., Robla, J. I., & Lunadei, L. (2010). Testing ZigBee Motes for Monitoring Refrigerated Vegetable Transportation Under Real Conditions. *Journal of Sensors*, *10*(5), 4968–4982. doi:10.3390100504968 PMID:22399917

Shih, C.-W., & Wang, C.-H. (2016). Integrating wireless sensor networks with statistical quality control to develop a cold chain system in food industries. *Computer Standards & Interfaces*, *45*, 62–78. doi:10.1016/j.csi.2015.12.004

Stilmant. (2013). *Pharmaceutical Cold Chain*. Retrieved from http://www.coldchain.be/guidelines-and-regulations/some-history.html

Tennermann, J. (2012). *Cold Chain for Beginners*. Vaisala. Retrieved from https://www.rdmag.com/article/2012/06/cold-chain-beginners

Tools.ietf.org. (2018). *TCP Usage Guidance in the Internet of Things (IoT)*. Retrieved from: https://tools.ietf.org/id/draft-ietf-lwig-tcp-constrained-node-networks-01.html

Verma, R., & Srivastava, K. (2017). Middleware, Operating System and Wireless Sensor Networks for Internet of Things. *International Journal of Computers and Applications*, *167*(11), 11–17. doi:10.5120/ijca2017914356

World Health Organization. (2010). *WHO guide to good storage practices for pharmaceuticals. WHO Expert Committee on Specific cations for Pharmaceutical Preparations (WHO Technical Report Series, No. 920)*. World Health Organization.

Wu, M. M. (2015). The Design and Implementation of Food Cold Chain Monitoring System Based on ZigBee. *Journal of Applied Mechanics and Materials*, *751*, 281–286. doi:10.4028/www.scientific.net/AMM.751.281

ADDITIONAL READING

Dong, H. (2009). China's agricultural products Cold-chain logistics status, Problems and Solutions. *Journal of Ecological Economy*, *10*, 255–257.

Lei, Y., Cheng, L., Zhang, Z., Guosheng, L., & Jun, L. (2009). livestock product supply chain safety control studies based on RFID traceability system. *Zhongguo Xumu Zazhi*.

Liu, L., & Li, J. (2008). Summary of Development Pattern and Government Behavior of Cold Chain Logistics of Agricultural Products. *Journal of Food Science*, *29*(9), 680–683.

Singh, A., & Singh, G. (2016). Review on Temperature & Humidity Sensing using IoT. *International Journal of Advanced Research in Computer Science and Software Engineering*, *6*(2).

KEY TERMS AND DEFINITIONS

AVR: Is a family of microcontrollers developed by Atmel beginning in 1996.

GPS: The global positioning system enables to locate the latitude and longitude coordinates of the location.

HACCP: Is a management system in which food safety is addressed through the analysis and control of biological, chemical, and physical hazards from raw material production, procurement and handling, to manufacturing, distribution, and consumption of the finished product.

HTTP: The hypertext transfer protocol (HTTP) is an application protocol for distributed, collaborative, and hypermedia information systems. HTTP is the foundation of data communication for the world wide web.

IDE: An integrated development environment is a software application that provides comprehensive facilities to computer programmers for software development.

TCP/IP: The transmission control protocol/internet protocol is a suite of communication protocols used to interconnect network devices on the internet.

ZigBee: Is newly developed technology that works on IEEE standard 802.15.4, which can be used in the wireless sensor network (WSN).

Chapter 8

Learning-Aided IoT Set-Up for Home Surveillance Applications

Jutika Borah
Gauhati University, India

Kandarpa Kumar Sarma
Gauhati University, India

Pulak Jyoti Gohain
Gauhati University, India

ABSTRACT

Of late, home surveillance systems have been enhanced considerably by resorting to increased use of automated systems. The automation aspect has reduced human intervention and made such systems reliable and efficient. With the proliferation of wireless devices, networking among the connected devices is leading to the formation of internet of things (IoT). This has made it essential that home surveillance systems be also automate using IoT. The decision support system (DSS) in such platforms necessitates that automation be extensive. It necessitates the use of learning-aided systems. This chapter reports the design of IoT-driven learning-aided system for home surveillance application.

INTRODUCTION

Most, security systems required an automated approach of monitoring, verification and execution. A significant part of it involves real-time monitoring, capturing hundreds and thousands of images each day, recording the contents as streams of videos of different objects and deriving decisions. It is relevant for all sensitive areas like home, an office, institutions, traffic point, airport entrance, defense installations, hospitals, roadsides, buildings, elevators, or any other property/asset or resource used and accessed by human beings. Most of the time the primary sensor or pickup device used for surveillance and monitoring is the camera which may be placed at different locations. With tremendous growth in information and communication technology (ICT) and the proliferation of human habitation, the demand for increasing use of innovative security aids have become an often observed phenomena. The role of Information

DOI: 10.4018/978-1-5225-6210-8.ch008

and Communication Technologies (ICT) is significantly increasing in our everyday lives and it has a predominant influence on the development of the economy and information society (Ilnas, 2018). The positive impact across various economic sectors in the interdisciplinary applications is only possible with the growth of these technologies. In Luxembourg, ICT is largely used for the development of innovative products and services in order to address societal, market, and business challenges. Nowadays, IoT is considered to have a potential to advance the quality of life of the citizens and economic growth of the country. Adoption of IoT technology in various domains, such as Smart cities, Smart transportation, Smart logistics, Smart industry, Smart meter and Smart grid improves their current operational efficiency and interaction with the people.

Security systems thus talks using the language of images it captures and processes the image to derive some decision as done by the brain. Security and safety are two intertwined terms. It is a common belief that when a place or system is secure, it is safe. Security and safety are always intertwined and it is impossible to design a security system without taking into account the safety of the object or person into consideration. Security whether it be in industry or government or any other sensitive areas including home or personal assets has myriads of context ranging from individuals to nation-wide. AI and machine learning (ML) technologies are now being widely employed and developed across the spectrum of security are an unavoidable and important matter of concern of the world. For the purpose of identification of unknown process or factors can be done by training the network to predict the sequences originated from the sources. The perception of human motion is one of the most important skills people possess and the visualization system of the people provides rich information. Human motion analysis has received much attention in last few decades due to the plethora of its applications. The immense amount of video data being recorded and collected every day from surveillance security cameras it has become an essential task to automatically analyze and understand the contents. The paper reports the work related to the integration of three devices for physical intrusion detection. This paper throws light on the means of increasing the level of security in sensitive areas including home. This paper intends to show that a system with more than one security device in place tends to prevent unauthorized access.

The surveillance system in the proposed work is formulated using an embedded system connected to a control unit. Most security arrangements based on vision require human intervention for decision making. Therefore, there is a necessity to urgently automate the mechanism using learning aided tools so that the system is independent of human intervention once it is deployed. The primary mechanism of which will revolve around the working of the learning aided decision support system (DSS) which continuously learns to discriminate between authorized and unauthorized entries.

Of late, automation has triggered many changes in the existing technologies. These, due to their user-friendly nature and the facilitation of access to information, have become indispensable elements of Information and Communication Technology (ICT) systems. Further, catalyzed by connected states of systems and networking between devices, DSS have become real-time. Most networked devices are being provided with the ability to adapt to the deployed environment. With the ability of network devices to sense and collect data from around the world, and then share that data across the internet, a host of applications are evolving. We are now entering into the era of 'Internet of Things (IoT)', and Artificial Intelligence (AI) working together.

Providing security relies on two main elements:

1. Equipment or technology
2. People

Human security (Oludele, Ayodele, Oladele, & Olurotimi, 2009), has the tendency to want to cover more ground than actually securing the ground. Human security has several reoccurring problems which include:

- Disgruntled employees
- Professionalism
- Job characteristics
- Security structure and climate for security

These reoccurring problems tend to disturb or halt the work to be done or carried out.

The capabilities of home surveillance systems have been enhanced considerably by resorting to increase use of automated systems. The automation aspect have reduced human intervention and made such systems reliable and efficient. With the proliferation of wireless devices, networking among the connected devices is leading to the formation of Internet of Things (IoT). This has made it essential that home surveillance systems be also automate using IoT. The Decision Support System (DSS) in such platforms necessitate that automation be extensive. It necessitates the use of learning aided systems. This work reports the design of IoT driven learning aided system for home surveillance application.

REVIEW OF PREVIOUSLY REPORTED WORKS

Various works have been done around the globe during the last few decades which deals with remote monitoring, controlling and accessing and also provides analysis and categorization of security and surveillance systems. A few of the related works are included here. These are related to the present work and are expected to form the background of the study.

Review of Previous Work Done on Security and Surveillance System With Arduino, Raspberry Pi Using Bluetooth, ZigBee, GSM Technology, Wireless Technology and Internet of Things (IoT)

The following section provides a detailed survey on the study of the literature related to the work with surveillance and security system.

1. Abu, Nordin, Suboh, Md Yid and Ramli (2018). Here in this paper, the authors have reported their work on the development of a home security system based on IoT via Favoriot platform. Their work involved the development of a home security system using IoT with online database server, for which FAVORIOT is needed. The devices will be equipped with Passive Infrared sensor and Infrared sensor which monitor the presence of intruder and any unauthorized entry. The data received through the FAVORIOT platform can help the user to monitor the house and sending a real-time alert to the users.
2. Listyorini and Rahim (2018). The authors here have reported their work on the development of a device that can detect fire hotspots by using IoT. and fuzzy logic. Their developed prototypecould detect the hotspots in the peatlands by the use of fire sensors, temperature sensors, servo motors,

buzzers and surveillance cameras controlled by a WEMOS ESP8266 microcontroller and by applying the fuzzy logic method. Here they have analyzed the intensity of the flames detected

3. Keerthikanth, SaiSanath and Manikandaswamy (2018). The authors have reported their work on the need for self - controlled robots for military or investigation purposes. They have demonstrated the building of a self-controlled robot that could undertake missions like border patrol, surveillance, etc., that could in act both as a standalone unit by implementing real coordination with humans and utilizing IoT is used for the way of communication. Their developed system has the abilities of sensing motion, detect bombs, monitor the environment through visuals, capture the audio in a particular room, automated capabilities, GPS location detection etc.

4. Basyal, Kaushal and Singh (2018). The authors have reported their work on voice recognition technology in single voice command that could perform a real world operation. They have reported that the conversion of input voice signal to its corresponding text through an android application could be dealt by the voice recognition and that the text message is transmitted through Bluetooth. The authors have discussed on the concept of real-time surveillance and automation.

5. Diego, Coral, Rodriguez, Cabra and Colorado (2017), This paper presents the development of a novel system based on IoT to Human Activity Recognition (HAR) by monitoring vital signs remotely. They have employed the machine learning algorithms to determine the activity done within four pre-established categories (lie, sit, walk and jog). The system was able to give feedback during and after the activity was performed, using a remote monitoring component with remote visualization and programmable alarms.

6. Quadri and Sathish (2017). Here the authors have reported their work on IoT that offers user interoperability and connectivity between devices, systems, services, networks and involves enhancing the network to proficiently collect and analyze the data from various sensors and actuators then sends the data to the mobile phone or a personal computer over a wireless connection. They have discussed the importance of IoT on developing security aids that has become an important issue due to the rising possibilities of intrusion.

7. Bashal, Jilani and Arun (2016). The authors have presented an intelligent door system using IoT that notifies intrusion by sending out email notification to the owner. In the system the changes in the motion of the door is detected by ADXL345 accelerometer and the raspberry pi read the sensor intrusion data and communicate to the Amazon Web Service Internet of Things (AWS IoT) console. The AWS Simple Notification Service(SNS) will send out email notification based on the message from the AWS IoT console to the concerned owner based on AWS IoT console message.

8. S. and G. (2016) have worked on the design of a smart surveillance system, monitored by owner remotely. The system utilizes IOT technology and whenever an intrusion is detected inside the room the notification is sent. The authorized user who knows the details can access to their monitoring system remotely and monitor the situation on application via internet with help of mobile phone. The entire work is done on Raspberry Pi with Raspbian operating system ported on it.

9. Sharma and Thanaya (2016) reported the design and implementation of sensor based security system with an IOT environment, which is expected to resolve various security issues like unauthorized intruder entry, fire detection etc. Therefore, continuous monitoring of the home/apartment is possible. The system is cost effective, reliable and has low power consumption.

10. Shaik and D. (2016) have presented a system with door accessibility and voice alerting through Smart Phone and have received captured image of visitor at door as alert message through email. The system uses a PIR motion sensor with camera module for the detection of motion and captures

images to make the security system alive. The user can monitor and control the door accessibility on active SSH (Secure Shell) page designed on android platform and enhanced with JavaScript. The system uses ARM1176JZF-S microcontroller.

11. Widyantara and Sastra (2015). The authors have presented their work on the design and implementation of IoT for intelligent traffic monitoring system (ITMS) in the Denpasar city, Bali, Indonesia. The goal of their work was to develop a monitoring system that would be capable enough to visualize the traffic on the Web-based GPS/GPRS. The authors have discussed on the implementation of the work of IoT.

12. Sugapriya and Amsavalli (2015) report the security and authentication for individuals especially bank lockers. The work used techniques like pattern recognition comparing these existing traits, there is still need for considerable computer vision. Image processing is used and keypad password is needed for another level of security.

13. Kadu, Dekhane, Dhanwala and Awate (2015) have presented a system that has four hardware components: ARM processor to transfer signals to home appliances, an android smart phone as a Web server to store records and support services to the other components, user's android mobile with running Android application and Bluetooth module to provide wireless remote access from smart phone to ARM controller. Smart phone connected to the ARM controller via Bluetooth module enables wireless system communication with graphical user interface (GUI) on smart phone.

14. Ramlee, Leong, Singh, Othman, H., Misran and Meor (2013), have demonstrated an overall design of Home Automation System (HAS) with low cost and wireless remote control. The main control system implements wireless Bluetooth technology to provide remote access from PC/laptop or smart phone. The design remains the existing electrical switches and provides more safety control on the switches with low voltage activating method.

Basic Factors Related to the Design a Surveillance Set-Up

Every security system must essentially be reliable and possess allsafety features. While developing surveillance or security system it should have a level of guarantee that it would behave as expected (Oludele, Avodele, Oladele & Olurotimi, 2009). A segment of generating a countermeasure should be inbuilt so as to stop a threat from triggering a risk event beforehand. It is essential to take into consideration every single risk that could cause a possible loss and prevent situations that might be dangerous.

The key concern fields are (Oludele, Avodele, Oladele & Olurotimi, 2009):

- **Ease of Access:** The doors and windows in the environment shouldn't make the system unsafe.
- **Lack of Intrusion Detection Alerts:** A proper intrusion detection system should alert the responsible quarters so as to prevent the occurrence of a dangerous situation.
- **Inefficient Monitoring Method:** Monitoring method and its reliability is the key to prevent dangerous situations. Hence all monitoring systems must have a continuous mode of observation.

Attributes of a Reliable Security System

A reliable security system must have the following attributes (Oludele, Avodele, Oladele & Olurotimi, 2009):

- **Sensitivity:** The system must be sensitive enough to detect threats or changes in the environment.
- **Reliability:** The system must be dependable i.e. it must work in the environment it's placed in.
- **Durability:** It must be "rugged" i.e. work efficiently for a long time or a reasonable period.
- **Ease of Deployment:** It must be easy to transport and set up.

AN OVERVIEW OF INTERNET OF THINGS (IOT), SURVEILLANCE SYSTEM, AND AUTOMATION

Here we discuss briefly the basic concepts related to the proposed IoT based surveillance and automation system aided by a decision support system (DSS) driven by learning aided mechanism.

Internet of Things (IoT)

IoT is a universal global network set-up within a network by integration of connection oriented devices which may share a cloud or certain space that intelligently connects various devices or processes and comprises of smart machines interacting and communicating with other machines, environments, objects and infrastructures including radio frequency identification (RFID) and sensor network technologies (Sharma & Tiwari, 2016).

In today's IoT system architectures (IEC, 2016), the concept of an IoT platform is typically expressed as referring to the central hub of domains that collectively constitute the physical realization of the functional view of an architecture encompassing one or more aggregated edge environments. The IoT platform is an integrated physical/virtual entity system employing various applications and components to provide fully interoperable IoT services and management of those services. Nowadays, the concept of the "edge" refers to the aspect that comprises the operational domain of the overall IoT system. The edge typically consists of sensors, controllers, actuators, tag and tag readers, communication components, gateways and the physical devices themselves. The edge is where operational components connect, communicate and interact with each other, with the platform and in some cases directly with components in other edges.

More sophisticated data analysis techniques using deep learning and artificial intelligence will require significant enhancements employing new approaches (IEC, 2016). Autonomous devices such as self-driving cars and fully recombinant plant equipment are creating unparalleled demands for system responsiveness to support real-time behavior. This in turn requires the ability to sift through massive amounts of data streamed in real time and stored in memory for low or zero latency access. Real time IoT applications need real-time platform support that allows for sophisticated processing within the proximity networks as well as across the full network range. Cross-industrial application domain usage of data, (e.g. data generated in the smart home industrial application area is used in the automotive domain), can enable the development of new business models.

In this work, the focus is to design IoT based surveillance and DSS based on learning tools.

Figure 1, shows the flow diagram of the Internet of Things, how the devices are connected through the internet to came communication possible.

Figure 1. Flow diagram of Internet of Things (IoT)

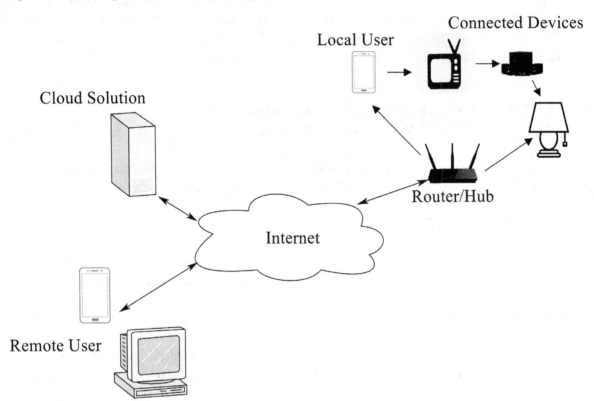

Various Platforms and Tools Used

Python

Python (Dave Kuhlman, 2013) is one of the most popular languages in the world and is a general purpose programming language started by Guido van Rossum. The primary reason behind its popularity is its simplicity and code readability that enables the programmer to express ideas in fewer lines of code without reducing readability. It is heavily used in academic environments and is a widely supported platform in modern applications, especially utilities, and desktop and Web applications.

Applications of Python (Dave Kuhlman, 2013)

- GUI based desktop applications
- Image processing and graphic design applications
- Scientific and computational applications
- Games
  - Web frameworks and web applications
  - Enterprise and business applications
  - Operating systems
  - Language development
  - Prototyping

Advantages/Benefits of Python (Dave Kuhlman, 2013)

Some of the benefits of programming in Python include:

- **Extensive Support Libraries:** Python provides a large standard library which includes areas like internet protocols, string operations, web services tools and operating system interfaces.
- **Open Source and Community Development:** Python language is developed under an OSI-approved open source license, which makes it free to use and distribute, including for commercial purposes.
- **Learning Ease and Support Available:** Python offers excellent readability and uncluttered simple-to-learn syntax which helps beginners to utilize this programming language.
- **User-Friendly Data Structures:** Python has built-in list and dictionary data structures which can be used to construct fast runtime data structures
- **Productivity and Speed:** Python has clean object-oriented design, provides enhanced process control capabilities, and possesses strong integration and text processing capabilities and its own unit testing framework, all of which contribute to the increase in its speed and productivity. Python is considered a viable option for building complex multi-protocol network applications.

OpenCV

OpenCV (Open Source Computer Vision Library) (Bradski & Kaehler, 2008) is released under a Berkeley Software Distribution (BSD) license and hence it's free for both academic and commercial use. It has C++, C, Python and Java interfaces and supports Windows, Linux, Mac OS, iOS and Android. OpenCV was designed for computational efficiency and with a strong focus on real-time applications. Written in optimized C/C++, the library can take advantage of multi-core processing. Enabled with OpenCL, it can take advantage of the hardware acceleration of the underlying heterogeneous compute platform.

OpenCV python is a library of python bindings designed to solve computer vision problems. Python is general purpose programming language started by Guido van Rossum It enables the programmer to express ideas in fewer lines of code without reducing readability. OpenCV now supports a multitude of algorithms related to Computer Vision and Machine Learning.

IoT Based Surveillance System

Large-scale, real time video based monitoring arrangements have become indispensable for safety of human lives and assets. Such a system requires continuously growing transmission data rate and storage requirements. Such a demand can be fulfilled by designing and deploying a multi-layer mechanism which combines various technologies and provides required support. Most of the ub-blocks under such a mechanism when unified as IoT facilitate smooth operation. If the pick-up devices in such a framework are the video cameras these become "the things" which continuously stream video feed to a central unit where storage and decision making take place. It can be cloud based connected via Internet. Lately, the devices connected in such arrangements prefer wireless links which adds to the efficiency while most of the wired connections are discarded as these create inconveniences at times and require dedicated support. As a result, the security and surveillance industry has grown in leaps and bounds as demands for such systems are increasing each day. Present day solutions have evolved from the rudimentary alarm based surveillance to more sophisticated IoT aided monitoring with decision support and process control. Live video streaming and related remote security mechanisms have enhanced the reliability of such systems for which these are preferred by organizations for protection of human life, assets, and premises. The IoT is enabling the creation of safer homes, communities, neighborhoods and cities by ensuring round the clock monitoring to securely and remotely secure facilities and public spaces. Some of the major benefits derived by the use of IoT in security and surveillance systems by real estate managers, institutes, business concerns and security concerns are:

1. Remote management and regulation of surveillance mechanisms for monitoring every attribute of a set-up.
2. Facilitate AI driven decision support for ensuring the appropriate course of action with real-time process control.
3. Make physical inspection useless and thereby ensuring greater safety to personnel and assets especially in case of law enforcement.
4. Saving of time and money while providing security cover.
5. Continuous analysis and improvement of capabilities of the system depending upon the requirements.

One of the biggest advantages derived out of the use of using IoT based monitoring and surveillance is that the system is able to ensure minimum loss of time and resources including human lives even in hazardous conditions. In all premises where IoT security solutions are deployed, it facilitates:

- Continuous vigil regarding entry, exit and activity in real-time.
- Consistently regulate and check the working of the facility conditions from remote location with round the clock access.
- Initiate corrective measures in case of an emergency.

Some of the recent works related to IoT and surveillance systems are as below:

1. Yang, Seasholtz, Luo and Li (2018), the authors have reported the rapid expansion of IoT-enabled home automation that accompanies substantial security and privacy risks. The authors have presented their work on the design of multipath Onion IoT gateway and split channel Onion IoT gateway to tackle the issue of security and privacy risks in home automation. Their first design implements a customized multipath routing protocol in Tor to construct a multi-circuit anonymous tunnel between the user and the Onion gateway to support applications that require low latency and high bandwidth and the second scheme splits command and data channels so that small-sized command packets are transmitted through the more secure channel over the Tor hidden service, while the less secure data channel over the public network is used for outbound very-high-bandwidth data traffic.
2. Shitole, Kamatchi and Iyer (2018), the author here describes their work on a smart home context-aware system. This paper reports a rule-based service customization strategy that uses a rule coincidence method based on semantic distance to make decisions about the context and a set theory method based on set theory to monitor service customization. Their designed hypothesis lies on reducing the bandwidth of the network and the precondition of the capacity of the device in an attempt to guarantee accuracy and a certain degree of security of delivery. Their work lies in the improvement of the quality of life by providing a profitable life, including security and entertainment through the use of the AES algorithm.

3. A (2017), the author has described the application of IoT in developing reliable and dependable home security system and for industrial security as well. The author mentioned that the system informs the owner about any unauthorized access by sending notification to the user. The various components used in the security system involves a microcontroller known as Arduino Uno that is used to interface the components, a magnetic Reed sensor to monitor the status, a buzzer for sounding the alarm, and a Wi-Fi module, ESP8266 to connect and communicate using the Internet.

4. Srilakshmi and Padma (2017), have described their work on smart surveillance system based on IoT, whereby they have aimed to design a system that fulfill the needs of the user for particular surveillance. In the developed system the motion detected in the surveillance area is captured and GCM notification is sent to the user informing about the motion detection. The image of which can be viewed by the user from the remote area with the help of internet or Wi-Fi. The authors have mentioned that the Android Application works in two modes one is Auto mode and other is Manual mode, user receives the notifications only in Auto mode in order to avoid frequent interruptions.

5. Moubara and Desouky (2016), have presented their work that is focused on smart home automation i.e. increasing home security using Internet of Things (IoT), integrating that with computer vision, web services and cross-platform mobile services. They have embedded intelligence using Raspberry Pi that assist interaction of end users and home devices through cross-platform mobile application which is developed using Ionic Framework by connecting the two client sides i.e. the end user and devices, through publish/subscribe model using PubNub Data Stream Network.

6. Venugopal and Pattewale (2016), have discussed about their work that focuses on developing a home automation and security system based on IoT. The authors have aimed at developing a reliable system to provide a reliable solution for the home automation. They have discussed home automation systems that have achieved a large scale transformation from panic switches to sending fixed messages to specified recipients during emergency, remote controlled switches for machines, systems based on GSM networked devices to comprehensive home server for monitoring and control of domestic environment.

7. Darbari, Yagyasen, and Tiwari (2015), have described their work on IoT based monitoring system that controls the traffic due to sudden rise in the use of vehicles that have raised due to rise in population. The authors have highlighted the different issue of Intelligent Traffic monitoring system using the technologies like IoT, Multi Agent system and Semantic Web. They have also stated the connection between IoT sensors using ZigBee protocol, whereby the traffic movements are continuously monitored by control center using Granular classification in Ontology.

Automation and Surveillance System

Automation is the set of method, systems or processes used for replacement of humans with technology or machines. It is used in all spheres of day to day life. Automation has already started to have impacts on day-to-day lives and has percolated to each aspect of the daily life of the common man in a way which is barely noticeable. Automation is here to stay for a long time and shall spread even further as industries continue to develop and adopt new technologies to find ways and means to replace the human role with machine driven processing.

During the last two decades the world has witnessed major advances in artificial intelligence (AI) and robotics which are now essential ingredients of the automation industry. The future is expected to be filled with more spectacular developments which shall contribute towards transforming of the ways and means of doing work around the world. The world is moving towards intelligent automation where there are three components:

1. Machine Vision which is a computer based mechanism is used to understand visual input. The machine learns data (images) for classification or identification. Examples are face recognition in some mobile devices, Facebook etc. which analyzes images, extracts attributes and then places them as per classes which facilitates recognition.
2. Natural Language Processing (NLP) is a set of mechanism used to understand human voice and text inputs. Examples are Apple's Siri, Google Assistant, and Amazon Alexa etc.
3. Machine Learning is the method to enable machines to learn from the surrounding, retain the learning and use it subsequently to make intelligent decisions. Machine learning improves the efficiency of decision making.

The above three aspects help in designing intelligent automation system. These sets of devices are also essential for designing an automated intelligent surveillance system. Many automated intelligent surveillance systems are designed to work on face recognition principles. These are based on a DSS which executes process control using the knowhow acquired from a set of faces held in a database. Certain systems are trained to detect suspicious behavior.

Popular video surveillance systems have one noticeable common feature i.e. these require human intervention. There should be operator (s) to deal with the monitoring and handle the process control. As a result, the efficiency and effectiveness of these systems are dictated by human behavior and constraints. Further, the vigilance of the person deployed is largely responsible for the working of the system. Moreover, the areas under surveillance and number of cameras that can be used is dependent on the personnel count which in certain cases may turn out to be undesirable. At many situations the user may seek to avoid such a situation. To reduce these dependencies, the combination of computer vision, NLP and machine learning have emerged as an alternative for automated intelligent surveillance.

Some of the recent works related to automation and surveillance systems are as below:

1. Ayed, Elkosantini and Abid (2017), have demonstrated their work of a specific System on Chip architecture for surveillance system based on Multi-Processor (MPSOC) and hardware accelerator. They have aimed at accelerating the processing and obtain reliable and an accelerated suspicious behavior of recognition. The system architecture is based on multi-processor approach. The implementation of a specific architecture based on MPSOC in a single chip is accomplished by FPGA. The architecture of the system consists of three main functional blocks: Object detection Unit, Tracking Unit and Behavior exploration application.
2. Kodali, Boppana and Jain (2016), have reported their work on IoT connected remotely and monitoring real world objects or things through the Internet. Their work is focused on building a smart wireless home security system that sends alerts to the owner by using Internet in case of any trespass and raises an alarm optionally. They have also reported that the same could also be utilized for home automation by making use of the same set of sensors. The microcontroller used in the system is the TI-CC3200 Launchpad board with an embedded micro-controller and an onboard Wi-Fi shield.
3. Chuimurkar and Bagdi (2016), have demonstrated their work on implementation and the results of smart surveillance monitoring system using Raspberry pi and PIR sensor for mobile devices. The Raspberry Pi with Open Source Computer Vision (OpenCV) software handles the image process-

ing, control algorithms for the alarms and captured image is send to user's email via Wi- Fi. Their work on home security system that captures information and transmits that via a 3G Dongle to a Smart phone using web application.

4. Nagarajan and Surendran (2015), have reported their work on the design and implementation of an automated security system that would facilitate a healthy, flexible, comfortable and a secure environment to the residents. Their designed system incorporates a SIRC (Sony Infrared Remote Control) protocol based infrared remote controller for the wireless operation and control of electrical appliances. The appliances on the other hand are monitored and controlled via a laptop using a GUI (Graphical User Interface) application.

5. Domadia and Mehta (2014), have reported their work on automated video surveillance systems that are of most importance in the field of security, the task of which depends on detecting moving objects in surveillance area. They have mentioned that in video surveillance, detection of moving objects from a video is necessary for object classification, target tracking, activity recognition, as well as behavior understanding. Computer application for automatic detection of human face from digital image or video frame from video source has been used in the system. The idea of their work revolves in developing human motion detection algorithm using image for which they have applied methods: Gaussian Mixture Modeling and Optical flow.

6. Pathari and Bojewar (2014), have reported their work on monitoring and recording suspicious movement in a company during the closing hours of the company. They have reported the work of computer vision technology, intelligent video surveillance architecture to protect personnel and infrastructure to automate the process of watching web cam. They have implemented motion detection algorithm that acted as the security tool.

7. ElShafee and Hamed (2012), have presented their work on the design and prototype implementation of home automation system using WiFi technology as a network infrastructure connecting its parts. Their system consisted of two main components; the first part is the server present at the system core that manages, controls, and monitors users' home. The software of their work on home automation system is divided into server application software, and Microcontroller (Arduino) firmware.

8. Chiu, Ku and Wang (2010), have reported the design of a real-time traffic surveillance system for the detection, recognition, and tracking of multiple vehicles in roadway images. They have discussed on the application of CCD surveillance cameras. In their system the segmentation and recognition method used are the length, width, and roof size to classify vehicles as vans, utility vehicles, sedans, mini trucks, or large vehicles, even when occlusive vehicles are continuously merging from one frame to the next. The system integrates image capture, an object segmentation algorithm, an occlusive vehicle segmentation method, a vehicle recognition method, and a vehicle tracking method.

9. Shah, Omar and Khurram (2007), have reported their work on using video cameras for monitoring and surveillance which is common in both federal agencies and private firms. On that ground to overcome those limitations they have reported the use of computer vision and artificial intelligence. In their work they have introduced the key logical components of a general automated surveillance system. The Knight which is commercial, off-the-shelf surveillance system detects, categorizes, and tracks moving objects in the scene using state-of-the-art computer vision techniques.

Artificial Intelligence (AI) and Surveillance Operation

As already mentioned above, AI is already an accepted element in surveillance operations and systems. The heart of the AI block is an ANN which is a non-parametric tool with the ability to map inputs non-linearly to the outputs. The mapping is associated with some learning rule which is crucial to a DSS. An ANN is formed by a network of artificial neurons which are arranged in layers and linked in connectionist arrangements and is adaptive in nature. As like the human brain, a typical neuron collects signals from the dendrites and transmits that signal through axons that splits into thousands of branches whereby the synapses convert the activity from axon into effects that excite activity in other connected axons. ANNs as like the human brain typically is composed of interconnected nodes or units connected to a link which has a numeric weight associated with it. The weights are the primary means of long-term storage in ANN, and learning usually takes place by updating the weights (Russell & Norvig, 1995). The weights are modified so as to try to bring the network's input or output behavior more into line with that of the environment providing the inputs. Each unit has a set of input links from other units, a set of output links to other units, a current activation level, and a means of computing the activation level at the next step in time, given its inputs and weights (Russell & Norvig, 1995). ANN finds application in different task due to its efficiency by learning complex input output mappings (Sharma & Sarma, 2016). The training procedures that is applied and theoretical properties of neural network are of utmost importance for its performance. For a large variety of classification task which can be enhanced by discriminative property, has shown reliable and good performances. The parameters of the system are estimated by the training algorithms. For the purpose of identification of unknown process or factors, it can be done by training the network to predict the sequences originated from the source.

Some of the works related to neural network and surveillance operation are as below:

1. Ondrej, Vollmer and Milos (2009), have discussed on the resiliency and security in control systems in the world of hackers and malware and the computer systems that are used within critical infrastructures. They have presented an IDS-NNM i.e. Intrusion Detection System using Neural Network based Modeling. The authors have discussed on various factors such as the use and analyses of real network data, the development of a specific window based feature extraction technique, the construction of training dataset using randomly generated intrusion vectors and the use of a combination of two neural network learning algorithms i.e. the Error-Back Propagation and Levenberg- Marquardt, for normal behavior modeling. They have demonstrated the robustness of the artificial neural network as a cluster boundary modeling tool and the suitability of the ANN architecture in the domain of their work.

2. Jan (2004), have discussed on the reliable detection of suspicious human behavior by automated visual surveillance systems. They have discussed the better performance of flexible models such as artificial neural network (ANN) models, computational requirement of which are prohibitively large for real- time video processing. The author here has used the Modified Probabilistic Neural Network (MPNN). They have mentioned that the MPNN achieved good classification but it has much reduced computation compared to other ANN models. In their work, they have worked on the detection of suspicious behavior. They have evaluated the use of ANN based classifiers for assessment of abnormal or suspicious behaviors in an automated visual surveillance application.

3. Teschioni, Oberti and Regazzoni (1999) have described about the need of real time solution of outdoor environment monitoring system for complex computer vision problems. The authors here

have discussed about the advanced visual surveillance systems for detecting, tracking of moving objects and interpretation of their behavioral pattern. They have presented a method based on neural networks for classification of moving tracked objects. The images are fed into a database which would be utilized and the sequences acquired from selected image would obtain the particular result. The authors have measured the performances in terms of capabilities of object classification and discrimination through the percentage of correct object recognition.

4.   Lin and Kung (1997), have presented a face recognition system based on probabilistic decision based neural networks (PDBNN). They have discussed the technological advances on microelectronic and vision system, high performance automatic techniques on biometric recognition that have become economically feasible. The authors have described about their work on PDBNN face recognition system that has three modules namely a face detector, an eye localizer and the third module a face recognizer. They have applied PDBNN effectively to all the three modules that adopted a hierarchical network structure. They have also presented automatic face recognition that performed human face detection, eye localization, and face recognition. They have applied the PDBNN which is a probabilistic variant of the decision based neural network to implement the major modules of their work.

5.   Moghaddam and Pentland (1995), have presented an unsupervised technique for visual learning that is based on density estimation in high dimensional spaces using an Eigen space decomposition. The authors have derived two types of density estimates for modeling the training data i.e. a multivariate Gaussian and a multivariate Mixture of Gaussians model, whose probabilities are then used to formulate a maximum likelihood for visual search and target detection for automatic object recognition. The authors have described a density estimation technique for unsupervised visual learning which exploits the intrinsic low dimensionality of the training imagery to form a computationally simple estimator.

System Architecture

The working of the system is described using a system model depicted in Figure 2. The system has several camera units used as primary sensors, an embedded block with a Raspberry Pi as the primary processor, a control unit, networking resources and a DSS driven by a learning based mechanism.

Figure 2. Functional Block diagram of the home surveillance system model

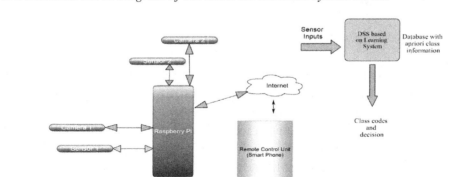

Figure 2, shows the functional block diagram of the home surveillance system which consist of the units.

The surveillance system consists of two main units.

1. Embedded unit
2. Networking Resources
3. Decision Support System (DSS) based on Learning Systems
4. Control unit

1. **Embedded Unit:** The embedded unit is the main system unit which comprises of Raspberry Pi set up with the Raspbian Operating System including the PIR motion sensor and camera as the primary sensor to detect intruder and captures image respectively. The captured image will be saved on the Pi. Raspberry pi configured for enabling the SSH and camera.

2. **Networking Resources:** The different wired and wireless links constitute the network resources. The inputs from the sensors are passed on to the remote controller using the network resources. Also, the sensor data are continuously fed to the DSS which is a decision support system based on learning aided characteristics. The DSS executes the control over the remote access mechanisms through the networking resources which in this case are Wi-Fi, Bluetooth and Zigbee based for close range operation. For extended range operation, internet connectivity is used through service provider as is available in an actual situation.

3. **Learning Aided DSS:** This block is used to continuously learn input patterns of visual pickups and is trained to discriminate between authorized and unauthorized entries. The DSS is formed using a feedforward (FF) Artificial Neural Network (ANN) trained using (error) back propagation algorithm. The FF ANN has one two hidden layers and has log-sigmoid activation functions. The ANN is trained with a few numbers of faces and are also tested. The training time performance is critical because it shall later on determine the ability of the network to discriminate between legal and illegal entry. If an illegal entry is recorded an alert is generated and the controller initiates action in form of passing an email to the remote user.

4. **Control Unit:** The SSH is a secure protocol and most commonly used to administrate and communicate with Linux server. The GUI (Graphical User Interface) send predefined Linux terminal commands through SSH to Embedded control unit. The control unit is a remote unit which is software implemented on user smart phone.

The workings of the system in terms of constituent systems are described below:

1. **Raspberry Pi:** It is a fully functioned computer (Simon Monk, 2014) a System-on-Chip (SoC) device, which runs on Linux operating system specially designed for it, named Raspbian. Raspbian is the official operating system for Raspberry Pi, where other operating systems such as Android, Ubuntu can be installed on Pi. Like a computer it has memory, processor, USB ports, audio output, HDMI video and audio output it run on Linux. Raspberry Pi is capable of doing multiple tasks at a time like a computer. The processor at the heart of Raspberry Pi is Broadcom BCM2837 SoC multimedia processor with 1.2GHz Quad-Core ARM cortex-A53 (64 bit). It has 40 pin 2.54mm

header expansion slots providing 27 GPIO pins that allows other peripheral devices such as LEDS, sensors etc. to be interfaced to Pi as per the requirement. Four USB ports output of which maximum is 1.2 A. 10/100BaseT Ethernet sockets for internet Access. It has also an inbuilt integrated video core 4 graphics GPU capable of playing. Comparing the speed, raspberry pi is 40 times faster than Arduino. It does not require external hardware for most of the function. It can be accessed via SSH and file can easily be transferred over FTP. The Pi 3 comes with 40 GPIO pins that can be used to interface with various hardware devices—for both receiving from and or writing data to them. Figure 3, shows the model diagram of support system designed with the Raspberry Pi processor. It can support a number of devices such as smart-phones, lamps, sensors etc.

2. **Raspberry PiCamera Module:** The Raspberry has a 15 pin MIPI camera serial interface on the upper surface that supports the PiCamera module to be interfaced Pi board. This interface uses the dedicated CSI interface. This interfacing medium is designed especially for interfacing to cameras. The CSI bus capable of carrying extremely high data and it exclusively carries pixel data. The camera is incorporated in a printed circuited board which is connected to an expandable ribbon cable which connects to the Pi itself on its own port. The camera on the board is very small usually of 5MP. It uses 250mA, externally powering the Pi should be sufficient enough for the camera.

3. **PIR Motion Sensor:** PIR sensor allows to sense motion, and is almost always used to detect whether a human has moved in or out of the sensors range. They are small, inexpensive, low-power, easy to use and don't wear out. For that reason, they are commonly found in appliances and gadgets used in homes or businesses. They are often referred to as PIR, "Passive Infrared", "Pyroelectric", or "IR motion" sensors.

Everything emits some low level of radiation, and hotter something is, the more radiation is emitted (Simon Monk, 2014). The sensor in a motion detector is actually split into two halves. The two halves are wired up so that they cancel each other. The motion in case detected gives a high signal at the single I/O pin. It can detect up to a range of about 10 meters. The output pin can be connected to GPIO pins of various platforms to monitor the signal. PIR sensor has three onboard pins, the +5V, OUT, GROUND.

The PIR sensor (Lady Ada, 2017) itself has two slots in it, each slot is made of a special material that is sensitive to IR. The two slots can 'see' out past some distance (basically the sensitivity of the sensor). When the sensor is idle, both slots detect the same amount of IR, the ambient amount radiated from the room or walls or outdoors. When a warm body like a human or animal passes by, it first intercepts

Figure 3. Model diagram of support system designed with a Raspberry Pi processor

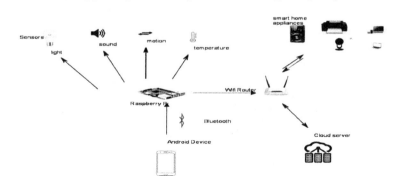

one half of the PIR sensor, which causes a positive differential change between the two halves. When the warm body leaves the sensing area, the reverse happens, whereby the sensor generates a negative differential change. These change pulses are what is detected.

4. **USB Camera:** The USB camera module used in this system which is directly plugs into the USB port of the Raspberry pi. Webcam comes with USB cable, User documentation. Camera display on screen. Simple plug-and-play setup and an easy-to-use universal clip. High-resolution snapshots at up-to 5 megapixels (software enhanced). The images stay razor sharp, even in close-ups with built-in autofocus. It is versatile and portable. The overall block diagram of the system is as shown in Figure 2. The sensors are installed at the different location in the home. The cameras and PIR sensors that are installed at the doors of the home interfaced with the Raspberry pi. When PIR sensor is high i.e. motion detected by the sensor is above a threshold level, the camera is on and captures the image of the person.

5. **Feed Forward (FF) Artificial Neural Network (ANN):** The DSS is formed using a FF ANN which is trained with a number of sensor inputs. The FF ANN is a computational technique which is configured to learn from the input patterns, retain the learning and use it subsequently. The computational part is taken care by numerous artificial neuron which mimic the biological neurons. The artificial neurons called perceptron is packed in multiple layers. All the perceptron is interconnected by certain connectionist links which adapt as per the learning taking place till the expected outcome is achieved. This is learning. In this case, the learning happens in between multiple layers and the shared. Figure 4 shows a FF ANN which has been used as a DSS for the present work.

Figure 4, shows the generic FF ANN used as DSS.

System Implementation

The System implemented on a Raspberry pi development board in Linux environment, that supports SMTP (Simple Mail Transfer Protocol), TCP/IP, HTTP.

Installing OS and Configuring Raspberry Pi:

1. After successfully installing Raspbian OS on Raspberry Pi, we need to update software.

Figure 4. Generic FF ANN used as DSS

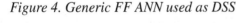
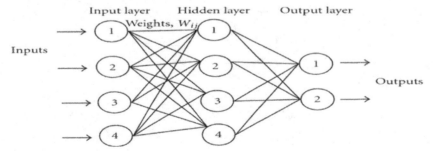

The following Linux commands is used:

$ sudo apt-get update $ sudo apt-get upgrade

2. Raspberry Pi Camera Configuring- After successfully installing Raspbian OS on Raspberry Pi, we need to install PiCamera Library files. To do this we need to run following Linux commands:

$ sudo apt-get install motion

$ sudo apt-get install python-picamera

$ sudo apt-get install python3-picamera

After installing Picamera Library files, we need to enable camera by running command:

$ sudo raspi-config

To test that the system is installed correctly and is in working condition, try the following command:

$ rasistill -v -o test.jpg

3. Installing Software for sending Email alert-Now after setting up the Pi Camera, we will install software for sending the Email. Here we are using SMTP, which is an easy and good solution for sending Email using command line or using Python Script.

We need to install two Libraries for sending mails using SMTP:

$ sudo apt-get install ssmtp

$ sudo apt-get install mailutils

After installing libraries, user needs to open ssmtp.conf file and edit this configuration file as shown below and then save the file.
To save and exit the file, Press 'CTRL+x', then 'y' and then press 'enter'

$ sudo nano /etc/ssmtp/ssmtp.conf

The Python Program of this project plays a very important role to perform all the operations. First of all, we include required libraries for email, initialize variables and define pins for PIR, LED and other components. For sending simple email, SMTP Library is enough but if we want to send mail in cleaner way with subject line, attachment etc. then we need to use MIME (Multipurpose Internet Mail Extensions).

Figure 5. Application Flow chart of system model

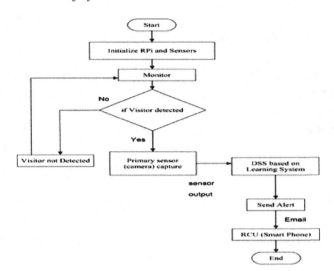

Software Implementation for Remote Control Unit

Software tool for Remote Control Unit implemented to provide GUI (Graphical User Interface) of Secure Shell (SSH) client to send predefined Linux Terminal Commands via SSH to ECU (Shaik & D., 2016). SSH Client is implemented on android platform using Java Script on JDK (Java Development Kit). Android is the first complete, open, and free mobile platform.

Process Logic in a Flow Chart

Figure 5, shows the application flow chart of the system model.

The hardware components interfaced which involves Raspberry pi module, PIR sensor, and camera. The primary pickup device i.e. the camera detects any kind of intruder or visitor. The PIR sensor is configured and connected to the GPIO pins of Raspberry pi to sense any kind of suspicious motion by the visitor or intruder at the door or window or entrance or at any kind of personal assets. The constituent systems thus initialize, the camera from its vision captures the image of any person at the entrance other than the owners that are being fed to the DSS which continuously discriminate through its learning mechanism between any kinds of legal or illegal entry with access to authorized users. The captured image is sent to the controller which through the raspberry pi with the help of predefined server is directly sent to the user as an Email with attachments to user which may be a remote control user. The stored photo is forwarded via email to the user. The flow chart given in the Figure 5 works as same as described. If no visitor or intruder is detected by the pickup sensor the camera the process is repeated under the loop.

Experimental Details

The camera based surveillance system detects the intruder or visitors at the door or any kind of entrance or personal assets and captures the same other than the owners and processed by the DSS and then an email is sent to the authorized user about the authorized and unauthorized access. The system is simple and easy to use. While using python in software design made it more convenient to write the codes due to its extensive support library function and user friendly data structure. There are various parameters which can be adjusted in the software. Streaming of videos is also possible with this software. The developed IoT based surveillance system gives good response to the sensor and sends Email when it needed, the unauthorized access or detection of intrusion at any kind of entrance or personal assets. The time taken by the system to deliver the email is dependent on the coverage area or range of the specified mobile network.

The ECU sends the Email alert indicating the update of the authorized or unauthorized access (Shaik & D., 2016). As the software tool RCU that provide GUI of SSH send predefined Linux Terminal commands via SSH to ECU. The SSH client is setup by knowing static IP address and Port. When connected through SSH, it is the shell session which is a text based interface with the other server takes place. For the duration of SSH session any command that is typed into local terminal are sent through an encrypted SSH tunnel and executed on server.

A crucial part of the work is configuring the DSS which as described above is formed by a FF ANN. The working of the DSS has two phases. In the first phase, the ANN compares the present output with the expected result. The difference is fed back to the previous layers to update the weight values existing in between the layers. While the training continues, a stage comes, where the present results match the

Figure 6. A set of face samples used for training the DSS

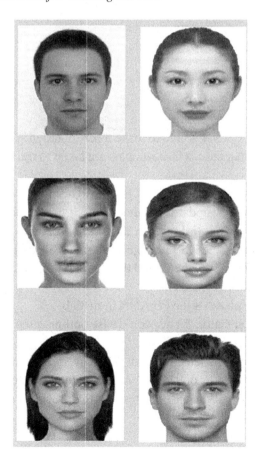

Figure 7. Execution of the training phase by the FF ANN

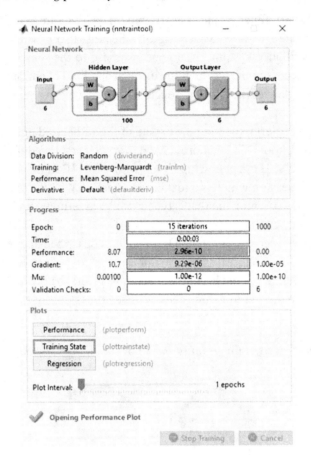

expected output. At this stage the ANN is able to make discrimination between legal and illegal entries. In the present case, for a particular case, a face samples are taken to train the ANN. Figure 6 shows the face samples.

Figure 6, shows the sample of a set of faces that is used to train the DSS. With the set of faces fed to the support system, the network now updates its decision each time a face is recognized. The FF ANN attains the learning goal quite fast. With less than 20 epochs, it attains the mean square error (MSE) convergence limit. During training, the DSS is subjected to several passes. The ANN set-up at the time of training is shown in Figure 7. The attributes and the training time state of the ANN is clearly shown in the figure.

Figure 7, shows the training phase of the FF ANN in matlab.

Figure 8, shows the confusion matrix for a specific case outlining the test results of the face recognition processes.

Figure 9, shows the MSE convergence plot. With this convergence, the DSS is found to demonstrate accuracy in the high nineties. For faces outside the database, the DSS doesn't provide a detection decision and an alert is sounded. For all the cases of testing, the proposed system is found to be accurate and reliable.

Figure 8. Confusion Matrix for a specific case outlining the test result face recognition system

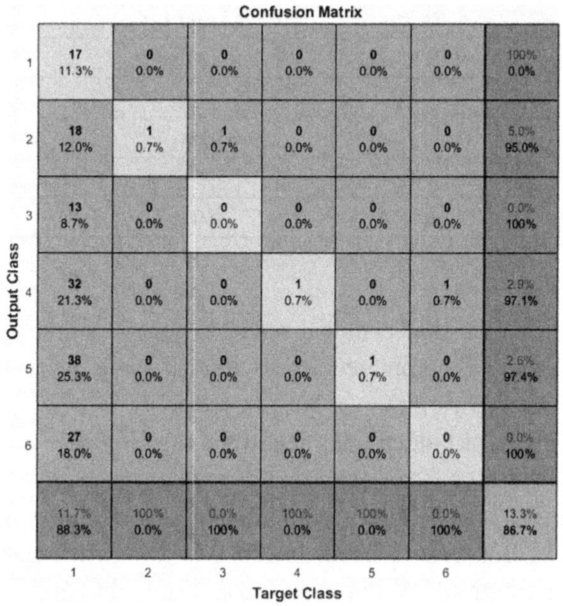

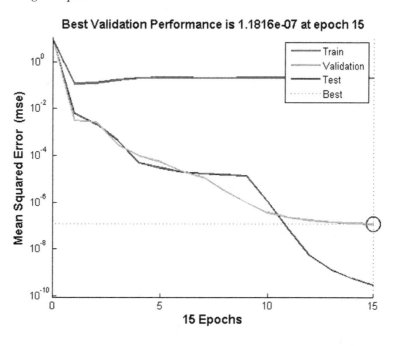

Figure 9. MSE convergence plot

The classifier takes varied number of epochs to reach the desired convergence goal. The DSS executes its work from a controller PC which acts as the interface for integrating all the constituent blocks of the system. In a modified form, the DSS may be deployed in a cloud server with access to authorized users. Figure 9 shows a schematic regarding the use of a cloud based architecture for deployment of the system

Table 1. Effect of Hidden Layer Length on the classifier training

Sl. No.	Number of Epochs	Hidden Layer Length	Average Success Rate (in %)
1	08	100	88
2	08	90	86
3	12	80	93.3
4	11	70	96.7
5	7	60	81.3

for greater access. This modification shall enable the system become suitable for actual deployment. The smooth working of the DSS enables automated access control using the present arrangement.

Figure 9, shows MSE convergence plot.

The Table 1, shows the effect of hidden layer length on the classifier training while performing the experiment. As seen in the table a series of experiments are performed to ascertain the effect of hidden layer on the training. As shown in the Table 1, with a hidden layer of 100, the classifier takes eight epochs to reach an MSE of 10^{-7}. But it provides an accuracy of 88% when tested for six different classes. Similarly, for a hidden layer length of 90, the epochs count of eight generating 10^{-7} MSE convergence lowers accuracy to 86%. With a hidden layer length of 80, the epoch count goes upto twelve, but accuracy improves to 93.3%. With a hidden layer length of 70, the epoch count is eleven and the accuracy reaches to 96.7%. This is the optimal configuration adopted for the system. In the case of hidden layer length of 60, the accuracy decreases to 81.3% though the train takes place fast. It indicates that a slower learning contributes towards better results.

Figure 10, shows the communication through the remote cloud server. The cloud based decision support system and data base. The data received is continuously synced through the data fed in the database.

Figure 10. Communication through remote cloud server

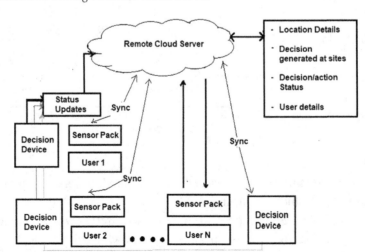

CONCLUSION

Here, we have discussed the design and implementation of a home surveillance system designed using legacy devices connected in line of IoT framework. There are multiple sub blocks like embedded unit, control unit, networking resources, DSS etc. which enable continuous monitoring and access control. The significant part of the work is its integration to a DSS which is learning based. A FF ANN has been trained to verify a set of faces in a database and trigger remote access inside a premise. We have performed a series of experiments to fix the configuration of the recognition block which is a multi-layer set-up. Several configurations have been adopted and the optimal design ascertained. Experimental results have shown that the system is reliable. The entire system is integrated using a PC where the DSS runs as well. In a modified form, the DSS may be deployed in a cloud server which shall make it more accessible and suitable for actual deployment.

REFERENCES

Abu, Suboh, & Ramli. (2018). Design and Development of Home Security Systems based on Internet of Things Via Favoriot Platform. *International Journal of Applied Engineering Research, 13*(2), 1253-1260.

Ada, L. (2017). *PIR Motion Sensor Created.* Adafruit Industries.

Ayed, Elkosantini, & Abid. (2017). An Automated Surveillance System based on Multi-Processor System-on-Chip and Hardware Accelerator. *International Journal of Advanced Computer Science and Applications., 8*(9), 59.

Bashal, Jilani, & Arun. (2016). An Intelligent Door System using Raspberry Pi and Amazon Web Services IoT. *International Journal of Engineering Trends and Technology.*

Basyal, Kaushal, & Singh. (2018). Voice Recognition Robot with Real Time Surveillance and Automation. *International Journal of Creative Research Thoughts, 6*(1), 2320–2882.

Bradski & Kaehler. (2008). *Learning OpenCV.* Academic Press.

Castro, Coral, Rodriguez, Cabra, & Colorado. (2017). Wearable-Based Human Activity Recognition Using an IoT Approach. *Journal Sensor and Actuator Networks, 6*(28).

Chiu, Ku, & Wang. (2010). Automatic Traffic Surveillance System for Vision-Based Vehicle Recognition and Tracking. *Journal of Information Science and Engineering, 26,* 611–629.

Domadia & Mehta. (2014). Automated Video Surveillance System for Human Motion Detection with Face Detection. *International Journal of Advance Engineering and Research Development, 1*(5).

Elshafee & Hamed. (2012). Design and Implementation of a WiFi Based Home Automation System. World Academy of Science, Engineering and Technology. *International Journal of Computer, Electrical, Automation, Control and Information Engineering, 6*(8).

Evans, D. (2011). *The Internet of Things How the Next Evolution of the Internet Is Changing Everything.* Cisco.

Industrial Internet Consortium. (n.d.). *Industrial Internet Reference Architecture*. Available: http://www.iiconsortium.org/IIRA.htm

Jan. (2004). Neural Network Based Threat Assessment for Automated Visual Surveillance. *Neural Networks, 2004. Proceedings. 2004 IEEE International Joint Conference on*. doi: . doi:10.1109/IJCNN.2004.1380133

Kadu, Dekhane, Dhanwala, & Awate. (2015). Real Time Monitoring and Controlling System. *International Journal of Engineering and Science, 4*(2), 15-18.

Keerthikanth, SaiSanath, & Manikandaswamy. (2018). Multiple Motion Control System of a Rover Based on IoT to Produce Cloud Service. *International Journal of Pure and Applied Mathematics, 119*(12), 13171-13173.

Kodali, Bose, & Boppana. (2016). IoT Based Smart Security and Home Automation System. *International Conference on Computing, Communication and Automation (ICCCA2016)*.

Kuhlman, D. (2013). *A Python Book: Beginning Python*. Advanced Python, and Python Exercises.

Lin & Kung. (1997). Face Recognition/Detection by Probabilistic Decision-Based Neural Network. *IEEE Transactions on Neural Networks, 8*(1), 1045–9227. PMID:18255615

Listyorini & Rahim. (2018). A prototype fire detection implemented using the Internet of Things and fuzzy logic. World Transactions on Engineering and Technology Education, 16(1), 42-46.

Lynggaard, P. (2017). *Artificial intelligence and Internet of Things in a "smart home" context: A Distributed System Architecture*. Available: vbn.aau.dk

Moghaddam & Pentland. (1995). Probabilistic Visual Learning for Object Detection. *IEEE Transactions on Pattern Analysis and Machine Intelligence, 19*(7).

Monk. (2014). *Raspberry Pi Cookbook*. Academic Press.

Nagarajan & Surendran. (2015). A High End Building Automation and Online Video Surveillance Security System. *International Journal of Engineering and Technology, 7*(1).

Oludele, Avodele, Oladele, & Olurotimi. (2009). Design of an Automated Intrusion Detection System incorporating an Alarm. *Journal of Computers, 1*(1), 2151–9617.

Ondrej & Milos. (2009). Neural Network Based Intrusion Detection System for Critical Infrastructures. *Proceedings of International Joint Conference on Neural Networks*.

Pathari & Bojewar. (2014). Video Surveillance in Public Transport Areas using Semantic Based Approach. *International Journal of Engineering Research and Technology, 4*(1).

Ramlee, L., Singh, I., Othman, S., & Misran, M. (2013). Bluetooth Remote Home Automation System Using Android Application. *International Journal of Engineering and Science, 1*, 149-153.

Russell, S. J., & Norvig, P. (1995). *Artificial Intelligence a Modern Approach*. Prentice Hall.

S., & G. (2016). Motion Detection Using IoT and Embedded System Concepts. *International Journal of Advanced Research in Electrical, Electronics and Instrumentation, 5*(10), 3297.

Shah, Omar, & Khurram. (2007). *Automated Visual Surveillance in Realistic Scenarios*. IEEE Computer Society.

Shaik & D. (2016). IoT based Smart Home Security System with Alert and Door Access Control using Smart Phone. *International Journal of Engineering Research & Technology, 5*(12).

Sharma & Sarma. (2016). Soft-Computational Techniques and Spectro-Temporal Features for Telephonic Speech Recognition: An Overview and Review of Current State of the Art. Handbook of Research on Advanced Hybrid Intelligent Techniques and Applications.

Shitole, Kamatchi, & Iyer. (2018). Smart Home Context-Aware Automation by Customization Strategy. *International Conference on Emerging Trends in Computing Technology (ICETCT- 2018)*.

Singh & Verma. (2012). Tracking of Moving object in Video scene using Neural Network. *International Journal of Advanced Research in Computer Engineering & Technology, 1*(10), 2278–1323.

Teschioni, Oberti, & Regazzoni. (1991). *A Neural-Network Approach for Moving Objects Recognition in Color Image Sequences for Surveillance Applications*. Academic Press.

Widyantara & Sastra. (2015). Internet of Things for Intelligent Traffic Monitoring System: A Case Study in Denpasar. *International Journal of Computer Trends and Technology, 30*(3).

Yang, Luo, & Li. (2018). Hide Your Hackable Smart Home from Remote Attacks: The Multipath Onion IoT Gateways. *23rd European Symposium on Research in Computer Security, ESORICS 2018*.

Chapter 9
Application of Predictive Intelligence in Water Quality Forecasting of the River Ganga Using Support Vector Machines

Anil Kumar Bisht
MJP Rohilkhand University, India

Ravendra Singh
MJP Rohilkhand University, India

Rakesh Bhutiani
Gurukul Kangri Vishwavidhayalaya, India

Ashutosh Bhatt
Birla Institute of Applied Sciences, India

ABSTRACT

Predicting the water quality of rivers has attracted a lot of researchers all around the globe. A precise prediction of river water quality may benefit the water management bodies. However, due to the complex relationship existing among various factors, the prediction is a challenging job. Here, the authors attempted to develop a model for forecasting or predicting the water quality of the river Ganga using application of predictive intelligence based on machine learning approach called support vector machine (SVM). The monthly data sets of five water quality parameters from 2001 to 2015 were taken from five sampling stations from Devprayag to Roorkee in the Uttarakhand state of India. The experiments are conducted in Python 2.7.13 language (Anaconda2 4.3.1) using the radial basis function (RBF) as a kernel for developing the non-linear SVM-based classifier as a model for water quality prediction. The results indicated a prediction performance of 96.66% for best parameter combination which proved the significance of predictive intelligence in water quality forecasting.

DOI: 10.4018/978-1-5225-6210-8.ch009

INTRODUCTION

For sustainable development of the environment it is crucial for the human being to protect the key water resource i.e. rivers. Predicting the water quality of rivers has been considered as one of critical and challenging application of time series based predictive intelligence. The reason behind is that the determination of water quality of rivers is itself a nonlinear and complex phenomenon in nature. Basically the water quality is characterized by three important components i.e. physical, biological and chemical with reverence to their proposed use and set of corresponding standards (Gazzaz, 2012). Recently, there have been a tremendous increase in the number of research in the field of ecological and environmental modelling. Researchers have made remarkable efforts in the field of water quality. (Maier, 2010) discussed their research in detail and conducted a detailed survey of 210 journal papers and indicated that artificial neural networks (ANNs) have been used progressively for modelling problems in water and ecological domain. They concluded that majority of studies more than 90% of the papers focused on water quantity with only few focused on to water quality.

This research work will address the problem associated with present water related challenge in India i.e. of 'water quality'. The major motivational factor behind the present study is: "water pollution" in rivers which is attracting a lot of attention in all around especially in India. The second motivating factor which inspired the most is the orders of the Supreme Court of India to the Government of India for finding out technical solutions to the water related challenges (Union Ministry of Science and Technology Govt. of India, 2009). Finally the most striking motivational factor to carry out this research is the fact that only a limited efforts and little research has been carried out to date for the Indian rivers and as far as to the best knowledge of authors concern no efforts have been made till date for assessment, prediction and modelling the water quality of GANGA river in India using technical approaches based on machine learning.

The objectives of this chapter is to contribute to the development of various prediction models for forecasting or predicting the quality of the river Ganga in prospective of India based on collection of the previous historical times-series authentic data and then selecting the best one on the basis of their forecasting performance. In this paper authors, first of all emphasis is on one of the modern approach of machine learning named Support Vector Machines (SVM). Secondly, the research will determine an efficient predictive model among the developed models by comparing their performances via several experiments. Finally, try to propose an optimal model that can be used as a decision support system for proactive planning and performing actions in order to maintain the water quality of rivers.

BACKGROUND

During the past years the quality of water is deteriorating day-by-day that resulted in serious problem of water pollution. Therefore this issue of water security attracted a lot of attention of the researchers and academicians all around the world. A variety of research work in this fields has been going on using different techniques. Because of much difficult and highly non-linear nature of environmental systems the deterministic models which have been constructed so far are not up to the mark (Sarkar & Pandey, 2015). In addition to this, limited availability of water data and high cost in monitoring are main drawbacks associated with the process based modelling methodologies (Palani, 2008). Now-a-days various machine learning techniques are common in practice which use the given data in order to derive a solution for the given problem. Most of the water researches which were intended for water quantity modelling used the concept of artificial neural networks (ANNs). The ANNs have become tremendously popular and being used in many fields especially as an ecological modelling tool to predict/forecast water resource variables. The models based on ANN method are data-driven, nonlinear, flexible, require minimal human involvement and no detailed information regarding the system under concern (Yan, 2012). ANN based water quality models are faster, lucrative and requisite a low input data as compared with the process based models (Palani, 2008). Consequently, the modelling methods based on data driven principle are more in demand.

In last few decades extensive work have been done on water movement prediction with only limited research on quality of water (Maier, 2010). There exist a vast literature which focused on prediction of flow of rivers (Jayawardena, & Fernando, 2001; Chang, 2002; Riad & Mania, 2004; Abrahart & See, 2007; Shamseldin, 2010; Krishna, 2011; Moalafhi, 2014; Reyes, 2016). Though, now the research community is more focused towards the assessment water quality using ANNs (Palani, 2008; Rankovi, Radulovic, Radojevic, Ostojic, & Comic, 2010; Banejad & Olyaie, 2011; Yan, 2012; Guru & Jha, 2013; Sarkar & Pandey, 2015). Considering the scenario of Indian rivers very limited research work have been done by utilizing ANNs as a tool for water quality modelling purpose (Sarkar & Pandey, 2015).

As far as to the best awareness of writers of this paper no efforts have been made till date for assessment, modelling and prediction for the water quality of national River GANGA in India using machine learning based technical approaches like ANNs or SVMs utilizing an authentic time series data. Recently, researchers have twisted their interest from ANNs into another growing domain of training the machines known as support vector machines (SVMs) in order to solve the water quality problems. Various researchers reported several drawbacks of ANNs like it may only find a local optimum while SVMs are capable of finding a global optimum (Madge, 2015). Moreover, ANN may also have the problem of slower speed of training, ineffective generalization and low rate of accuracy (Liao, 2011). Besides this it also require excessive amount of training data due to having complex network structure. Compared to ANN, SVM has several benefits like small amount of samples requirement, high prediction accuracy to solve the complex and highly nonlinear data problems of water quality modeling and prediction.

The forecasting or prediction of water quality is a multivariable and nonlinear type of problem to be solved. In this study, we attempted to develop first ever (as far the best knowledge of authors) SVM-based predictive model to predict the water quality of the river Ganga using data from five different regions in Uttarakhand, India. The experimental data sets from 2001 to 2015 were used to train and test the model. SVM is a state-of-the-art machine-learning system proposed by V. Vapnik and his team of AT&T's Bell Labs (Junping, L.) based on statistical learning theory (SLT) utilizing the principle of structural risk minimization, which has good generalization ability (Malek, 2014). At present SVM has been applied successfully in a range of research areas.

Liao et al., (2011), presented a water quality assessment technique based on bio-monitoring and multiclass Support Vector Machine. They have conducted experiments on the study of the behavioral of fish (Zebrafish) based on the computer vision technology and multi-classification method using SVM. The organic observation process was used for generating the initial caution messages based on which various preventive actions can be initiated for regulating the pollution. Authors gave a concluding remark that as compared to the older water quality estimation procedures the methods like this based on biological monitoring where the fish responses have been studied, a highly cost effective results will be developed which demands minimum human involvement.

Malek et al., (2014) proposed a method for predicting the dissolved oxygen (DO) for the two lakes namely Chini and Bera in Malaysia. They have taken data sample from 2005 to 2009 consisting 11 water quality parameters. The Authors conducted the experiments using SVM model based on Anova kernel. Their results showed an accuracy of 74%. They concluded that using SVM based water quality model it is possible to achieve a greater efficiency for predicting the DO and SVM is turns out to be an effective technique for prediction and forecasting.

Junping et al., performed a research on groundwater Quality Assessment at the Niangziguan fountain region of Haihe River basin using the method support vector machine. They have considered eight assessment factors to develop the sample data set. The results proved the importance of SVM which classified all test samples correctly.

Liao et al., (2012), performed an experiment for determining the water quality based on the application of biomonitoring and support vector machine. They studied behavior of one of the water spices i.e. of zebrafish in toxic environments to access the water quality using SVM method. In this study, acute toxicity experiments using four kinds of metal ions were performed on zebrafish. The response of zebrafish to one of the metal ions was found to be strong, concluding a fast worsening in water quality. Authors concluded that this becomes a good technique to access the water quality. The achieved results were found to be satisfactory. Their developed model attains a high classification accuracy of 80%.

Tan et al., (2012) performed an experiment over the water quality of rivers for prediction of total phosphorus using three different techniques BP (Back Propagation), RBF (Radial Basis Function) network and LS-SVM (Least Squares Support Vector Machine). The results showed that out of these three methods the least squares support vector machine method outperforms the other two methods. The water quality model based on LS-SVM have least prediction error among other two models and thus achieved a high prediction performance accuracy. The results of this study highlighted the fact that the SVM based methodology is more advantageous than the ANN based method when the sample size of the problem domain to consider is small. Thus, SVM is now-a-days growing to be a vital tool for solving various types of ecological problems.

Therefore, the above said literature survey results in a conclusion that for Indian rivers only a little effort have been done till date for prediction and forecasting their water quality. Additionally, no research work was available exclusively for the modelling the water quality of the river Ganga based on machine learning methodologies like ANN or SVM. Therefore, in this paper the authors try to bridge this research gap by developing SVM based model for forecasting the water quality of the river Ganga.

MATERIALS AND METHODS

Study Zone and the Data Used

For the purpose of research, the biggest river basin in India i.e. Ganga River was selected in this paper. Apart from National River the Ganga River is also awarded the status of living entity in 2017. This river comprises almost one-fourth of the country's total land mass and supports 43% of its population along the 11 states in India. A major portion of this river is lies in India while only 21% of the remaining part is lies in Nepal and Bangladesh (Ministry of Environment and Forests, 2009). Figure 1 displayed the area covered by the river Ganga in India.

Figure 1. The View of Ganga River
Source: http://www.all-about-india.com/Route-of-Ganges-River.html

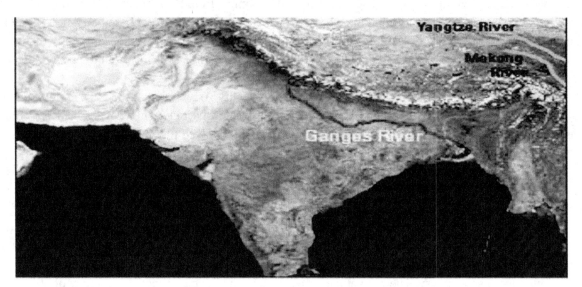

The journey of Ganga River is started from the Uttarakhand state towards the Uttar Pradesh, Bihar, Jharkhand and West Bengal and terminated into the Bay of Bengal covering a distance of 2525 km. Initiating from Garhwal Himalayas, the River Bhagirathi joined with river Alaknanda to form the river Ganga at Devprayag region (CPCB, 2013). The Devprayag, Rishikesh, Haridwar, Jwalapur and Roorkee are the five sampling places taken under consideration for this research work in the Uttarakhand state. The monthly data sets of size 900 records consisting of five water quality parameters from these stations sampled over a period of 2001 to 2015 is used in this experiment examined by Limnology & Ecological Modelling Laboratory, department of Zoology and Environment Science, Gurukul Kangri Vishwavidhyalaya, Haridwar, Uttarakhand, India (Bisht, 2017).

Support Vector Machine Based Model Development

Support vector machines (SVMs) is an emerging machine learning approach for solving both linear and non-linear types of classification problems. In linear problems the data can be separated linearly and thus for such problems the linear methods are used that define a linear decision boundaries between the classes. While the non-linear problems can be solved using non-linear algorithms where data can't be separated linearly can be solved. The machine-learning models based on SVM are supervised and non-parametric in nature. The supervised methods involve a training set with a known target (or output) and the non-parametric models don't make strict assumptions about the structure of the data as in the real world there is no smooth relationship between the input and the target variable. Instead these models adapts as per the input-output relationships among the data. As a result these non-parametric approaches fit the data in best manner and generating accurate prediction performances (Brink, 2017)

Existing approaches to machine learning like Back-Propagation Neural Networks (BPNNs), Naive Bayes, K-Nearest Neighbors (KNN), Random Forest may not be suited in case of small sized sample data set while SVM works well. This attractive concept of SVM was developed by Vapnik in 1995 based on the Statistical Learning Theory (SLT). The concepts behind SLT is to find solution for the learning based on finite sample. SLT considers issues like that of generalization, topology selection, local minimum, over fitting and others in order to address the small sample learning problem.

SVM becomes more popular because of the following features: (Malek, 2014; Liao, 2011).

- It can classify highly nonlinear and complex data.
- Works well even small size sample is available.
- Faster training speed.
- Good generalization ability.
- High prediction accuracy.

All these features made SVM as a promising tool for classification purpose in several applications of Machine Learning (ML) as compared to ANN model and other approaches.

A SVM based classifier performs classification of specified data set by dividing it into two classes by drawing a straight line called hyperplane.

Let us assume there exist a set of input data/training sample called input vectors: (Kara, 2011).

$$(x_1, y_1), (x_2, y_2), (x_3, y_3) \ldots (x_n, y_n):$$

x_i belongs to R^d and i=1,2,3,......n

means there are n-vectors of d-dimension having its corresponding output data called labels as:

y_i belongs $\{-1,1\}$.

Having x_i as feature vector and y_i as label the principal working of SVM is to determine such a hyperplane which performs optimal classification such that -1 and +1 denotes two output classes into which the input data is classified (Liao, 2011).

The main focus of SVM is on drawing such a hyperplane as a dividing boundary so that it maximizes the distance among the nearest data points of both classes to this hyperplane. These nearest data points belonging to the two different classes are called as support vectors (Liao, 2012). This distance is said to define a margin as shown in the Figure 2 and the objective is to maximize this margin to achieve an optimal classification (Kara, 2011). In this way SVM can classify the linearly separable data. For the non-linear data sets which can't be separated linearly Vapnik (1995) proposed to use the non-linear classifier based on SVM using the kernel function. The hyperplane which maximizes the margin between two different classes is said to define as a best hyperplane providing best classification.

In general, most of the real world problems are non-linear in nature i.e. they can't be classified into linearly separable classes as above. In those cases, the concept of nonlinear SVM based on kernel function is to be used where the input sample is transformed into a high-dimensional feature space by applying nonlinear mapping then as usual an optimal hyperplane is to be constructed that separates data into two classes as shown in Figure 3 (Lieo, 2011; Liao, 2012). The mapping is performed by the kernel function. There exist various kinds of kernel functions, among which the radial basis function (RBF) is most commonly used by the researchers. The RBF is defined as follows:

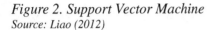

Figure 2. Support Vector Machine
Source: Liao (2012)

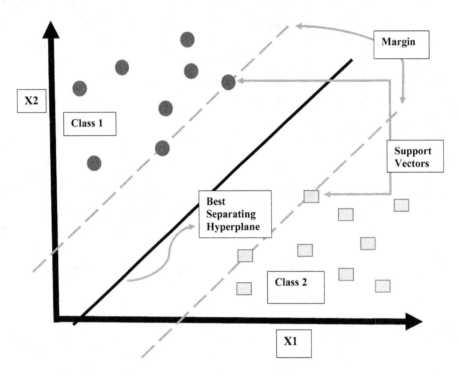

$$K(x, x_{i)} = e^{-\gamma \|x-xi\|}{}_2$$

where γ is the constant in RBF must be greater than zero and $|\,x\text{-}x_i\,|$ denotes the Euclidean distance from center x to the input vector $x_{i.}$ (Liao, 2012).

EXPERIMENTS, RESULTS AND DISCUSSIONS

The experiments are conducted in Python 2.7.13 language (Anaconda2 4.3.1) (https://www.python.org) applying the Radial Basis Function (RBF) as a kernel for Support Vector Machine. The flow chart in the Figure 4 shows the working flow of the proposed forecasting scheme.

The initial data set containing total 900 tuples was divided into two parts using 60%-40% data partitioning strategy where 60% data is used for training purpose i.e. to develop the model whereas using the remaining 40% data testing is performed to evaluate the efficiency of the constructed model. Temperature, pH, dissolved oxygen (DO), biochemical oxygen demand (BOD) and total coliform (TC) are the input parameters with WQ (water quality) as the output parameter. The support vector machine (SVM) based program was developed in Python 2.7.13 language (Anaconda2 4.3.1). For defining the output parameter, the water quality (WQ) standards prescribed by Central pollution control board (CPCB) is used. Central Pollution Control Board (CPCB), categorized the Water Quality into five different classes which is described in Table 1.

Figure 3. Non Linear Transformation
Source: Lieo (2011) and Liao (2012)

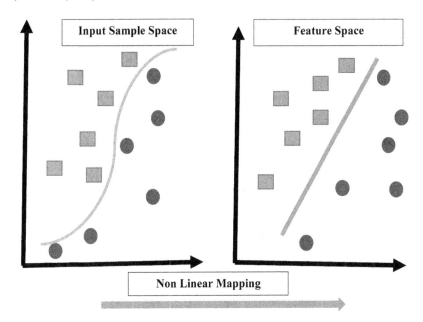

For developing the SVM based water quality prediction model one of the well-known kernel function called radial basis function (RBF) was used. Based on this a total number of 80 different experimental investigations have been conducted following various training parameters. The model was developed by initiating the training process applying various parameters like dataset, (γ) constant in RBF kernel function and (C) regularization parameter in RBF kernel. Various ranges of parameters γ and C tested for selecting best parameter combination to develop the SVM model for WQ prediction as shown in the Table 2.

First the training is done applying the 60% of the data (comprising 540 data instances) from the total available dataset. Once the training is completed, the testing of developed model is done using the remaining 40% dataset (i.e. 360 data instances). Thus, as soon as the proposed model is developed, it is tested upon the testing dataset and the corresponding performance is measured. If the performance is acceptable than the model is accepted as best one otherwise again training phase is required to be performed by setting up the parameters in such a way that it could reach the highest performance on testing (unseen) data set.

Finally the prediction performance of the developed WQ model based on SVM using RBF kernel was calculated for different parameter combinations as shown in the Table 3. Twenty different levels of (γ) constant and four different levels of (C) regularization parameter in RBF kernel have been experimented and corresponding to each combination their prediction performance was determined as tabulated in the Table 3.

Out of these several developed models a model that attained the greater prediction accuracy is concluded as the ideal WQ prediction model. This table is showing a clear trend that as the value of 'γ' parameter in RBF kernel increases for every value of the 'C' i.e. regularization parameter corresponding result i.e. the prediction accuracy performance is gradually decreases. Figure 5 shows the experimental

Figure 4. Flowchart of proposed work explaining the working flow

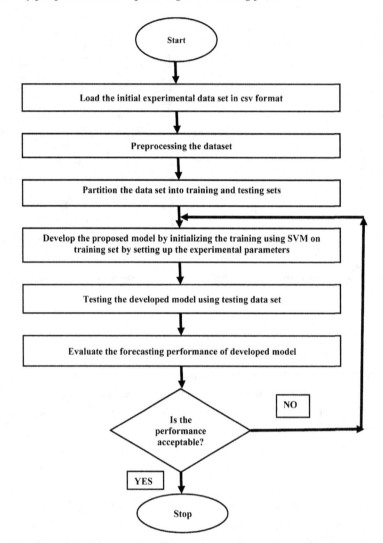

Table 1. Water Quality Classification

Sr. No.	Class	Usefulness
1.	A	Drinking Water Source without conventional treatment
2.	B	Outdoor bathing
3.	C	Drinking water source after conventional treatment
4.	D	Wild life and Fisheries
5.	E	Irrigation and Industrial Cooling

Table 2. Various ranges of parameters tested for selecting best parameter combination to develop the SVM model using RBF Kernel

Parameters	Ranges of Parameters
(γ) constant in RBF kernel function	0.1, 0.2, 0.3,............, 2.0
(C) regularization parameter in RBF kernel	1, 10, 100, 1000

Table 3. Prediction Performance (%) of WQ Prediction Model based on SVM using RBF kernel

C	γ	Prediction Accuracy (%)	C	γ	Prediction Accuracy (%)	C	γ	Prediction Accuracy (%)	C	γ	Prediction Accuracy (%)
1	0.1	94.72	**10**	**0.1**	**96.66**	100	0.1	94.66	1000	0.1	93.88
1	0.2	94.16	**10**	**0.2**	**96.66**	100	0.2	94.88	1000	0.2	90.83
1	0.3	92.22	10	0.3	95.83	100	0.3	94.22	1000	0.3	90.27
1	0.4	90.27	10	0.4	95.83	100	0.4	93.77	1000	0.4	92.5
1	0.5	89.16	10	0.5	95.55	100	0.5	92.44	1000	0.5	93.05
1	0.6	87.5	10	0.6	95.27	100	0.6	91.11	1000	0.6	93.05
1	0.7	85.55	10	0.7	93.88	100	0.7	89.77	1000	0.7	92.77
1	0.8	84.72	10	0.8	90.83	100	0.8	88	1000	0.8	91.94
1	0.9	84.44	10	0.9	89.44	100	0.9	86.44	1000	0.9	89.72
1	1	83.88	10	1	87.77	100	1	86.22	1000	1	88.88
1	1.1	84.16	10	1.1	86.94	100	1.1	86.66	1000	1.1	88.33
1	1.2	84.72	10	1.2	86.38	100	1.2	87.55	1000	1.2	87.5
1	1.3	84.72	10	1.3	86.66	100	1.3	87.77	1000	1.3	87.22
1	1.4	86.11	10	1.4	88.05	100	1.4	88.88	1000	1.4	87.22
1	1.5	87.22	10	1.5	89.72	100	1.5	81.55	1000	1.5	89.16
1	1.6	77.77	10	1.6	78.05	100	1.6	79.77	1000	1.6	78.61
1	1.7	76.94	10	1.7	77.5	100	1.7	78.22	1000	1.7	76.66
1	1.8	75.55	10	1.8	77.22	100	1.8	78	1000	1.8	76.38
1	1.9	75.55	10	1.9	76.38	100	1.9	78	1000	1.9	76.66
1	2	75.27	10	2	75	100	2	77.55	1000	2	75

Where, 'γ' denotes a constant and 'C' is a regularization parameter used in RBF kernel.

snapshot of the developed model using SVM in Python for the best parameter combination among the others providing a best efficiency of 96.66%.

The prediction performance of the worst and the best SVM model among all other models is displayed in the Table 4.

The results indicated a best prediction performance of 96.66 for two different combination of parameters i.e. when the value of γ is =0.1 and C=10 and when γ =0.2 and C is =10. However, when the value of γ is increased to 2, the developed model had shown a very poor performance of 75% in both cases when C =10 as well as when C =1000 which is lowest among the all other developed model.

Figure 5. Experimental window showing output of the proposed model (case of best model) in Python

```
svc = svm.SVC(kernel='rbf', C=10,gamma=0.1, verbose=False).fit(X1, y)
coun=0
for i in range(X_test.shape[0]):
    tt=svc.predict(X_test[i])
    observed.append(int(tt))
    if(tt==Y_test[i]):
        #observed.append(svc.predict(X_test[i]))
        #print("hi")
        coun=coun+1
months=[]
for i in range(Y_test.shape[0]):
    months.append(i)
print((1.0*coun*100)/Y_test.shape[0])
plt.plot(months,observed)
plt.xlabel('Months')
plt.ylabel('Predicted')
plt.show()
    DeprecationWarning)
96.6666666667
```

Table 4. Prediction performance of the worst and the best SVM model for WQ Prediction

C	Γ	Prediction Accuracy (%)
10	0.1	96.66 (Best Result)
	0.2	
10	2	75 (Worst Result)
1000		

Hence we can say that SVM is proved to be an efficient machine learning method for developing the prediction or forecasting models.

CONCLUSION AND FUTURE SCOPE

In this chapter, authors have proposed and developed first ever (as far the best knowledge of authors) water quality forecasting model based on SVM for Ganga River. The main focus of this work is to solve the issues in the river Ganga. A variety of experiments have been conducted following 60%-40% data partitioning policy and different combinations of (γ) constant and different levels of (C) regularization parameter using RBF kernel in SVM. The monthly water quality dataset for the period of 2001 to 2015 covering five different stations Devprayag, Rishikesh, Haridwar, Jwalapur and Roorkee in the Uttarakhand state of India comprises of five water quality parameters is used for this research work. For developing the SVM based WQ prediction model total 80 experiments are conducted in Python 2.7.13 language (Anaconda2 4.3.1) using the Radial Basis Function (RBF) as a kernel adopting different combinations of two main parameters involved in this kernel i.e. 'γ' parameter and regularization parameter 'C'. The combination of 'γ' and 'C' which resulted in greatest prediction performance will be considered as a best training parameters.

After extensive experiments a prediction performance of 96.66 is achieved for best parameter combination of 'γ' and 'C'. Thus we concluded from this research work that the predictive intelligence is applied successfully for the water quality prediction or forecasting of the river Ganga using one of the emerging machine learning method i.e. SVM. This research will definitely going to be of much importance for the researchers. As a future scope of this work authors can explore the possibilities of other parameters for the RBF kernel, a totally different training and testing data patterns as well as they may have a more number of experiments utilizing another mapping functions for improving the accuracy. In upcoming research one can also apply this framework of research for solving another ecological problems.

The present work also contributes useful information related with the river water quality that is of great importance for the authorities related with water problem in order to adopt various decisions keeping in view the benefits of rivers as well as that of the mankind.

REFERENCES

Abrahart, R.J. & See, L.M. (2007). Neural network emulation of a rainfall-runoff model. *The Journal of Hydrology and Earth System Sciences, 4*, 287–326.

Banejad, H., & Olyaie, E. (2011). Application of an Artificial Neural Network Model to Rivers Water Quality Indexes Prediction – A Case Study. *The Journal of American Science, 7*(1).

Bisht, A. K. (2017). Development of an Automated Water Quality Classification Model for the river Ganga. In *3rd International Conference on Next Generation Computing Technologies*. Springer.

Brink, H. (2017). *Real-World Machine Learning*. Manning publications Co.

Chang, F. J. (2002). Hydrological Processes. *Hydrological Processes, 16*, 2577–2588. doi:10.1002/hyp.1015

Gazzaz, N. M. (2012). Artificial neural network Modelling of the water quality index for Kinta River (Malaysia) using water quality variables as predictors. Marine Pollution Bulletin.

Guru, N., & Jha, R. (2013). Simulation of BOD-DO Modelling in Mahanadi River System lying in Odisha using ANN, India. *IOSR Journal Of Environmental Science, Toxicology And Food Technology, 2*(4), 52-57.

Heydari, M. (2013). Development of a Neural Network Technique for Prediction of Water Quality Parameters in the Delaware River, Pennsylvania. *Middle East Journal of Scientific Research, 13*(10), 1367–1376.

Jayawardena, A. W., & Fernando, T. M. K. G. (2001). River flow prediction: an artificial neural network Approach. In *Proceedings of a symposium held during die Sixth IAHS Scientific Assembly at Maastricht, The Netherlands*. IAHS Publication no. 268..

Kara, Y., Acar Boyacioglu, M., & Baykan, Ö. K. (2011). Predicting direction of stock price index movement using artificial neural networks and support vector machines: The sample of the Istanbul Stock Exchange. *Expert Systems with Applications, 38*(5), 5311–5319. doi:10.1016/j.eswa.2010.10.027

Krishna, B., Rao, Y. R. S., & Nayak, P. C. (2011). Time Series Modeling of River Flow Using Wavelet Neural Networks. *Journal of Water Resource and Protection, 3*(01), 50–59. doi:10.4236/jwarp.2011.31006

Liao, Y. (2012). Application of biomonitoring and support vector machine in water quality assessment. *Journal of Zhejiang University (Biomed & Biotechnol), 13*(4), 327-334.

Liao, Y., Xu, J., & Wang, W. (2011). A Method of Water Quality Assessment Based on Biomonitoring and Multiclass Support Vector Machine. *Procedia Environmental Sciences, Elsevier, 10*, 451–457. doi:10.1016/j.proenv.2011.09.074

Madge, S. (2015). *Predicting Stock Price Direction using Support Vector Machines*. Independent Work Report Spring.

Maier, H. R. (2010). Methods used for the development of neural networks for the prediction of water resource variables in river systems: Current status and future directions. In Environmental Modelling & Software 25 (pp. 891–909). Elsevier.

Malek, S. (2014). Dissolved Oxygen Prediction Using Support Vector Machine. *International Journal of Bioengineering and Life Sciences Vol, 8*(1).

Ministry of Environment and Forests, Government of India. (2009). *Status Paper On River Ganga, "State of Environment and Water Quality," National River Conservation Directorate*. Author.

Moalafhi, D. B. (2014). A Hybrid Stochastic-ANN Approach For Flow Partotioning In The Okavango Delta Of Botswana. *Global NEST Journal*.

Palani, S. (2008). An ANN application for water quality forecasting. *Bulletin, 56*, 1586–1597. PMID:18635240

Rankovi, V., Radulovic, J., Radojevic, I., Ostojic, A., & Comic, L. (2010). Neural network Modelling of Dissolved oxygen in the Gruza reservoir, Serbia. *Ecological Modelling, 221*, 1239–1244.

Reyes, J. V. (2016). Artificial Neural Networks applied to flow prediction: A use case for the Tomebamba river. *Procedia Engineering, 162*, 153–161. doi:10.1016/j.proeng.2016.11.031

Riad, S., Mania, J., Bouchaou, L., & Najjar, Y. (2004). Rainfall-Runoff Model Using an Artificial Neural Network Approach. *Mathematical and Computer Modelling, 40*(7-8), 839–846. doi:10.1016/j.mcm.2004.10.012

Sarkar, A., & Pandey, P. (2015). River Water Quality Modelling using Artificial Neural Network Technique. In *International Conference on Water Resources And Ocean Engineering (ICWRCOE)*. ELSEVIER.

Shamseldin, A. Y. (2010). Artificial neural network model for river flow forecasting in a developing country. *Journal of Hydroinformatics, 12*(1).

Tan, G., Yan, J., Gao, C., & Yang, S. (2012). Prediction of water quality time series data based on least squares support vector machine. *Procedia Engineering, 31*, 1194–1199. doi:10.1016/j.proeng.2012.01.1162

Union Ministry of Science and Technology Government of India. (2009). *Technology Mission: Winning, Augmentation and Renovation*. Technology Mission: WAR for Water, Plan Document Prepared by, On the directive of Supreme Court of India Order on Writ Petition (C) No 230 of 2001.

Yan, W. (2012). Toward Automatic Time-Series Forecasting Using Neural Networks. *IEEE Transactions on Neural Networks and Learning Systems, 23*(7). Retrieved from https://www.python.org

Chapter 10
Interference Management Techniques for Device-to-Device Communications

Weston Mwashita
Vaal University of Technology, South Africa

Marcel Ohanga Odhiambo
Vaal University of Technology, South Africa

ABSTRACT

The snowballing of many different electronic gadgets connected to different networks and to the internet is a clear indication that the much-anticipated internet of things (IoT) is fast becoming a reality. It is generally agreed that the next generation mobile networks should offer wireless connection to anything and anyone with a proper enabling device at any time leading to the full realization of IoT. Device-to device (D2D) communication is one technology that the research community believes will aid the implementation of the next generation of mobile networks, specifically 5G. Full roll out of D2D is however being impeded by the resulting interference. This chapter looks at the state-of-the-art research works on interference management technologies proposed for device-to-device communications. A comprehensive analysis of the proposed schemes is given and open challenges and issues that need to be considered by researchers in D2D communication for it to become a key enabler for 5G technology are highlighted and recommendations provided.

INTRODUCTION

When the fifth generation of mobile networks (5G) hits the market in 2020, it is generally agreed by academia and industry experts that by that time, there will be a 1000-fold increase in mobile traffic compared to what is being experienced today. This strategically positions 5G to become the backbone of the Internet of Things. What is currently hindering an expansive roll out of the Internet of Things are short range technologies such as Radio Frequency Identification (RFID), Bluetooth, etc which cannot be expected to offer seamless connection in large smart cities. This is where 5G comes in. 5G will be more

DOI: 10.4018/978-1-5225-6210-8.ch010

than a fast radio access technology. It will be a revolutionary change in the whole network architectures which will trigger highly innovative and revenue generating services. It is predicted that over 50 billion devices will be connected directly to cellular networks all over the world (Evans, 2011). A larger percentage of these devices will incorporate sensors for the measurement of temperature, pressure, speed or stress. 5G will allow for the remote monitoring of buildings, roads and bridges for structural changes. For the unlocking of IoT, 5G must address issues like latency, bandwidth and security. The revolutionary nature of 5G will usher in technologies like D2D. Figure 1 shows some of the technologies that will make 5G achieve most of users' expectations. D2D communications is when devices can directly communicate with each other without routing their communication via a base station. This is good for the Internet of Things. This allows sensors to directly send harvested information to processing equipment located at strategic points in smart cities and other environments. The integration of D2D communication into the legacy networks as well as in the next generation networks presents technical challenges and because of this, the implementation of D2D is still far. The biggest challenge is interference. There must be an effective interference management and mitigation of other challenges for the technology to achieve optimal system performance. Researchers have suggested several solutions but the fact that there hasn't been any meaningful D2D deployment speaks volumes of the ineffectiveness of these proposed schemes.

A qualitative comparison of the latest interference mitigation schemes is presented, and the technical challenges analysed. Open challenges and issues that need to be considered by researchers in D2D for it to become a key enabler for 5G technology are highlighted and recommendations provided in this chapter.

Various issues related to D2D are discussed and plans by researchers to integrate D2D into wireless sensor networking explored.

Figure 1. The 5G roadmap by METIS
Source: Osserain, Boccardi, Braun, Kusume, Marsch, Matermia,…. Fallgen (2014)

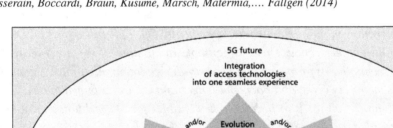

The target audience for this chapter are academicians, researchers and technology developers interested in developing practical technologies that can be used to deal with interference affecting D2D communications so that the D2D technology can be rolled out commercially to enable 5G to meet the expected data rate expectations. It is anticipated that researchers will find this chapter useful in furthering their research in the field of IoT.

BACKGROUND

With D2D communications, devices that are close to each other can establish a D2D link with or without the assistance of a base station (BS) or access point (AP). A D2D is an infrastructure-less communication technology. Figure 2 shows two users, UE_1 and UE_2 engaged in D2D communication. For traditional cellular networks, the BS must be involved in all communications even when communicating devices are located a few millimetres away from each other. This arrangement can work well for low data applications like voice and text but presents problems to modern mobile users who exchange high volumes of data especially in the form of video files. D2D communication system is a paradigm technology that increases network spectral efficiency (Cai, Zheng & Zhang, 2015), throughput and energy efficiency (Charar, Guennoun & Aniba, 2015) for users that are close to each other. Figure 3 shows some of the many uses of D2D communication.

The idea of D2D communications was first recorded by Lin and Hsu (2000) and its first implementation appeared in the work of Wu, Tavildar, Shakkottai, Richardson, Li, Laroia and Jovicic (2010). Table 1 presents the several types of D2D communications.

Inband D2D communication utilises the licensed frequency band. The main disadvantage of Inband D2D communications is the interference that is introduced to the cellular network.

A D2D communication link can be established via either licensed or unlicensed links. The unlicensed links involve the usage of the unlicensed frequency band and thus does not suffer from interference. The main problem with using the unlicensed band is the requirement of an extra interface. Bluetooth, Wi-Fi

Figure 2. D2D communications
Source: Chaudhari and Prashant (2017)

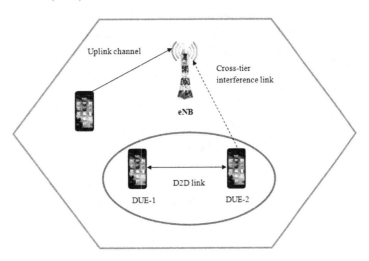

Figure 3. Application scenarios for D2D-enhanced IoT environments
Source: Militano, Araniti, Condoluci, Farris, & Iera (2015)

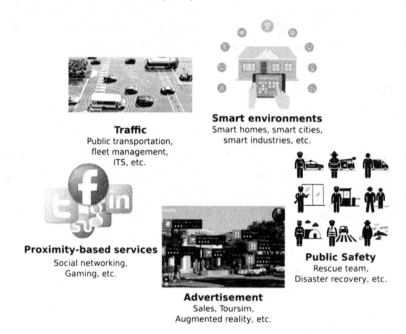

Table 1. D2D communication types

	D2D communications			
	Inband		Outband	
	Underlay	**Overlay**	**Controlled**	**Autonomous**
Frequency band	Licensed band	Licensed band	Unlicensed band is used	Unlicensed band is used
Spectrum resources	Cellular and D2D users use the same spectrum resources	Cellular users and D2D users use separate resources	Cellular spectrum is used	Industrial, Scientific and Medical (ISM) band is used

Direct and ZigBee are some of the technologies that can be used to provide the extra interface. The IoT applications that require the involvement of the user of a device in selecting certain applications can use the unlicensed frequency band. The IoT applications that do not require the intervention of users can make use of the licensed frequency band. The main problem with the licensed link is the interference experienced each time a licensed frequency band is used for D2D communications. Two types of interference affect In-band D2D communications (Shamrao & Kumar, 2017). There is cross-tier interference which results from D2D User Equipment (DUEs) and Cellular User Equipment (CUEs) sharing either uplink or downlink channels. Figure 4 depicts the interference that is introduced to the cellular network by D2D communications

Another type of interference is co-tier interference. This is the interference that affects DUEs coming from other DUEs. The next section looks at the main interference mitigation schemes that have been advanced by various researchers in terms of their strengths and weaknesses and their suitability in IoT.

Figure 4. Interference introduced by D2D communications
Source: Ghazanfar, Masood, Mujahid and Muhammad (2016)

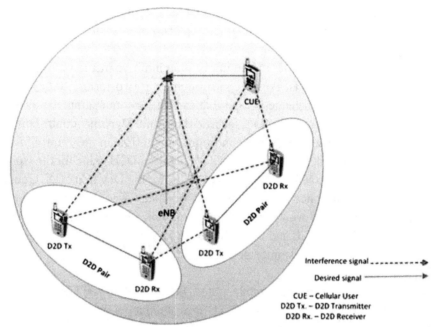

THE STATE-OF-THE ART IN INTERFERENCE MANAGEMENT SCHEMES

To address the issue of interference affecting D2D, the research community has been focusing on developing novel interference management techniques to mitigate the interference. Several techniques have been advanced.

Power Control

A proper power control mechanism is one technique that can be used to deal with cross-tier as well as co-tier interference. According to Song, Niyato, Han, and Hossain, (2015), power control can be achieved using basically two methods:

1. **Self-Organised:** DUEs make power changes by themselves in accordance with a predefined signal-to-interference-plus-noise ratio (SINR) to meet a stipulated Quality of Service (QoS). CUEs do not participate in the process. This method is simpler but not so efficient.
2. **Network Managed:** Both CUEs and DUEs dynamically change their transmit powers following a SINR report. The iterative users' process stops when all participating users have met their SINR requirements. The method is more efficient but more complex as an exchange of information among DUEs, CUEs and the BS is required.

In 3G mobile networks, power control is a critical component in the handling of the near-far problem. The near-far problem results from UEs transmitting to a BS such that weak transmissions from the cell edges will be obliterated or overwhelmed by strong signals from those UEs that are close to the BS. 4G does not have problems with intra-cell interference since orthogonal resources are used in the uplink. Power control is however still needed in 4G to compensate for shadowing and path loss. New techniques like fast scheduling have however been introduced to replace power control techniques in 4G (Sesia, Toufik & Baker, 2011).

The issue of power control has been rekindled in 5G as an intuitive method of reducing interference emanating from D2D communications. Power control comes in two forms; static or dynamic. With static power control, a fixed power scheme is used that can utilise some parameter as a reference. The transmitting power of DUEs can be limited to a specific threshold. Dynamic control on the other hand, has some form of feedback that uses prevailing conditions in real time in the controlling of power.

Power control strategy largely depends on the distance between D2D pairs, for the Uplink (UL) reuse case and the distance between the DUEs and the BS or CUE, for the Downlink (DL) reuse case. Where D2D pairs are an appreciable distance from the BS and the DUEs are in very close proximity to each other, a reduction of power control won't affect D2D communication performance. For a case where DUEs are very close to the BS or CUE and the distance between the D2D pair is large, a power control that results in the reduction of the transmitter powers of the DUEs would most likely result in no D2D communication taking place.

A power control strategy can be implemented on the already standardised UL power control schemes for LTE. The UL power control incorporated into LTE aims at reducing the near-far problem - a scenario that arises when UEs from various locations within a cell transmit to the same BS at the same time with the same amount of power. There is a tendency of the stronger signals from the mobiles closer to the BS to obliterate the weaker signals from the cell edges.

The standardised LTE power control utilises open loop control and closed loop control to set the UE transmitter power. Path loss, the modulation schemes used, and the network transmit power control (TPC) signals are all factored into establishing the power at which the UEs need to transmit at in the UL to establish effective communication. Options that can be incorporated into network assisted D2D communications are:

1.   Fixed SINR target (FST).
2.   Open loop with fractional path loss.
3.   Closed loop power control.

Hongnian and Hakola (2010) evaluated the effectiveness of power control schemes in networks incorporating D2D and concluded that power control schemes cannot be implemented alone in such networks. Power control schemes need to be complemented by other schemes like mode selection or resource scheduling. Fodor, Penda, Belleschi, Johansson, and Abrardo (2013) concluded that flexible power control schemes can be effective in network assisted D2D communications with CUEs being the biggest beneficiaries ahead of DUEs.

Lee, Lin, Andrews, and Heath (2015) proposed centralised and decentralised power control schemes. With a centralised power control strategy, the Device to Device links are managed centrally by a BS under the assumption that D2D pairs can give feedback of the normalised channel gains as well as target SINR to the central BS. The transmitter power used for the uplink user and the D2D transmitters is computed by the BS. Stochastic geometry was used to develop a centralised power control scheme by Lee et al., (2015) The scheme involves the BS as the central entity in collecting global channel state information

(CSI). DUEs send their normalised channel gains and target SINR figures to the central BS. Using this information, the BS then computes the power that DUEs and CUEs must transmit at for minimum interference amongst the communicating devices. One main problem with this centralised power control method is that the method incurs a very high CSI feedback overhead that has the capability of disrupting the efficient functioning of the network. To fix this problem, Lee et al., (2015) then proposed a distributed on-off power control mechanism that does not require any sharing of CSI coordination between D2D pairs. In the proposed scheme, the D2D pairs get to choose transmit powers to maximize their rates towards their targeted receivers. The D2D pairs select the transmit powers from a decision set using the individual DUEs' direct link information in addition to a prescribed non-negative threshold that is known to all D2D pairs. Each D2D pair only uses these two pieces of information to decide on which power to transmit at. Evaluation of the two schemes by the authors showed that the centralised power control scheme improves the cellular network throughput performance with a drawback of increased complexity. The distributed power control scheme was found to outperform the centralised power control in system throughput and it is has lower complexity compared to the centralised power control.

Feng, Lu, Yuan-Wu, Li, Feng, and Li (2013) also proposed a centralised power control scheme for use in conjunction with a resource allocation technique. It was proposed that the allocation of resources and the controlling of user equipment (UE) transmit powers be undertaken centrally by the BS. The scheme involves D2D links sharing uplink resources. With D2D pairs sharing the uplink, it becomes easier for the BS to control the DUEs' transmit power. The BS chooses a back off factor parameter that it instructs to apply. A large back off factor is associated with very low interference to uplink transmissions, but it implies that the D2D link range is reduced. A boosting factor is however incorporated for compensation so that the D2D link range may not be critically reduced. Power boosting is only applied where there might be ongoing D2D transmissions and to resource blocks (RBs) being shared by D2D pairs. The uplink power control scheme ensures that all DUEs and CUEs connected to a BS enjoy similar SINR. A similar power control scheme cannot be implemented on the downlink as it would require a significant overhead. The authors evaluated the proposed scheme using extensive simulations and were able to conclude that by properly choosing the maximum power that can be used on a D2D link, a high D2D link is achieved with very minimum impact on the network.

Chen, Liu, Li, Li, and Li (2016) proposed a power control scheme that calculates the minimum power required to establish D2D communication. A minimum required SINR and the interference that comes from a CUE sharing RB resources with a specific link are the values needed to calculate the minimum transmit power. The maximum D2D transmit power is then calculated using the BS interference threshold.

A set of CUEs and DUEs that can share RB resources is established and three groups are formed:

Group 1: D2D pairs and CUEs that cannot share resources because of the interference threshold and SINR threshold requirements.
Group 2: D2D pairs that can share resources with some CUEs.
Group 3: D2D pairs in this group can share resources with all CUEs.

For groups 1 and 2, Chen et al., (2016), designed algorithms that adjust transmit powers of D2D pairs such that the interference is kept to a minimum. On simulating the proposed scheme, it was shown that the scheme can achieve a high network capacity which means that the scheme is effective in interference management. The designed algorithms are simple, making the process of implementation easier.

Power control schemes, whether centralised or distributed, cannot effectively deal with interference that is imposed on DUEs by the network (Safdar, Ur-Rehman, Muhammad, Imran, &Tafazolli, 2016). They are not effective when it comes to interference from CUEs to DUEs. Power control techniques are mostly effective when the DUEs are very close to each other and/or are at an appropriate distance from a CUE or a BS. Hongnian and Hakola (2010) stated that power control schemes must be considered jointly with other interference mitigation schemes like mode selection, link adaptation and resource scheduling. On the positive side, power control systems are easy to implement and have low computational cost.

Mathematical Modelling and Designing Techniques

Mathematical theories can be used to design automated decisions for interference management in D2D-enabled cellular networks. The most commonly used mathematical tool is game theory. The theory avails mathematical tools that can be used to model and analyse complex interactions among rational players leading to the players' choices of strategies. This enables game theory to be used in the development of strategies to reduce interference in wireless networks. Leyton-Brown and Shoham (2008) described game theory as a systematic study of decisions that can be made by rational players that are under competition.

Two branches of game theory exist; cooperative or coalitional game theory and non-cooperative game theory. Cooperative game theory provides analytical tools that enable the study of the behaviour of cooperating rational players. The weighting or power that is held by the players is very important in deciding the outcome. Non-cooperative game theory is concerned with strategic choices that result from actions of competing players. The timing and ordering of competing players play a crucial role in the process of determining the outcome.

Leyton-Brown and Shoham (2008) presented four sub-disciplines of game theory as shown in Figure 5.

Combinatorial game theory and classical game theory have been used to design schemes for the minimization of interference in communication systems (Huang, Zhao, & Sohraby, 2014).

Combinatorial Auction-Based Resource Allocation Theory

Combinatorial auction-based resource allocation theory, being a sub-discipline of game theory can be used in the trading of available channels to DUEs and CUEs such that interference is minimised resulting in a high sum rate. Huang et al., (2014) proposed a mechanism that involves BSs competing to obtain demand to allocate their resources to DUEs and CUEs. DUEs and CUEs initially announce a price for each resource block that they require from the BSs that they are associated with. If the demand for RB

Figure 5. The sub-disciplines of Game Theory
Source: Leyton-Brown and Shoham (2008)

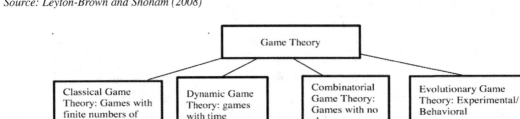

resources exceeds the supply from BSs, or the demand for RBs is exceeded by supply, DUEs and CUEs adjust their prices accordingly so that the auction can proceed to the next round. Multiple iterations determine the allocation of RB resources. The following are the properties of the proposed scheme:

1. A solution is reached after a finite number of iterations.
2. Adjustment of prices leads to an improvement in efficiency.
3. The complexity is given by O $(n\,(2^m - 1) + t)$, where m is the number of RBs to be allocated, n is the number of bidders, and t is the total number of iterations.

Simulations performed by Song et al., (2015) and Huang et al., (2014) show that the use of combinatorial auction increases the system performance as the number of DUEs and CUEs increases.

Classical Game Theory

Zhao et al., (2014) made use of classical game theory to design a mechanism that can be used to allocate channel resources in an efficient way under realistic conditions to reduce interference. In a D2D-enabled cellular network, DUEs are likely to report their channel quality untruthfully to gain an unfair advantage over other participants. Zhao et al., (2014) used game theory to study the interference that results from this cheating by the DUEs. In legacy mobile networks, because all communication is via a BS, the BS knows the channel quality being experienced by all the UEs actively participating in the network. The BS then gets to decide what resources to allocate and to which UE to allocate those resources. The unfair reporting of channel quality by DUEs leads to the problem of Unknown Channel Quality (UCQ). Zhao et al., (2014) successfully used classical game theory to model the selfish behaviour of DUEs and CUEs in channel reporting and to derive equilibrium.

Equipped with this equilibrium point, the researchers designed an algorithm which resulted in reduced interference which in turn increased system efficiency. Simulations were used to validate the proposed scheme.

Ye, Al-Shalash, Caramanis, and Andrews (2015) also used a classical game theory approach to obtain distributed algorithms for interference management. The scheme that they adopted requires very little coordination overhead with very low complexity in its implementation.

In a cellular network, the uplink spectrum is usually underutilised when compared to the downlink. Marques, Bastos, and Gameiro (2008) capitalised on this theory and suggested that making D2D links use the uplink is likely to result in an improved resource allocation which leads to reduced levels of interference. BSs send out a fictional price to DUEs. DUEs then optimise an objective function based on the fictional price. High chances are that the individual D2D links are optimised selfishly hence the justification to use game theory.

CUEs and DUEs then agree to be players of a game utilising the fictional price coming from the BSs. The scheme that was designed by Marques et al., (2008) does not require any cooperation from other D2D links. D2D links with strong interference are discouraged from acquiring more RBs. On performance evaluation of the proposed algorithm, it was discovered that a large throughput gain was achieved implying that the interference management was effective. The proposed strategy is a distributed one in that DUEs autonomously control the interference that results from the introduction of D2D communications into the cellular network. Distributed resource allocation schemes when compared with centralised schemes, have low overheads and are less complex hence are the ones that are likely to be used in large networks with high volumes of D2D communications.

Graph Theory

Graph theory is another mathematical tool that can be used in dealing with interference affecting D2D communications in cellular networks. According to Nouran and Nordin (2016), interference affecting DUEs' and CUEs' communication links can be shown on a graph and the resulting graph can then be used to develop strategies to reduce cross-tier and co-tier interferences. With graph theory, CUEs and DUEs appear as vertices in a graph with edges representing the interference between the vertices. The interference between the vertices can be represented by the weights of the edges. Channel resources can then be allocated iteratively.

Guo, Sun, and Gao (2014) proposed a scheme that utilises graph theory in interference management. For a network making use of the proposed scheme, BSs acquire the channel state information (CSI) of channels between D2D pairs and CUEs. To reduce the feedback overheard, DUEs report to the BS, the interference on channels that are lower than a specified threshold. Using the reported CSIs on channels in use, the BS constructs a weighted bipartite graph with DUEs and CUEs making up the vertices of the graph and the weighted edges representing the relationships in terms of interference between the vertices. The CSI feedback of channels is used to construct two matrices, matrix X1 and matrix X2. In matrix X1, information of which UE does not cause interference to which D2D pair, and which cellular resource is available, is appended. Information on whether a D2D pair will cause severe interference to another pair upon sharing a channel is appended in the second matrix X2. Using the weighted bipartite graph and the two matrices, resources are then allocated using an iteration algorithm. Resources are allocated considering the level of interference existing in the channels. When the scheme was simulated, and results compared with other schemes, it was shown that the proposed scheme produced an interference level that is very close to optimal.

Hyper Graph Theory

According to Zhang, Song, and Han (2016), the conventional graph theory does not completely characterise the interference from multiple DUEs and CUEs hence the need to rope in hyper graph theory. Zhang et al., (2016) argued that the use of edges in the conventional graph theory is not accurate in interference modelling due to the cumulative effect of the interference from several neighbouring DUEs and CUEs. With hyper graph colouring, cumulative interference emanating from several D2D pairs can be modelled and subsequently eliminated. The conventional graph resource allocation scheme usually takes two steps (Zhang, Song, & Han, 2016). This is shown in Table 2. For the parameters used in Table 2, graph G is taken as a pair (C, P) where C is a set made up of vertices:

$C = \{ c_1, c_2, \ldots\ldots\ldots c_n \}$, and P is a set of 2-element subsets of C called edges
$P = \{ p_1, p_2, \ldots\ldots\ldots p_n \}$

Edges give the indication that the interference existing between connected vertices may not allow the use of the same channel at the same time as that would result in severe interference.

Table 2. Graph-based resource allocation method

Step 1: Graph Construction

* CUEs CUE_n and Uj form an edge, $\forall U_n$, U_j, where n ≠ j.

* A cellular UE U_n and a D2D pair D_m form an edge if SINR is below a specified threshold.

* D2D pairs D_i and D_m form an edge if the interference from another D2D pair is not strong, these two D2D pairs can share the same channel otherwise they cannot share.

Step 2: Graph Colouring Algorithm

* i = 1. Find a vertex of the maximum degree and label it x_i.

* repeat

1. Set i = i + 1. Select from the unexamined subgraph a vertex x which has the maximum degree, and label it x_i.

2. Break the edges which connect to vertex x_i;

* until All the vertices in the graph are examined.

* Starting from i = 1, select a colour randomly from the available colour set to colour X_i. If the available colour set is empty, leave the vertex X_i uncoloured.

Source: Zhang, Song, & Han (2016)

The analysis performed by Zhang et al., (2016) led them to conclude that the hypergraph-based resource allocation method takes place in cubic polynomial time as opposed to the traditional graph-based resource allocation method that takes place in quadratic polynomial time. On further comparison, simulation results showed that the hypergraph-based method posted a 33% cell capacity increase.

Stochastic Geometry

Stochastic geometry is another mathematical tool that can be used in the mitigation of interference in D2D-enabled cellular networks. It is a branch of applied probability that is intrinsically related to the theory of random point patterns.

ElSawy and Hossain (2013) pointed out that stochastic geometry is the only computational tool that can be used to model large scale wireless networks. The model can be used to capture network performance metrics. Stochastic geometry provides averages of quantities of interest like SINR and outage probability. ElSawy, Hossain, and Haenggi (2013) elaborated as to how stochastic geometry can be used to capture the topological randomness in cellular networks.

ElSawy and Hossain (2013) proposed a mode selection strategy that is effective in reducing interference in D2D-enabled cellular networks. A D2D mode is chosen by a potential D2D transmitter only if the link quality is acceptable. The link quality must be at least equal to or greater than a cellular uplink quality. A bias factor is incorporated into the decision-making process. A bias factor is a parameter that is used to control the volume of traffic offloading from the cellular infrastructure to use the D2D infrastructure. If the bias factor is set to zero, then no D2D communication takes place. The mode selection strategy correlates the D2D transmitters' locations and D2D link distances to the locations of BSs to ensure that there is interference protection in the cellular uplink. Using stochastic geometry, ElSawy and Hossain (2013) concluded that designing a mode selection strategy that only relies on link distance between a D2D pair does not provide the desired interference levels in a D2D-enabled cellular network. Optimal levels of interference are achieved if a link distance and a suitable bias factor are used to control mode selection. A suitable bias factor can be chosen using the analytical framework presented by the authors. The proposed scheme achieved a 25% reduction in SINR outage probability for CUEs.

Spectrum Splitting

Spectrum splitting is the easiest method that can be used to reduce cross-tier interference in a D2D-enabled cellular network (Nouran & Nordin, 2016). Lin, Andrews, and Ghosh (2014) used an analytical approach to tackle the spectrum sharing optimisation problem in a bid to effectively deal with interference. A tractable hybrid network model that positions mobiles using a random spatial Poisson process was developed.

The model was used to capture important characteristics in network assisted D2D communication systems like the characteristic of mode selection that involves D2D pairs in choosing whether to communicate directly or to communicate via a BS. The researchers then designed an analytical framework that they used to derive analytical rate expressions. The analytical expressions were then used to optimise the spectrum sharing parameters. They derived an optimal D2D mode selection threshold that is then used to reduce DUEs' transmit power to the lowest level that allows communication to take place but with minimum interference. The authors studied overlay and underlay in-band D2D communication systems. For the overlay in-band D2D communication, the uplink is split into two portions that are orthogonal to each other. One portion of the spectrum is reserved for D2D pairs and the other is taken by CUEs. For the underlay in-band D2D communication, D2D pairs use frequency hopping to reduce interference on other communicating devices. Lin et al., (2014) concluded that in the underlay mode, a linear increase in spectrum resources leads to a linear rate increase. The rate of D2D connections is however limited by interference. For CUEs, the rate is sensitive to a spectrum reduction in the overlay but more robust to the D2D interference that exists in the underlay. Lin et al., (2014) were able to identify the trade-off between mode selection and the underlay D2D spectrum access by using the model they developed. This was achieved using traditional homogeneous cellular networks consisting of five macro BSs. There is need to test performance of the proposed scheme in heterogeneous networks since 5G networks will be heterogeneous networks.

Mode Selection

At what point, should two devices that are close to each other switch from cellular mode to D2D mode after discovering each other? Being near each other does not necessarily mean that it would be optimal for the two devices to switch to D2D mode. The most commonly used selection metrics are SINR and channel quality condition. For network-assisted D2D communications, the BS can select the mode to be used by a D2D pair. To achieve this task, the BS uses channel quality information that comes from DUEs and CUEs. For autonomous D2D, the DUEs are the ones that get to decide when to change from one mode to another. If the process is not handled properly, interference will affect the communication (Safdar, Ur-Rehman, Muhammad, Imran, & Tafazolli, 2016). For in-band D2D communications, three modes of operation exist:

1. **Overlay/Dedicated Mode:** Dedicated spectrum is allocated to DUEs.
2. **Underlay/Reuse Mode:** DUEs reuse available resources.

3. **Cellular Mode:** UEs communicate in the normal way, i.e. by relaying messages to each other via a BS.

Huang, Nasir, Durrani, and Zhou (2016) proposed a mode selection technique that selects the overlay method if DUEs are close to each other and orthogonal resources are available. The BS decides whether any two UEs that are near each other can participate in D2D communication. The UEs can only connect and communicate if the stipulated conditions are met. The devices can then use the dedicated or reuse method to connect otherwise they will remain in cellular mode. The strategy devised by Huang et al., (2016) also ropes in power control and resource allocation techniques to effectively deal with interference.

This means that once a mode has been decided upon, the BS then controls the transmit powers of the participating devices to meet a specified Quality of Service (QoS) requirement for all receivers in the vicinity. The BS then goes on to allocate available resources to the DUEs and CUEs in a way that eliminates interference. Reuse can only be permitted if a D2D pair is outside an interference zone such that the resulting interference from D2D communications is lower than a specified threshold. Simulation results showed the dedicated mode delivers a higher sum rate when DUEs are close to each other and are an appreciable distance from the BS.

Wang, Liu, Cao, Tian and Cheng (2015) proposed that the issue of social interaction should seriously be considered in the allocation of network resources. At times, devices that are geographically close to each other do not necessarily need to connect to each other directly to form a D2D pair. Wang et al., (2015) argued that social properties should also be considered when deciding whether any two devices should connect and participate in D2D communication. The decision should not only be based on the distance between the devices and the link quality. A D2D link that is established between two friends is likely to be of longer duration compared to a D2D link between strangers. Figure 6 depicts the connection of devices following the social traits of the users. A longer contact time ensures that more data is delivered. This means that the social property and the geographical distance should be put into account when allocating resources to DUEs.

Figure 6. System architecture. Dashed arrows denote D2D links which are intermittent due to human mobility from a social network perspective
Source: Wang et al. (2015)

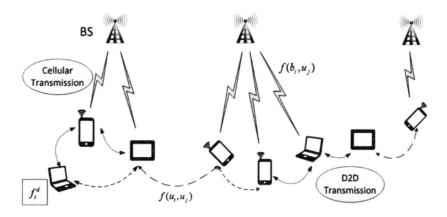

A D2D link between friends that are near each other will be a more reliable link. This is because the contact time is likely to be longer compared to a D2D link between strangers. Wang et al., (2015) went on to use contact time to model the sociality of D2D transmission links to maximise the resource utilisation. Using extensive numerical results, they concluded that both the user's social property and the geographical location do affect network performance and the allocation of resources. The authors proposed a sociality-based network model that they used to calculate an average contact time between any two users within a time slot. The average contact time of each D2D link was then used to construct resource allocation constraints. The formulated linear optimisation problem was then solved by use of CPLEX off-the-shelf tool. The results obtained showed that social-aware optimisation strategy outperforms methods that do not take sociality aspect into account.

Li, Su, and Chen (2014) proposed a similar spectrum sharing technique that CUEs and DUE pairs can use to minimise interference in networks where D2D is being used. The researchers called the scheme, "Optimal Social-Community-Aware Resource Allocation" that they shortened to OSRA. OSRA capitalises on the fact that it is usually human beings who would want to participate in D2D communications and it is a fact that human beings exhibit well defined social structures. The proposed scheme then exploits human behaviour in trying to solve the resource allocation problem in the process of reducing interference. The social information about D2D users that is collected over time is then used to form social characteristics of communities. The collected information is then used to divide a cellular network into communities as shown in Figure 7.

Extensive simulations were used to evaluate the performance of the proposed algorithm. The results obtained show that the overall system performance can substantially be improved with regards to D2D transmission time. The proposed scheme can be effective if it is used for gaming, social media, file exchange and other social activities. Attempting to use the scheme in densely populated areas like shopping malls can become problematic. This can be problematic because collection of social information of people who visit shopping malls or stadia and expecting to use that information to form social communities is in itself a mammoth task. Regular visitors to crowded areas are usually people who work there, and this forms a very small community to the actual number of people who are found at these places at any given point in time.

Figure 7. A social-aware D2D system is projected onto two domains
Source: Li et al. (2015)

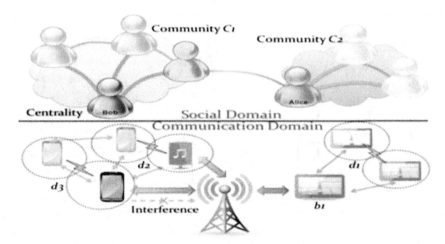

Token Method

D2D communication has multiple advantages especially for devices that are in close proximity which have to share information. D2D communication however becomes a bother for the DUEs if participation in the D2D communication process is solely for the relaying of information. UEs are reluctant to participate in the D2D communications since participation comes with costs. To overcome this, Yuan, Yang, Feng, Hu, Zhang, Wang, and Lu (2017) proposed a scheme that can be used to incentivise the UEs so that they can provide D2D service and in the process keeping interference at a very minimum level. A token-based incentive was devised that involves UEs exchanging electronic tokens for the provision of D2D service. In the scheme, for UEs to transmit data via a D2D link, they must pay electronic tokens and they gain tokens when they participate in cooperative relaying of information. The researchers formulated a Markov decision process to characterise the D2D interactions. Upon the arrival of traffic, a UE must decide whether it can accept the request or not. A UE can only allow a request to participate in relaying information if it is in idle state and if the participation does not cause interference to overshoot a specified threshold. A UE is rewarded for providing a D2D service to other UEs. The proposed scheme provides a good incentive for users within a cellular network, to allow their devices to participate in the relaying of data. The scheme is simple and has considerably low complexity. The scheme was systematically evaluated in various deployment scenarios. The simulation results obtained suggest that UEs have the greatest appetite to participate in the cooperative process when there is a high volume of UEs with high relay energy budgets and in networks with high mobility users like those in automobiles. Yuan et al., (2017) showed that the proposed strategy increases throughput per area per user by reducing interference. The scheme protects UEs from relaying D2D information more than they receive relayed information themselves. The provision of a relay service should match the reception of a relay service to prevent the UEs from ending up with high negative average utilities.

Beamforming Techniques

Array beamforming strategies exist that can produce multiple beams which can be made to have very high gain or to have a controlled beamwidth. Adaptive beamforming methods can be used to reject interfering signals coming from a direction that is different from the desired direction. The phase and amplitude can then be controlled by a beam finder into a high direction beam directed towards the intended recipient and no signal in the direction of interference. This concept of beam forming can be adapted and used in D2D-enabled mobile networks to deal with cross-tier and co-tier interference. This is illustrated in Figure 8.

Song, Zhu, and Chen (2014) designed and investigated a joint power control and beamforming method to mitigate interference in a D2D-enabled cellular network. A scheme to deal with interference in a single cell like the one depicted in Figure 9 was proposed.

The BS in Figure 9 is equipped with multiple antennas with the UEs having a single antenna each. The scheme is a centralised strategy in that the BS controls the beamforming as well as controlling the transmit powers of UEs. The following steps are taken:

1. The BS performs beamforming to DUEs to prevent them from receiving interference from the BS.
2. DUEs and CUEs report DOWNLINK CSI to the BS.

Figure 8. Schematic representation of beamforming with the BSs and DUEs equipped with multiple antenna elements
Source: Safdar et al. (2016)

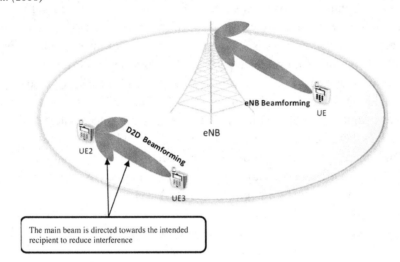

Figure 9. A cell where beamforming is employed
Source: Song et al. (2014)

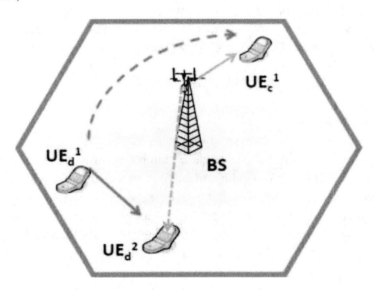

3. Transmit power is then calculated by the BS for the system sum rate maximisation. This is achieved by considering SINR threshold of the links of DUEs and CUEs.

The implementation process of the proposed scheme is shown in Figure 10.

Results of simulations showed that the proposed joint beamforming and power control scheme improves the system performance. System throughput increases since interference is reduced. Beamforming is a robust interference reduction solution that requires a comprehensive precoder design and this

Figure 10. The implementation process
Source: Song et al. (2014)

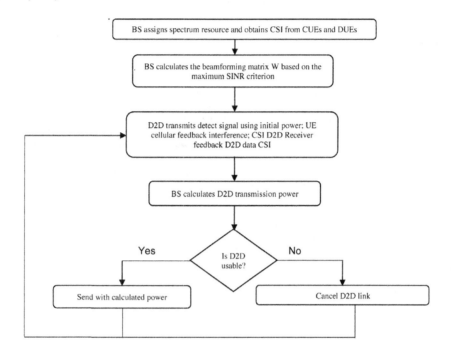

attracts a heavy computational overhead. The scheme requires an accurate CSI of all the involved links. The multiple antenna elements increase the cost of hardware implementation.

Load Balancing Technology

Liu, Kawamoto, Nishiyama, Kato, and Kadowaki (2014) proposed to solve the problem of interference by use of an efficient four step load balancing algorithm. The first step involves the BS attempting to offload a requesting UE to an uncongested cell that is adjacent to the requesting UE. The BS first checks for the availability of an uncongested cell adjacent to the requesting UE as depicted in Figure 11.

If there exists an uncongested Macro BS, Pico BS or Femto BS, location of the requesting UE is multicast by the Macro BS to potential BSs via the X2 interface. After an elaborate collaboration among the requesting UE, an uncongested BS and the Macro BS, traffic is offloaded to an uncongested BS. In Figure 11, the congested Macro BS has managed to offload traffic to UE_3 and UE_5 via the lightly loaded BSs. If there is no uncongested BS around the requesting UE, the algorithm proceeds to the next step. For step 2, the newly established CUE and DUE links should offer comparable Quality of Service (QoS). If there is a deterioration in QoS, then the newly released RB is allocated to a requesting UE as shown in Figure 12.

If there is an indication that there are some observable changes in Quality of Experience (QoE) to the user UE_1, then step 3 is activated. Step 3 involves the collaboration of three BSs as shown in Figure 13.

Figure 11. Illustration of step 1
Source: Liu et al. (2014)

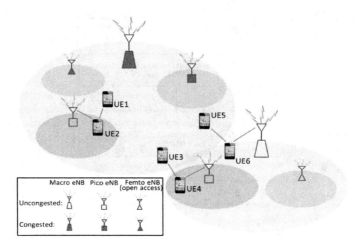

Figure 12. Illustration of step 2
Source: Liu et al. (2014)

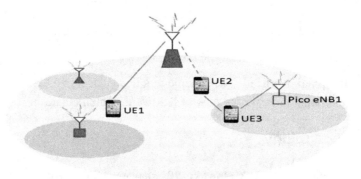

Figure 13. Illustration of step 3
Source: Liu et al. (2014)

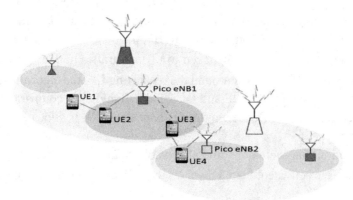

A congested BS attempts to offload a requesting UE by factoring in the element of distance. The requesting UE is offloaded to a congested BS to which it is very close. At the same time another UE is moved from the congested BS to an uncongested BS as shown in Figure 14. If step 3 fails due to channel inferior quality, insufficient RBs, considerable D2D delay, then the algorithm goes to step 4 that is illustrated in Figure 14.

In Figure 14, After pico eNB_1 has offloaded the currently served UE_4 via UE_5 to the uncongested pico eNB_2 macro eNB allocates to the requesting UE_1 the resource blocks newly released by offloading the currently being served macro tier UE_2 to the pico eNB_1 via UE_3. The dashed line denotes a newly released link.

On simulating the proposed scheme, Liu et al., (2014) concluded that after applying steps 1, 2, 3 and 4, 86% of requesting UEs were able to access the Internet at the same time. If the steps are not applied, it was discovered that only 65% could access the Internet at the same time. An increase in the number of devices that can access the Internet at the same time means the proposed scheme managed to use D2D that introduces very little interference to the network.

Other Interference Mitigation Technologies

To solve the problem of interference in D2D communications, Katsinis, Tsiropoulou, and Papavassiliou (2017) proposed a two-step approach that involves an efficient allocation of RBs and transmission power allocation by a BS which oversees the allocation of RBs to users. Interference occurs each time an RB is reused by cellular users in adjacent cells or by D2D users making use of some of the same RBs in the neighbouring cells or in the same cell. Though spectrum economy is promoted by RBs' reuse, co-sharing users may experience SINR degradation. The proposed algorithm does not limit the number of D2D pairs that can reuse an RB allocated to a cellular link. The proposed scheme allows D2D links to reuse

Figure 14. Illustration of step 4
Source: Liu et al. (2014)

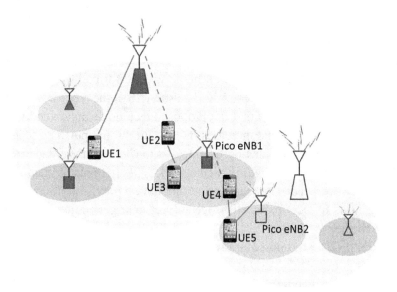

RBs reserved by cellular links many times. This has the effect of increasing the spectrum efficiency. For the second step, Katsinis et al., (2017) adopted Foschine-Miljanic algorithm appearing in Foschini and Miljanic (1993) which they used to solve the total power minimisation problem in a distributed way. The algorithm can either work out a feasible solution or the users whose SINR requirements cannot be met are pushed to the maximum power level so that a SINR that is close to their SINR requirement is achieved. The iterative efficient approximation algorithm that chooses an RB assignment of users in a cell is based on Equation (1) as given by Katsinis et al., (2017).

$$\mathbf{s}_1\left(\mathbf{u}, \mathbf{k}\right) = \begin{cases} 1 & if\,user\,u\,of\,cell\,i\,uses\,RB\,k \\ 0 & otherwise \end{cases} \tag{1}$$

The algorithm converges after several iterations at the minimum of the total interference. For the algorithm to be implementable, BSs exchange control information via the X2 interface. The convergence of the algorithm is guaranteed but it does not necessarily do so in polynomial time. Performance evaluation of the proposed interference management strategy showed that a 93% interference reduction was achieved. On implementation of the second step, it was observed that there was a 57% reduction in total power consumption and that and there was 86% increase of users meeting their SINR requirements.

The scheme may be effective with 4G but may encounter problems with 5G networks. Most 5G networks will use multiple antenna systems and this was not considered in designing the scheme and in the simulations performed.

Wang and Hou (2017) proposed a scheme that uses relay assistance and network coding to reduce interference in a D2D under-laid cellular network. The scheme identifies helper nodes that assist in the transmission of cellular and D2D traffic. According to Wang and Hou (2017), helper nodes are nodes that are idle and happen to be enjoying cellular coverage. With the proposed scheme, a specific frequency resource that is assigned to a cellular user can only be reused by one D2D communication pair. Helpers are not chosen randomly. The quality of individual links is carefully considered. A helper can only become a candidate for information relaying if the link quality packet error rate (PER) meets specified requirements. When helper nodes close to CUEs overhear signals, they encode the received packets and send these to a BS when prompted to do so.

This ensures that all the packets from CUEs including the lost ones arrive at their destinations. The proposed scheme does not allow D2D communications if resulting interference on CUEs is severe. Evaluation of the effectiveness of the proposed scheme was performed by comparing the number of packets sent versus the number of packets received. The strength of the received signal is also compared to the distance travelled. Results showed that the proposed technique can extend the distance that can be covered by D2D communications and increases the system throughput. The scheme is however designed to deal with the interference emanating from DUEs to CUEs. Interference from CUEs to DUEs is not considered. The relaying of messages in the network is likely to result in an increased end to end delay and an unnecessary overhead. The scheme does not have a provision of dealing with interference coming from cellular users to D2D pairs. Heterogeneity of next generation mobile networks was not factored in into the scheme.

Jeon, Ko, Lee, and Kim (2013) proposed an advanced distributed resource allocation scheme to mitigate interference which they coined DICRA (Distributed Interference Channel Based Resource Allocation). The scheme avoids the bulky overhead that is associated with centralised approaches of interference management by using interference channel coding scheme that enables distributed channel-aware spatial scheduling. The smaller overhead further increases the performance gap. Neighbouring pairs are grouped to reduce the control overhead and the interference channel coding is used to deal with intra-group interference. Results obtained by the researchers showed better performance compared to similar schemes given by Wu et al., (2010). Simulations carried out confirmed that the proposed scheme increases spectral efficiency and reduces interference emanating from the presence of D2D communications. The scheme is likely to fail to deliver the desired results if it were to be used for sensor networking, because, with sensor networking, some centralisation is needed for the coordination of the complex process.

A scheme that is based on interference suppression area (ISA) was proposed in Sun and Gao, 2014. Since D2D communications is between proximate devices, the interference that is created from such communications is quite limited. The scheme defines ISAs for D2D pairs to indicate areas with severe interference. D2D pairs and cellular user equipment (CUE) within the same ISA will interfere with each other and hence require to be allocated with orthogonal resources to prevent interference. The scheme also controls the transmit power of the user equipment (UE). D2D communication is then permitted if the UE transmit power requirements are met. The scheme also reduces interference in the network by allocating resources intelligently. Whenever the interference between D2D pairs and CUEs is inevitable, only orthogonal resources are allocated. Certain resources then become forbidden to D2D communications but can be made available to the downlink. The scheme was compared with a scheme that uses random scheduling. The results showed that the proposed scheme has high performance. With heterogeneous networks, the BS is likely be burdened by the processes involved resulting in a compromised performance.

Kim, Karim, and Cho (2017) proposed a hybrid mechanism that makes use of fractional frequency reuse (FFR) and almost blank sub-frames (ABS) to deal with inter-cell interference as well as inter-sector interference. The scheme was designed to specifically deal with CUEs from one cell interfering with the communication of DUE pairs at the edges of an adjacent cell. The scheme has three phases:

1. Soft Fractional Frequency Reuse.
2. Almost Blank Sub-frames.
3. Data transmission.

In phase one, the BS allocates frequencies to the UEs using a soft FFR technique. Soft FFR involves dividing the cell into an inner region (cell centre) and an outer region (cell-edge) and dividing the entire frequency band into four portions. Orthogonal resources are used to mitigate against interference. Mitigating against inter-sector interference is achieved by using ABS-a technique that adaptively partitions resources in the time domain. During the data transmission phase, the CUEs that are likely to cause severe interference are made to be silent in ABS to minimise throughput loss.

This ensures that overall system throughput is increased and the Quality-of-Service (QoS) of D2D pairs and CUE transmissions is guaranteed. Mathematical analysis and computer simulations were used for the evaluation of the scheme. It was shown that the system throughput as well as signal-to-noise-plus-interference ratio (SINR) were higher compared to a conventional method that uses FFR only. A 60% increase in throughput was observed. The mathematical analysis proved that a balance between DUEs and CUEs can be reached by use of the ABS ratio. The scheme however, did not consider the heterogeneity and randomness of next generation networks.

Transmission control is used in Safdar et al., (2016) to mitigate cross-tier interference. The proposed scheme prioritises QoS requirements of the CUEs. Power management schemes are used to control the transmission power of DUEs so that CUEs' QoS is not compromised. The proposed algorithm switches OFF DUEs that would have received power that is less than their receiver sensitivity. The algorithm only controls DUEs' transmission power. The CUEs' transmission power remains fixed. This is meant to mitigate cross-tier interference at the BS. Controlling the DUEs' transmission power is achieved by use of the instantaneous channel state information. The authors performed Monte Carlo simulations in MATLAB and the results obtained show that cross-tier interference can effectively be reduced.

Asadi, Wang, and Mancuso (2014) also proposed a transmission control scheme that leaves the transmission power of CUE fixed like the scheme proposed by Safdar et al., (2016). The DUEs' transmit power is then optimised accordingly to control interference. A brute-force enumeration algorithm that uses statistical CSI on the current location of DUEs was adopted. Instantaneous CSI is not used since it increases power consumption as well as signalling overhead. The algorithm allows DUEs that are a considerable distance away from a BS to continue with their communications since this does not cause interference to the BS. DUEs that are close to the BS are made to revert to communicating to each other via the BS. Performance evaluation of the scheme showed that the same spectrum can be shared by multiple D2D links and one cellular link without performance being degraded. The scheme uses a small signalling overhead that does not fast track battery deterioration of the devices involved.

Another interference management scheme was proposed by Janis, Yu, Doppler, Rebeiro, Wijting, Hugl, Tirkkonen, and Koivunen (2009). The base station is responsible for managing the allocation of Orthogonal Frequency Division Multiple Access (OFDMA) resource blocks. The D2D transmission power is limited using the cellular Uplink (UL). This is done in a bid to contain the interference on the base station. The mobile network UL power control framework is not used to control the D2D transmit powers. The researchers simulated the proposed scheme and the results obtained show that D2D communication can be introduced into cellular networks without negatively impacting on the network operations. However, the scheme was designed to reduce interference from D2D to cellular and not interference from cellular to D2D pairs. In as much as D2D communications should not introduce interference to CUEs, DUEs engaged in communication also need to enjoy interference-free sessions.

Two schemes that can be used for interference management in a hybrid network were advanced by (Peng, Lu, Wang, Xu, & Wang, 2009). The first scheme requires that DUEs decode uplink radio resource management information that is meant for CUEs. This information is used to perform smart resource allocation to avoid D2D interference. Each D2D pair measures and maps the interference coming from the different UEs. The recorded interference is then used for smart resource allocation. For the second mechanism, the BS calculates the interference level coming from DUEs' transmissions for each uplink resource unit. The acquired information is then broadcast to enable smart resource allocation. The results obtained from extensive simulations showed that the proposed interference management schemes can reduce mutual interference in a cellular network with an underlay D2D. The BSs' broadcasting that is performed in the process of reducing interference is likely to cause some congestion in the network. The proposed scheme was not evaluated in a heterogeneous network (HetNet) environment.

The interference dynamics are likely to be complex in a HetNet and it is therefore important to techniques that work in such next generation networks.

Dacheng, Xin, Zhesheng, Xiaoyue, and Si (2012) proposed a scheme that increases system throughput as a method of reducing interference in D2D-enabled cellular mobile networks. The proposed strategy focuses on the following:

1. Resource allocation.

2.   Power control.
3.   Self-optimisation system.

   D2D receivers measure the interference appearing in the whole allocated band. D2D pairs use this information to select suitable resource block sets to be used for spectrum sharing. The resource block information and D2D property messages are broadcast by the BS. The broadcast messages will carry UEs' locations and priorities. UEs then use the broadcast information to discover partners for pairing. The best transmit resource blocks that introduce the least interference to the nearby CUEs are chosen by the D2D pairs. To ensure that D2D pairs in the same cluster do not cause interference, a priority mechanism is used. The SINR is measured and the information is used by D2D pairs to decide whether a power increase request to a BS can be made. A power increase can only be allowed if that move does not end up affecting other DUEs and CUEs. Extensive simulations were used to evaluate the performance of the scheme and a 220%-430% gain in system capacity was observed. Interference reduction caused this marked gain in system capacity. The proposed scheme however could not handle a sizeable number of DUEs intending to communicate in a small area. This shows that the scheme was not designed for densified networks and hence might fail to post satisfactory results when used in 5G networks.

Table 3. Comparison of interference management schemes

Interference Management Techniques		Complexity of Scheme	Interference Control Type	Spectrum Efficiency	Applicability to 5G Networks
Power control		Medium	Both fixed and dynamic can be used. Control can be central being controlled by BS or distributive, with the UEs involved	Medium	Useful in 3G. Used in 4G for shadowing and rekindled in 5G to deal with interference from D2D communications
Mathematical modelling	Combinatorial Auction based	High	Suitable for centralised and distributive control	High	Highly applicable. Can work for heterogeneous networks as well
	Classical Game theory	High	Suitable for distributive algorithms in controlling interference	High	Highly applicable to 5G networks
	Graph Theory	Medium	For both centralised and distributive	Medium	Highly applicable to 5G networks
	Stochastic Geometry	Medium	For both centralised and distributive	High	Highly applicable to 5G networks
Spectrum splitting		Easy to implement	Suitable for centralised control	Medium	Tested in homogeneous cellular networks.
Mode selection		Medium	Both centralised and distributive control possible	High	Very applicable to 5G networks
Token methods		Medium	Distributive control	Medium	Works well for 3G and 4G networks but problematic with highly densified networks
Beam forming techniques		Medium	Works well for centralised systems where the BS is in full control of resources	High	One of the latest techniques that can be used to deal with interference in 5G networks
Load balancing techniques		Medium		Medium	Robust interference mitigation technique that is also suitable for 5G networks

CONCLUSION

This chapter has presented the state-of-the-art of interference management schemes in D2D-enabled cellular networks that have been advanced by academia and industry experts. These schemes are summarised in Table 3. D2D communication is a promising technology that is positioned to enhance spectral efficiency. Most of the proposed schemes have however, ignored the heterogeneity of the next generation of mobile networks. 5G will be heterogeneous in nature. D2D communication has the potential of depleting UEs' batteries but the proposed schemes have failed to introduce some battery saving schemes into the interference mitigation equation. The proposed schemes have also failed to incorporate mmWave technology. The mmWave band communication will feature prominently in the next generation mobile networks and as such should be incorporated into schemes that are supposed to work with 5G networks.

REFERENCES

Asadi, A., Wang, Q., & Mancuso, V. (2014). A survey on device-to-device communication in cellular networks. *IEEE Communications Surveys and Tutorials*, *16*(4), 1801–1819. doi:10.1109/COMST.2014.2319555

Cai, X., Zheng, J., & Zhang, Y. (2015). A Graph colouring-based resource allocation algorithm for D2D communication in cellular networks. In *Proceedings of the IEEE International Conference on Communications (ICC)* (pp. 5429-5434). London: IEEE.

Charar, M. A., Guennoun, Z., & Aniba, G. (2015). Achieving energy efficiency for Device-to-Device communications using power control: A low complexity algorithm. In *Proceedings of the 10th International Conference on Intelligent Systems: Theories and Applications (SITA)* (pp. 1-6). Rabat: IEEE.

Chaudhari, S., & Prashant, K. (2017). Joint Mode Selection and Power Control Scheme for Interference Alleviation in Device-to-Device Communications. *International Journal of Electronics, Electrical and Computational System.*, *6*(3), 136–141.

Chen, J., Liu, C., Li, H., Li, X., & Li, S. (2016). A Categorized Resource Sharing Mechanism for Device-to-Device Communications in Cellular Networks. *Mobile Information Systems.*, *2016*, 1–10.

Dacheng, Y., Xin, Z., Zhesheng, L., Xiaoyue, Z., & Si, W. (2012). Optimization of interference coordination schemes in Device-to-Device(D2D) communication. In *Proceedings of the 2013 8th International Conference on Communications and Networking in China (CHINACOM)* (pp. 542-547). Kun Ming: IEEE.

ElSawy, H., & Hossain, E. (2017). Analytical modelling of mode selection and power control for underlay D2D communication in cellular networks. *IEEE Transactions on Communications*, *2*, 1–7.

ElSawy, H., Hossain, E., & Haenggi, M. (2013). Stochastic geometry for modelling, analysis, and design of multi-tier and cognitive cellular wireless networks: A Survey. *IEEE Communications Surveys and Tutorials*, *15*(3), 996–1019. doi:10.1109/SURV.2013.052213.00000

Evans, D. (2011). *The Internet of Things: How the next evolution of the Internet is changing everything.* Cisco Internet Business Solutions Group. Retrieved on March 12, 2018 from https://www.cisco.com/c/dam/en_us/about/ac79/docs/innov/IoT_IBSG_0411FINAL.pdf

Feng, D., Lu, L., Yuan-Wu, Y. G., Li, G. Y., Feng, G., & Li, S. (2013). Device-to-Device Communications Underlaying Cellular Networks. *IEEE Transactions on Communications*, *61*(8), 3541–3551. doi:10.1109/TCOMM.2013.071013.120787

Fodor, G., Penda, D. D., Belleschi, M., Johansson, M., & Abrardo, A. (2013). A comparative study of power control approaches for device-to-device communications. In *Proceedings of the 2013 IEEE International Conference on Communications (ICC)* (pp. 6008-6013). Budapest: IEEE. 10.1109/ICC.2013.6655561

Foschini, G. J., & Miljanic, Z. (1993). A simple distributed autonomous power control algorithm and its convergence. *IEEE Transactions on Vehicular Technology*, *42*(4), 641–646. doi:10.1109/25.260747

Guo, G., Sun, S., & Gao, Q. (2014). Graph-Based Resource Allocation for D2D Communications Underlying Cellular Networks in Multiuser Scenario. *International Journal of Antennas and Propagation*, *2014*, 1–27. doi:10.1155/2014/783631

Hongnian, X., & Hakola, S. (2010). The investigation of power control schemes for a device-to-device communication integrated into OFDMA cellular system. In *Proceedings of the 21st Annual IEEE International Symposium on Personal, Indoor and Mobile Radio Communications* (pp.1775-1780). Istanbul: IEEE. 10.1109/PIMRC.2010.5671643

Huang, H., Nasir, A. A., Durrani, S., & Zhou, X. (2016). Mode selection, resource allocation, and power control for D2D-enabled two-tier cellular network. *IEEE Transactions on Communications*, *64*(8), 3534–3547. doi:10.1109/TCOMM.2016.2580153

Huang, J., Zhao, Y., & Sohraby, K. (2014). Resource allocation for intercell device-to-device communication underlaying cellular network: A game-theoretic approach. In *Proceedings of the 2014 23rd International Conference on Computer Communication and Networks (ICCCN)* (pp. 1-8). Shanghai: IEEE.

Janis, P., Yu, C. H., Doppler, K., Rebeiro, C., Wijting, C., Hugl, K., ... Koivunen, V. (2009). Device-to-Device communication underlaying cellular communication. *International Journal of Communications, Networks and System Sciences*, *3*, 169–179. doi:10.4236/ijcns.2009.23019

Jeon, J., Ko, B. H., Lee, S. R., & Kim, K. S. (2013). Distributed interference channel-based resource allocation for network-assisted device-to-device communications. In *Proceedings on 2013 IEEE International Workshop on Signal Design and its Applications* (pp. 96-98). Tokyo: IEEE.

Katsinis, G., Tsiropoulou, E. E., & Papavassiliou, S. (2017). Multicell Interference Management in device-to-device underlay cellular networks. *Future Internet*, *9*(44), 1–20.

Kim, J., Karim, N. A., & Cho, S. (2017). An interference mitigation scheme of device-to-device communications for sensor networks underlaying LTE-A. *Sensor*, *2017*(17), 1088–1105.

Lee, N., Lin, X., Andrews, J. G., & Heath, R. W. (2015). Power control for D2D underlaid cellular networks: Modeling, algorithms, and analysis. *IEEE Journal on Selected Areas in Communications*, *33*(1), 1–13. doi:10.1109/JSAC.2014.2369612

Leyton-Brown, K., & Shoham, Y. (2008). *Essentials of Game Theory*. Morgan & Claypool.

Li, Y., Su, S., & Chen, S. (2015). Social-aware resource allocation for device-to-device communications underlaying cellular networks. *IEEE Wireless Communications Letters, 4*(3), 293–296. doi:10.1109/LWC.2015.2410768

Lin, X., Andrews, J. G., & Ghosh, A. (2014). Spectrum sharing for device-to-device communication in cellular networks. *IEEE Transactions on Wireless Communications, 13*(12), 6727–6740. doi:10.1109/TWC.2014.2360202

Lin, Y. D., & Hsu, Y. C. (2000). Multi-hop Cellular: A new architecture for wireless communications. *Proceedings - IEEE INFOCOM, 3*, 1273–1282.

Liu, J., Kawamoto, Y., Nishiyama, H., Kato, N., & Kadowaki, N. (2014). Device-to-device communications achieve efficient load balancing in LTE-advanced networks. *IEEE Wireless Communications Magazine, 21*(2), 57–65. doi:10.1109/MWC.2014.6812292

Marques, P., Bastos, J., & Gameiro, A. (2008). Opportunistic use of 3G uplink Licensed Bands. In *Proceedings of the 2008 IEEE International Conference on Communications* (pp. 3588-3592). Beijing: IEEE. 10.1109/ICC.2008.675

Militano, L., Araniti, G., Condoluci, M., Farris, I., & Iera, A. (2015). Device-to-Device Communications for 5G Internet of Things. *EAI Endorsed Transactions on Internet of Things., 1*(4), 1–16.

Nouran, M., & Nordin, R. (2016). A survey on interference management for Device-to-Device (D2D) communication and its challenges in 5G networks. *Journal of Network and Computer Applications, 71*, 130–150. doi:10.1016/j.jnca.2016.04.021

Osserain, A., Boccardi, F., Braun, V., Kusume, K., Marsch, P., Matermia, M., ... Fallgen, M. (2014). Scenari.os for 5G mobile and wireless communications: The vision of the METIS project. *IEEE Communications Magazine, 52*(5), 26–35. doi:10.1109/MCOM.2014.6815890

Peng, T., Lu, Q., Wang, H., Xu, S., & Wang, W. (2009). Interference avoidance mechanisms in the hybrid cellular and device-to-device systems. In *Proceedings of the 2009 IEEE 20th International Symposium on Personal, Indoor and Mobile Radio Communications* (pp. 617-621). Tokyo: IEEE. 10.1109/PIMRC.2009.5449856

Safdar, G. A., Ur-Rehman, M., Muhammad, M., Imran, M. A., & Tafazolli, R. (2016). Interference Mitigation in D2D Communication Underlaying LTE-A Network. *IEEE Access: Practical Innovations, Open Solutions, 4*, 7967–7987. doi:10.1109/ACCESS.2016.2621115

Sesia, S., Toufik, I., & Baker, M. (2011). *LTE-The UMTS Long Term Evolution: From theory to practice.* London: John Wiley & Sons Ltd. doi:10.1002/9780470978504

Shamrao, C., & Kumar, P. (2017). Interference mitigation by switching the underlaying transmitter in D2D communications. In *Proceedings of the 2017 Innovations in Power and Advanced Computing Technologies (i-PACT2017)* (pp. 1-6). Vellore: IEEE.

Song, L., Niyato, D., Han, Z., & Hossain, E. (2015). *Wireless Device-to-Device Communications and Networks.* New York: Cambridge University Press. doi:10.1017/CBO9781107478732

Song, L., Zhu, H., & Chen, X. (2014). *Resource mmanagement for device-to-device underlay communication*. Retrieved on March 12, 2018 from http://adsabs.harvard.edu/abs/2013arXiv1311.1018X

Sun, B. S., & Gao, S. S. Q. (2014). Interference management for device-to-device communications underlaying networks at cell edge. In *Proceedings on the International Conference on Wireless and Mobile Communications* (pp. 118-123), Seville: IARIA.

Wang, L., Liu, L., Cao, X., Tian, X., & Cheng, Y. (2015). Sociality-aware resource allocation for device-to-device communications in cellular networks. *IET Communications*, *9*(3), 342–349. doi:10.1049/iet-com.2014.0436

Wang, S., & Hou, R. (2017). Network coding-based interference management scheme in Device-to-Device communications. *ZTE Communications*, *15*(2), 48–54.

Wu, X., Tavildar, S., Shakkottai, S., Richardson, T., Li, T., Laroia, R., & Jovicic, A. (2010). FlashLinQ: A synchronous distributed scheduler for peer-to-peer ad hoc networks. In *Proceedings on IEEE International Conference on Communication Control and Computing Technologies (ICCCCT)* (pp. 524-521). Tamil Nadu: IEEE.

Ye, Q., Al-Shalash, M., Caramanis, C., & Andrews, J. G. (2015). Distributed resource allocation in device-to-device enhanced cellular networks. *IEEE Transactions on Communications*, *63*(2), 441–454. doi:10.1109/TCOMM.2014.2386874

Yuan, Y., Yang, T., Feng, H., Hu, B., Zhang, J., & Wang, B., & Lu, Q. (2017). Traffic-aware transmission mode selection in D2D-enabled cellular networks with token system. In *Proceedings 2017 25th European Signal Processing Conference (EUSIPCO)* (pp.2249-2253). Kos: IEEE. 10.23919/EUSIPCO.2017.8081610

Zhang, H., Song, L., & Han, Z. (2016). Radio resource allocation for device-to-device underlay communication using hypergraph theory. *IEEE Transactions on Wireless Communications*, *15*(70), 4852–4861.

Compilation of References

Abdous, M., He, W., & Yen, C. J. (2012). Using Data Mining for Predicting Relationships between Online Question Theme and Final Grade. *Journal of Educational Technology & Society*, *15*(3), 77–88. Available Online at www.sciencedirect.com

Abrahart, R.J. & See, L.M. (2007). Neural network emulation of a rainfall-runoff model. *The Journal of Hydrology and Earth System Sciences, 4*, 287–326.

Abu, Suboh, & Ramli. (2018). Design and Development of Home Security Systems based on Internet of Things Via Favoriot Platform. *International Journal of Applied Engineering Research, 13*(2), 1253-1260.

Ada, L. (2017). *PIR Motion Sensor Created*. Adafruit Industries.

Agarwal, R., & Dhar, V. (2014). Editorial – big data, data science, and analytics: The opportunity and challenge for is research. *Information Systems Research*, *25*(3), 443–448. doi:10.1287/isre.2014.0546

Ahmed, R., & Karypis, G. (2012). Algorithms for Mining the Evolution of Conserved Relational States in Dynamic Networks. *Knowledge and Information Systems, 33*(3), 603–630. doi:10.100710115-012-0537-2

Aickelin, U., & Dowsland, K. A. (2004). An indirect genetic algorithm for a nurse scheduling problem. *Computers & Operations Research*, *31*(5), 761–778. doi:10.1016/S0305-0548(03)00034-0

Akkerman, F., Farahani, P., & Grunow, M. (2010). Quality, safety and sustainability in food distribution: A review of quantitative operations management approaches and challenges. *OR-Spektrum*, *32*(4), 863–904. doi:10.100700291-010-0223-2

Akulwar, K. (2016). *5 ways Internet of Things is helping logistics industry around the globe*. DreamOrbit. Retrieved from: http://dreamorbit.com/5-ways-internet-of-things-is-helping-logistics-industry-around-the-globe/

Alemdar & Ersoy. (2010). Wireless Sensor Networks for Healthcare: A Survey. *Computer Networks*, *54*(15), 2688–710.

Angelov, S., Grefen, P., & Greefhorst, D. (2012). A framework for analysis and design of software reference architectures. *Journal of Information and Software Technology*, *54*(4), 417–431. doi:10.1016/j.infsof.2011.11.009

Apte, C., & Hong, S. J. (1995). *Predicting Equity Returns from Securities Data with Minimal Rule Generation. In Advances in Knowledge Discovery and Data Mining.* AAAI Press.

Armstrong, P. (2015). Teacher characteristics and student performance: An analysis using hierarchical linear modelling. *South African Journal of Childhood Education, 5*(2).

Arnold, S. E. (1992). Information manufacturing: The road to database quality. *Database, 15*(5), 32–39.

Asadi, A., Wang, Q., & Mancuso, V. (2014). A survey on device-to-device communication in cellular networks. *IEEE Communications Surveys and Tutorials, 16*(4), 1801–1819. doi:10.1109/COMST.2014.2319555

Atzori, L., Iera, A., & Morabito, G. (2005). The Internet of Things: A survey. *Journal of Computer Networks, 54*(15), 2787–2805. doi:10.1016/j.comnet.2010.05.010

Aung, M. M., & Chang, Y. S. (2014). Temperature Management for The Quality Assurance of a Perishable Food Supply Chain. *Journal of Food Control, 40*, 198–207. doi:10.1016/j.foodcont.2013.11.016

Avitesh, A. (2017). A Method of WSN and Sensor Cloud System to Monitor Cold Chain Logistics as Part of The IoT Technology. *International Journal of Multimedia and Ubiquitous Engineering, 9*(10), 145–152.

Ayed, Elkosantini, & Abid. (2017). An Automated Surveillance System based on Multi-Processor System-on-Chip and Hardware Accelerator. *International Journal of Advanced Computer Science and Applications., 8*(9), 59.

Ayhan, S. (2013). Predictive analytics with aviation big data. *2013 Integrated Communications, Navigation and Surveillance Conference (ICNS)*, 1-13.

Baesens, A. (2014). *Analytics in a big data world: The essential guide to data science and its applications.* Hoboken, NJ: John Wiley & Sons.

Bakhshinategh, B., Zaiane, O. R., Elatia, S., & Ipperciel, D. (2018). Educational data mining applications and tasks: A survey of the last 10 years. *Education and Information Technologies, 23*(1), 537–553. doi:10.100710639-017-9616-z

Bala, M., & Ojha, D. B. (2012). Study of applications of Data Mining Techniques in Education. *International Journal of Research in Science and Technology, 1*(4).

Ballou, D. P., & Pazer, H. L. (1985). Modeling data and process quality in multi-input, multi-output information systems. *Management Science, 31*(2), 150–162. doi:10.1287/mnsc.31.2.150

Ballou, D. P., Wang, R., & Pacer, H. (1998). Modeling information manufacturing systems to determine information product quality. *Management Science, 44*(4), 462–484. doi:10.1287/mnsc.44.4.462

Banejad, H., & Olyaie, E. (2011). Application of an Artificial Neural Network Model to Rivers Water Quality Indexes Prediction – A Case Study. *The Journal of American Science, 7*(1).

Barbierato, E., Gribaudo, M., & Iacono, M. (2014). Performance evaluation of No SQL big data applications using multi-formalism models. *Future Generation Computer Systems, 37*, 345–353. doi:10.1016/j.future.2013.12.036

Barnaghi, P., Sheth, A., & Henson, C. (2013). From data to actionable knowledge: Big data challenges in the web of things. *IEEE Intelligent Systems, 28*(6), 6–11. doi:10.1109/MIS.2013.142

Bashal, Jilani, & Arun. (2016). An Intelligent Door System using Raspberry Pi and Amazon Web Services IoT. *International Journal of Engineering Trends and Technology*.

Basyal, Kaushal, & Singh. (2018). Voice Recognition Robot with Real Time Surveillance and Automation. *International Journal of Creative Research Thoughts, 6*(1), 2320–2882.

Battani, C., Cappelli, C., Francians, C., & Maurino, A. (2009). Methodologies for data quality assessment and improvement. *Association for Computing Machinery Computing Surveys, 41*(3), 1–52.

Bechini, Marcelloni, & Segatori. (2016). A MapReduce solution for associative classification of big data. *Information Sciences, 332*(1), 33–55.

Bhardwaj, B. K., & Pal, S. (2011). Mining Educational Data to Analyze Students Performance. *International Journal of Advanced Computer Science and Applications, 2*(6), 2011.

Bhosale, H. S., & Gadekar, D. P. (2014). A Review Paper on Big Data and Hadoop. *IJSRP, 4*(10).

Bisht, A. K. (2017). Development of an Automated Water Quality Classification Model for the river Ganga. In *3rd International Conference on Next Generation Computing Technologies*. Springer.

Blaisdell, R. (2018). *The risks of IoT. Rick's Cloud*. Retrieved from: https://rickscloud.com/the-risks-of-iot/

Blake, R., & Mangiameli, P. (2011). The effects and interactions of data quality and problem complexity on classification. *Association for Computing Machinery Journal of Data and Information Quality, 2*(2), 1–28. doi:10.1145/1891879.1891881

Blockow, D. (2018). *Big Data Architecture Principles*. Data to Decision CRC. Retrieved from https://www.d2dcrc.com.au/blog/big-data-architecture-principles/

Boyd & Crawford. (2012). *Six Provocations for Big Data. Proceeding of A Decade in Internet Time: Symposium on the Dynamics of the Internet and Society*. Retrieved from: https://papers.ssrn.com/sol3/papers.cfm?abstract_id=1926431

Bradski & Kaehler. (2008). *Learning OpenCV*. Academic Press.

Brink, H. (2017). *Real-World Machine Learning*. Manning publications Co.

Brown, B., Chui, M., & Manyika, J. (2011). Are you ready for the era of Big Data? *The McKinsey Quarterly, 4*, 24–35.

Buhler, P. (2016). *Big Data Fundamentals: Concepts, Drivers & Techniques*. Prentice Hall.

Cai, X., Zheng, J., & Zhang, Y. (2015). A Graph colouring-based resource allocation algorithm for D2D communication in cellular networks. In *Proceedings of the IEEE International Conference on Communications (ICC)* (pp. 5429-5434). London: IEEE.

Caldeira, J. M. L. P. (2012). Toward ubiquitous mobility solutions for body sensor network health care. *IEEE Communications Magazine, 50*(5), 108 – 115. Doi:10.1109/MCOM.2012.6194390

Castro, Coral, Rodriguez, Cabra, & Colorado. (2017). Wearable-Based Human Activity Recognition Using an IoT Approach. *Journal Sensor and Actuator Networks, 6*(28).

Chandra, S. (2018). *India's Biometric Identity Program Is Rooting Out Corruption.* Retrieved from: https://slate.com/technology/2018/08/aadhaar-indias-biometric-identity-program-is-working-but-privacy-concerns-remain.html

Chang, F. J. (2002). Hydrological Processes. *Hydrological Processes, 16,* 2577–2588. doi:10.1002/hyp.1015

Charar, M. A., Guennoun, Z., & Aniba, G. (2015). Achieving energy efficiency for Device-to-Device communications using power control: A low complexity algorithm. In *Proceedings of the 10th International Conference on Intelligent Systems: Theories and Applications (SITA)* (pp. 1-6). Rabat: IEEE.

Chaudhari, S., & Prashant, K. (2017). Joint Mode Selection and Power Control Scheme for Interference Alleviation in Device-to-Device Communications. *International Journal of Electronics, Electrical and Computational System., 6*(3), 136–141.

Cheeseman, P., & Stutz, J. (1996). Bayesian Classification (AUTOCLASS): Theory and Results. In *Advances in Knowledge Discovery and Data Mining.* AAAI Press.

Chen, C. L. P., & Zhang, C. Y. (2014). Data-intensive applications, challenges, techniques and technologies: A survey on big data. *Information Sciences, 275,* 314–347. doi:10.1016/j.ins.2014.01.015

Chen, J., Chen, Y., Du, X., Li, C., Lu, J., Zhao, S., & Zhou, X. (2013). Big data challenge: A data management perspective. *Frontiers of Computer Science, 7*(2), 157–164. doi:10.100711704-013-3903-7

Chen, J., Liu, C., Li, H., Li, X., & Li, S. (2016). A Categorized Resource Sharing Mechanism for Device-to-Device Communications in Cellular Networks. *Mobile Information Systems., 2016,* 1–10.

Chen, M., Mao, S., & Liu, Y. (2014). Big data: A survey. *Mobile Networks and Applications, 19*(2), 171–209. doi:10.100711036-013-0489-0

Chen, W., Wang, Y.-J., & Jan, J.-K. (2014). A novel deployment of smart cold chain system using 2G-RFID-Sys. *Journal of Food Engineering, 141,* 113–121. doi:10.1016/j.jfoodeng.2014.05.014

Chen, X. (2012). Article. *Research on Key Technology and Applications for Internet of Things, 33,* 561–566.

Chiu, Ku, & Wang. (2010). Automatic Traffic Surveillance System for Vision-Based Vehicle Recognition and Tracking. *Journal of Information Science and Engineering, 26,* 611–629.

Chung, C., Khatkar, P., Xing, T., Lee, J., & Huang, D. (2013). NICE: Network Intrusion Detection and Countermeasure Selection in Virtual Network Systems. *IEEE Transactions on Dependable and Secure Computing*, *10*(4), 198–211. doi:10.1109/TDSC.2013.8

Cisco. (2017). *The Zettabyte Era: Trends and Analysis*. Retrieved from: http://www.cisco.com/c/en/us/solutions/collateral/service-provider/visual-networking-index-vni/VNI_Hyperconnectivity_WP.html

Cooke, J. A. (2013). Three trends to watch in 2013, Perspective. *Supply Chain Quarterly*, *1*, 11.

Crosby, P. (1995). *Philip Crosby's Reflections on Quality*. McGraw-Hill.

Dacheng, Y., Xin, Z., Zhesheng, L., Xiaoyue, Z., & Si, W. (2012). Optimization of interference coordination schemes in Device-to-Device(D2D) communication. In *Proceedings of the 2013 8th International Conference on Communications and Networking in China (CHINACOM)* (pp. 542-547). Kun Ming: IEEE.

Daniel, B. K. (2017). Thoughts on Recent Trends and Future Research Perspectives in Big Data and Analytics in Higher Education. In *Big Data and Learning Analytics in Higher Education* (pp. 7–17). Cham: Springer. doi:10.1007/978-3-319-06520-5_1

Danubianu, M., Pentiuc, S. G., & Tobolcea, I. (2011). *Mining Association Rules Inside a Relational Database – A Case Study, ICCGI 2011. Sixth International Multi-Conference on Computing in the Global Information Technology*.

Davenport, T. H., Barth, P., & Bean, R. (2012, Fall). How Big Data is different. *MIT Sloan Management Review*, 22–24.

Davenport, T. H., & Harris, J. G. (2007). *Competing on analytics – the new science of wining*. Boston: Harvard Business School Publishing Corporation.

Davenport, T. H., Harris, J. G., & Morison, R. (2010). *Analytics at work – smart decisions, better results*. Boston: Harvard Business Press.

Davenport, T. H., & Prusiks, L. (2000). *Working knowledge: how organizations manage what they know*. Boston: Harvard Business Press.

Dean, J., & Ghemawat, S. (2010). *MapReduce: Simplified Data Processing on Large Clusters*. Google, Inc.

Del Din, S., Godfrey, A., Mazzà, C., Lord, S., & Rochester, L. (2016). Free-living monitoring of Parkinson's disease: Lessons from the field. *Movement Disorders*, *31*(9), 1293–1313. doi:10.1002/mds.26718 PMID:27452964

Deloitte & MHI. (2014). *The 2014 MHI Annual Industry Report – Innovation the driven supply chain*. Charlotte, NC: MHI.

Deloitte & MHI. (2016). *The 2016 MHI Annual Industry Report – Accelerating change: How innovation is driving digital, always-on Supply Chains*. MHI.

Deming, W. E. (2000). *The New Economics for Industry, Government, Education* (2nd ed.). MIT Press.

Department of Atmospheric Sciences. (2010). *Relative Humidity*. University of Illinois at Urbana-Champaign. Retrieved from: http://ww2010.atmos.uiuc.edu/%28Gh%29/guides/mtr/cld/dvlp/rh.rxml

Department of Defence. (2012). *Big Data Across the Federal Government*. Executive Office of the President. Retrieved from: https://www.hsdl.org/?view&did=742609

Dhar, V. (2013). Data Science and Prediction. *Communication of the ACM, 56*(12), 64-73. doi:10.1145/2500499

Dietrich, B., Plachy, E. C., & Norton, M. F. (2014). *Analytics across the enterprise: How IBM realize business value from big data and analytics*. Boston: IBM Press Books.

Dobre, C., & Xhafa, F. (2014). Intelligent services for big data science. *Future Generation Computer Systems, 37*, 267–281. doi:10.1016/j.future.2013.07.014

Domadia & Mehta. (2014). Automated Video Surveillance System for Human Motion Detection with Face Detection. *International Journal of Advance Engineering and Research Development, 1*(5).

Domingo, M. C. (2012). An overview of the Internet of Things for people with disabilities. *Journal of Network and Computer Applications, 35*(2), 584–596. doi:10.1016/j.jnca.2011.10.015

Dringus, L. P., & Ellis, T. (2005). Using data mining as a strategy for assessing asynchronous discussion forums. *Computers & Education, 45*(1), 141–160. doi:10.1016/j.compedu.2004.05.003

Edoh, T. (2017). Smart Medicine Transportation and Medication Monitoring System in EPharmacyNet. *2017 International Rural and Elderly Health Informatics Conference (IREHI)*, 1-9.

Educause. (2010). *7 Things you should know about analytics*. Retrieved October 1, 2010 from https://www.educause.edu/ir/library/pdf/ELI7059.pdf

Elder, J. (n.d.). Non Linear Classification and Regression. In *Introduction to Machine Learning and Pattern Recognition*. CSE 4404/5327.

Elias, T. (2011). Learning Analytics: Definintions, Processes and Potential. *Learning*, 1-22.

ElSawy, H., & Hossain, E. (2017). Analytical modelling of mode selection and power control for underlay D2D communication in cellular networks. *IEEE Transactions on Communications, 2*, 1–7.

ElSawy, H., Hossain, E., & Haenggi, M. (2013). Stochastic geometry for modelling, analysis, and design of multi-tier and cognitive cellular wireless networks: A Survey. *IEEE Communications Surveys and Tutorials, 15*(3), 996–1019. doi:10.1109/SURV.2013.052213.00000

Elshafee & Hamed. (2012). Design and Implementation of a WiFi Based Home Automation System. World Academy of Science, Engineering and Technology. *International Journal of Computer, Electrical, Automation, Control and Information Engineering, 6*(8).

Emery, J. C. (1969). *Organizational planning and control systems: Theory and management*. New York: Macmillan.

Enterprise, H. P. (2017). *The Exponential Growth of Data*. Retrieved from: https://insidebigdata.com/2017/02/16/the-exponential-growth-of-data/

Eskofier, Lee, Daneault, Golabchi, Ferreira-Carvalho, Vergara-Diaz, ... Bonato. (2016). Recent machine learning advancements in sensor-based mobility analysis: Deep learning for Parkinson's disease assessment. *2016 38th Annual International Conference of the IEEE Engineering in Medicine and Biology Society (EMBC)*, 655–658.

Evans, D. (2011). *The Internet of Things: How the next evolution of the Internet is changing everything*. Cisco Internet Business Solutions Group. Retrieved on March 12, 2018 from https://www.cisco.com/c/dam/en_us/about/ac79/docs/innov/IoT_IBSG_0411FINAL.pdf

Evans, D. (2011). *The Internet of Things How the Next Evolution of the Internet Is Changing Everything*. Cisco.

Fairhurst, G. (2003). *Transmission Control Protocol (TCP)*. Retrieved from: https://erg.abdn.ac.uk/users/gorry/course/inet-pages/tcp.html

Fayyad, U., Shapiro, G. P., & Smyth, P. (1996). From Data Mining to Knowledge Discovery in Databases. *American Association for Artificial Intelligence*, *17*(3), 1996.

Feng, D., Lu, L., Yuan-Wu, Y. G., Li, G. Y., Feng, G., & Li, S. (2013). Device-to-Device Communications Underlaying Cellular Networks. *IEEE Transactions on Communications*, *61*(8), 3541–3551. doi:10.1109/TCOMM.2013.071013.120787

Fernandez-Gago, M., Moyano, F., & Lopez, J. (2017). Modelling trust dynamics in the Internet of Things. *Information Sciences*, *396*, 72–82. doi:10.1016/j.ins.2017.02.039

Filzmoser, P. (2008). Linear and Nonlinear Methods for Regression and Classification and applications in R. *Forschungsbericht CS-2008-3*.

Fleisch, B. (2004). Does higher education expenditure generate higher learner achievement?A study of historically disadvantaged schools in Gauteng. *South African Journal of Education*, *24*(4), 264–269.

Fodor, G., Penda, D. D., Belleschi, M., Johansson, M., & Abrardo, A. (2013). A comparative study of power control approaches for device-to-device communications. In *Proceedings of the 2013 IEEE International Conference on Communications (ICC)* (pp. 6008-6013). Budapest: IEEE. 10.1109/ICC.2013.6655561

Food and Drug Administration. (2018). *Hazard Analysis Critical Control Point System (HACCP)*. Food and Drug Administration. Retrieved from http://www.who.int/foodsafety/fs_management/haccp/en/

Forrest, C. (2016). 5 architectural principles for building big data systems on AWS. *TechRepublic*. Retrieved from: https://www.techrepublic.com/article/5-architectural-principles-for-building-big-data-systems-on-aws/

Foschini, G. J., & Miljanic, Z. (1993). A simple distributed autonomous power control algorithm and its convergence. *IEEE Transactions on Vehicular Technology*, *42*(4), 641–646. doi:10.1109/25.260747

Gandomi, A., & Haider, M. (2015). *Beyond the hype: Big data concepts, methods, and analytics*. Academic Press.

Gandomi, A., & Haider, M. (2015). Beyond the hype: Big data concepts, methods, and analytics. *International Journal of Information Management*, *35*(2), 137–144. doi:10.1016/j.ijinfomgt.2014.10.007

Ganguli, S. (2016). *Worldwide IoT in Logistics Market: Drivers, Opportunities, Trends, and Forecasts.* Infoholic Research LLP. Retrieved from https://www.infoholicresearch.com/worldwide-iot-in-logistics-market-to-grow-at-a-cagr-of-35-5-over-the-period-2016-2022-to-aggregate-1050-95-billion-by-2022/

Gantz, J., & Reinsel, D. (2012). *The Digital Universe in 2020: Big data, bigger digital shadows, and biggest growth in the Far East.* IDC – EMC Corporation. Available at http://www.emc.com/collateral/analyst-reports/idc-the-digital-universe-in2020.pdf

Gao, X. & Ma. (2017). A new approach of cloud control systems: CCSs based on data-driven predictive control. *2017 Chinese Automation Congress (CAC)*, 3419-3422.

García, E., Romero, C., Ventura, S., & Castro, C. D. (2011). A collaborative educational association rule mining tool. *Internet and Higher Education*, *14*(2), 77–88. doi:10.1016/j.iheduc.2010.07.006

Gazzaz, N. M. (2012). Artificial neural network Modelling of the water quality index for Kinta River (Malaysia) using water quality variables as predictors. Marine Pollution Bulletin.

Goh, D. H., & Ang, R. P. (2007). An introduction to association rule mining: An application in counseling and help-seeking behavior of adolescents. *Behavior Research Methods*, *39*(2), 259–266. doi:10.3758/BF03193156 PMID:17695353

Greenough, J. (2014). *The 'Internet of Things' Will Be The World's Most Massive Device Market And Save Companies Billions Of Dollars. BI Intelligence reports.* Retrieved form: https://www.businessinsider.in/The-Internet-of-Things-Will-Be-The-Worlds-Most-Massive-Device-Market-And-Save-Companies-Billions-Of-Dollars/articleshow/44766662.cms

Gros, B. (2016). The design of smart educational environments. *Smart Learning Environments*, *3*(1), 15. doi:10.118640561-016-0039-x

Guo, G., Sun, S., & Gao, Q. (2014). Graph-Based Resource Allocation for D2D Communications Underlying Cellular Networks in Multiuser Scenario. *International Journal of Antennas and Propagation*, *2014*, 1–27. doi:10.1155/2014/783631

Guru, N., & Jha, R. (2013). Simulation of BOD-DO Modelling in Mahanadi River System lying in Odisha using ANN, India. *IOSR Journal Of Environmental Science, Toxicology And Food Technology*, *2*(4), 52-57.

Ha, S. H., Bae, S. M., & Park, S. C. (2000). Web mining for distance education. In IEEE international conference on management of innovation and technology (pp. 715–719). IEEE.

Hadoop. (2017). Retrieved from http://hadoop.apache.org

Hart & Martinez. (2006). Environmental Sensor Networks: A revolution in the earth system science. *Journal of Earth-Science Reviews, 78*(3), 177–191.

Hashem, I., Yaqoob, I., Anuar, N. B., Mokhtar, S., Gani, A., & Ullah Khan, S. (2015). The rise of "big data" on cloud computing: Review and open research issues. *Information Systems, 47*, 98–115. doi:10.1016/j.is.2014.07.006

Haug, A., & Arlbjorn, J. S. (2011). Barriers to master data quality. *Journal of Enterprise Information Management, 24*(3), 288–303. doi:10.1108/17410391111122862

Haugh, A., Arlbjorn, J. S., & Pedersen, A. (2009). A classification model of ERP system data quality. *Industrial Management & Data Systems, 109*(8), 1053–1068. doi:10.1108/02635570910991292

HBR. (2012, October). Getting Control of Big Data. *Harvard Business Review*.

Henard, F., & Roseveare, D. (2012). *Fostering Quality Teaching in Higher Education:Policies and Practices*. OECD,.

Heydari, M. (2013). Development of a Neural Network Technique for Prediction of Water Quality Parameters in the Delaware River, Pennsylvania. *Middle East Journal of Scientific Research, 13*(10), 1367–1376.

Hilbert, M. (2015). What is Big Data. *YouTube*. Retrieved from: https://www.youtube.com/watch?v=XRVIh1h47sA

Hilbert, M. (2016). Big Data for Development: A Review of Promises and Challenges. *Development Policy Review, 34*(1), 135–174. doi:10.1111/dpr.12142

Hongnian, X., & Hakola, S. (2010). The investigation of power control schemes for a device-to-device communication integrated into OFDMA cellular system. In *Proceedings of the 21st Annual IEEE International Symposium on Personal, Indoor and Mobile Radio Communications* (pp.1775-1780). Istanbul: IEEE. 10.1109/PIMRC.2010.5671643

How the Internet of Things impacts the logistics business. (2018). Softweb Solutions. Retrieved from: https://www.softwebiot.com/iot-use-cases/how-iot-impacts-transportation-and-logistics-industry/

Hu, R. (2010). Medical Data Mining Based on Association Rules. *Computer and Information Science, 3*(4).

Huang, H., Nasir, A. A., Durrani, S., & Zhou, X. (2016). Mode selection, resource allocation, and power control for D2D-enabled two-tier cellular network. *IEEE Transactions on Communications, 64*(8), 3534–3547. doi:10.1109/TCOMM.2016.2580153

Huang, J., Zhao, Y., & Sohraby, K. (2014). Resource allocation for intercell device-to-device communication underlaying cellular network: A game-theoretic approach. In *Proceedings of the 2014 23rd International Conference on Computer Communication and Networks (ICCCN)* (pp. 1-8). Shanghai: IEEE.

Huh, Y. U., Keller, F. R., Redman, T. C., & Watkins, A. R. (1990). Data quality. *Information and Software Technology, 32*(8), 559–565. doi:10.1016/0950-5849(90)90146-I

Hwang, G.-J. (2014). Definition, framework and research issues of smart learning environments-a context-aware ubiquitous learning perspective. *Smart Learning Environments, 1*(1), 4. doi:10.118640561-014-0004-5

Imminent, A., Pacemen, P., & Alaska, E. (2015). Evaluating the quality of social media data in big data architecture. *IEEE Access: Practical Innovations, Open Solutions, 3*, 2028–2043. doi:10.1109/ACCESS.2015.2490723

Industrial Internet Consortium. (n.d.). *Industrial Internet Reference Architecture.* Available: http://www.iiconsortium.org/IIRA.htm

Instruments, T. (2014). *Single, Dual, and Quad General Purpose, Low-Voltage, Rail-to-Rail Output Operational Amplifiers. Datasheet of LMV321/358/324.* Texas Instruments.

Islam, M., Mukhopadhyay, S. C., & Suryadevara, N. K. (2017). Smart Sensors and Internet of Things: A Postgraduate Paper. *IEEE Sensors Journal, 17*(3), 577–584. doi:10.1109/JSEN.2016.2630124

Jadeja & Modi. (2012). Cloud computing - concepts, architecture and challenges. *2012 International Conference on Computing, Electronics and Electrical Technologies (ICCEET)*, 877-880.

Jain, A. K., Murty, M. N., & Flynn, P. J. (1999). Data clustering: A review. *ACM Computing Surveys, 31*(3), 264–323. doi:10.1145/331499.331504

Jan. (2004). Neural Network Based Threat Assessment for Automated Visual Surveillance. *Neural Networks, 2004. Proceedings. 2004 IEEE International Joint Conference on.* doi: . doi:10.1109/IJCNN.2004.1380133

Janis, P., Yu, C. H., Doppler, K., Rebeiro, C., Wijting, C., Hugl, K., ... Koivunen, V. (2009). Device-to-Device communication underlaying cellular communication. *International Journal of Communications, Networks and System Sciences, 3*, 169–179. doi:10.4236/ijcns.2009.23019

Jayawardena, A. W., & Fernando, T. M. K. G. (2001). River flow prediction: an artificial neural network Approach. In *Proceedings of a symposium held during die Sixth IAHS Scientific Assembly at Maastricht, The Netherlands.* IAHS Publication no. 268..

Jeon, J., Ko, B. H., Lee, S. R., & Kim, K. S. (2013). Distributed interference channel-based resource allocation for network-assisted device-to-device communications. In *Proceedings on 2013 IEEE International Workshop on Signal Design and its Applications* (pp. 96-98). Tokyo: IEEE.

Jia, Tian, Shenc, & Tran. (2016). Leveraging MapReduce to efficiently extract associations between biomedical concepts from large text data. *Microprocessors and Microsystems.*

Jiang, H., Chen, Y., Qiao, Z., Weng, T. H., & Li, K. C. (2015). Scaling up MapReduce-based big data processing on multi-GPU systems. *Cluster Computing, 18*(1), 369–383. doi:10.100710586-014-0400-1

Jin, X., Wah, B. W., Cheng, X., & Wang, Y. (2015). Significance and challenges of big data research. *Big Data Research, 2*(2), 59–64. doi:10.1016/j.bdr.2015.01.006

Jones-Farmer, L. A., Ezell, J. D., & Hazen, B. T. (2013). Applying control chart methods to enhance data quality. *Technometrics*.

Jurak, J. M., & Godfrey, A. B. (1999). *Juran's Quality Handbook* (5th ed.). McGraw-Hill.

Kadu, Dekhane, Dhanwala, & Awate. (2015). Real Time Monitoring and Controlling System. *International Journal of Engineering and Science*, *4*(2), 15-18.

Kahan, B. K., Strong, D. M., & Wang, R. Y. (2002). Information quality benchmarks: Product and service performance. *Communications of the ACM*, *45*(4), 184–192. doi:10.1145/505248.506007

Kalil, T. (2012). *Big Data is a Big Deal*. The White House. Retrieved from: https://obamawhitehouse.archives.gov/blog/2012/03/29/big-data-big-deal

Kapasa, R. (2016). Predictive Analytics as a Security Management Tool in Virtualised Environment. *International Conference on Developments of E-Systems Engineering (DeSE)*, 102-106.

Kaplan, R. S., & Norton, D. P. (1993, September). Putting the Balanced Scorecard to Work. *Harvard Business Review*, 4–17.

Kara, Y., Acar Boyacioglu, M., & Baykan, Ö. K. (2011). Predicting direction of stock price index movement using artificial neural networks and support vector machines: The sample of the Istanbul Stock Exchange. *Expert Systems with Applications*, *38*(5), 5311–5319. doi:10.1016/j.eswa.2010.10.027

Katsinis, G., Tsiropoulou, E. E., & Papavassiliou, S. (2017). Multicell Interference Management in device-to-device underlay cellular networks. *Future Internet*, *9*(44), 1–20.

Kaufman, L. (2009). Data security in the world of cloud computing. *IEEE Security and Privacy*, *7*(4), 61–64. doi:10.1109/MSP.2009.87

Keerthikanth, SaiSanath, & Manikandaswamy. (2018). Multiple Motion Control System of a Rover Based on IoT to Produce Cloud Service. *International Journal of Pure and Applied Mathematics, 119*(12), 13171-13173.

Khemapech, I. (2005). *A Survey of Wireless Sensor Networks Technology. 6th Annual Postgraduate Symposium on the Convergence of Telecommunications, Networking and Broadcasting*, Liverpool, UK.

Khurana, N., Rathi, A., & Akshatha, P. S. (2011). Genetic algorithm: A search of complex spaces, international. *Jisuanji Yingyong*, *25*, 13–17.

Kim, G. H., Trimi, S., & Chung, J. H. (2014). Big-data applications in the government sector. *Communications of the ACM*, *57*(3), 78–85. doi:10.1145/2500873

Kim, J., Karim, N. A., & Cho, S. (2017). An interference mitigation scheme of device-to-device communications for sensor networks underlaying LTE-A. *Sensor*, *2017*(17), 1088–1105.

Klein, J. (2017). *Reference Architectures for Big Data Systems.* Carnegie Mellon University Software Engineering Institute. Retrieved from: https://insights.sei.cmu.edu/sei_blog/2017/05/reference-architectures-for-big-data-systems.html

Ko. (2010). *Wireless Sensor Networks for Healthcare.* IEEE.

Kodali, Bose, & Boppana. (2016). IoT Based Smart Security and Home Automation System. *International Conference on Computing, Communication and Automation (ICCCA2016).*

Kouskoumvekaki, I. (2011). *Non-linear Classification and Regression Methods.* Academic Press.

Krishna, B., Rao, Y. R. S., & Nayak, P. C. (2011). Time Series Modeling of River Flow Using Wavelet Neural Networks. *Journal of Water Resource and Protection, 3*(01), 50–59. doi:10.4236/jwarp.2011.31006

Kubota, K. J., Chen, J. A., & Little, M. A. (2016). Machine learning for large-scale wearable sensor data in Parkinson's disease: Concepts, promises, pitfalls, and futures. *Movement Disorders, 31*(9), 1314–1326. doi:10.1002/mds.26693 PMID:27501026

Kuhlman, D. (2013). *A Python Book: Beginning Python.* Advanced Python, and Python Exercises.

Kumar, V., & Chadha, A. (2012). Mining Association Rules in Student's Assessment Data. *International Journal of Computer Science Issues, 9*(5).

Kumar, A., Niu, F., & Ré, C. (2013). Hazy: Making it easier to build and maintain big-data analytics. *Communications of the ACM, 56*(3), 40–49. doi:10.1145/2428556.2428570

Kune, R., Konugurthi, P. K., Agarwal, A., Chillarige, R. R., & Buyya, R. (2016). The anatomy of big data computing. *Software, Practice & Experience, 46*(1), 79–105. doi:10.1002pe.2374

Labrinidis, A., & Jagadish, H. V. (2012). Challenges and opportunities with big data. *Proceeding of VLDB Endowment, 5*(12), 2032–2033.

LeCun, Y., Bengio, Y., & Hinton, G. (2015, May 28). Deep learning. *Nature, 521*(7553), 436–444. doi:10.1038/nature14539 PMID:26017442

Lee, N., Lin, X., Andrews, J. G., & Heath, R. W. (2015). Power control for D2D underlaid cellular networks: Modeling, algorithms, and analysis. *IEEE Journal on Selected Areas in Communications, 33*(1), 1–13. doi:10.1109/JSAC.2014.2369612

Lee, Y. W., Pipino, L., Strong, D. M., & Wang, R. Y. (2004). Process-embedded data integrity. *Journal of Database Management, 15*(1), 87–103. doi:10.4018/jdm.2004010104

Lee, Y. W., Strong, D. M., Kahn, B. K., & Wang, R. Y. (2002). AIMQ: A methodology for information quality assessment. *Information & Management, 40*(2), 133–146. doi:10.1016/S0378-7206(02)00043-5

Leyton-Brown, K., & Shoham, Y. (2008). *Essentials of Game Theory.* Morgan & Claypool.

Li, Shi, & Wang. (2012). Automatic ARIMA Time Series Modeling for Data Aggregation in Wireless Sensor Networks. *International Journal of Digital Content Technology and its Applications, 6*(23), 438-447.

Li, Song, Zhang, Ouyang, & Khan. (2016). MapReduce-based fast fuzzy c-means algorithm for large-scale underwater image segmentation. *Future Generation Computer Systems*.

Liao, Y. (2012). Application of biomonitoring and support vector machine in water quality assessment. *Journal of Zhejiang University (Biomed & Biotechnol), 13*(4), 327-334.

Liao, Y., Xu, J., & Wang, W. (2011). A Method of Water Quality Assessment Based on Biomonitoring and Multiclass Support Vector Machine. *Procedia Environmental Sciences, Elsevier, 10*, 451–457. doi:10.1016/j.proenv.2011.09.074

Lin & Kung. (1997). Face Recognition/Detection by Probabilistic Decision-Based Neural Network. *IEEE Transactions on Neural Networks, 8*(1), 1045–9227. PMID:18255615

Lin, I., & Doniz, H. Vicente, & Doyle. (n.d.). *Applying human factors to the Linklabs IoT In Health Care: What You Should Know*. Retrieved from https://www.link-labs.com/blog/IoT-in-healthcare

Lin, X., Andrews, J. G., & Ghosh, A. (2014). Spectrum sharing for device-to-device communication in cellular networks. *IEEE Transactions on Wireless Communications, 13*(12), 6727–6740. doi:10.1109/TWC.2014.2360202

Lin, Y. D., & Hsu, Y. C. (2000). Multi-hop Cellular: A new architecture for wireless communications. *Proceedings - IEEE INFOCOM, 3*, 1273–1282.

Listyorini & Rahim. (2018). A prototype fire detection implemented using the Internet of Things and fuzzy logic. World Transactions on Engineering and Technology Education, 16(1), 42-46.

Liu, B., & Wong, C. K. (2000). *Improving an association rule based classifier*. Journal In Principles of Data Mining and Knowledge Discovery.

Liu, J., Kawamoto, Y., Nishiyama, H., Kato, N., & Kadowaki, N. (2014). Device-to-device communications achieve efficient load balancing in LTE-advanced networks. *IEEE Wireless Communications Magazine, 21*(2), 57–65. doi:10.1109/MWC.2014.6812292

Liu, M. C., & Huang, Y. M. (2017). *The use of data science for education: The case of social-emotional learning. Smart Learning Environments, 4(1)*. doi:10.118640561-016-0040-4

Li, Y., Su, S., & Chen, S. (2015). Social-aware resource allocation for device-to-device communications underlaying cellular networks. *IEEE Wireless Communications Letters, 4*(3), 293–296. doi:10.1109/LWC.2015.2410768

Lopes & Ribeiro. (2015). GPUMLib: An Efficient Open-source GPU Machine Learning Library. *Machine Learning for Adaptive Many-Core Machines - A Practical Approach, 7*, 15–36.

Low, Y., Bickson, D., Gonzalez, J., Guestrin, C., Kyrola, A., & Hellerstein, J. M. (2012). Distributed GraphLab: A framework for machine learning and data mining in the cloud. *Proceedings of the VLDB Endowment International Conference on Very Large Data Bases, 5*(8), 716–727. doi:10.14778/2212351.2212354

Lu, Y. (2015). Integrating predictive analytics and social media. *IEEE Conference on Visual Analytics Science and Technology (VAST)*, 193-202.

Lynggaard, P. (2017). *Artificial intelligence and Internet of Things in a "smart home" context: A Distributed System Architecture.* Available: vbn.aau.dk

Madge, S. (2015). *Predicting Stock Price Direction using Support Vector Machines.* Independent Work Report Spring.

Maier, H. R. (2010). Methods used for the development of neural networks for the prediction of water resource variables in river systems: Current status and future directions. In Environmental Modelling & Software 25 (pp. 891–909). Elsevier.

Malek, S. (2014). Dissolved Oxygen Prediction Using Support Vector Machine. *International Journal of Bioengineering and Life Sciences Vol, 8*(1).

Mali, A. R. (2016). A novel approach for temperature sensing and monitoring through wireless sensor using IoT. *Journal of Engineering and Computer Science, 5*(12), 19657–19659.

Mampadi, F., Chen, S. Y. H., Ghinea, G., & Chen, M. P. (2011). Design of adaptive hypermedia learning systems: a cognitive style approach. *Computers & Education, 56*(4), 1003–1011. doi:10.1016/j.compedu.2010.11.018

Manjulatha, B., Venna, A., & Soumya, K. (2016). Implementation of Hadoop Operations for Big Data Processing in Educational Institutions. *International Journal of Innovative Research in Computer and Communication Engineering, 4*(4).

Manyika. (2011). *Big data: The next frontier for innovation, competition, and productivity.* McKinsey Global Institute. Retrieved from: http://www.mckinsey.com/insights/business_technology/big_data_the_next_frontier_for_innovation

March, S. T., & Hevner, A. R. (2007). Integrated decision support systems: A data warehousing perspective. *Decision Support Systems, 43*(3), 1031–1043. doi:10.1016/j.dss.2005.05.029

Marques, P., Bastos, J., & Gameiro, A. (2008). Opportunistic use of 3G uplink Licensed Bands. In *Proceedings of the 2008 IEEE International Conference on Communications* (pp. 3588-3592). Beijing: IEEE. 10.1109/ICC.2008.675

Massano & Bhatia. (2012). Clinical Approach to Parkinson's Disease: Features, Diagnosis, and Principles of Management. *Cold Spring Harb Perspect Med, 2*(6).

Mayer, V., Schonberger, K., & Cukier, K. (2013). *Big data: A revolution that will transform how we live,work,and think.* Boston: Houghton Mifflin Harcourt.

McAfee, A., & Brynjolfsson, E. (2012). Big data: The management revolution. *Harvard Business Review*, *90*(10), 61–68. PMID:23074865

Mehta, S., Sahni, J., & Khanna, K. (2018). Internet of Things: Vision, Applications and Challenges. *Procedia Computer Science*, *132*, 1263–1269. doi:10.1016/j.procs.2018.05.042

Militano, L., Araniti, G., Condoluci, M., Farris, I., & Iera, A. (2015). Device-to-Device Communications for 5G Internet of Things. *EAI Endorsed Transactions on Internet of Things.*, *1*(4), 1–16.

Ministry of Environment and Forests, Government of India. (2009). *Status Paper On River Ganga, "State of Environment and Water Quality," National River Conservation Directorate.* Author.

Mishra & Silakari. (2012). Predictive analytics: A survey, trends, applications, opportunities & challenges. *International Journal of Computer Science and Information Technologies*, *3*(3), 4434–4438.

Moalafhi, D. B. (2014). A Hybrid Stochastic-ANN Approach For Flow Partotioning In The Okavango Delta Of Botswana. *Global NEST Journal.*

Moghaddam & Pentland. (1995). Probabilistic Visual Learning for Object Detection. *IEEE Transactions on Pattern Analysis and Machine Intelligence*, *19*(7).

Monitoring Motor Fluctuations in Patients With Parkinson's Disease Using Wearable Sensors. (2009). *IEEE Transactions on Information Technology in Biomedicine*, *13*(6), 864–873. doi:10.1109/TITB.2009.2033471 PMID:19846382

Monk. (2014). *Raspberry Pi Cookbook.* Academic Press.

Morris, H. (2014). *A Software Platform for Operational Technology Innovation.* International Data Corporation. Retrieved from: https://www.predix.com/sites/default/files/IDC_OT_Final_whitepaper_249120.pdf

Mullich, J. (2013). *Closing the Big Data Gap in Public Sector.* SAP, Bloomberg Inc.

Murphy, C., Kaiser, G., Hu, L., & Wu, L. (2008). Properties of machine learning applications for use in metamorphic testing. *Proceeding of the 20th Internal Conference on Software Engineering and Knowledge Engineering (SEKE)*, 867-872.

Nagarajan & Surendran. (2015). A High End Building Automation and Online Video Surveillance Security System. *International Journal of Engineering and Technology*, *7*(1).

Nasser, T., & Tariq, R. S. (2015). Big data challenges. *Journal of Computer Engineering & Information Technology.* doi:10.4172/2324-9307.1000135

National Science Foundation. (2012). *Core Techniques and Technologies for Advancing Big Data Science & Engineering (BIGDATA)* (Publication Number: 12-499). Retrieved from: http://www.nsf.gov/pubs/2012/nsf12499/nsf12499.pdf

National Security Agency, Central Security Services. (2011). *Groundbreaking Ceremony Held for $1.2 Billion Utah Data Center*. NSA Press. Retrieved from: https://www.nsa.gov/news-features/press-room/press-releases/2011/utah-groundbreaking-ceremony.shtml

National Semiconductor. (2000). *Precision Centigrade Temperature Sensors*. National Semiconductor.

NCTM (National Council of Teachers of Mathematics). (2000). *Principles and standards for school mathematics*. Reston, VA: NCTM.

Nielsen & Chuang. (2000). Quantum Computation and Quantum Information. Cambridge University Press.

NIST. (2015). *NIST Big Data Interoperability Framework: Use Cases and General Requirements*. NIST Big Data Public Working Group (Publication number 1500-3). Retrieved from: https://bigdatawg.nist.gov/_uploadfiles/NIST.SP.1500-3.pdf

NIST. (2018). *National Institute of Standards and Technology - Computer Security Resource Center*. Retrieved form: www.csrc.nist.gov

Normandeau. (2013). *Beyond Volume, Variety and Velocity is the Issue of Big Data Veracity*. Big Data Innovation Summit. Retrieved from: https://insidebigdata.com/2013/09/12/beyond-volume-variety-velocity-issue-big-data-veracity/

Nouran, M., & Nordin, R. (2016). A survey on interference management for Device-to-Device (D2D) communication and its challenges in 5G networks. *Journal of Network and Computer Applications, 71*, 130–150. doi:10.1016/j.jnca.2016.04.021

Nowak & Spiller. (2017). *Two Billion People Coming Together on Facebook*. Facebook News.

Oladipupo, O.O., & Oyelade, O.J. (n.d.). Knowledge Discovery from Students' Result Repository: Association Rule Mining Approach. *International Journal of Computer Science & Security, 4*(2).

Oludele, Avodele, Oladele, & Olurotimi. (2009). Design of an Automated Intrusion Detection System incorporating an Alarm. *Journal of Computers, 1*(1), 2151–9617.

Ondrej & Milos. (2009). Neural Network Based Intrusion Detection System for Critical Infrastructures. *Proceedings of International Joint Conference on Neural Networks*.

Oracle Corporation. (2015). *An Enterprise Architect's Guide to Big Data*. Oracle Corporation. Retrieved from: https://www.oracle.com/technetwork/topics/entarch/articles/oea-big-data-guide-1522052.pdf

Osserain, A., Boccardi, F., Braun, V., Kusume, K., Marsch, P., Matermia, M., ... Fallgen, M. (2014). Scenari.os for 5G mobile and wireless communications: The vision of the METIS project. *IEEE Communications Magazine, 52*(5), 26–35. doi:10.1109/MCOM.2014.6815890

Ossig, C., Antonini, A., Buhmann, C., Classen, J., Csoti, I., Falkenburger, B., ... Storch, A. (2016). Wearable sensor-based objective assessment of motor symptoms in Parkinson's disease. *Journal of Neural Transmission (Vienna, Austria), 123*(1), 57–64. doi:10.100700702-015-1439-8 PMID:26253901

Palani, S. (2008). An ANN application for water quality forecasting. *Bulletin, 56*, 1586–1597. PMID:18635240

Pal, K. (2017). A Semantic Web Service Architecture for Supply Chain Management. *Procedia Computer Science, 109C*, 999–1004. doi:10.1016/j.procs.2017.05.442

Pang, Z., Tian, J., & Chen, Q. (2014). Intelligent packaging and intelligent medicine box for medication management towards the Internet-of-Things. *Proc. 16th International Conference in Advance Communication Technology (ICACT)*. 10.1109/ICACT.2014.6779193

Papanikolaou, K. A., Grigoriadou, M., Magoulas, G. D., & Kornilakis, H. (2002). Towards new forms of knowledge communication:the adaptive dimension of a web-based learning environment. *Computers & Education, 39*(4), 333–360. doi:10.1016/S0360-1315(02)00067-2

Parssian, A. (2006). Managerial decision support with knowledge of accuracy and completeness of the relational aggregate functions. *Decision Support Systems, 42*(3), 1494–1502. doi:10.1016/j.dss.2005.12.005

Pathari & Bojewar. (2014). Video Surveillance in Public Transport Areas using Semantic Based Approach. *International Journal of Engineering Research and Technology, 4*(1).

Patil, S. M., & Kumar, P. (2017). Data Mining Model for Effective Data Analysis of Higher Education Students Using MapReduce. *IJERMT, 6*(4).

Pearce, M., Zeadally, S., & Hunt, R. (2013). Virtualization: Issues, security threats, and solutions. *ACM Computing Surveys, 45*(2), 1–39. doi:10.1145/2431211.2431216

Peng, J. (2009). Comparison of several cloud computing platforms. *Information Science and Engineering (ISISE), 2009 Second International Symposium on*, 23-27. 10.1109/ISISE.2009.94

Peng, T., Lu, Q., Wang, H., Xu, S., & Wang, W. (2009). Interference avoidance mechanisms in the hybrid cellular and device-to-device systems. In *Proceedings of the 2009 IEEE 20th International Symposium on Personal, Indoor and Mobile Radio Communications* (pp. 617-621). Tokyo: IEEE. 10.1109/PIMRC.2009.5449856

Penumarthi, H. (2017). *Indian Cold Chain Industry – Challenges and Opportunities*. Food Marketing & Technology. Retrieved from http://fmtmagazine.in/indian-cold-chain-industry-challenges-opportunities/

Pereira, A., Bergeret, E., Benzaim, O., Routin, J., Haon, O., Tournon, L., ... Depres, G. (2018). Near-field communication tag development on a paper substrate—application to cold chain monitoring. *Flexible and Printed Electronics, 3*(1), 014003. doi:10.1088/2058-8585/aaaeca

Picciano, A. G. (2012). The evolution of big data and learning analytics in American Higher Education. *Journal of Asynchronous Learning Networks, 16*(3), 9–20.

Pipino, L. L., Lee, Y. W., & Wang, R. Y. (2002). Data quality assessment. *Communications of the ACM, 45*(4), 211–218. doi:10.1145/505248.506010

Plotz. (2015). PD Disease State Assessment in Naturalistic Environments Using Deep Learning. In *Proceedings of the Twenty-Ninth AAAI Conference on Artificial Intelligence (AAAI'15)*. AAAI Press.

Prakash, B.R., Hanumanthappa, M., & Kavitha, V. (2014). Big data in Educational Data Mining and Learning Analytics. *International Journal of Innovative Research in Computer and Communication Engineering*, *2*(12).

Provost, F., & Fawcett, T. (2013). Data science and its relationship to big data and data-driven decision making. *Big Data*, *1*(1), 51–59. doi:10.1089/big.2013.1508 PMID:27447038

Ramlee, L., Singh, I., Othman, S., & Misran, M. (2013). Bluetooth Remote Home Automation System Using Android Application. *International Journal of Engineering and Science*, *1*, 149-153.

Rankovi, V., Radulovic, J., Radojevic, I., Ostojic, A., & Comic, L. (2010). Neural network Modelling of Dissolved oxygen in the Gruza reservoir, Serbia. *Ecological Modelling*, *221*, 1239–1244.

Redman, T. C. (1996). *Data Quality for the Information Age*. Norwood, MA: Artech House Publishers.

Reeves, C. (2003). *Genetic algorithms. Handbook of metaheuristics*. Springer. doi:10.1007/0-306-48056-5_3

Reyes, J. V. (2016). Artificial Neural Networks applied to flow prediction: A use case for the Tomebamba river. *Procedia Engineering*, *162*, 153–161. doi:10.1016/j.proeng.2016.11.031

Riad, S., Mania, J., Bouchaou, L., & Najjar, Y. (2004). Rainfall-Runoff Model Using an Artificial Neural Network Approach. *Mathematical and Computer Modelling*, *40*(7-8), 839–846. doi:10.1016/j.mcm.2004.10.012

Rijmenam, M. (2018). *A Short History Of Big Data*. Retrieved from: https://datafloq.com/read/big-data-history/239

Rohling, G. (2014). *Facts and Forecasts: Billions of Things, Trillions of Dollars*. Siemens - Internet of Things: Facts and Forecasts. Retrieved from: https://www.siemens.com/innovation/en/home/pictures-of-the-future/digitalization-and-software/internet-of-things-facts-and-forecasts.html

Romero, C., & Ventura, S. (2007). Educational data mining: A survey from 1995 to 2005. *Expert Systems with Applications*, *33*(1), 135–146. doi:10.1016/j.eswa.2006.04.005

Romero, C., Ventura, S., & Bra, P. D. (2004). Knowledge Discovery with Genetic Programming for Providing Feedback to Courseware Authors. *User Modeling and User-Adapted Interaction*, *14*(5), 425–464. doi:10.100711257-004-7961-2

Ronen, B., & Spiegler, I. (1991). Information as inventory: A new conceptual view. *Information & Management*, *21*(4), 239–247. doi:10.1016/0378-7206(91)90069-E

Rotariu, C., & Manta, V. (2012). Wireless system for remote monitoring of oxygen saturation and heart rate. *Proceedings of the Federated Conference on Computer Science and Information Systems (FedCSIS)*, 193–196.

Ruiz-Garcia, L., Barreiro, P., Robla, J. I., & Lunadei, L. (2010). Testing ZigBee Motes for Monitoring Refrigerated Vegetable Transportation Under Real Conditions. *Journal of Sensors*, *10*(5), 4968–4982. doi:10.3390100504968 PMID:22399917

Russell, S. J., & Norvig, P. (1995). *Artificial Intelligence a Modern Approach*. Prentice Hall.

S., & G. (2016). Motion Detection Using IoT and Embedded System Concepts. *International Journal of Advanced Research in Electrical, Electronics and Instrumentation*, *5*(10), 3297.

S4. (2017). Retrieved from http://incubator.apache.org/s4

Safdar, G. A., Ur-Rehman, M., Muhammad, M., Imran, M. A., & Tafazolli, R. (2016). Interference Mitigation in D2D Communication Underlaying LTE-A Network. *IEEE Access: Practical Innovations, Open Solutions*, *4*, 7967–7987. doi:10.1109/ACCESS.2016.2621115

Sahlberg, P. (2007). Education policies for raising student learning: The Finnish approach. *Journal of Education Policy*, *22*(2), 147–171. doi:10.1080/02680930601158919

Sandhu, R., & Sood, S. K. (2014). Scheduling of big data applications on distributed cloud based on QoS parameters. *Cluster Computing*, *18*, 1–12.

Sarkar, A., & Pandey, P. (2015). River Water Quality Modelling using Artificial Neural Network Technique. In *International Conference on Water Resources And Ocean Engineering (ICWRCOE)*. ELSEVIER.

Sarkin & Maistry. (2016). A Pragmatic Overview of Predictive Analytics Applications. *20th Asian Actuarial Conference*.

Sarma, P. K. D., & Roy, R. (2010). A Data Warehouse for Mining Usage Pattern in Library Transaction Data. *Assam University Journal of Science &Technology: Physical Sciences and Technology*, *6*(2), 125–129.

Sathi, A. (2012). Big data analytics: Disruptive technologies for changing the game. MC Press Online, LLC.

Satish, M., & Hegadi. (2017). E-Solution for Next Line of Business and Education Using Cloud Computing. *2017 World Congress on Computing and Communication Technologies (WCCCT)*, 105-110. 10.1109/WCCCT.2016.33

Savitz, E. (2012a). *Gartner: Top 10 strategic technology trends for 2013*. Available at http://www.forbes.com/sites/ericsavitz/2012/10/23/gartner-top-10-strategictechnology-rends-for-2013/

Savitz, E. (2012b). *Gartner: 10 critical tech trends for the next five years*. Available at http://www.forbes.com/sites/ericsavitz/2012/10/22/gartner-10-critical-techtrends-for-the-next-five-years

Scannapieco, M., & Catarci, T. (2002). Data quality under a computer science perspective, *Archivi and Computer*, 21-15.

Scheffel, M., Drachsler, H., Stoyanov, S., & Specht, M. (2014). Quality indicators for learning analytics. *Journal of Educational Technology & Society*, *17*(4), 117–132.

Schmidt, E. (2010). *Techonomy*. Retrieved from: https://www.youtube.com/watch?utm_source=datafloq&utm_medium=ref&utm_campaign=datafloq&v=UAcCIsrAq70

Sesia, S., Toufik, I., & Baker, M. (2011). *LTE-The UMTS Long Term Evolution: From theory to practice*. London: John Wiley & Sons Ltd. doi:10.1002/9780470978504

Shah, Omar, & Khurram. (2007). *Automated Visual Surveillance in Realistic Scenarios*. IEEE Computer Society.

Shahrivari, S., & Jalili, S. (2016). Single-pass and linear-time k-means clustering based on MapReduce. *Information Systems*, *60*, 1–12. doi:10.1016/j.is.2016.02.007

Shaik & D. (2016). IoT based Smart Home Security System with Alert and Door Access Control using Smart Phone. *International Journal of Engineering Research & Technology*, *5*(12).

Shamrao, C., & Kumar, P. (2017). Interference mitigation by switching the underlaying transmitter in D2D communications. In *Proceedings of the 2017 Innovations in Power and Advanced Computing Technologies (i-PACT2017)* (pp. 1-6). Vellore: IEEE.

Shamseldin, A. Y. (2010). Artificial neural network model for river flow forecasting in a developing country. *Journal of Hydroinformatics*, *12*(1).

Shapiro, P. (1999). The Data-Mining Industry Coming of Age. *IEEE Intelligent Systems*, *14*(6), 32–34. doi:10.1109/5254.809566

Sharma & Sarma. (2016). Soft-Computational Techniques and Spectro-Temporal Features for Telephonic Speech Recognition: An Overview and Review of Current State of the Art. Handbook of Research on Advanced Hybrid Intelligent Techniques and Applications.

Shih, C.-W., & Wang, C.-H. (2016). Integrating wireless sensor networks with statistical quality control to develop a cold chain system in food industries. *Computer Standards & Interfaces*, *45*, 62–78. doi:10.1016/j.csi.2015.12.004

Shitole, Kamatchi, & Iyer. (2018). Smart Home Context-Aware Automation by Customization Strategy. *International Conference on Emerging Trends in Computing Technology (ICETCT- 2018)*.

Shmueli, G. (2010). To explain or to predict? *Statistical Science*, *25*(3), 289–310. doi:10.1214/10-STS330

Shmueli, K., & Koppius. (2011). Predictive analytics in information systems research. *Management Information Systems Quarterly*, *35*(3), 553–572. doi:10.2307/23042796

Siegel, E. (2013). *Predictive analytics: The power to predict who will click, buy, lie or die*. Hoboken, NJ: John Wiley & Sons Inc.

Sin, K., & Muthu, L. (2015). Application of Big Data in Education Data Mining and Learning Analytics – A Literature Review. *ICTACT Journal on Soft Computing, 5*(4).

Singh & Verma. (2012). Tracking of Moving object in Video scene using Neural Network. *International Journal of Advanced Research in Computer Engineering & Technology, 1*(10), 2278–1323.

Slater, H., Davies, N., & Burgess, S. (2009). *Do teachers matter? Measuring the variation in teacher effectiveness in England*. Centre for Market and Public organisation (CMPO), Working paper series no. 09/212.

Slater, S., Joksimovic, S., Kovanovic, V., Baker, R. S., & Gasevic, D. (2017). Tools for Educational Data Mining: A Review. *Journal of Educational and Behavioral Statistics, 42*(1), 85–106. doi:10.3102/1076998616666808

Smith & Hallman. (2013). NSA Spying Controversy Highlights Embrace Of Big Data. *The Huffington Post*. Retrieved from: https://www.huffingtonpost.in/entry/nsa-big-data_n_3423482

Smith, T. P. (2013). *How big is big and how small is small, the size of everything and why*. Oxford University Press.

Smith, W. B. (1993). Total Customer Satisfaction as a Business Strategy. *Quality and Reliability Engineering International, 9*(1), 49–53. doi:10.1002/qre.4680090109

Song, L., Zhu, H., & Chen, X. (2014). *Resource mmanagement for device-to-device underlay communication*. Retrieved on March 12, 2018 from http://adsabs.harvard.edu/abs/2013arXiv1311.1018X

Song, L., Niyato, D., Han, Z., & Hossain, E. (2015). *Wireless Device-to-Device Communications and Networks*. New York: Cambridge University Press. doi:10.1017/CBO9781107478732

Spark. (2017). Retrieved from https://spark.incubator.apache.org

Stilmant. (2013). *Pharmaceutical Cold Chain*. Retrieved from http://www.coldchain.be/guidelines-and-regulations/some-history.html

Stock, J. R. (2013). Supply chain management: A look back, a look ahead. *Supply Chain Quarterly, 2*, 22–26.

Storm. (2017). Retrieved from https://storm.incubator.apache.org

Stout. (2018). *Social Media Statistics 2018: What You Need to Know*. Retrieved from: https://dustn.tv/social-media-statistics/

Sun, B. S., & Gao, S. S. Q. (2014). Interference management for device-to-device communications underlaying networks at cell edge. In *Proceedings on the International Conference on Wireless and Mobile Communications* (pp. 118-123), Seville: IARIA.

Svilvar, M., Charkraborty, A. & Kanioura, A. (2013). Big data analytics in marketing. OR/MS Today, October 22-25.

Tajunisha, N., & Anjali, M. (2015). Predicting Student Performance Using MapReduce. *IJECS*, *4*(1), 9971–9976.

Tan, Y. (2012). PREPARE: Predictive Performance Anomaly Prevention for Virtualized Cloud Systems. *2012 IEEE 32nd International Conference on Distributed Computing Systems*, 285-294.

Tang, T. Y., & Gordon, M. (2002). Student modeling for a web-based learning environment: a data mining approach. *AAAI*, 967-968.

Tan, G., Yan, J., Gao, C., & Yang, S. (2012). Prediction of water quality time series data based on least squares support vector machine. *Procedia Engineering*, *31*, 1194–1199. doi:10.1016/j.proeng.2012.01.1162

Tennermann, J. (2012). *Cold Chain for Beginners*. Vaisala. Retrieved from https://www.rdmag.com/article/2012/06/cold-chain-beginners

Teschioni, Oberti, & Regazzoni. (1991). *A Neural-Network Approach for Moving Objects Recognition in Color Image Sequences for Surveillance Applications*. Academic Press.

Tole, A. A. (2013). Big Data Challenges. Database Systems Journal, 4(3).

Tomlinson, C. A., & Kalbfleisch, M. L. (1998). Teach Me, Teach my Brain: A call for differential classrooms. *Educational Leadership*, *56*(3), 52–55.

Tomlinson, C. A., & McTighe, J. (2006). *Integrating differentiated instruction & understanding by design: Connecting content and kids*. Alexandria, VA: ASCD.

Tools.ietf.org. (2018). *TCP Usage Guidance in the Internet of Things (IoT)*. Retrieved from: https://tools.ietf.org/id/draft-ietf-lwig-tcp-constrained-node-networks-01.html

U.S. Department of Education. (2012). *Enhancing Teaching and Learning Through Educational Data Mining and Learning Analytics*: *An Issue Brief*. Available online: https://tech.ed.gov/wp-content/uploads/2014/03/edm-la-brief.pdf

Umadevi & Chaturvedi. (2017). Predictive load balancing algorithm for cloud computing. *2017 International conference on Microelectronic Devices, Circuits and Systems (ICMDCS)*, 1-5.

Union Ministry of Science and Technology Government of India. (2009). *Technology Mission: Winning, Augmentation and Renovation*. Technology Mission: WAR for Water, Plan Document Prepared by, On the directive of Supreme Court of India Order on Writ Petition (C) No 230 of 2001.

Verma, R., & Srivastava, K. (2017). Middleware, Operating System and Wireless Sensor Networks for Internet of Things. *International Journal of Computers and Applications*, *167*(11), 11–17. doi:10.5120/ijca2017914356

Wand, Y., & Wang, R. Y. (1996). Anchoring data quality dimensions in ontological foundations. *Communications of the ACM, 39*(11), 86–95. doi:10.1145/240455.240479

Wang, J. (2017). Big Data Driven Smart Transportation: the Underlying Story of IoT Transformed Mobility. *The WIOMAX SmartIoT Blog*. Retrieved from: http://www.wiomax.com/big-data-driven-smart-transportation-the-underlying-big-story-of-smart-iot-transformed-mobility/

Wang, Ozcan, Wan, & Harrison. (n.d.). *Trends in Hospital Efficiency among Introduction to Human Factors in Medical Devices*. US Department of Health and Human.

Wang, B., Fedele, J., Pridgen, B., Williams, A., Rui, T., Barnett, L., ... Poplin, B. (2010). Evidence-based maintenance: part I: measuring maintenance effectiveness with failure codes. *Journal of Clinical Engineering, 35*(3), 132–144. doi:10.1097/JCE.0b013e3181e6231e

Wang, L., Liu, L., Cao, X., Tian, X., & Cheng, Y. (2015). Sociality-aware resource allocation for device-to-device communications in cellular networks. *IET Communications, 9*(3), 342–349. doi:10.1049/iet-com.2014.0436

Wang, R. Y. (1998). A product perspective on total data quality management. *Communications of the Association for Computer Machinery, 41*(2), 58–65. doi:10.1145/269012.269022

Wang, R. Y., & Kon, H. B. (1993). Towards total data quality management (TDQM). In R. Y. Wanf (Ed.), *Information technology in action: Trends and perspectives*. Englewood Cliffs, NJ: Prentice-Hall.

Wang, R. Y., Storey, V. C., & Firth, C. P. (1995). A framework for analysis of data quality research. *IEEE Transactions on Knowledge and Data Engineering, 7*(4), 623–640. doi:10.1109/69.404034

Wang, R. Y., & Strong, D. M. (1996). Beyond Accuracy: What data quality means to data consumers. *Journal of Management Information Systems, 12*(4), 5–33. doi:10.1080/07421222.1996.11518099

Wang, S., & Hou, R. (2017). Network coding-based interference management scheme in Device-to-Device communications. *ZTE Communications, 15*(2), 48–54.

Watson, M., Lewis, S., Cacioppo, P., & Jayaraman, J. (2013). *Supply chain network design – applying optimization and analytics to the global supply chain*. FT Press.

Watts, S., Shankaranarayanan, G., & Even, A. (2009). Data quality assessment in context: A cognitive perspective. *Decision Support Systems, 48*(1), 202–211. doi:10.1016/j.dss.2009.07.012

Wedutenko & Keeing. (2014). *Big data and the public sector: strategy and guidance*. Clayton Utz Insights.

We, H. (2014). *SAP and Hortonworks Reference Architecture*. SAP AG.

Weiss, S. M., & Kulikowski, C. A. (1991). *Computer systems that learn: classification and prediction methods from statistics, neural nets, machine learning, and expert systems*. Morgan Kaufman Publishers.

Widyantara & Sastra. (2015). Internet of Things for Intelligent Traffic Monitoring System: A Case Study in Denpasar. *International Journal of Computer Trends and Technology, 30*(3).

Williamson, B. (2017). *Big data in education: The digital future of learning, policy and practice.* Sage.

Williamson, O. (1996). *The Mechanisms of Governance.* New York: Oxford University Press.

Wixom, B. H., & Ross, J. W. (2017). How to Monetize Your Data, MIT Sloan Management Review. *Spring Issue, 58*(3), 10–13.

Woo, J. (2012). Apriori-Map/Reduce Algorithm. *Proceedings of the International Conference on Parallel and Distributed Processing Techniques and Applications (PDPTA).*

World Health Organization. (2010). *WHO guide to good storage practices for pharmaceuticals. WHO Expert Committee on Specific cations for Pharmaceutical Preparations (WHO Technical Report Series, No. 920).* World Health Organization.

Wu, M. M. (2015). The Design and Implementation of Food Cold Chain Monitoring System Based on ZigBee. *Journal of Applied Mechanics and Materials, 751,* 281–286. doi:10.4028/www.scientific.net/AMM.751.281

Wu, X. (2014). Data Mining with Big Data. *IEEE Transactions on Knowledge and Data Engineering, 26*(1), 97–107. doi:10.1109/TKDE.2013.109

Wu, X., Tavildar, S., Shakkottai, S., Richardson, T., Li, T., Laroia, R., & Jovicic, A. (2010). FlashLinQ: A synchronous distributed scheduler for peer-to-peer ad hoc networks. In *Proceedings on IEEE International Conference on Communication Control and Computing Technologies (ICCCCT)* (pp. 524-521). Tamil Nadu: IEEE.

Xin, Wang, Qu, Yu, & Kang. (2016). A-ELM: Adaptive Distributed Extreme Learning Machine with MapReduce. *Neurocomputing, 174*(A), 368–374.

Yan, W. (2012). Toward Automatic Time-Series Forecasting Using Neural Networks. *IEEE Transactions on Neural Networks and Learning Systems, 23*(7). Retrieved from https://www.python.org

Yang, Luo, & Li. (2018). Hide Your Hackable Smart Home from Remote Attacks: The Multipath Onion IoT Gateways. *23rd European Symposium on Research in Computer Security, ESORICS 2018.*

Yang, X. Y., Liu, Z., & Fu, Y. (2010). MapReduce as a Programming Model for Association Rules Algorithm on Hadoop. In *Information Sciences and Interaction Sciences (ICIS) 2010: Proceedings of 3rd International Conference.* IEEE.

Yaseen, Swathi, & Kumar. (2017). IoT based condition monitoring of generators and predictive maintenance. *2017 2nd International Conference on Communication and Electronics Systems (ICCES),* 725-729.

Ye, Q., Al-Shalash, M., Caramanis, C., & Andrews, J. G. (2015). Distributed resource allocation in device-to-device enhanced cellular networks. *IEEE Transactions on Communications, 63*(2), 441–454. doi:10.1109/TCOMM.2014.2386874

Yi, X., Liu, F., Liu, J., & Jin, H. (2014). Building a network highway for big data: Architecture and challenges. *IEEE Network*, 28(4), 5–13. doi:10.1109/MNET.2014.6863125

YouTube. (2017). *YouTube by the Numbers*. Retrieved from: https://www.youtube.com/yt/about/press/

Yuan, Y., Yang, T., Feng, H., Hu, B., Zhang, J., & Wang, B., & Lu, Q. (2017). Traffic-aware transmission mode selection in D2D-enabled cellular networks with token system. In *Proceedings 2017 25th European Signal Processing Conference (EUSIPCO)* (pp.2249-2253). Kos: IEEE. 10.23919/EUSIP-CO.2017.8081610

Zeithaml, V. A., Berry, L. L., & Parasuraman, A. (1990). *Delivering quality service: Balancing customer perceptions and expectations*. New York: Free Press.

Zhan, C.-Y., Philip Chen, C. L., Chen, D., & Kin Tek, N. G. (1996). MapReduce based distributed learning algorithm for Restricted Boltzmann Machine" Neurocomputing Available online 17 March 2016 In Press, Corrected Proof — Note to users computer-based medical devices. *Human Factors*, 38(4), 574–592. PMID:8976622

Zhang, H. (2013). Environmental Effect Removal Based Structural Health Monitoring in the Internet of Things. *Innovative Mobile and Internet Services in Ubiquitous Computing (IMIS), 2013 Seventh International Conference on*. DOI: 10.1109/IMIS.2013.91

Zhang, H., Song, L., & Han, Z. (2016). Radio resource allocation for device-to-device underlay communication using hypergraph theory. *IEEE Transactions on Wireless Communications*, 15(70), 4852–4861.

Zhang, J., Johnson, T. R., Patel, V. L., Paige, D. L., & Kubose, T. (2003). Using usability heuristics to evaluate patient safety of medical devices. *Journal of Biomedical Informatics*, 36(1-2), 23–30. doi:10.1016/S1532-0464(03)00060-1 PMID:14552844

Zhang, Y. (2011). HomeAlone: Co-residency Detection in the Cloud via Side-Channel Analysis. *2011 IEEE Symposium on Security and Privacy*, 313-328. 10.1109/SP.2011.31

Zhang, Y., Oussena, S., Clark, T., & Kim, H. (2010). Use Data Mining to improve student retention in higher education – A Case Study. *Proceedings of the 12th International Conference on Enterprise Information Systems*, 1,.

Zhu, Z.-T., Yu, M.-H., & Riezebos, P. (2016). A research framework of smart education. *Smart Learning Environments*, 3(4). doi:10.118640561-016-0026-2

Zhu, Z. T., & He, B. (2012). Smart Education: New frontier of educational informatization. *E-education Research*, 12, 1–13.

Related References

To continue our tradition of advancing information science and technology research, we have compiled a list of recommended IGI Global readings. These references will provide additional information and guidance to further enrich your knowledge and assist you with your own research and future publications.

Aasi, P., Rusu, L., & Vieru, D. (2017). The Role of Culture in IT Governance Five Focus Areas: A Literature Review. *International Journal of IT/Business Alignment and Governance, 8*(2), 42-61. doi:10.4018/IJITBAG.2017070103

Abdrabo, A. A. (2018). Egypt's Knowledge-Based Development: Opportunities, Challenges, and Future Possibilities. In A. Alraouf (Ed.), *Knowledge-Based Urban Development in the Middle East* (pp. 80–101). Hershey, PA: IGI Global. doi:10.4018/978-1-5225-3734-2.ch005

Abu Doush, I., & Alhami, I. (2018). Evaluating the Accessibility of Computer Laboratories, Libraries, and Websites in Jordanian Universities and Colleges. *International Journal of Information Systems and Social Change, 9*(2), 44–60. doi:10.4018/IJISSC.2018040104

Adeboye, A. (2016). Perceived Use and Acceptance of Cloud Enterprise Resource Planning (ERP) Implementation in the Manufacturing Industries. *International Journal of Strategic Information Technology and Applications, 7*(3), 24–40. doi:10.4018/IJSITA.2016070102

Adegbore, A. M., Quadri, M. O., & Oyewo, O. R. (2018). A Theoretical Approach to the Adoption of Electronic Resource Management Systems (ERMS) in Nigerian University Libraries. In A. Tella & T. Kwanya (Eds.), *Handbook of Research on Managing Intellectual Property in Digital Libraries* (pp. 292–311). Hershey, PA: IGI Global. doi:10.4018/978-1-5225-3093-0.ch015

Adhikari, M., & Roy, D. (2016). Green Computing. In G. Deka, G. Siddesh, K. Srinivasa, & L. Patnaik (Eds.), *Emerging Research Surrounding Power Consumption and Performance Issues in Utility Computing* (pp. 84–108). Hershey, PA: IGI Global. doi:10.4018/978-1-4666-8853-7.ch005

Afolabi, O. A. (2018). Myths and Challenges of Building an Effective Digital Library in Developing Nations: An African Perspective. In A. Tella & T. Kwanya (Eds.), *Handbook of Research on Managing Intellectual Property in Digital Libraries* (pp. 51–79). Hershey, PA: IGI Global. doi:10.4018/978-1-5225-3093-0.ch004

Agarwal, R., Singh, A., & Sen, S. (2016). Role of Molecular Docking in Computer-Aided Drug Design and Development. In S. Dastmalchi, M. Hamzeh-Mivehroud, & B. Sokouti (Eds.), *Applied Case Studies and Solutions in Molecular Docking-Based Drug Design* (pp. 1–28). Hershey, PA: IGI Global. doi:10.4018/978-1-5225-0362-0.ch001

Ali, O., & Soar, J. (2016). Technology Innovation Adoption Theories. In L. Al-Hakim, X. Wu, A. Koronios, & Y. Shou (Eds.), *Handbook of Research on Driving Competitive Advantage through Sustainable, Lean, and Disruptive Innovation* (pp. 1–38). Hershey, PA: IGI Global. doi:10.4018/978-1-5225-0135-0.ch001

Alsharo, M. (2017). Attitudes Towards Cloud Computing Adoption in Emerging Economies. *International Journal of Cloud Applications and Computing*, 7(3), 44–58. doi:10.4018/IJCAC.2017070102

Amer, T. S., & Johnson, T. L. (2016). Information Technology Progress Indicators: Temporal Expectancy, User Preference, and the Perception of Process Duration. *International Journal of Technology and Human Interaction*, 12(4), 1–14. doi:10.4018/IJTHI.2016100101

Amer, T. S., & Johnson, T. L. (2017). Information Technology Progress Indicators: Research Employing Psychological Frameworks. In A. Mesquita (Ed.), *Research Paradigms and Contemporary Perspectives on Human-Technology Interaction* (pp. 168–186). Hershey, PA: IGI Global. doi:10.4018/978-1-5225-1868-6.ch008

Anchugam, C. V., & Thangadurai, K. (2016). Introduction to Network Security. In D. G., M. Singh, & M. Jayanthi (Eds.), Network Security Attacks and Countermeasures (pp. 1-48). Hershey, PA: IGI Global. doi:10.4018/978-1-4666-8761-5.ch001

Anchugam, C. V., & Thangadurai, K. (2016). Classification of Network Attacks and Countermeasures of Different Attacks. In D. G., M. Singh, & M. Jayanthi (Eds.), Network Security Attacks and Countermeasures (pp. 115-156). Hershey, PA: IGI Global. doi:10.4018/978-1-4666-8761-5.ch004

Anohah, E. (2016). Pedagogy and Design of Online Learning Environment in Computer Science Education for High Schools. *International Journal of Online Pedagogy and Course Design*, 6(3), 39–51. doi:10.4018/IJOPCD.2016070104

Anohah, E. (2017). Paradigm and Architecture of Computing Augmented Learning Management System for Computer Science Education. *International Journal of Online Pedagogy and Course Design*, 7(2), 60–70. doi:10.4018/IJOPCD.2017040105

Anohah, E., & Suhonen, J. (2017). Trends of Mobile Learning in Computing Education from 2006 to 2014: A Systematic Review of Research Publications. *International Journal of Mobile and Blended Learning*, 9(1), 16–33. doi:10.4018/IJMBL.2017010102

Assis-Hassid, S., Heart, T., Reychav, I., & Pliskin, J. S. (2016). Modelling Factors Affecting Patient-Doctor-Computer Communication in Primary Care. *International Journal of Reliable and Quality E-Healthcare*, 5(1), 1–17. doi:10.4018/IJRQEH.2016010101

Bailey, E. K. (2017). Applying Learning Theories to Computer Technology Supported Instruction. In M. Grassetti & S. Brookby (Eds.), *Advancing Next-Generation Teacher Education through Digital Tools and Applications* (pp. 61–81). Hershey, PA: IGI Global. doi:10.4018/978-1-5225-0965-3.ch004

Balasubramanian, K. (2016). Attacks on Online Banking and Commerce. In K. Balasubramanian, K. Mala, & M. Rajakani (Eds.), *Cryptographic Solutions for Secure Online Banking and Commerce* (pp. 1–19). Hershey, PA: IGI Global. doi:10.4018/978-1-5225-0273-9.ch001

Baldwin, S., Opoku-Agyemang, K., & Roy, D. (2016). Games People Play: A Trilateral Collaboration Researching Computer Gaming across Cultures. In K. Valentine & L. Jensen (Eds.), *Examining the Evolution of Gaming and Its Impact on Social, Cultural, and Political Perspectives* (pp. 364–376). Hershey, PA: IGI Global. doi:10.4018/978-1-5225-0261-6.ch017

Banerjee, S., Sing, T. Y., Chowdhury, A. R., & Anwar, H. (2018). Let's Go Green: Towards a Taxonomy of Green Computing Enablers for Business Sustainability. In M. Khosrow-Pour (Ed.), *Green Computing Strategies for Competitive Advantage and Business Sustainability* (pp. 89–109). Hershey, PA: IGI Global. doi:10.4018/978-1-5225-5017-4.ch005

Basham, R. (2018). Information Science and Technology in Crisis Response and Management. In M. Khosrow-Pour, D.B.A. (Ed.), Encyclopedia of Information Science and Technology, Fourth Edition (pp. 1407-1418). Hershey, PA: IGI Global. doi:10.4018/978-1-5225-2255-3.ch121

Batyashe, T., & Iyamu, T. (2018). Architectural Framework for the Implementation of Information Technology Governance in Organisations. In M. Khosrow-Pour, D.B.A. (Ed.), Encyclopedia of Information Science and Technology, Fourth Edition (pp. 810-819). Hershey, PA: IGI Global. doi:10.4018/978-1-5225-2255-3.ch070

Bekleyen, N., & Çelik, S. (2017). Attitudes of Adult EFL Learners towards Preparing for a Language Test via CALL. In D. Tafazoli & M. Romero (Eds.), *Multiculturalism and Technology-Enhanced Language Learning* (pp. 214–229). Hershey, PA: IGI Global. doi:10.4018/978-1-5225-1882-2.ch013

Bennett, A., Eglash, R., Lachney, M., & Babbitt, W. (2016). Design Agency: Diversifying Computer Science at the Intersections of Creativity and Culture. In M. Raisinghani (Ed.), *Revolutionizing Education through Web-Based Instruction* (pp. 35–56). Hershey, PA: IGI Global. doi:10.4018/978-1-4666-9932-8.ch003

Bergeron, F., Croteau, A., Uwizeyemungu, S., & Raymond, L. (2017). A Framework for Research on Information Technology Governance in SMEs. In S. De Haes & W. Van Grembergen (Eds.), *Strategic IT Governance and Alignment in Business Settings* (pp. 53–81). Hershey, PA: IGI Global. doi:10.4018/978-1-5225-0861-8.ch003

Bhatt, G. D., Wang, Z., & Rodger, J. A. (2017). Information Systems Capabilities and Their Effects on Competitive Advantages: A Study of Chinese Companies. *Information Resources Management Journal*, *30*(3), 41–57. doi:10.4018/IRMJ.2017070103

Bogdanoski, M., Stoilkovski, M., & Risteski, A. (2016). Novel First Responder Digital Forensics Tool as a Support to Law Enforcement. In M. Hadji-Janev & M. Bogdanoski (Eds.), *Handbook of Research on Civil Society and National Security in the Era of Cyber Warfare* (pp. 352–376). Hershey, PA: IGI Global. doi:10.4018/978-1-4666-8793-6.ch016

Boontarig, W., Papasratorn, B., & Chutimaskul, W. (2016). The Unified Model for Acceptance and Use of Health Information on Online Social Networks: Evidence from Thailand. *International Journal of E-Health and Medical Communications*, *7*(1), 31–47. doi:10.4018/IJEHMC.2016010102

Brown, S., & Yuan, X. (2016). Techniques for Retaining Computer Science Students at Historical Black Colleges and Universities. In C. Prince & R. Ford (Eds.), *Setting a New Agenda for Student Engagement and Retention in Historically Black Colleges and Universities* (pp. 251–268). Hershey, PA: IGI Global. doi:10.4018/978-1-5225-0308-8.ch014

Burcoff, A., & Shamir, L. (2017). Computer Analysis of Pablo Picasso's Artistic Style. *International Journal of Art, Culture and Design Technologies*, 6(1), 1–18. doi:10.4018/IJACDT.2017010101

Byker, E. J. (2017). I Play I Learn: Introducing Technological Play Theory. In C. Martin & D. Polly (Eds.), *Handbook of Research on Teacher Education and Professional Development* (pp. 297–306). Hershey, PA: IGI Global. doi:10.4018/978-1-5225-1067-3.ch016

Calongne, C. M., Stricker, A. G., Truman, B., & Arenas, F. J. (2017). Cognitive Apprenticeship and Computer Science Education in Cyberspace: Reimagining the Past. In A. Stricker, C. Calongne, B. Truman, & F. Arenas (Eds.), *Integrating an Awareness of Selfhood and Society into Virtual Learning* (pp. 180–197). Hershey, PA: IGI Global. doi:10.4018/978-1-5225-2182-2.ch013

Carlton, E. L., Holsinger, J. W. Jr, & Anunobi, N. (2016). Physician Engagement with Health Information Technology: Implications for Practice and Professionalism. *International Journal of Computers in Clinical Practice*, 1(2), 51–73. doi:10.4018/IJCCP.2016070103

Carneiro, A. D. (2017). Defending Information Networks in Cyberspace: Some Notes on Security Needs. In M. Dawson, D. Kisku, P. Gupta, J. Sing, & W. Li (Eds.), Developing Next-Generation Countermeasures for Homeland Security Threat Prevention (pp. 354-375). Hershey, PA: IGI Global. doi:10.4018/978-1-5225-0703-1.ch016

Cavalcanti, J. C. (2016). The New "ABC" of ICTs (Analytics + Big Data + Cloud Computing): A Complex Trade-Off between IT and CT Costs. In J. Martins & A. Molnar (Eds.), *Handbook of Research on Innovations in Information Retrieval, Analysis, and Management* (pp. 152–186). Hershey, PA: IGI Global. doi:10.4018/978-1-4666-8833-9.ch006

Chase, J. P., & Yan, Z. (2017). Affect in Statistics Cognition. In *Assessing and Measuring Statistics Cognition in Higher Education Online Environments: Emerging Research and Opportunities* (pp. 144–187). Hershey, PA: IGI Global. doi:10.4018/978-1-5225-2420-5.ch005

Chen, C. (2016). Effective Learning Strategies for the 21st Century: Implications for the E-Learning. In M. Anderson & C. Gavan (Eds.), *Developing Effective Educational Experiences through Learning Analytics* (pp. 143–169). Hershey, PA: IGI Global. doi:10.4018/978-1-4666-9983-0.ch006

Chen, E. T. (2016). Examining the Influence of Information Technology on Modern Health Care. In P. Manolitzas, E. Grigoroudis, N. Matsatsinis, & D. Yannacopoulos (Eds.), *Effective Methods for Modern Healthcare Service Quality and Evaluation* (pp. 110–136). Hershey, PA: IGI Global. doi:10.4018/978-1-4666-9961-8.ch006

Cimermanova, I. (2017). Computer-Assisted Learning in Slovakia. In D. Tafazoli & M. Romero (Eds.), *Multiculturalism and Technology-Enhanced Language Learning* (pp. 252–270). Hershey, PA: IGI Global. doi:10.4018/978-1-5225-1882-2.ch015

Cipolla-Ficarra, F. V., & Cipolla-Ficarra, M. (2018). Computer Animation for Ingenious Revival. In F. Cipolla-Ficarra, M. Ficarra, M. Cipolla-Ficarra, A. Quiroga, J. Alma, & J. Carré (Eds.), *Technology-Enhanced Human Interaction in Modern Society* (pp. 159–181). Hershey, PA: IGI Global. doi:10.4018/978-1-5225-3437-2.ch008

Cockrell, S., Damron, T. S., Melton, A. M., & Smith, A. D. (2018). Offshoring IT. In M. Khosrow-Pour, D.B.A. (Ed.), Encyclopedia of Information Science and Technology, Fourth Edition (pp. 5476-5489). Hershey, PA: IGI Global. doi:10.4018/978-1-5225-2255-3.ch476

Coffey, J. W. (2018). Logic and Proof in Computer Science: Categories and Limits of Proof Techniques. In J. Horne (Ed.), *Philosophical Perceptions on Logic and Order* (pp. 218–240). Hershey, PA: IGI Global. doi:10.4018/978-1-5225-2443-4.ch007

Dale, M. (2017). Re-Thinking the Challenges of Enterprise Architecture Implementation. In M. Tavana (Ed.), *Enterprise Information Systems and the Digitalization of Business Functions* (pp. 205–221). Hershey, PA: IGI Global. doi:10.4018/978-1-5225-2382-6.ch009

Das, A., Dasgupta, R., & Bagchi, A. (2016). Overview of Cellular Computing-Basic Principles and Applications. In J. Mandal, S. Mukhopadhyay, & T. Pal (Eds.), *Handbook of Research on Natural Computing for Optimization Problems* (pp. 637–662). Hershey, PA: IGI Global. doi:10.4018/978-1-5225-0058-2.ch026

De Maere, K., De Haes, S., & von Kutzschenbach, M. (2017). CIO Perspectives on Organizational Learning within the Context of IT Governance. *International Journal of IT/Business Alignment and Governance, 8*(1), 32-47. doi:10.4018/IJITBAG.2017010103

Demir, K., Çaka, C., Yaman, N. D., İslamoğlu, H., & Kuzu, A. (2018). Examining the Current Definitions of Computational Thinking. In H. Ozcinar, G. Wong, & H. Ozturk (Eds.), *Teaching Computational Thinking in Primary Education* (pp. 36–64). Hershey, PA: IGI Global. doi:10.4018/978-1-5225-3200-2.ch003

Deng, X., Hung, Y., & Lin, C. D. (2017). Design and Analysis of Computer Experiments. In S. Saha, A. Mandal, A. Narasimhamurthy, S. V, & S. Sangam (Eds.), Handbook of Research on Applied Cybernetics and Systems Science (pp. 264-279). Hershey, PA: IGI Global. doi:10.4018/978-1-5225-2498-4.ch013

Denner, J., Martinez, J., & Thiry, H. (2017). Strategies for Engaging Hispanic/Latino Youth in the US in Computer Science. In Y. Rankin & J. Thomas (Eds.), *Moving Students of Color from Consumers to Producers of Technology* (pp. 24–48). Hershey, PA: IGI Global. doi:10.4018/978-1-5225-2005-4.ch002

Devi, A. (2017). Cyber Crime and Cyber Security: A Quick Glance. In R. Kumar, P. Pattnaik, & P. Pandey (Eds.), *Detecting and Mitigating Robotic Cyber Security Risks* (pp. 160–171). Hershey, PA: IGI Global. doi:10.4018/978-1-5225-2154-9.ch011

Dores, A. R., Barbosa, F., Guerreiro, S., Almeida, I., & Carvalho, I. P. (2016). Computer-Based Neuropsychological Rehabilitation: Virtual Reality and Serious Games. In M. Cruz-Cunha, I. Miranda, R. Martinho, & R. Rijo (Eds.), *Encyclopedia of E-Health and Telemedicine* (pp. 473–485). Hershey, PA: IGI Global. doi:10.4018/978-1-4666-9978-6.ch037

Doshi, N., & Schaefer, G. (2016). Computer-Aided Analysis of Nailfold Capillaroscopy Images. In D. Fotiadis (Ed.), *Handbook of Research on Trends in the Diagnosis and Treatment of Chronic Conditions* (pp. 146–158). Hershey, PA: IGI Global. doi:10.4018/978-1-4666-8828-5.ch007

Doyle, D. J., & Fahy, P. J. (2018). Interactivity in Distance Education and Computer-Aided Learning, With Medical Education Examples. In M. Khosrow-Pour, D.B.A. (Ed.), Encyclopedia of Information Science and Technology, Fourth Edition (pp. 5829-5840). Hershey, PA: IGI Global. doi:10.4018/978-1-5225-2255-3.ch507

Elias, N. I., & Walker, T. W. (2017). Factors that Contribute to Continued Use of E-Training among Healthcare Professionals. In F. Topor (Ed.), *Handbook of Research on Individualism and Identity in the Globalized Digital Age* (pp. 403–429). Hershey, PA: IGI Global. doi:10.4018/978-1-5225-0522-8.ch018

Eloy, S., Dias, M. S., Lopes, P. F., & Vilar, E. (2016). Digital Technologies in Architecture and Engineering: Exploring an Engaged Interaction within Curricula. In D. Fonseca & E. Redondo (Eds.), *Handbook of Research on Applied E-Learning in Engineering and Architecture Education* (pp. 368–402). Hershey, PA: IGI Global. doi:10.4018/978-1-4666-8803-2.ch017

Estrela, V. V., Magalhães, H. A., & Saotome, O. (2016). Total Variation Applications in Computer Vision. In N. Kamila (Ed.), *Handbook of Research on Emerging Perspectives in Intelligent Pattern Recognition, Analysis, and Image Processing* (pp. 41–64). Hershey, PA: IGI Global. doi:10.4018/978-1-4666-8654-0.ch002

Filipovic, N., Radovic, M., Nikolic, D. D., Saveljic, I., Milosevic, Z., Exarchos, T. P., ... Parodi, O. (2016). Computer Predictive Model for Plaque Formation and Progression in the Artery. In D. Fotiadis (Ed.), *Handbook of Research on Trends in the Diagnosis and Treatment of Chronic Conditions* (pp. 279–300). Hershey, PA: IGI Global. doi:10.4018/978-1-4666-8828-5.ch013

Fisher, R. L. (2018). Computer-Assisted Indian Matrimonial Services. In M. Khosrow-Pour, D.B.A. (Ed.), Encyclopedia of Information Science and Technology, Fourth Edition (pp. 4136-4145). Hershey, PA: IGI Global. doi:10.4018/978-1-5225-2255-3.ch358

Fleenor, H. G., & Hodhod, R. (2016). Assessment of Learning and Technology: Computer Science Education. In V. Wang (Ed.), *Handbook of Research on Learning Outcomes and Opportunities in the Digital Age* (pp. 51–78). Hershey, PA: IGI Global. doi:10.4018/978-1-4666-9577-1.ch003

García-Valcárcel, A., & Mena, J. (2016). Information Technology as a Way To Support Collaborative Learning: What In-Service Teachers Think, Know and Do. *Journal of Information Technology Research*, 9(1), 1–17. doi:10.4018/JITR.2016010101

Gardner-McCune, C., & Jimenez, Y. (2017). Historical App Developers: Integrating CS into K-12 through Cross-Disciplinary Projects. In Y. Rankin & J. Thomas (Eds.), *Moving Students of Color from Consumers to Producers of Technology* (pp. 85–112). Hershey, PA: IGI Global. doi:10.4018/978-1-5225-2005-4.ch005

Garvey, G. P. (2016). Exploring Perception, Cognition, and Neural Pathways of Stereo Vision and the Split–Brain Human Computer Interface. In A. Ursyn (Ed.), *Knowledge Visualization and Visual Literacy in Science Education* (pp. 28–76). Hershey, PA: IGI Global. doi:10.4018/978-1-5225-0480-1.ch002

Ghafele, R., & Gibert, B. (2018). Open Growth: The Economic Impact of Open Source Software in the USA. In M. Khosrow-Pour (Ed.), *Optimizing Contemporary Application and Processes in Open Source Software* (pp. 164–197). Hershey, PA: IGI Global. doi:10.4018/978-1-5225-5314-4.ch007

Ghobakhloo, M., & Azar, A. (2018). Information Technology Resources, the Organizational Capability of Lean-Agile Manufacturing, and Business Performance. *Information Resources Management Journal*, *31*(2), 47–74. doi:10.4018/IRMJ.2018040103

Gianni, M., & Gotzamani, K. (2016). Integrated Management Systems and Information Management Systems: Common Threads. In P. Papajorgji, F. Pinet, A. Guimarães, & J. Papathanasiou (Eds.), *Automated Enterprise Systems for Maximizing Business Performance* (pp. 195–214). Hershey, PA: IGI Global. doi:10.4018/978-1-4666-8841-4.ch011

Gikandi, J. W. (2017). Computer-Supported Collaborative Learning and Assessment: A Strategy for Developing Online Learning Communities in Continuing Education. In J. Keengwe & G. Onchwari (Eds.), *Handbook of Research on Learner-Centered Pedagogy in Teacher Education and Professional Development* (pp. 309–333). Hershey, PA: IGI Global. doi:10.4018/978-1-5225-0892-2.ch017

Gokhale, A. A., & Machina, K. F. (2017). Development of a Scale to Measure Attitudes toward Information Technology. In L. Tomei (Ed.), *Exploring the New Era of Technology-Infused Education* (pp. 49–64). Hershey, PA: IGI Global. doi:10.4018/978-1-5225-1709-2.ch004

Grace, A., O'Donoghue, J., Mahony, C., Heffernan, T., Molony, D., & Carroll, T. (2016). Computerized Decision Support Systems for Multimorbidity Care: An Urgent Call for Research and Development. In M. Cruz-Cunha, I. Miranda, R. Martinho, & R. Rijo (Eds.), *Encyclopedia of E-Health and Telemedicine* (pp. 486–494). Hershey, PA: IGI Global. doi:10.4018/978-1-4666-9978-6.ch038

Gupta, A., & Singh, O. (2016). Computer Aided Modeling and Finite Element Analysis of Human Elbow. *International Journal of Biomedical and Clinical Engineering*, *5*(1), 31–38. doi:10.4018/IJBCE.2016010104

H., S. K. (2016). Classification of Cybercrimes and Punishments under the Information Technology Act, 2000. In S. Geetha, & A. Phamila (Eds.), *Combating Security Breaches and Criminal Activity in the Digital Sphere* (pp. 57-66). Hershey, PA: IGI Global. doi:10.4018/978-1-5225-0193-0.ch004

Hafeez-Baig, A., Gururajan, R., & Wickramasinghe, N. (2017). Readiness as a Novel Construct of Readiness Acceptance Model (RAM) for the Wireless Handheld Technology. In N. Wickramasinghe (Ed.), *Handbook of Research on Healthcare Administration and Management* (pp. 578–595). Hershey, PA: IGI Global. doi:10.4018/978-1-5225-0920-2.ch035

Hanafizadeh, P., Ghandchi, S., & Asgarimehr, M. (2017). Impact of Information Technology on Lifestyle: A Literature Review and Classification. *International Journal of Virtual Communities and Social Networking*, *9*(2), 1–23. doi:10.4018/IJVCSN.2017040101

Harlow, D. B., Dwyer, H., Hansen, A. K., Hill, C., Iveland, A., Leak, A. E., & Franklin, D. M. (2016). Computer Programming in Elementary and Middle School: Connections across Content. In M. Urban & D. Falvo (Eds.), *Improving K-12 STEM Education Outcomes through Technological Integration* (pp. 337–361). Hershey, PA: IGI Global. doi:10.4018/978-1-4666-9616-7.ch015

Haseski, H. İ., Ilic, U., & Tuğtekin, U. (2018). Computational Thinking in Educational Digital Games: An Assessment Tool Proposal. In H. Ozcinar, G. Wong, & H. Ozturk (Eds.), *Teaching Computational Thinking in Primary Education* (pp. 256–287). Hershey, PA: IGI Global. doi:10.4018/978-1-5225-3200-2.ch013

Hee, W. J., Jalleh, G., Lai, H., & Lin, C. (2017). E-Commerce and IT Projects: Evaluation and Management Issues in Australian and Taiwanese Hospitals. *International Journal of Public Health Management and Ethics*, 2(1), 69–90. doi:10.4018/IJPHME.2017010104

Hernandez, A. A. (2017). Green Information Technology Usage: Awareness and Practices of Philippine IT Professionals. *International Journal of Enterprise Information Systems*, 13(4), 90–103. doi:10.4018/IJEIS.2017100106

Hernandez, A. A., & Ona, S. E. (2016). Green IT Adoption: Lessons from the Philippines Business Process Outsourcing Industry. *International Journal of Social Ecology and Sustainable Development*, 7(1), 1–34. doi:10.4018/IJSESD.2016010101

Hernandez, M. A., Marin, E. C., Garcia-Rodriguez, J., Azorin-Lopez, J., & Cazorla, M. (2017). Automatic Learning Improves Human-Robot Interaction in Productive Environments: A Review. *International Journal of Computer Vision and Image Processing*, 7(3), 65–75. doi:10.4018/IJCVIP.2017070106

Horne-Popp, L. M., Tessone, E. B., & Welker, J. (2018). If You Build It, They Will Come: Creating a Library Statistics Dashboard for Decision-Making. In L. Costello & M. Powers (Eds.), *Developing In-House Digital Tools in Library Spaces* (pp. 177–203). Hershey, PA: IGI Global. doi:10.4018/978-1-5225-2676-6.ch009

Hossan, C. G., & Ryan, J. C. (2016). Factors Affecting e-Government Technology Adoption Behaviour in a Voluntary Environment. *International Journal of Electronic Government Research*, 12(1), 24–49. doi:10.4018/IJEGR.2016010102

Hu, H., Hu, P. J., & Al-Gahtani, S. S. (2017). User Acceptance of Computer Technology at Work in Arabian Culture: A Model Comparison Approach. In M. Khosrow-Pour (Ed.), *Handbook of Research on Technology Adoption, Social Policy, and Global Integration* (pp. 205–228). Hershey, PA: IGI Global. doi:10.4018/978-1-5225-2668-1.ch011

Huie, C. P. (2016). Perceptions of Business Intelligence Professionals about Factors Related to Business Intelligence input in Decision Making. *International Journal of Business Analytics*, 3(3), 1–24. doi:10.4018/IJBAN.2016070101

Hung, S., Huang, W., Yen, D. C., Chang, S., & Lu, C. (2016). Effect of Information Service Competence and Contextual Factors on the Effectiveness of Strategic Information Systems Planning in Hospitals. *Journal of Global Information Management*, 24(1), 14–36. doi:10.4018/JGIM.2016010102

Ifinedo, P. (2017). Using an Extended Theory of Planned Behavior to Study Nurses' Adoption of Healthcare Information Systems in Nova Scotia. *International Journal of Technology Diffusion*, 8(1), 1–17. doi:10.4018/IJTD.2017010101

Ilie, V., & Sneha, S. (2018). A Three Country Study for Understanding Physicians' Engagement With Electronic Information Resources Pre and Post System Implementation. *Journal of Global Information Management*, 26(2), 48–73. doi:10.4018/JGIM.2018040103

Inoue-Smith, Y. (2017). Perceived Ease in Using Technology Predicts Teacher Candidates' Preferences for Online Resources. *International Journal of Online Pedagogy and Course Design*, 7(3), 17–28. doi:10.4018/IJOPCD.2017070102

Islam, A. A. (2016). Development and Validation of the Technology Adoption and Gratification (TAG) Model in Higher Education: A Cross-Cultural Study Between Malaysia and China. *International Journal of Technology and Human Interaction*, *12*(3), 78–105. doi:10.4018/IJTHI.2016070106

Islam, A. Y. (2017). Technology Satisfaction in an Academic Context: Moderating Effect of Gender. In A. Mesquita (Ed.), *Research Paradigms and Contemporary Perspectives on Human-Technology Interaction* (pp. 187–211). Hershey, PA: IGI Global. doi:10.4018/978-1-5225-1868-6.ch009

Jamil, G. L., & Jamil, C. C. (2017). Information and Knowledge Management Perspective Contributions for Fashion Studies: Observing Logistics and Supply Chain Management Processes. In G. Jamil, A. Soares, & C. Pessoa (Eds.), *Handbook of Research on Information Management for Effective Logistics and Supply Chains* (pp. 199–221). Hershey, PA: IGI Global. doi:10.4018/978-1-5225-0973-8.ch011

Jamil, G. L., Jamil, L. C., Vieira, A. A., & Xavier, A. J. (2016). Challenges in Modelling Healthcare Services: A Study Case of Information Architecture Perspectives. In G. Jamil, J. Poças Rascão, F. Ribeiro, & A. Malheiro da Silva (Eds.), *Handbook of Research on Information Architecture and Management in Modern Organizations* (pp. 1–23). Hershey, PA: IGI Global. doi:10.4018/978-1-4666-8637-3.ch001

Janakova, M. (2018). Big Data and Simulations for the Solution of Controversies in Small Businesses. In M. Khosrow-Pour, D.B.A. (Ed.), Encyclopedia of Information Science and Technology, Fourth Edition (pp. 6907-6915). Hershey, PA: IGI Global. doi:10.4018/978-1-5225-2255-3.ch598

Jha, D. G. (2016). Preparing for Information Technology Driven Changes. In S. Tiwari & L. Nafees (Eds.), *Innovative Management Education Pedagogies for Preparing Next-Generation Leaders* (pp. 258–274). Hershey, PA: IGI Global. doi:10.4018/978-1-4666-9691-4.ch015

Jhawar, A., & Garg, S. K. (2018). Logistics Improvement by Investment in Information Technology Using System Dynamics. In A. Azar & S. Vaidyanathan (Eds.), *Advances in System Dynamics and Control* (pp. 528–567). Hershey, PA: IGI Global. doi:10.4018/978-1-5225-4077-9.ch017

Kalelioğlu, F., Gülbahar, Y., & Doğan, D. (2018). Teaching How to Think Like a Programmer: Emerging Insights. In H. Ozcinar, G. Wong, & H. Ozturk (Eds.), *Teaching Computational Thinking in Primary Education* (pp. 18–35). Hershey, PA: IGI Global. doi:10.4018/978-1-5225-3200-2.ch002

Kamberi, S. (2017). A Girls-Only Online Virtual World Environment and its Implications for Game-Based Learning. In A. Stricker, C. Calongne, B. Truman, & F. Arenas (Eds.), *Integrating an Awareness of Selfhood and Society into Virtual Learning* (pp. 74–95). Hershey, PA: IGI Global. doi:10.4018/978-1-5225-2182-2.ch006

Kamel, S., & Rizk, N. (2017). ICT Strategy Development: From Design to Implementation – Case of Egypt. In C. Howard & K. Hargiss (Eds.), *Strategic Information Systems and Technologies in Modern Organizations* (pp. 239–257). Hershey, PA: IGI Global. doi:10.4018/978-1-5225-1680-4.ch010

Kamel, S. H. (2018). The Potential Role of the Software Industry in Supporting Economic Development. In M. Khosrow-Pour, D.B.A. (Ed.), Encyclopedia of Information Science and Technology, Fourth Edition (pp. 7259-7269). Hershey, PA: IGI Global. doi:10.4018/978-1-5225-2255-3.ch631

Karon, R. (2016). Utilisation of Health Information Systems for Service Delivery in the Namibian Environment. In T. Iyamu & A. Tatnall (Eds.), *Maximizing Healthcare Delivery and Management through Technology Integration* (pp. 169–183). Hershey, PA: IGI Global. doi:10.4018/978-1-4666-9446-0.ch011

Kawata, S. (2018). Computer-Assisted Parallel Program Generation. In M. Khosrow-Pour, D.B.A. (Ed.), Encyclopedia of Information Science and Technology, Fourth Edition (pp. 4583-4593). Hershey, PA: IGI Global. doi:10.4018/978-1-5225-2255-3.ch398

Khanam, S., Siddiqui, J., & Talib, F. (2016). A DEMATEL Approach for Prioritizing the TQM Enablers and IT Resources in the Indian ICT Industry. *International Journal of Applied Management Sciences and Engineering, 3*(1), 11–29. doi:10.4018/IJAMSE.2016010102

Khari, M., Shrivastava, G., Gupta, S., & Gupta, R. (2017). Role of Cyber Security in Today's Scenario. In R. Kumar, P. Pattnaik, & P. Pandey (Eds.), *Detecting and Mitigating Robotic Cyber Security Risks* (pp. 177–191). Hershey, PA: IGI Global. doi:10.4018/978-1-5225-2154-9.ch013

Khouja, M., Rodriguez, I. B., Ben Halima, Y., & Moalla, S. (2018). IT Governance in Higher Education Institutions: A Systematic Literature Review. *International Journal of Human Capital and Information Technology Professionals, 9*(2), 52–67. doi:10.4018/IJHCITP.2018040104

Kim, S., Chang, M., Choi, N., Park, J., & Kim, H. (2016). The Direct and Indirect Effects of Computer Uses on Student Success in Math. *International Journal of Cyber Behavior, Psychology and Learning, 6*(3), 48–64. doi:10.4018/IJCBPL.2016070104

Kiourt, C., Pavlidis, G., Koutsoudis, A., & Kalles, D. (2017). Realistic Simulation of Cultural Heritage. *International Journal of Computational Methods in Heritage Science, 1*(1), 10–40. doi:10.4018/IJCMHS.2017010102

Korikov, A., & Krivtsov, O. (2016). System of People-Computer: On the Way of Creation of Human-Oriented Interface. In V. Mkrttchian, A. Bershadsky, A. Bozhday, M. Kataev, & S. Kataev (Eds.), *Handbook of Research on Estimation and Control Techniques in E-Learning Systems* (pp. 458–470). Hershey, PA: IGI Global. doi:10.4018/978-1-4666-9489-7.ch032

Köse, U. (2017). An Augmented-Reality-Based Intelligent Mobile Application for Open Computer Education. In G. Kurubacak & H. Altinpulluk (Eds.), *Mobile Technologies and Augmented Reality in Open Education* (pp. 154–174). Hershey, PA: IGI Global. doi:10.4018/978-1-5225-2110-5.ch008

Lahmiri, S. (2018). Information Technology Outsourcing Risk Factors and Provider Selection. In M. Gupta, R. Sharman, J. Walp, & P. Mulgund (Eds.), *Information Technology Risk Management and Compliance in Modern Organizations* (pp. 214–228). Hershey, PA: IGI Global. doi:10.4018/978-1-5225-2604-9.ch008

Landriscina, F. (2017). Computer-Supported Imagination: The Interplay Between Computer and Mental Simulation in Understanding Scientific Concepts. In I. Levin & D. Tsybulsky (Eds.), *Digital Tools and Solutions for Inquiry-Based STEM Learning* (pp. 33–60). Hershey, PA: IGI Global. doi:10.4018/978-1-5225-2525-7.ch002

Lau, S. K., Winley, G. K., Leung, N. K., Tsang, N., & Lau, S. Y. (2016). An Exploratory Study of Expectation in IT Skills in a Developing Nation: Vietnam. *Journal of Global Information Management, 24*(1), 1–13. doi:10.4018/JGIM.2016010101

Lavranos, C., Kostagiolas, P., & Papadatos, J. (2016). Information Retrieval Technologies and the "Realities" of Music Information Seeking. In I. Deliyannis, P. Kostagiolas, & C. Banou (Eds.), *Experimental Multimedia Systems for Interactivity and Strategic Innovation* (pp. 102–121). Hershey, PA: IGI Global. doi:10.4018/978-1-4666-8659-5.ch005

Lee, W. W. (2018). Ethical Computing Continues From Problem to Solution. In M. Khosrow-Pour, D.B.A. (Ed.), Encyclopedia of Information Science and Technology, Fourth Edition (pp. 4884-4897). Hershey, PA: IGI Global. doi:10.4018/978-1-5225-2255-3.ch423

Lehto, M. (2016). Cyber Security Education and Research in the Finland's Universities and Universities of Applied Sciences. *International Journal of Cyber Warfare & Terrorism*, *6*(2), 15–31. doi:10.4018/IJCWT.2016040102

Lin, C., Jalleh, G., & Huang, Y. (2016). Evaluating and Managing Electronic Commerce and Outsourcing Projects in Hospitals. In A. Dwivedi (Ed.), *Reshaping Medical Practice and Care with Health Information Systems* (pp. 132–172). Hershey, PA: IGI Global. doi:10.4018/978-1-4666-9870-3.ch005

Lin, S., Chen, S., & Chuang, S. (2017). Perceived Innovation and Quick Response Codes in an Online-to-Offline E-Commerce Service Model. *International Journal of E-Adoption*, *9*(2), 1–16. doi:10.4018/IJEA.2017070101

Liu, M., Wang, Y., Xu, W., & Liu, L. (2017). Automated Scoring of Chinese Engineering Students' English Essays. *International Journal of Distance Education Technologies*, *15*(1), 52–68. doi:10.4018/IJDET.2017010104

Luciano, E. M., Wiedenhöft, G. C., Macadar, M. A., & Pinheiro dos Santos, F. (2016). Information Technology Governance Adoption: Understanding its Expectations Through the Lens of Organizational Citizenship. *International Journal of IT/Business Alignment and Governance, 7*(2), 22-32. doi:10.4018/IJITBAG.2016070102

Mabe, L. K., & Oladele, O. I. (2017). Application of Information Communication Technologies for Agricultural Development through Extension Services: A Review. In T. Tossy (Ed.), *Information Technology Integration for Socio-Economic Development* (pp. 52–101). Hershey, PA: IGI Global. doi:10.4018/978-1-5225-0539-6.ch003

Manogaran, G., Thota, C., & Lopez, D. (2018). Human-Computer Interaction With Big Data Analytics. In D. Lopez & M. Durai (Eds.), *HCI Challenges and Privacy Preservation in Big Data Security* (pp. 1–22). Hershey, PA: IGI Global. doi:10.4018/978-1-5225-2863-0.ch001

Margolis, J., Goode, J., & Flapan, J. (2017). A Critical Crossroads for Computer Science for All: "Identifying Talent" or "Building Talent," and What Difference Does It Make? In Y. Rankin & J. Thomas (Eds.), *Moving Students of Color from Consumers to Producers of Technology* (pp. 1–23). Hershey, PA: IGI Global. doi:10.4018/978-1-5225-2005-4.ch001

Mbale, J. (2018). Computer Centres Resource Cloud Elasticity-Scalability (CRECES): Copperbelt University Case Study. In S. Aljawarneh & M. Malhotra (Eds.), *Critical Research on Scalability and Security Issues in Virtual Cloud Environments* (pp. 48–70). Hershey, PA: IGI Global. doi:10.4018/978-1-5225-3029-9.ch003

McKee, J. (2018). The Right Information: The Key to Effective Business Planning. In *Business Architectures for Risk Assessment and Strategic Planning: Emerging Research and Opportunities* (pp. 38–52). Hershey, PA: IGI Global. doi:10.4018/978-1-5225-3392-4.ch003

Mensah, I. K., & Mi, J. (2018). Determinants of Intention to Use Local E-Government Services in Ghana: The Perspective of Local Government Workers. *International Journal of Technology Diffusion, 9*(2), 41–60. doi:10.4018/IJTD.2018040103

Mohamed, J. H. (2018). Scientograph-Based Visualization of Computer Forensics Research Literature. In J. Jeyasekar & P. Saravanan (Eds.), *Innovations in Measuring and Evaluating Scientific Information* (pp. 148–162). Hershey, PA: IGI Global. doi:10.4018/978-1-5225-3457-0.ch010

Moore, R. L., & Johnson, N. (2017). Earning a Seat at the Table: How IT Departments Can Partner in Organizational Change and Innovation. *International Journal of Knowledge-Based Organizations, 7*(2), 1–12. doi:10.4018/IJKBO.2017040101

Mtebe, J. S., & Kissaka, M. M. (2016). Enhancing the Quality of Computer Science Education with MOOCs in Sub-Saharan Africa. In J. Keengwe & G. Onchwari (Eds.), *Handbook of Research on Active Learning and the Flipped Classroom Model in the Digital Age* (pp. 366–377). Hershey, PA: IGI Global. doi:10.4018/978-1-4666-9680-8.ch019

Mukul, M. K., & Bhattaharyya, S. (2017). Brain-Machine Interface: Human-Computer Interaction. In E. Noughabi, B. Raahemi, A. Albadvi, & B. Far (Eds.), *Handbook of Research on Data Science for Effective Healthcare Practice and Administration* (pp. 417–443). Hershey, PA: IGI Global. doi:10.4018/978-1-5225-2515-8.ch018

Na, L. (2017). Library and Information Science Education and Graduate Programs in Academic Libraries. In L. Ruan, Q. Zhu, & Y. Ye (Eds.), *Academic Library Development and Administration in China* (pp. 218–229). Hershey, PA: IGI Global. doi:10.4018/978-1-5225-0550-1.ch013

Nabavi, A., Taghavi-Fard, M. T., Hanafizadeh, P., & Taghva, M. R. (2016). Information Technology Continuance Intention: A Systematic Literature Review. *International Journal of E-Business Research, 12*(1), 58–95. doi:10.4018/IJEBR.2016010104

Nath, R., & Murthy, V. N. (2018). What Accounts for the Differences in Internet Diffusion Rates Around the World? In M. Khosrow-Pour, D.B.A. (Ed.), Encyclopedia of Information Science and Technology, Fourth Edition (pp. 8095-8104). Hershey, PA: IGI Global. doi:10.4018/978-1-5225-2255-3.ch705

Nedelko, Z., & Potocan, V. (2018). The Role of Emerging Information Technologies for Supporting Supply Chain Management. In M. Khosrow-Pour, D.B.A. (Ed.), Encyclopedia of Information Science and Technology, Fourth Edition (pp. 5559-5569). Hershey, PA: IGI Global. doi:10.4018/978-1-5225-2255-3.ch483

Ngafeeson, M. N. (2018). User Resistance to Health Information Technology. In M. Khosrow-Pour, D.B.A. (Ed.), Encyclopedia of Information Science and Technology, Fourth Edition (pp. 3816-3825). Hershey, PA: IGI Global. doi:10.4018/978-1-5225-2255-3.ch331

Nozari, H., Najafi, S. E., Jafari-Eskandari, M., & Aliahmadi, A. (2016). Providing a Model for Virtual Project Management with an Emphasis on IT Projects. In C. Graham (Ed.), *Strategic Management and Leadership for Systems Development in Virtual Spaces* (pp. 43–63). Hershey, PA: IGI Global. doi:10.4018/978-1-4666-9688-4.ch003

Nurdin, N., Stockdale, R., & Scheepers, H. (2016). Influence of Organizational Factors in the Sustainability of E-Government: A Case Study of Local E-Government in Indonesia. In I. Sodhi (Ed.), *Trends, Prospects, and Challenges in Asian E-Governance* (pp. 281–323). Hershey, PA: IGI Global. doi:10.4018/978-1-4666-9536-8.ch014

Odagiri, K. (2017). Introduction of Individual Technology to Constitute the Current Internet. In *Strategic Policy-Based Network Management in Contemporary Organizations* (pp. 20–96). Hershey, PA: IGI Global. doi:10.4018/978-1-68318-003-6.ch003

Okike, E. U. (2018). Computer Science and Prison Education. In I. Biao (Ed.), *Strategic Learning Ideologies in Prison Education Programs* (pp. 246–264). Hershey, PA: IGI Global. doi:10.4018/978-1-5225-2909-5.ch012

Olelewe, C. J., & Nwafor, I. P. (2017). Level of Computer Appreciation Skills Acquired for Sustainable Development by Secondary School Students in Nsukka LGA of Enugu State, Nigeria. In C. Ayo & V. Mbarika (Eds.), *Sustainable ICT Adoption and Integration for Socio-Economic Development* (pp. 214–233). Hershey, PA: IGI Global. doi:10.4018/978-1-5225-2565-3.ch010

Oliveira, M., Maçada, A. C., Curado, C., & Nodari, F. (2017). Infrastructure Profiles and Knowledge Sharing. *International Journal of Technology and Human Interaction*, *13*(3), 1–12. doi:10.4018/IJTHI.2017070101

Otarkhani, A., Shokouhyar, S., & Pour, S. S. (2017). Analyzing the Impact of Governance of Enterprise IT on Hospital Performance: Tehran's (Iran) Hospitals – A Case Study. *International Journal of Healthcare Information Systems and Informatics*, *12*(3), 1–20. doi:10.4018/IJHISI.2017070101

Otunla, A. O., & Amuda, C. O. (2018). Nigerian Undergraduate Students' Computer Competencies and Use of Information Technology Tools and Resources for Study Skills and Habits' Enhancement. In M. Khosrow-Pour, D.B.A. (Ed.), Encyclopedia of Information Science and Technology, Fourth Edition (pp. 2303-2313). Hershey, PA: IGI Global. doi:10.4018/978-1-5225-2255-3.ch200

Özçınar, H. (2018). A Brief Discussion on Incentives and Barriers to Computational Thinking Education. In H. Ozcinar, G. Wong, & H. Ozturk (Eds.), *Teaching Computational Thinking in Primary Education* (pp. 1–17). Hershey, PA: IGI Global. doi:10.4018/978-1-5225-3200-2.ch001

Pandey, J. M., Garg, S., Mishra, P., & Mishra, B. P. (2017). Computer Based Psychological Interventions: Subject to the Efficacy of Psychological Services. *International Journal of Computers in Clinical Practice*, *2*(1), 25–33. doi:10.4018/IJCCP.2017010102

Parry, V. K., & Lind, M. L. (2016). Alignment of Business Strategy and Information Technology Considering Information Technology Governance, Project Portfolio Control, and Risk Management. *International Journal of Information Technology Project Management*, *7*(4), 21–37. doi:10.4018/IJITPM.2016100102

Patro, C. (2017). Impulsion of Information Technology on Human Resource Practices. In P. Ordóñez de Pablos (Ed.), *Managerial Strategies and Solutions for Business Success in Asia* (pp. 231–254). Hershey, PA: IGI Global. doi:10.4018/978-1-5225-1886-0.ch013

Patro, C. S., & Raghunath, K. M. (2017). Information Technology Paraphernalia for Supply Chain Management Decisions. In M. Tavana (Ed.), *Enterprise Information Systems and the Digitalization of Business Functions* (pp. 294–320). Hershey, PA: IGI Global. doi:10.4018/978-1-5225-2382-6.ch014

Paul, P. K. (2016). Cloud Computing: An Agent of Promoting Interdisciplinary Sciences, Especially Information Science and I-Schools – Emerging Techno-Educational Scenario. In L. Chao (Ed.), *Handbook of Research on Cloud-Based STEM Education for Improved Learning Outcomes* (pp. 247–258). Hershey, PA: IGI Global. doi:10.4018/978-1-4666-9924-3.ch016

Paul, P. K. (2018). The Context of IST for Solid Information Retrieval and Infrastructure Building: Study of Developing Country. *International Journal of Information Retrieval Research*, *8*(1), 86–100. doi:10.4018/IJIRR.2018010106

Paul, P. K., & Chatterjee, D. (2018). iSchools Promoting "Information Science and Technology" (IST) Domain Towards Community, Business, and Society With Contemporary Worldwide Trend and Emerging Potentialities in India. In M. Khosrow-Pour, D.B.A. (Ed.), Encyclopedia of Information Science and Technology, Fourth Edition (pp. 4723-4735). Hershey, PA: IGI Global. doi:10.4018/978-1-5225-2255-3.ch410

Pessoa, C. R., & Marques, M. E. (2017). Information Technology and Communication Management in Supply Chain Management. In G. Jamil, A. Soares, & C. Pessoa (Eds.), *Handbook of Research on Information Management for Effective Logistics and Supply Chains* (pp. 23–33). Hershey, PA: IGI Global. doi:10.4018/978-1-5225-0973-8.ch002

Pineda, R. G. (2016). Where the Interaction Is Not: Reflections on the Philosophy of Human-Computer Interaction. *International Journal of Art, Culture and Design Technologies*, *5*(1), 1–12. doi:10.4018/IJACDT.2016010101

Pineda, R. G. (2018). Remediating Interaction: Towards a Philosophy of Human-Computer Relationship. In M. Khosrow-Pour (Ed.), *Enhancing Art, Culture, and Design With Technological Integration* (pp. 75–98). Hershey, PA: IGI Global. doi:10.4018/978-1-5225-5023-5.ch004

Poikela, P., & Vuojärvi, H. (2016). Learning ICT-Mediated Communication through Computer-Based Simulations. In M. Cruz-Cunha, I. Miranda, R. Martinho, & R. Rijo (Eds.), *Encyclopedia of E-Health and Telemedicine* (pp. 674–687). Hershey, PA: IGI Global. doi:10.4018/978-1-4666-9978-6.ch052

Qian, Y. (2017). Computer Simulation in Higher Education: Affordances, Opportunities, and Outcomes. In P. Vu, S. Fredrickson, & C. Moore (Eds.), *Handbook of Research on Innovative Pedagogies and Technologies for Online Learning in Higher Education* (pp. 236–262). Hershey, PA: IGI Global. doi:10.4018/978-1-5225-1851-8.ch011

Radant, O., Colomo-Palacios, R., & Stantchev, V. (2016). Factors for the Management of Scarce Human Resources and Highly Skilled Employees in IT-Departments: A Systematic Review. *Journal of Information Technology Research*, *9*(1), 65–82. doi:10.4018/JITR.2016010105

Rahman, N. (2016). Toward Achieving Environmental Sustainability in the Computer Industry. *International Journal of Green Computing*, 7(1), 37–54. doi:10.4018/IJGC.2016010103

Rahman, N. (2017). Lessons from a Successful Data Warehousing Project Management. *International Journal of Information Technology Project Management*, 8(4), 30–45. doi:10.4018/IJITPM.2017100103

Rahman, N. (2018). Environmental Sustainability in the Computer Industry for Competitive Advantage. In M. Khosrow-Pour (Ed.), *Green Computing Strategies for Competitive Advantage and Business Sustainability* (pp. 110–130). Hershey, PA: IGI Global. doi:10.4018/978-1-5225-5017-4.ch006

Rajh, A., & Pavetic, T. (2017). Computer Generated Description as the Required Digital Competence in Archival Profession. *International Journal of Digital Literacy and Digital Competence*, 8(1), 36–49. doi:10.4018/IJDLDC.2017010103

Raman, A., & Goyal, D. P. (2017). Extending IMPLEMENT Framework for Enterprise Information Systems Implementation to Information System Innovation. In M. Tavana (Ed.), *Enterprise Information Systems and the Digitalization of Business Functions* (pp. 137–177). Hershey, PA: IGI Global. doi:10.4018/978-1-5225-2382-6.ch007

Rao, Y. S., Rauta, A. K., Saini, H., & Panda, T. C. (2017). Mathematical Model for Cyber Attack in Computer Network. *International Journal of Business Data Communications and Networking*, 13(1), 58–65. doi:10.4018/IJBDCN.2017010105

Rapaport, W. J. (2018). Syntactic Semantics and the Proper Treatment of Computationalism. In M. Danesi (Ed.), *Empirical Research on Semiotics and Visual Rhetoric* (pp. 128–176). Hershey, PA: IGI Global. doi:10.4018/978-1-5225-5622-0.ch007

Raut, R., Priyadarshinee, P., & Jha, M. (2017). Understanding the Mediation Effect of Cloud Computing Adoption in Indian Organization: Integrating TAM-TOE- Risk Model. *International Journal of Service Science, Management, Engineering, and Technology*, 8(3), 40–59. doi:10.4018/IJSSMET.2017070103

Regan, E. A., & Wang, J. (2016). Realizing the Value of EHR Systems Critical Success Factors. *International Journal of Healthcare Information Systems and Informatics*, 11(3), 1–18. doi:10.4018/IJHISI.2016070101

Rezaie, S., Mirabedini, S. J., & Abtahi, A. (2018). Designing a Model for Implementation of Business Intelligence in the Banking Industry. *International Journal of Enterprise Information Systems*, 14(1), 77–103. doi:10.4018/IJEIS.2018010105

Rezende, D. A. (2016). Digital City Projects: Information and Public Services Offered by Chicago (USA) and Curitiba (Brazil). *International Journal of Knowledge Society Research*, 7(3), 16–30. doi:10.4018/IJKSR.2016070102

Rezende, D. A. (2018). Strategic Digital City Projects: Innovative Information and Public Services Offered by Chicago (USA) and Curitiba (Brazil). In M. Lytras, L. Daniela, & A. Visvizi (Eds.), *Enhancing Knowledge Discovery and Innovation in the Digital Era* (pp. 204–223). Hershey, PA: IGI Global. doi:10.4018/978-1-5225-4191-2.ch012

Riabov, V. V. (2016). Teaching Online Computer-Science Courses in LMS and Cloud Environment. *International Journal of Quality Assurance in Engineering and Technology Education, 5*(4), 12–41. doi:10.4018/IJQAETE.2016100102

Ricordel, V., Wang, J., Da Silva, M. P., & Le Callet, P. (2016). 2D and 3D Visual Attention for Computer Vision: Concepts, Measurement, and Modeling. In R. Pal (Ed.), *Innovative Research in Attention Modeling and Computer Vision Applications* (pp. 1–44). Hershey, PA: IGI Global. doi:10.4018/978-1-4666-8723-3.ch001

Rodriguez, A., Rico-Diaz, A. J., Rabuñal, J. R., & Gestal, M. (2017). Fish Tracking with Computer Vision Techniques: An Application to Vertical Slot Fishways. In M. S., & V. V. (Eds.), Multi-Core Computer Vision and Image Processing for Intelligent Applications (pp. 74-104). Hershey, PA: IGI Global. doi:10.4018/978-1-5225-0889-2.ch003

Romero, J. A. (2018). Sustainable Advantages of Business Value of Information Technology. In M. Khosrow-Pour, D.B.A. (Ed.), Encyclopedia of Information Science and Technology, Fourth Edition (pp. 923-929). Hershey, PA: IGI Global. doi:10.4018/978-1-5225-2255-3.ch079

Romero, J. A. (2018). The Always-On Business Model and Competitive Advantage. In N. Bajgoric (Ed.), *Always-On Enterprise Information Systems for Modern Organizations* (pp. 23–40). Hershey, PA: IGI Global. doi:10.4018/978-1-5225-3704-5.ch002

Rosen, Y. (2018). Computer Agent Technologies in Collaborative Learning and Assessment. In M. Khosrow-Pour, D.B.A. (Ed.), Encyclopedia of Information Science and Technology, Fourth Edition (pp. 2402-2410). Hershey, PA: IGI Global. doi:10.4018/978-1-5225-2255-3.ch209

Rosen, Y., & Mosharraf, M. (2016). Computer Agent Technologies in Collaborative Assessments. In Y. Rosen, S. Ferrara, & M. Mosharraf (Eds.), *Handbook of Research on Technology Tools for Real-World Skill Development* (pp. 319–343). Hershey, PA: IGI Global. doi:10.4018/978-1-4666-9441-5.ch012

Roy, D. (2018). Success Factors of Adoption of Mobile Applications in Rural India: Effect of Service Characteristics on Conceptual Model. In M. Khosrow-Pour (Ed.), *Green Computing Strategies for Competitive Advantage and Business Sustainability* (pp. 211–238). Hershey, PA: IGI Global. doi:10.4018/978-1-5225-5017-4.ch010

Ruffin, T. R. (2016). Health Information Technology and Change. In V. Wang (Ed.), *Handbook of Research on Advancing Health Education through Technology* (pp. 259–285). Hershey, PA: IGI Global. doi:10.4018/978-1-4666-9494-1.ch012

Ruffin, T. R. (2016). Health Information Technology and Quality Management. *International Journal of Information Communication Technologies and Human Development, 8*(4), 56–72. doi:10.4018/IJICTHD.2016100105

Ruffin, T. R., & Hawkins, D. P. (2018). Trends in Health Care Information Technology and Informatics. In M. Khosrow-Pour, D.B.A. (Ed.), Encyclopedia of Information Science and Technology, Fourth Edition (pp. 3805-3815). Hershey, PA: IGI Global. doi:10.4018/978-1-5225-2255-3.ch330

Safari, M. R., & Jiang, Q. (2018). The Theory and Practice of IT Governance Maturity and Strategies Alignment: Evidence From Banking Industry. *Journal of Global Information Management, 26*(2), 127–146. doi:10.4018/JGIM.2018040106

Sahin, H. B., & Anagun, S. S. (2018). Educational Computer Games in Math Teaching: A Learning Culture. In E. Toprak & E. Kumtepe (Eds.), *Supporting Multiculturalism in Open and Distance Learning Spaces* (pp. 249–280). Hershey, PA: IGI Global. doi:10.4018/978-1-5225-3076-3.ch013

Sanna, A., & Valpreda, F. (2017). An Assessment of the Impact of a Collaborative Didactic Approach and Students' Background in Teaching Computer Animation. *International Journal of Information and Communication Technology Education, 13*(4), 1–16. doi:10.4018/IJICTE.2017100101

Savita, K., Dominic, P., & Ramayah, T. (2016). The Drivers, Practices and Outcomes of Green Supply Chain Management: Insights from ISO14001 Manufacturing Firms in Malaysia. *International Journal of Information Systems and Supply Chain Management, 9*(2), 35–60. doi:10.4018/IJISSCM.2016040103

Scott, A., Martin, A., & McAlear, F. (2017). Enhancing Participation in Computer Science among Girls of Color: An Examination of a Preparatory AP Computer Science Intervention. In Y. Rankin & J. Thomas (Eds.), *Moving Students of Color from Consumers to Producers of Technology* (pp. 62–84). Hershey, PA: IGI Global. doi:10.4018/978-1-5225-2005-4.ch004

Shahsavandi, E., Mayah, G., & Rahbari, H. (2016). Impact of E-Government on Transparency and Corruption in Iran. In I. Sodhi (Ed.), *Trends, Prospects, and Challenges in Asian E-Governance* (pp. 75–94). Hershey, PA: IGI Global. doi:10.4018/978-1-4666-9536-8.ch004

Siddoo, V., & Wongsai, N. (2017). Factors Influencing the Adoption of ISO/IEC 29110 in Thai Government Projects: A Case Study. *International Journal of Information Technologies and Systems Approach, 10*(1), 22–44. doi:10.4018/IJITSA.2017010102

Sidorkina, I., & Rybakov, A. (2016). Computer-Aided Design as Carrier of Set Development Changes System in E-Course Engineering. In V. Mkrttchian, A. Bershadsky, A. Bozhday, M. Kataev, & S. Kataev (Eds.), *Handbook of Research on Estimation and Control Techniques in E-Learning Systems* (pp. 500–515). Hershey, PA: IGI Global. doi:10.4018/978-1-4666-9489-7.ch035

Sidorkina, I., & Rybakov, A. (2016). Creating Model of E-Course: As an Object of Computer-Aided Design. In V. Mkrttchian, A. Bershadsky, A. Bozhday, M. Kataev, & S. Kataev (Eds.), *Handbook of Research on Estimation and Control Techniques in E-Learning Systems* (pp. 286–297). Hershey, PA: IGI Global. doi:10.4018/978-1-4666-9489-7.ch019

Simões, A. (2017). Using Game Frameworks to Teach Computer Programming. In R. Alexandre Peixoto de Queirós & M. Pinto (Eds.), *Gamification-Based E-Learning Strategies for Computer Programming Education* (pp. 221–236). Hershey, PA: IGI Global. doi:10.4018/978-1-5225-1034-5.ch010

Sllame, A. M. (2017). Integrating LAB Work With Classes in Computer Network Courses. In H. Alphin Jr, R. Chan, & J. Lavine (Eds.), *The Future of Accessibility in International Higher Education* (pp. 253–275). Hershey, PA: IGI Global. doi:10.4018/978-1-5225-2560-8.ch015

Smirnov, A., Ponomarev, A., Shilov, N., Kashevnik, A., & Teslya, N. (2018). Ontology-Based Human-Computer Cloud for Decision Support: Architecture and Applications in Tourism. *International Journal of Embedded and Real-Time Communication Systems*, *9*(1), 1–19. doi:10.4018/IJERTCS.2018010101

Smith-Ditizio, A. A., & Smith, A. D. (2018). Computer Fraud Challenges and Its Legal Implications. In M. Khosrow-Pour, D.B.A. (Ed.), Encyclopedia of Information Science and Technology, Fourth Edition (pp. 4837-4848). Hershey, PA: IGI Global. doi:10.4018/978-1-5225-2255-3.ch419

Sohani, S. S. (2016). Job Shadowing in Information Technology Projects: A Source of Competitive Advantage. *International Journal of Information Technology Project Management*, *7*(1), 47–57. doi:10.4018/IJITPM.2016010104

Sosnin, P. (2018). Figuratively Semantic Support of Human-Computer Interactions. In *Experience-Based Human-Computer Interactions: Emerging Research and Opportunities* (pp. 244–272). Hershey, PA: IGI Global. doi:10.4018/978-1-5225-2987-3.ch008

Spinelli, R., & Benevolo, C. (2016). From Healthcare Services to E-Health Applications: A Delivery System-Based Taxonomy. In A. Dwivedi (Ed.), *Reshaping Medical Practice and Care with Health Information Systems* (pp. 205–245). Hershey, PA: IGI Global. doi:10.4018/978-1-4666-9870-3.ch007

Srinivasan, S. (2016). Overview of Clinical Trial and Pharmacovigilance Process and Areas of Application of Computer System. In P. Chakraborty & A. Nagal (Eds.), *Software Innovations in Clinical Drug Development and Safety* (pp. 1–13). Hershey, PA: IGI Global. doi:10.4018/978-1-4666-8726-4.ch001

Srisawasdi, N. (2016). Motivating Inquiry-Based Learning Through a Combination of Physical and Virtual Computer-Based Laboratory Experiments in High School Science. In M. Urban & D. Falvo (Eds.), *Improving K-12 STEM Education Outcomes through Technological Integration* (pp. 108–134). Hershey, PA: IGI Global. doi:10.4018/978-1-4666-9616-7.ch006

Stavridi, S. V., & Hamada, D. R. (2016). Children and Youth Librarians: Competencies Required in Technology-Based Environment. In J. Yap, M. Perez, M. Ayson, & G. Entico (Eds.), *Special Library Administration, Standardization and Technological Integration* (pp. 25–50). Hershey, PA: IGI Global. doi:10.4018/978-1-4666-9542-9.ch002

Sung, W., Ahn, J., Kai, S. M., Choi, A., & Black, J. B. (2016). Incorporating Touch-Based Tablets into Classroom Activities: Fostering Children's Computational Thinking through iPad Integrated Instruction. In D. Mentor (Ed.), *Handbook of Research on Mobile Learning in Contemporary Classrooms* (pp. 378–406). Hershey, PA: IGI Global. doi:10.4018/978-1-5225-0251-7.ch019

Syväjärvi, A., Leinonen, J., Kivivirta, V., & Kesti, M. (2017). The Latitude of Information Management in Local Government: Views of Local Government Managers. *International Journal of Electronic Government Research*, *13*(1), 69–85. doi:10.4018/IJEGR.2017010105

Tanque, M., & Foxwell, H. J. (2018). Big Data and Cloud Computing: A Review of Supply Chain Capabilities and Challenges. In A. Prasad (Ed.), *Exploring the Convergence of Big Data and the Internet of Things* (pp. 1–28). Hershey, PA: IGI Global. doi:10.4018/978-1-5225-2947-7.ch001

Teixeira, A., Gomes, A., & Orvalho, J. G. (2017). Auditory Feedback in a Computer Game for Blind People. In T. Issa, P. Kommers, T. Issa, P. Isaías, & T. Issa (Eds.), *Smart Technology Applications in Business Environments* (pp. 134–158). Hershey, PA: IGI Global. doi:10.4018/978-1-5225-2492-2.ch007

Thompson, N., McGill, T., & Murray, D. (2018). Affect-Sensitive Computer Systems. In M. Khosrow-Pour, D.B.A. (Ed.), Encyclopedia of Information Science and Technology, Fourth Edition (pp. 4124-4135). Hershey, PA: IGI Global. doi:10.4018/978-1-5225-2255-3.ch357

Trad, A., & Kalpić, D. (2016). The E-Business Transformation Framework for E-Commerce Control and Monitoring Pattern. In I. Lee (Ed.), *Encyclopedia of E-Commerce Development, Implementation, and Management* (pp. 754–777). Hershey, PA: IGI Global. doi:10.4018/978-1-4666-9787-4.ch053

Triberti, S., Brivio, E., & Galimberti, C. (2018). On Social Presence: Theories, Methodologies, and Guidelines for the Innovative Contexts of Computer-Mediated Learning. In M. Marmon (Ed.), *Enhancing Social Presence in Online Learning Environments* (pp. 20–41). Hershey, PA: IGI Global. doi:10.4018/978-1-5225-3229-3.ch002

Tripathy, B. K. T. R., S., & Mohanty, R. K. (2018). Memetic Algorithms and Their Applications in Computer Science. In S. Dash, B. Tripathy, & A. Rahman (Eds.), Handbook of Research on Modeling, Analysis, and Application of Nature-Inspired Metaheuristic Algorithms (pp. 73-93). Hershey, PA: IGI Global. doi:10.4018/978-1-5225-2857-9.ch004

Turulja, L., & Bajgoric, N. (2017). Human Resource Management IT and Global Economy Perspective: Global Human Resource Information Systems. In M. Khosrow-Pour (Ed.), *Handbook of Research on Technology Adoption, Social Policy, and Global Integration* (pp. 377–394). Hershey, PA: IGI Global. doi:10.4018/978-1-5225-2668-1.ch018

Unwin, D. W., Sanzogni, L., & Sandhu, K. (2017). Developing and Measuring the Business Case for Health Information Technology. In K. Moahi, K. Bwalya, & P. Sebina (Eds.), *Health Information Systems and the Advancement of Medical Practice in Developing Countries* (pp. 262–290). Hershey, PA: IGI Global. doi:10.4018/978-1-5225-2262-1.ch015

Vadhanam, B. R. S., M., Sugumaran, V., V., V., & Ramalingam, V. V. (2017). Computer Vision Based Classification on Commercial Videos. In M. S., & V. V. (Eds.), Multi-Core Computer Vision and Image Processing for Intelligent Applications (pp. 105-135). Hershey, PA: IGI Global. doi:10.4018/978-1-5225-0889-2.ch004

Valverde, R., Torres, B., & Motaghi, H. (2018). A Quantum NeuroIS Data Analytics Architecture for the Usability Evaluation of Learning Management Systems. In S. Bhattacharyya (Ed.), *Quantum-Inspired Intelligent Systems for Multimedia Data Analysis* (pp. 277–299). Hershey, PA: IGI Global. doi:10.4018/978-1-5225-5219-2.ch009

Vassilis, E. (2018). Learning and Teaching Methodology: "1:1 Educational Computing. In K. Koutsopoulos, K. Doukas, & Y. Kotsanis (Eds.), *Handbook of Research on Educational Design and Cloud Computing in Modern Classroom Settings* (pp. 122–155). Hershey, PA: IGI Global. doi:10.4018/978-1-5225-3053-4.ch007

Wadhwani, A. K., Wadhwani, S., & Singh, T. (2016). Computer Aided Diagnosis System for Breast Cancer Detection. In Y. Morsi, A. Shukla, & C. Rathore (Eds.), *Optimizing Assistive Technologies for Aging Populations* (pp. 378–395). Hershey, PA: IGI Global. doi:10.4018/978-1-4666-9530-6.ch015

Wang, L., Wu, Y., & Hu, C. (2016). English Teachers' Practice and Perspectives on Using Educational Computer Games in EIL Context. *International Journal of Technology and Human Interaction, 12*(3), 33–46. doi:10.4018/IJTHI.2016070103

Watfa, M. K., Majeed, H., & Salahuddin, T. (2016). Computer Based E-Healthcare Clinical Systems: A Comprehensive Survey. *International Journal of Privacy and Health Information Management, 4*(1), 50–69. doi:10.4018/IJPHIM.2016010104

Weeger, A., & Haase, U. (2016). Taking up Three Challenges to Business-IT Alignment Research by the Use of Activity Theory. *International Journal of IT/Business Alignment and Governance, 7*(2), 1-21. doi:10.4018/IJITBAG.2016070101

Wexler, B. E. (2017). Computer-Presented and Physical Brain-Training Exercises for School Children: Improving Executive Functions and Learning. In B. Dubbels (Ed.), *Transforming Gaming and Computer Simulation Technologies across Industries* (pp. 206–224). Hershey, PA: IGI Global. doi:10.4018/978-1-5225-1817-4.ch012

Williams, D. M., Gani, M. O., Addo, I. D., Majumder, A. J., Tamma, C. P., Wang, M., ... Chu, C. (2016). Challenges in Developing Applications for Aging Populations. In Y. Morsi, A. Shukla, & C. Rathore (Eds.), *Optimizing Assistive Technologies for Aging Populations* (pp. 1–21). Hershey, PA: IGI Global. doi:10.4018/978-1-4666-9530-6.ch001

Wimble, M., Singh, H., & Phillips, B. (2018). Understanding Cross-Level Interactions of Firm-Level Information Technology and Industry Environment: A Multilevel Model of Business Value. *Information Resources Management Journal, 31*(1), 1–20. doi:10.4018/IRMJ.2018010101

Wimmer, H., Powell, L., Kilgus, L., & Force, C. (2017). Improving Course Assessment via Web-based Homework. *International Journal of Online Pedagogy and Course Design, 7*(2), 1–19. doi:10.4018/IJOPCD.2017040101

Wong, Y. L., & Siu, K. W. (2018). Assessing Computer-Aided Design Skills. In M. Khosrow-Pour, D.B.A. (Ed.), Encyclopedia of Information Science and Technology, Fourth Edition (pp. 7382-7391). Hershey, PA: IGI Global. doi:10.4018/978-1-5225-2255-3.ch642

Wongsurawat, W., & Shrestha, V. (2018). Information Technology, Globalization, and Local Conditions: Implications for Entrepreneurs in Southeast Asia. In P. Ordóñez de Pablos (Ed.), *Management Strategies and Technology Fluidity in the Asian Business Sector* (pp. 163–176). Hershey, PA: IGI Global. doi:10.4018/978-1-5225-4056-4.ch010

Yang, Y., Zhu, X., Jin, C., & Li, J. J. (2018). Reforming Classroom Education Through a QQ Group: A Pilot Experiment at a Primary School in Shanghai. In H. Spires (Ed.), *Digital Transformation and Innovation in Chinese Education* (pp. 211–231). Hershey, PA: IGI Global. doi:10.4018/978-1-5225-2924-8.ch012

Yilmaz, R., Sezgin, A., Kurnaz, S., & Arslan, Y. Z. (2018). Object-Oriented Programming in Computer Science. In M. Khosrow-Pour, D.B.A. (Ed.), Encyclopedia of Information Science and Technology, Fourth Edition (pp. 7470-7480). Hershey, PA: IGI Global. doi:10.4018/978-1-5225-2255-3.ch650

Yu, L. (2018). From Teaching Software Engineering Locally and Globally to Devising an Internationalized Computer Science Curriculum. In S. Dikli, B. Etheridge, & R. Rawls (Eds.), *Curriculum Internationalization and the Future of Education* (pp. 293–320). Hershey, PA: IGI Global. doi:10.4018/978-1-5225-2791-6.ch016

Yuhua, F. (2018). Computer Information Library Clusters. In M. Khosrow-Pour, D.B.A. (Ed.), Encyclopedia of Information Science and Technology, Fourth Edition (pp. 4399-4403). Hershey, PA: IGI Global. doi:10.4018/978-1-5225-2255-3.ch382

Zare, M. A., Taghavi Fard, M. T., & Hanafizadeh, P. (2016). The Assessment of Outsourcing IT Services using DEA Technique: A Study of Application Outsourcing in Research Centers. *International Journal of Operations Research and Information Systems, 7*(1), 45–57. doi:10.4018/IJORIS.2016010104

Zhao, J., Wang, Q., Guo, J., Gao, L., & Yang, F. (2016). An Overview on Passive Image Forensics Technology for Automatic Computer Forgery. *International Journal of Digital Crime and Forensics, 8*(4), 14–25. doi:10.4018/IJDCF.2016100102

Zimeras, S. (2016). Computer Virus Models and Analysis in M-Health IT Systems: Computer Virus Models. In A. Moumtzoglou (Ed.), *M-Health Innovations for Patient-Centered Care* (pp. 284–297). Hershey, PA: IGI Global. doi:10.4018/978-1-4666-9861-1.ch014

Zlatanovska, K. (2016). Hacking and Hacktivism as an Information Communication System Threat. In M. Hadji-Janev & M. Bogdanoski (Eds.), *Handbook of Research on Civil Society and National Security in the Era of Cyber Warfare* (pp. 68–101). Hershey, PA: IGI Global. doi:10.4018/978-1-4666-8793-6.ch004

About the Contributors

P. K. Gupta is Post-Doctorate from University of Pretoria (South Africa-2015-16) in the Department of Electrical, Electronic and Computer Engineering. He is currently working as Associate Professor in the Department of Computer Science and Engineering at Jaypee University of Information Technology (JUIT). He has 15+ years of extensive experience in IT industry and Academics in India and abroad. He has completed his Ph.D. in Computer Science and Engineering 2012. He has extensive research experience in Internet-of-Things, Cloud Computing, Image Processing, and Pattern Recognition and authored more than forty research papers in referred journals and international conferences. Also, he has contributed his research work in number of renowned International conferences including IEEE TENCON-Singapore, IEEE-INDICON -India, ICT Innovations -Macedonia, WPMC -Japan etc. Dr. Gupta was the recipient of NRF-KIC South Africa-2015 grant. He was invited speaker at International Conference on Computer Science and Information Engineering (ICCSIE2015), Ningbo, China 2015. He is the recipient of award from Computer Society of India for maximum publications during year 2015-16. He was General Chair for IEEE 2017 Fourth International Conference on Image Information Processing 9ICIIP 2017), and 2015 IEEE International Conference on Computer Graphics, Vision and Information Security (CGVIS). He has organized a Special session on Smart and Ubiquitous Computing for Vehicle Navigation Systems at IEEE TENCON 2016, Singapore. He has also organized the special session on Context Aware and Ubiquitous Computing at IEEE International Smart Cities Conference at Guadalajara, Mexico. He has also organized a special session on Image processing and Machine Learning at 2015 IEEE INDIACom, NewDelhi, India. Dr. has organized more than 30 workshops on LINUX, PHP and MySQL, LaTeX, Python, SciLab and three Faculty development programs (FDPs) on LaTeX and SciLab. He is also a part of IIT Bombay's research team for "Spoken Tutorial Project" and working as a project ambassador for this project at JUIT. This project is the initiative of the "Talk to a Teacher" project of the National Mission on Education through ICT, launched by MHRD and Govt of India. Dr. Gupta is an Associate Editor of IEEE Access. He is also a Guest editor of Special issues from Springer, and Inderscience publishers. He is a regular reviewer of reputed Journals e.g. Springer Plus, Neural Computing and Applications, Multimedia Tools and Applications, Microelectronics, Journal of Medical Imaging and Health Informatics, etc. He has enthusiastically participated and acted as organizing committee member of numerous IEEE and other conferences. He is currently serving as a Life Member of Computer Society of India (CSI), Life member of Indian Science Congress Association (ISCA), Member of IEEE, Professional member of ACM, Senior member of IACSIT, and Member of Indian Society for Technical Education (ISTE).

Tuncer Ören is a professor emeritus of computer science at the School of Electrical Engineering and Computer Science of the University of Ottawa, Canada. He has been involved with simulation since 1965. Dr. Ören's Ph.D. is in Systems Engineering from the University of Arizona, Tucson, AZ (1971). His basic education is from Galatasaray Lisesi, a high school founded in his native Istanbul in 1481 and in Mechanical Engineering at the Technical University of Istanbul (1960). His research interests include advancing methodologies for modeling and simulation; agent-directed simulation; agents for cognitive and emotive simulations especially for conflict management training (including representations of human personality, understanding, misunderstanding, emotions, and anger mechanisms); reliability, QA, failure avoidance, ethics; as well as body of knowledge and terminology of modelling and simulation. He has well over 500 publications, including 46 books and proceedings –some translated in Chinese, German and Turkish. He has contributed to over 500 conferences and seminars held in 40 countries. He has been a keynote or invited speaker, or honorary chair in about half of them. Dr. Ören has been recognized, by IBM Canada, as a pioneer of computing in Canada where he has been also the Founding Chair of the Executive Committee of the Chairmen of the Canadian Computer Science Departments. He received "Information Age Award" from the Turkish Ministry of Culture and an "Honor Award" from the (Turkish) Language Association (2012). Dr. Ören is a Fellow of SCS (2016) and was inducted to "SCS Modeling and Simulation Hall of Fame" (Lifetime Achievement Award) in 2011. Some of his recent distinctions include the Golden Award of Excellence from the International Institute for Advanced Studies in Systems Research and Cybernetics (2018); SCS McLeod Founder's Award for Distinguished Service to the Profession (2017); and a book edited by Prof. Levent Yilmaz: Concepts and Methodologies for Modeling and Simulation: A Tribute to Tuncer Ören. Springer (2015).

Mayank Singh is currently working as a Post-Doctoral Fellow, Department of Electrical, Electronic and Computer Engineering, at University of KwaZulu-Natal, Durban, South Africa since September 2017. Prior, he worked as Professor and Head, Department of Computer Science and Engineering at Krishna Engineering College, Ghaziabad. He has 12+ years of extensive experience in IT industry and Academics in India. He completed his Ph.D. in Computer Science and Engineering from Uttarakhand Technical University in 2011. He obtained his M.E. (2007) in Software Engineering from Thapar University, Patiala and B.Tech. (2004) in Information Technology from Uttar Pradesh Technical University, Lucknow. He is currently also serving as a Life Member of Computer Society of India (CSI), Life Member of Indian Science Congress Association (ISCA), Member of IEEE, Senior Member of ACM, Senior Member of IACSIT, and Member of Indian Society for Technical Education (ISTE). He is also serving for IEEE Committees as a TPC Member and designated Reviewer for various IEEE Conferences. Dr. Singh is currently serving as Reviewer for IET Software, IEEE Communications, IEEE TENCON, IEEE Sensors, The Journal of Engineering, IET Wireless Sensor Networks, and Program Committee Member of innumerable IEEE & Springer International Journals and Conferences Worldwide.

* * *

Gopala Krishna Behara is an Enterprise Architect with 20+ years of extensive experience in the ICT industry which spans across Pre-Sales, Consulting, Enterprise Architecture, Service Oriented Architecture, Business Process Management, Solution Architecture, Project Management, Product Development and Systems Integration. He is certified in Open Group TOGAF, IBM Cloud Solutions. He serves as an Advisory Architect and Mentor on Enterprise Architecture, Application Portfolio Rationalization and Architecture Assurance initiatives and continues to work as a Subject Matter Expert and Author. He has worked on multiple architecture transformation engagements in the USA, UK, Europe, Asia Pacific and Middle East Regions that presented a phased roadmap to transformation that maximized the business value, while minimizing costs and risks. Dr. Gopal is currently working as Senior Enterprise Architect in Global Enterprise Architecture group of Wipro. Published White Papers in International Journals in SOA, BPM, Next Generation Technologies & e-Governance space and also done significant contribution for the SOA Reference Architecture definition across the organisation. Published books titled "Enterprise Architecture Practitioner Hand Book" and "Next Generation Enterprise Reference Architecture For Connected Government". Recipient of EA Hall of Fame - Individual Leadership in EA Practice, Promotion and Professionalisation Award, 13th Annual Enterprise Architecture Conference, Washington, DC, USA – 2015.

Ashutosh Bhatt is in Dept. of Computer Science and Engineering at Birla Institute of Applied Sciences, Bhimtal, Uttarakhand, India. He has done his Ph.D. in CSE in the field of Machine Learning. He is having a teaching experience of 20 years. He has a good number of reputed research publications. His Interest area are: Neural Networks, Web Applications. He has guided many research scholars.

Rakesh Bhutiani is currently working as Assistant Professor in Department of Zoology & Environmental Science Gurukula Kangri Vishwavidyalaya Haridwar (Uttarakhand) India. He has done his Ph.D. in Environmental Science "Limnological status of river Suswa with reference to its mathematical modelling" from Gurukula Kangri Vishwavidyalaya Haridwar, India. He has a total 15 years of teaching and research experience. He has more than 80 reputed publications in National and International Journals of repute and guided several scholars. Dr. Bhutiani is fellow of several academic societies and has several awards to his credit.

Anil Kumar Bisht is currently a Ph.D. research scholar and Asstt. Professor in the department of CS & IT, FET, Mahatma Jyotibha Phule Rohilkhand University, Bareilly, U.P. India. He has a teaching experience of about 14 years. He has done his M.Tech. in CSE from Uttarakhand Technical University, Dehradun, Uttarakhand, India. He has done his B.Tech in CSE from Uttar Pradesh Technical University, Lucknow, U.P., India. His research Areas are Artificial Intelligence, Machine Learning and Wireless Communications. He has completed online certificate course from Electronics and ICT Acedemy, IIT Kanpur on "Machine Learning". He has a total number of 17 research publications. He is a life time member of Computer Society of India (CSI).

Jutika Borah was born and brought up in the land of Assam, a land of rich cultural heritage and greenery, a part of the land of Seven Sisters i.e. North Eastern Region of India. Truly believe in the fact that "Leadership and Competence has no gender". Having a scientific temper, passion and a keen desire and zeal to serve the society and the nation with the potentials through learning and wisdom. Currently pursuing post graduation, Master of Science (M.Sc.) in Electronics and Communication Technology at Gauhati University, Assam, India.

Pulak Jyoti Gohain received his B.Sc degree in Electronics from the Dibrugarh University, Assam, India, in 2016 and is currently pursuing M.Sc degree in Electronics and Communication Technology from the Gauhati University. His interests are coding in Python, IoT.

Pratiyush Guleria is currently a Ph.D research scholar in Department of Computer Science,Himachal Pradesh University Shimla,India.He has done M. Tech in Computer Science with a Gold Medal from Himachal Pradesh University, Shimla, India. He has done B.Tech in Information Technology. Pratiyush Guleria has more than 9+ Years of Experience in IT Industry and Academics. He has, to his credit, approximately 15 research papers in peer reviewed International Journals and Conferences.His research interests include Data Mining, Machine Learning and Web Technologies.

Umang Kant has completed her B.Tech in 2009 from University of Mumbai and Master in 2013 from Gautam Buddha University, Greater Noida. She is having 8 years of extensive experience of IT Industry and Academics. She has participated in several International Conferences, Workshops, Training Programs and Faculty Development Programs. She has organized several college level technical and non-technical events.

Weston Mwashita is with Vaal University of Technology. He obtained a Bachelor of Technology degree in Electrical Engineering (Telecommunications) at the University of South Africa and went on to complete his Master of Technology degree in Electrical Engineering (Telecommunications) at the same university. Mr Mwashita is a registered member of the South Africa Institute of Electrical Engineers, a member of Institute of Electrical and Electronics Engineers, a member of Namibia Engineering Council, an associate member of Engineering Professions of Namibia. He has authored several publications. His research focus areas are; Internet of Things, Device-to-Device Communications, Green Cellular Networks and Wireless Sensor Networks. He is currently pursuing a PhD. degree in Electrical Engineering majoring in Wireless Communications.

Marcel Ohanga Odhiambo obtained a BSc degree in Electronic Engineering from University of Nairobi, Kenya in 1980, an MSc degree in Microprocessor Technology and Applications from Brighton University, UK in 1990 and a PhD degree in Parallel and Distributed Computer Architecture from University of Surrey, UK in 1998. He joined the department of Civil Aviation, Ministry of Transport and Communications, Kenya in 1980 as Trainee Engineer rising to the post of Planning Engineer responsible the planning, installation and commissioning Aircraft Navigation Aids systems around the country. He joined Moi University as a Lecturer in the department of Electrical and Communications Engineering in 1992, rising to the post of Senior Lecturer in 2001. At Moi University, Prof. Marcel Ohanga Odhiambo was appointed the Director: Information and Resources Management (IRM) Centre between May 2001 and April 2003. As IRM Director, he carried out preliminary design of Moi University (MU) backbone computer network, developed Moi University Information Management systems and chaired a committee to formulate ICT policy and ICT Master Plan for Moi University. He was appointed Manager: Academic Register Information System (ARIS) between September 2000 and April 2003 and head of department of Computer Engineering between May 2003 and June 2004. He joined Tshwane University of Technology, South Africa in 2004 as a Postdoctoral Fellow. In 2006, he joined the department of Electrical & Mining Engineering, University of South Africa (UNISA), South Africa as Senior Lecturer. At UNISA Prof. Marcel Ohanga Odhiambo was appointed Acting Director: School of Engineering between March – August 2007 and head of department of Electrical and Mining Engineering between January 1st 2009 to 31st December 2011. He was appointed Associate Professor in the same department in January 2012. He is currently an as Associate Professor and head: department of Process Control & Computer Systems, Vaal University of Technology, South Africa since December 2014. Prof. Marcel Ohanga Odhiambo is a Fellow of the Institution of Engineers and Technologists (IET), UK, senior member of South African Institute of Electrical Engineers (SAIEE) and a member of the Institution of Engineers of Kenya (IEK). He is a Registered Engineer (REng): Engineers Registration Board of Kenya (ERBK), a Chartered Engineer (CEng): Engineering Council (UK) and a Professional Engineer (PrEng): Engineering Council of South Africa (ECSA). Prof. Odhiambo research interest is in Parallel and Distributed Computer Architectures for Agents Execution, Electronic Systems/Devices and Wireless Communications (Quality of Service). He has over 57 scientific publications and continues to supervise postgraduate students/projects. Prof. Odhiambo has consulted for the industry.

Kamalendu Pal is with the Department of Computer Science, School of Mathematics, Computer Science and Engineering, City University London. Kamalendu received his BSc (Hons) degree in Physics from Calcutta University, India, Postgraduate Diploma in Computer Science from Pune, India; MSc degree in Software Systems Technology from Sheffield University, Postgraduate Diploma in Artificial Intelligence from Kingston University, MPhil degree in Computer Science from University College London, and MBA degree from University of Hull, United Kingdom. He has published dozens of research papers in international journals and conferences. His research interests include knowledge-based systems, decision support systems, computer integrated design, software engineering, and service oriented computing. He is a member of the British Computer Society, the Institution of Engineering and Technology, and the IEEE Computer Society.

Kandarpa Kumar Sarma, currently Professor and Head, Department of Electronics and Communication Engineering, GUIST, Gauhati University, India, specializes in mobile communication, speech processing, deep learning and antenna design. He completed MTech in Signal Processing in 2005 from IIT Guwahati, India from where he later on earned PhD in the area of mobile communication. He is the Editor in Chief of three major journals namely International Journal of Intelligent System Design and Computing, Inderscience, WSEAS Transactions on Computers and International Journal of Circuits and Electronics. He has been the chief investigator of several externally funded projects involving artificial intelligence driven paradigms of high data rate wireless communication. He is a Senior Member of IEEE (USA) and a fellow of Institution of Electronics and Telecommunication Engineers (IETE) (India). He has been the recipient of IETE N. V. Gadadhar Award (2014) for contributions in the area of wireless communication.

Dharmpal Singh received his Bachelor of Computer Science and Engineering and Master of Computer Science and Engineering from West Bengal University of Technology. He has about eight years of experience in teaching and research. At present, he is with JIS College of Engineering, Kalyani, and West Bengal, India as an Associate Professor. Currently, he had done his Ph. D from University of Kalyani. He has about 32 publications in national and international journals and conference proceedings. He is also the editorial board members of many reputed/ referred journal.

Ravendra Singh is an Associate Professor in the department of CS & IT, FET, Mahatma Jyotibha Phule Rohilkhand University, Bareilly, U.P. India. He has a teaching experience of about 20 years and 5 years experience in industry as Assistant Manager in Uptron India Ltd., Lucknow (U.P. Govt. Undertaking). His research Areas are At present, mainly engaged in Wired & Wireless networks, QoS based routing, ad hoc network, VANET, routing in under water and terrestrial sensor network, Admission control schemes for Real time communication and guided many scholars over the Internet, simulation and performance evaluation of wireless networks, Cost optimization & testing issues and Task allocation & scheduling in Distributed parallel computers. He is also working in the area related to association rules, cleaning & Integration of data in Data mining, & Data warehousing. He has a total number of more than 35 reputed publications. Also he had written 2 books with New Age International, N.Delhi. and University Science Press, N.Delhi.

Manu Sood is a Professor in the Department of Computer Science, HPU, India. He had held the additional charge of the Director, University Institute of Information Technoliogy, Himachal Pradesh University, Shimla, India for four and a half years. He had also remained the Chairman of Department of Computer Science, Himachal Pradesh University, Shimla, India for two terms of two years each. He is an Engineering graduate, has an M.Tech. degree in Information Systems from University of Delhi (DU) with Gold Medal. He also holds the degree of Ph.D, from the Faculty of Technology, DU, Dehli, India. He possesses around 5 years of Industry experience and more than 25 years of academics and diverse administrative experience. His areas of interest in research are Software Engineering, e-Learning, security in WANETs and SDNs.

Viranjay M. Srivastava is a Doctorate (2012) in the field of RF Microelectronics and VLSI Design, Master (2008) in VLSI design, and Bachelor (2002) in Electronics and Instrumentation Engineering. He has worked for the fabrication of devices and development of circuit design. Presently, he is a faculty in Department of Electronic Engineering, Howard College, University of KwaZulu-Natal, Durban, South Africa. He has more than 13 years of teaching and research experience in the area of VLSI design, RFIC design, and Analog IC design. He has supervised various Bachelors, Masters and Doctorate theses. He is a senior member of IEEE, and member of IEEE-HKN, IITPSA, ACEEE and IACSIT. He has worked as a reviewer for several Journals and Conferences both national and international. He is author/co-author of more than 110 scientific contributions including articles in international refereed Journals and Conferences and also author of following books, 1) VLSI Technology, 2) Characterization of C-V curves and Analysis, Using VEE Pro Software: After Fabrication of MOS Device, and 3) MOSFET Technologies for Double-Pole Four Throw Radio Frequency Switch, Springer International Publishing, Switzerland, October 2013.

Index

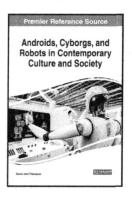

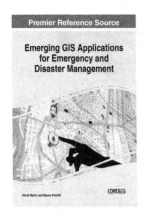

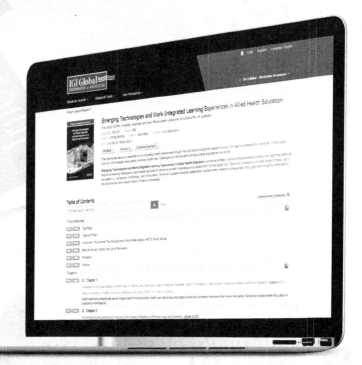

Printed in the United States
By Bookmasters